# AMERICA INVADED

## A State by State Guide to Fighting on American Soil

FROM THE AUTHORS OF *AMERICA INVADES*

Christopher Kelly & Stuart Laycock

HISTORY™
INVASIONS

*America Invaded: A State by State Guide
to Fighting on American Soil*

Copyright © 2017 by History Invasions, LLC


History Invasions Press
1455 NW Leary Way, Suite 400
Seattle, WA 98107
Phone 206 489 5335
www.AmericaInvaded.com

Printed in the United States of America

ISBN 978-0-692-90240-0 (hardback)

Editor: Elizabeth Barrett
Cover Designer: Blaine Donnelson
Book Design and Production: Gwyn Snider
Management: Vincent Driano

Dedicated to the memory of my ancestors—Jane Wells, killed at
Cherry Valley Massacre in 1778; and Captain Cortlandt Van Rensselaer,
who died in Nashville, Tennessee, likely from wounds received
at the Battle of Missionary Ridge in 1864.

*Captain Cortlandt Van Rensselaer, Albany Rural Cemetery, NY*
Source: Paula Lemire

# ACKNOWLEDGMENTS

I would like to acknowledge first and foremost my dear friend Stuart Laycock, who conceived the idea of "Invasion" books back in 2012 with his book *All the Countries We've Invaded*. Around 90 percent of the world's countries have, at some point, been invaded by Britain. I read and reviewed his work. We met in a pub in London, and then together we wrote *America Invades*, followed by *Italy Invades: How Italians Conquered the World*.

This work benefited from the input of friends and family around the world. My daughter Oona Kelly secured photographs from Mission Dolores in California. My son Marco Kelly accompanied me on a photo reconnaissance of Fort Ross on the coast of Sonoma County. Major Jack Coughlin (USAF Ret.) and I toured Oregon, visiting sites such as Fort Clatsop, Fort Stevens, and the Mitchell Monument. I visited the Albany Rural Cemetery in New York (where Captain Cortlandt Van Rensselaer of the Union Army is buried) with my aunt, Catherine Townsend. Ken Curtis helped with a photograph from North Carolina. My friend Tom Winmill secured photographs of Hannah Duston in New Hampshire. Miles Thomson, Stu's father-in-law, an expert on the Battle of Pea Ridge, contributed to our Arkansas chapter.

I am grateful for the assistance of my meticulous editor, Elizabeth Barrett. Our talented graphic designer, Blaine Donnelson, created our cover, maps, and website (www.americainvaded.com). Gwyn Snider did a super job on our layout. Keri Johns provided invaluable assistance in researching and compiling the tourist information found in this volume. Vincent Driano, my brother-in-law and business manager, was always invaluable and encouraging in this project.

Thanks much to Bob Cudmore of The Historians Podcast in New York and Charles Heller in Arizona for reviewing draft chapters of the work.

I am grateful to the National Park Service, which does an outstanding job of preserving the memory of our historic past, from Gettysburg to Little Bighorn, from Yorktown to Shanksville. Thanks to Susan Fernandez of the Chetco Community Public Library in Brookings, Oregon, for our inspection of the Fujita sword. I also appreciate the tranquil hospitality of Chris Blackwell's Goldeneye in Jamaica, where I edited much of the manuscript.

Thanks also to Sharon Bially and her team at Book Savvy for all their efforts with publicity.

Finally, this book would not have been possible without the patience and understanding of my dear wife, Maria Driano.

# INTRODUCTION

*by Christopher Kelly*

On July 28, 1996, some college kids in my adopted home state of Washington gathered on the banks of the Columbia River to watch a hydroplane race. One of them shocked his friends by pulling a human skull from the river. The police were quickly summoned, and the area was roped off with yellow tape and dubbed a crime scene. If it was the scene of a crime, its origins were surprisingly ancient. The local coroner called in an anthropologist, and the skeleton of what became known as Kennewick Man was determined by radiocarbon tests to be around 9,300 years old.

Kennewick Man was a source of considerable controversy after its skull was determined to have Caucasoid features. White supremacists got excited about the presence of an Aryan race in prehistoric North America. Native American groups sought to provide Kennewick Man with a traditional burial. Scientists pointed out that *Caucasoid* should not be confused with *Caucasian*, and Caucasoid features are found from North Africa to Northern Asia, as well as in Europe.

As a military historian, I was less intrigued by Kennewick Man's skull than by his pelvis. For lodged in his pelvis was a two-inch stone spear point. Kennewick Man had most likely died sometime in his late thirties. His pelvis wound, however, likely dated from his teenage years.

Was Kennewick Man a warrior? Was Kennewick Man an invader? Was he the victim of a warrior or invader? Or had he been accidentally injured in a hunt? These questions may never receive a satisfactory answer, but Kennewick Man seemed to provide evidence of fighting in Washington State over 9,000 years ago.

We Americans are often resistant to the notion that our country has ever been invaded. Sure, we've invaded other countries, from Normandy in 1944 to Iraq in 2003. In our earlier work, *America Invades,* my coauthor and I showed how Americans have invaded or fought in eighty-six different countries, representing 44 percent of all the countries in the world. And we have been militarily involved in a significant way with nearly all the rest. We have not, for example, invaded Portugal, but we have had military bases in the Azores since World War II, and they remain there to this day. The only three countries Americans do not seem to have affected militarily at all are Andorra, Bhutan, and the Principality of Liechtenstein.

*America Invades* addressed the question of America's military impact around the globe. What it left out was fighting within the boundaries of the United States. Our book did not deal with conflicts with indigenous people, the American Revolution, or the American Civil War.

*America Invaded: A State by State Guide to Fighting on American Soil* attempts to round out the picture by providing a snapshot of the waves of invasion that have touched all fifty American states and Washington DC. Both books together provide a 360-degree tour of American military action at home and abroad.

Humans first began arriving in North America less than twenty thousand years ago. Some of the earliest arrivals are thought to have crossed over the Bering Strait from Asia into what is now Alaska. The Clovis Culture that was based in present-day New Mexico dates back around thirteen thousand years.

Prior to the arrival of Europeans, a great deal of fighting took place in North America. Most of the details of this low-level warfare are lost to history due to the indigenous people's oral, as opposed to written, tradition. Arrowheads, spear points, and defensive establishments, however, give mute testament to fighting in prehistoric America. In the Hawaiian Islands, fighting was a highly ritualized and ceremonial process.

The arrival of Europeans changed the nature of warfare in many ways. Europeans voyaged to the New World in wooden sailing ships that bristled with cannon. They brought firearms. They introduced an animal—the horse— that changed forever the nature of hunting and warfare in North America.

The boundary between *exploration* and *invasion* can be a fine line determined largely by one's perspective. Lewis and Clark, aided by the Shoshone woman Sacagawea, managed to largely avoid violent conflicts with indigenous people. Captain Cook, on his second voyage to the Sandwich Islands, did not.

Technological advantages might be presumed to have given Europeans predominance in the combats that were to come. The conflict between European settlers and indigenous people is often presented as an asymmetrical contest. And the invasion of pathogens to which indigenous people lacked immunities did indeed ravage the native populations in both North and South America. But the triumph of the Europeans probably did not seem inevitable to those who lived during those times.

Native people also enjoyed their own tremendous advantages. Initially, they vastly outnumbered the scattered European settlers. Native people knew the lay of the land and were accustomed to the climactic conditions prevailing in North America. Millennia of warfare had also produced sharp warrior skills.

A number of early European settlements were wiped out, likely due to the resistance of indigenous people. Roanoke in North Carolina is remembered as the lost colony. Spanish settlements on the Sea Islands off Georgia disappeared, as did early French settlements in Texas.

European settlers quickly grew to both fear and respect the indigenous people of North America. Robert Rogers (1731–1795) learned to emulate Indian-style fighting techniques—Rogers' Rangers even took up scalping—and he later wrote Rogers Rules of Ranging, a guide to irregular warfare that inspires US Special Forces even in the twenty-first century. The Indian style of fighting relied upon stealth, camouflage, and hit-and-run attacks. Ambush and surprise were key ingredients for success. Frontal assaults against fixed fortifications and set-piece battles in open terrain were to be avoided. These sorts of tactics would prove invaluable when applied to the conflict against the British in the American Revolution.

But Indian-style fighting alone would be insufficient to dislodge the world's greatest empire of the eighteenth century from its control over the thirteen colonies. Baron von Steuben of Prussia instructed the Patriot soldiers in European-style drill tactics. Soldiers from Spain and France also played a critical role in assisting the Americans to win their revolution. The French fleet was decisive in closing the trap on Cornwallis at Yorktown.

The War of 1812 would be a sort of rematch of the American Revolution. This war included American invasions of Canada, and the British retaliating by burning the White House and very nearly capturing New Orleans. The death of Tecumseh, warrior leader of the Shawnee, in 1813 would open the path for westward expansion by the burgeoning American population. Land-hungry farmers streamed west, driving out native people, with conflicts flaring up on a regular basis. The US Army would be called upon to build fortifications to protect those on the frontier.

Native traditions in North America were jeopardized not merely by military activity, but also by cultural "invasions." Intermarriage, Western-style education, and religious conversion were all factors in the weakening of traditional native ways.

In the 1860s, America was convulsed by a great civil war. The bloodiest war in American history, whose casualty totals have been revised upward by recent scholarship to around 750,000 deaths, was fought on American soil. The Civil War began with soldiers in brightly colored uniforms being observed by Beltway picnickers (First Bull Run), and ended with grinding industrial warfare that would foreshadow the horrors of the trenches of World War I. Sherman's March to the Sea was a "total war" whose tactics—destruction of infrastructure and targeting of civilians—were a precursor to the world wars of the twentieth century.

The discovery of gold and other resources in the American West drove a mass of migration into what had previously been Indian lands. The grizzled and often cynical veterans of the Civil War were dispatched to tame the West. Both these factors inevitably led to brutal battles and multiple tragedies on the western frontier.

The collision between European warrior nations and the North American warrior tradition was full of tragedy and tears. But there was far more to it as well. Native Americans had a profound impact on the shaping of the American military mind. A statue of Tecumseh has pride of place at the US Naval Academy in Annapolis. A helicopter gunship was named *Apache*. The United States has Tomahawk cruise missiles; and in April 2017, President Donald Trump ordered fifty-nine of them fired at a Syrian airbase after Syria's president, Bashar al-Assad, was accused of using chemical weapons on Syrian people for the second time. Native Americans affected the way all Americans think about and conduct war.

Consider an example from World War II. In the closing days of the war in Europe, Dwight David Eisenhower, the Supreme Allied Commander, was pressured by Winston Churchill and other politicians to launch a frontal assault designed to capture Berlin. Eisenhower, aware of the tremendous casualties that would be incurred, refused this counsel. Let the Soviet Red Army have the honor and the casualties. Eisenhower had grown up in Abilene, Kansas. The Indian chieftains of the Plains thought in precisely parallel terms about warfare. They were reluctant to launch assaults on US forts, particularly if others could do the job for them. More braves would return to their squaws as a result. More American GIs would return home from Europe too.

America entered its overtly imperial phase after its quick victory in the Spanish-American War of 1898. The "water cure," a torture technique learned on the western frontier, was applied in the Philippines during the guerrilla war that raged there from 1899 until 1902. During this period, much of coastal America was fortified to defend against invasions that never materialized. While some regard this as pointless and wasteful, others appreciate the parks and wildlife refuges that were then bequeathed to posterity.

In 1917, President Wilson led America into the "war to end all wars." More than two million Americans served "Over There."

In World War II, America would take on fascism and Imperial Japan. American soil would be invaded in the remote Aleutian Islands, merchant ships would sink in view of the nightlights of Manhattan, and Japanese balloon bombs would rain down upon at least fifteen Western states. Hitler hoped to build Amerika jet bombers that would be capable of striking the United States. Japan actually built the largest submarines, which were underwater aircraft carriers capable of bombing the United States.

After the war, America would lead the West in the Cold War against Communism. There were widespread fears of espionage, sabotage, and betrayal in the new atomic age, but America was not really invaded.

America's status as a global superpower made her a target for attacks at the start of the twenty-first century. On 9/11/2001, the World Trade Center and the Pentagon were struck by hijacked commercial aircraft, damaging the latter and utterly destroying the former. America was attacked in a way never before imagined.

The nature of what constitutes an invasion has changed over time. Instead of targeting battleships and fortifications, enemies can now launch cyberattacks that target credit scores, corporations, the digital financial infrastructure, and even the democratic electoral process.

In *America Invades*, we defined an American invasion as "an armed attack or intervention in a country by American forces." In *America Invaded*, we took a more expansive approach to include invasions, attacks, and raids that took place within our borders, and even some fighting off American coasts.

A reader of *America Invaded* will often be reminded of the fluidity of political boundaries of the states. New Hampshire, Maine, and Vermont were eventually detached from Massachusetts. West Virginia was carved out of Virginia during the Civil War. Our methodology, as in *America Invades*, was to treat the current political boundaries as definitive. If, for example, an event occurred during the American Revolution in what is today West Virginia, we included it in the West Virginia chapter.

*America Invaded* was in many ways inspired by my personal journey of discovery of American military history. In 2014, I drove through thirty-six states on my book tour for *America Invades*. Walking the forests of Saratoga, New York, and along the Jackson Line near New Orleans proved invaluable in the writing of this work. Climbing Dorchester Heights to gaze on sweeping views of Boston Harbor helped me to appreciate Henry Knox's accomplishment in 1776. The Mitchell Monument near Bly, Oregon, where six Americans—five children and a pregnant woman—were killed by a Japanese balloon bomb, provided a poignant reminder of the wastefulness of war. Visiting Fort Missoula, the site of the Olive Oil Riot, furnished details that could not be captured by book searches. America's national parks are a tremendous resource for those curious about the past. Some of America's greatest historians are park rangers. In *America Invaded*, we have attempted to provide information that will facilitate the reader's own exploration of America's rich military history.

Our book does not purport to be a comprehensive account of *all* fighting in the United States. There were over 10,000 named battles and skirmishes in the Civil War alone. Our account has, of necessity, been selective. Our guiding principle was to include aspects that are of historic importance and interest to modern readers.

Our volume does include many incidents that were not, strictly speaking, invasions. The Gunfight at the O. K. Corral was not an invasion, but it is an episode of fighting on US soil. The struggle in the cockpit over Shanksville,

Pennsylvania, on 9/11 was not an invasion, but it is an important example of fighting in American airspace.

Our book also includes essential tourist information about sites connected to American military history in all fifty states and Washington DC. We cordially invite you to visit our website, www.americainvaded.com, which has more comprehensive listings and much more information.

Finally, we could not resist including some references to fictional invasions, from P. G. Wodehouse to Phillip K. Dick's *Man in the High Castle*. Imaginative works have always colored people's perceptions of the nature of war and invasion.

We invite you to see America for yourself and explore the many ways in which the country has been invaded and fought over. These invasions have, for good or ill, reshaped her and in many ways defined her.

# ALABAMA

Sweet home Alabama has been invaded and fought in many times over its history.

Humans first arrived in the area we know today as Alabama many thousands of years ago. Bows and arrows were introduced in the woodland era, from 300 BCE to AD 1000. The Mississippian culture, which began around AD 700, featured mound builders.

The Alabama, Choctaw, Cherokee, Chickasaw, and Creek (or Muscogee) were the principal tribes of Alabama. *Alabama* is a Muscogee word meaning *campsite*.

The first Europeans to explore the area were the Spanish. For instance, as early as 1519, Alonzo Álvarez de Pineda was venturing into Mobile Bay.

The Spanish explorer Hernando de Soto entered Alabama in 1540. It wasn't an entirely auspicious start to European settlement in Alabama. At the Battle of Mabila, located somewhere in what is now Alabama, de Soto found himself outwitted and forced to flee from an ambush by warriors under the command of the local ruler, Chief Tuskaloosa.

Other Spanish would follow him, but they too had little success in attempts to settle in the area. And then the French would arrive.

In 1702, the Le Moyne brothers—Pierre Le Moyne d'Iberville and Jean-Baptiste Le Moyne, Sieur de Bienville—founded Fort Louis de la Louisiane and its adjacent settlement, La Mobile, as the capital of New

France in the Louisiana territory. In 1711, after a flood inundated Fort Louis, Bienville moved Mobile to its current location.

However, while the French were trying to establish themselves in the region, the English had their own plans for the area, and English traders began to be active there.

The French would control Alabama until the conclusion of the Seven Years' War in 1763, when the territory passed to the British. Mobile briefly became the capital of British West Florida, thereby becoming part of the fourteenth British colony in the New World.

In January 1780, Captain William Pickles (great name!) of the Continental Navy rendezvoused with Spanish General Bernardo de Gálvez, who was leading over 750 Spanish troops. Their object was to attack the British outpost at Fort Charlotte in Mobile. The two-week siege lasted from March 2–14 and ended with British surrender. The city of Galveston, Texas, would later be named in honor of the Spanish general.

After the American Revolution, the southern half of what is now Alabama would form part of the Mississippi Territory. However, the section of Alabama that included the port of Mobile remained in Spanish hands.

The advance of American power in Alabama brought with it the usual process of pressuring Native Americans to relinquish control of their lands. Already, for instance, in 1805–6, lands were being opened up to settlers in large parts of western and northern Alabama, land that was held by Native American tribes such as the Muscogee and the Cherokee.

In 1811, Tecumseh, a Shawnee chief born in present-day Ohio, came down to Alabama in an effort to unite the Indian tribes against the encroachments of the American settlers. Most of the tribes ignored Tecumseh, but a portion of the Creek Nation known as the Upper Creeks did not. They allowed him to address their general meeting at Tukabatchee in what is today Elmore County. Tecumseh is reputed to have said:

> Brush from your eyelids the sleep of slavery; once more strike for vengeance; once more for your country. The red men have fallen as the leaves now fall. I hear their voices in those aged pines. Their tears drop from the weeping skies. Their bones bleach the hills of Georgia. Will no son of those brave men strike the pale face and quiet these complaining ghosts? Let

the white race perish! They seize your land; they corrupt your women; they trample on the bones of your dead! Back whence they came, upon a trail of blood, they must be driven!

The Creeks who were sympathetic to his message became known as the Red Sticks because of their red painted war clubs. The great comet of 1811 was seen by some as a portent for an uprising in the south; Tecumseh's name in Shawnee meant *shooting star*.

Tecumseh would align himself and the tribes of the Great Lakes with Britain against the Americans in the War of 1812.

The Creek War broke out in southern Alabama on July 27, 1813, with the Battle of Burnt Corn Creek. Colonel James Caller of the Alabama militia attacked a party of about two hundred Red Sticks led by Peter McQueen. The Alabama militia had some initial success, but the Red Sticks launched a counterattack, driving the militia from the field.

One of the deadliest attacks ever launched by Native Americans on settlers took place in Alabama during the Creek War. The Fort Mims Massacre, a reprisal for the Battle of Burnt Corn Creek, was fought on August 30, 1813. William Weatherford, known as Red Eagle, led thousands of Red Stick warriors against Fort Mims on the Alabama River. Around five hundred men, women, and children were killed that day with only about thirty of the settlers managing to escape the carnage. Fort Mims Park, featuring a partial reconstruction of the fort, is operated today by the Alabama Historical Commission.

On November 12, 1813, the small but memorable Canoe Fight occurred along Randon's Creek. Four Americans, led by Captain Sam Dale, fought and killed a canoe full of eleven Red Stick warriors. Among the Americans was a black man named Caesar, who paddled the boat through the hand-to-hand struggle.

The Battle of Holy Ground was fought on December 23, 1813, between the US militia and Weatherford's Red Sticks. Weatherford managed to escape by jumping, with his horse Arrow, off a fifteen-foot bluff.

The scale of the Fort Mims Massacre shocked Americans and drew national attention to Alabama. Andrew Jackson led a force of Tennessee militia south to fight the Creeks in Alabama. General John Floyd led elements of the Georgia militia west against the Creeks.

Andrew Jackson was a complicated man. He demonstrated both surprising compassion and horrific cruelty during the course of the Creek War. On November 3, 1813, Jackson oversaw a massacre of Red Sticks at the Battle of Tallushatchee. Nearly two hundred Red Sticks were killed in the space of a half hour. Jackson showed compassion on the field of battle by adopting an orphaned Creek boy and raising him as his own son, Lyncoya. Sadly, Lyncoya died of tuberculosis at age seventeen. Jackson and his wife Rachel had been planning to educate him at West Point.

On November 9, 1813, Jackson won a significant victory at the Battle of Talladega. Over three hundred Red Stick warriors were slain.

Andrew Jackson had another decisive victory over the Red Sticks on March 27, 1814, at the Battle of Horseshoe Bend. It must be noted that around six hundred Native American warriors from the Cherokee and Lower Creek tribes fought alongside Jackson against the Red Sticks. Approximately nine hundred Red Sticks were killed; Jackson's forces lost fewer than eighty men.

Jackson ordered the cutting off of nose tips after the Battle of Horseshoe Bend in order to count the bodies. Old Hickory became known to the Creeks as Sharp Knife for this harsh approach.

After the Battle of Horseshoe Bend, Weatherford, who was half Scottish and half Creek, walked into the American camp and surrendered. He declared to Jackson, "I am in your power." Sharp Knife chose to pardon Red Eagle, who lived peacefully in Alabama until his death in 1824.

The Americans strongly suspected the Europeans of encouraging the Red Sticks in the Creek War. American forces discovered correspondence between the Creeks and officials in Spanish Florida. Major General James Wilkinson was ordered to seize Spanish-occupied Mobile. On April 14, 1813, Wilkinson landed with four hundred American troops. The outnumbered Spanish garrison surrendered the next day. By the terms of the Treaty of Ghent, Mobile was the only territorial gain of the War of 1812.

In September of 1814, British forces under the command of Lieutenant Colonel Edward Nicolls landed in Alabama in an attempt to seize Fort Bowyer near Mobile. The attack was repelled. On December 5, 1814, British Admiral Alexander Cochrane penned a letter to the Creeks that was an attempt to fan the fire ignited by Tecumseh.

The Great King George, our beloved Father, has long wished to assuage the sorrows of his warlike Indian Children, and to assist them in regaining their rights and Possessions from their base and perfidious oppressors. ... If you want arms and ammunition to defend yourselves against your oppressors—come to us and we will provide you. ... And what think you we ask in return for this bounty of our Great Father, which we his chosen Warriors have so much pleasure in offering to you? Nothing more than that you should assist us manfully in regaining your lost lands,—the lands of your forefathers,—from the common enemy, the wicked People of the United States; and that you should hand down those lands to your children hereafter, as we hope we shall now be able to deliver them up to you, their lawful owners.

Even after Jackson's decisive American victory at the Battle of New Orleans (see Louisiana), the British did not abandon hope. In February 1815, British troops landed in Alabama and assaulted Fort Bowyer a second time, capturing the fort on February 11, 1815. The British would soon withdraw from Alabama after learning that the Treaty of Ghent, which ended the War of 1812, had been signed on December 24, 1814.

In 1819, Alabama became the twenty-second state to join the Union.

In the following decades, more Native American land was ceded to settlers. The years 1836–1837 saw the Second Creek War, which culminated in 1837 with the Battle of Hobdy's Bridge, the last battle against Native Americans that took place in Alabama. In 1838, Native Americans were sent westward on the Trail of Tears.

Alabama, a slave state, joined the Confederacy in February 1861. Montgomery briefly became the first capital of the Confederacy, from February until May of 1861, when she was succeeded by Richmond, Virginia. Around 120,000 Alabamians would serve in the gray armies of the Confederacy. Alabama was also a center of iron manufacturing, contributing much-needed artillery to the rebel cause. The state itself, however, was mostly on the periphery of military action during the Civil War.

However, some fighting did take place there.

In February 1862, Union gunboats moved up the Tennessee River to Florence. And the Union established a stronghold in parts of northern Alabama.

In April 1863, Colonel Abel Streight led Union forces on a raid on Confederate communication lines. Despite a Union victory in the Battle of Day's Gap, the raid turned into a disaster for Streight's men, who eventually were forced to surrender to Confederate troops.

In July 1864, Major General Harrison Lovell Rousseau led a Union raid on Confederate targets in north and east-central Alabama, disrupting Confederate communications and destroying supplies.

The year 1864 also saw Union land victories in the Battle of Athens and the Battle of Decatur.

The naval Battle of Mobile Bay was fought off the Alabama coast on August 5, 1864. At the battle's crisis, Rear Admiral David G. Farragut, the Union leader, famously exclaimed something like, "Damn the torpedoes, full speed ahead." This Union victory contributed to Lincoln's reelection in November of 1864.

The CSS *Alabama*, built near Liverpool, was the most famous Confederate commerce raider of the US Civil War. Her captain, Raphael Semmes, was born in Maryland but later adopted Alabama as his home. Under her bold captain, the *Alabama* terrorized Union shipping from the Atlantic to the Pacific for two years, capturing and burning sixty-five vessels. She was finally sunk on June 19, 1864, in the English Channel off Cherbourg by the armored Union ship *Kearsarge*.

In 1865, the war would hit Alabama even more severely. In March, Union Major General James H. Wilson launched a cavalry raid deep into Alabama, defeating Confederate forces and taking Selma before heading for Montgomery.

In April, after the Battle of Spanish Fort and the Battle of Fort Blakely, Mobile itself—one of the Confederacy's last deep-water ports—finally fell to the Union.

On May 4, 1865, General Richard Taylor, commanding the last major Confederate force in Alabama, surrendered at Citronelle.

The USS *Alabama* is a South Dakota-class battleship that was launched in 1942 and supported the liberation of the Philippines in World War II. She can be found today at the Battleship Memorial Park in Mobile.

The training of African-American airmen at Tuskegee is also a noteworthy feature of Alabama's war effort during World War II. In March of 1941, First Lady Eleanor Roosevelt was a passenger in a plane flown by an African-American pilot over Alabama.

German U-boats operated in the Gulf of Mexico in 1942 and 1943. During the month of May in 1942, they sank forty-one merchant ships in the Gulf.

## ALABAMA
## MILITARY HISTORY SITES

**Battleship Memorial Park (USS Alabama)**
Location: 2703 Battleship Parkway, Mobile, AL 36602
Web: ussalabama.com

**Citronelle Depot Museum & Grounds**
Location: 19000 South Center Street, Citronelle, AL 36522
Web: citronellehps.org

**Crooked Creek Civil War Museum**
Location: 516 CR 1127, Vinemont, AL 35179
Web: alabama.travel/places-to-go/crooked-creek-civil-war-museum

**First White House of the Confederacy**
Location: 644 Washington Avenue, Montgomery, AL 36130
Web: firstwhitehouse.org

**Fort Mims**
Location: 1813 Fort Mims Road, Tensaw, AL 36579
Web: ahc.alabama.gov/properties/ftmims/ftmims.aspx

**Fort Mims Restoration Association**
Web: fortmims.org

**TECUMSEH**
1768-1813
Visited Alabama in 1811
Source: akg-images/
Glasshouse Images

**FORT MIMS MASSACRE**
August 30, 1813
Source: akg-images/ClassicStock
Charles Phelps Cushing

**ANDREW JACKSON**
1767-1837
Source: iStock/GeorgiosArt

**USS ALABAMA** (BB-60)
Commissioned in 1942
Source: Author photo

Nickname: The Cotton State
Statehood: 1819
Capital: Montgomery

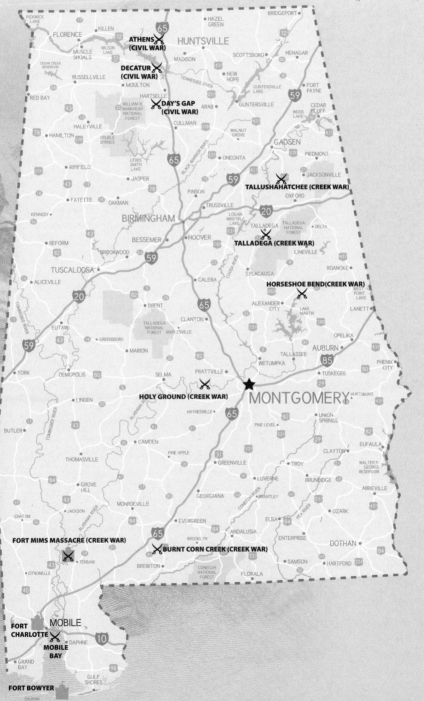

**Fort Mims State Historic Site**
Web: nps.gov/places/fort-mims.htm

**Holy Ground Battlefield Park**
Location: 300 Battlefield Road, Lowndesboro, AL 36752
Web: alabama.travel/places-to-go/holy-ground-battlefield-park

**Horseshoe Bend National Military Park**
Location: 11288 Horseshoe Bend Road, Daviston, AL 36256
Web: nps.gov/hobe

**Tuskegee Airmen National Historic Site**
Location: 1616 Chappie James Avenue, Tuskegee, AL 36083
Web: nps.gov/tuai

# ALASKA

The US Army officers who were planning Operation Landcrab, the 1943 invasion of the Aleutian island of Attu, must have received a shock when they studied maps of the invasion. Their route would pass through Massacre Bay. The bay received its name not on account of the 1942 invasion and occupation of the island, but due to a much earlier slaughter of the Aleut people by the Russians. The area we know today as Alaska had been subject to waves of invasions long before the 7th Motorized, or Hourglass, Division was assigned the task of liberating Attu from Japanese control in World War II.

Between 13,000 and 15,000 years ago, humans crossed the Bering Land Bridge from Siberia into the area now known as Alaska. These Paleolithic people adapted to the harsh climate and supported themselves by fishing and hunting. In the eighteenth century, it was Russian traders who arrived in Alaskan waters in pursuit of seals and fur-bearing animals.

In June of 1778, Captain James Cook of the HMS *Resolution* sailed into the inlet that now bears his name. He explored Alaskan waters, searching in vain for a northwest passage. In his Journals, Cook wrote that "several of the Natives paid us a visit, and brought with them a few skins some pieces of Salmon and Holibut which they exchanged with our people for old cloaths or whatever they could get." Cook traded with the wary natives, but did not really fight them. He also discovered evidence of Russian contact with the native tribes.

In 1732, Mikhail Gvozdev was the first Russian to investigate Alaskan waters. Vitus Bering, a Danish explorer who served in Czar Peter the Great's navy, explored the coast of Alaska in 1741. He died, probably of scurvy, on the voyage, and is buried on Bering Island. In 1784, the Russians established their first settlement in Alaska, at Three Saints Bay on Kodiak Island.

The Spanish were also taking an interest in the region, and a number of Spanish expeditions reached the area in the eighteenth century. In 1789, Alessandro Malaspina, an Italian explorer in the service of the Spanish crown, set out on a circumnavigation of the globe. He eventually made it to Alaskan waters, where he surveyed the coast and stopped at Yakutat Bay. The Malaspina Glacier is named after the Tuscan sailor.

In 1799, the Russian-American Company, a joint stock company, was founded. From 1804 to 1867, it enjoyed a monopoly on fur trading in Alaska. The Russians built forts, intermarried with some of the native people, and attempted to convert them to Orthodox Christianity.

Resistance by the indigenous people to Russian colonization dated nearly from the Russians' arrival. In 1802, the Tlingit tribe destroyed a Russian settlement at Redoubt Saint Michael. In 1804, the Russians won a victory at the Battle of Sitka, which was really more of a skirmish. At least twelve Russians were killed, and Governor Baronov was wounded. Tlingit casualties are unknown.

The Tlingit did not surrender after the battle. In 1805, the tribe wiped out a Russian settlement at Yakutat Bay. In spite of Russian pacification efforts, Tlingit resistance continued until 1858.

The British were also interested in the area. For instance, the Hudson's Bay Company established Fort Yukon in 1847.

And the American Civil War found its way to Alaskan waters. In fact, it continued in Alaskan waters after it had officially stopped elsewhere. The commander of the Confederate raider the CSS *Shenandoah* hadn't realized the war was finished when the ship entered the Bering Sea off Alaska. Between June 22 and 28, 1865, the *Shenandoah* captured over twenty ships and destroyed most of them. It wasn't until August 2 that the commander, James Iredell Waddell, had firm confirmation that the war had ended on May 9. After receiving the news, the CSS *Shenandoah* set sail for Britain, where it arrived in November, the only Confederate ship to circumnavigate the globe.

In 1867, Czar Alexander II, recognizing the growing power of the United States and unable to defend Russia's overseas empire, sold Alaska to the Americans. American critics were quick to condemn "Seward's folly," which added nearly 600,000 square miles to the Union at a bargain price of $7.2 million. The first American troops began arriving in Alaska in October of 1867. Regardless, Russian influence on Alaska is still felt today, with the onion-domed churches of Sitka and the predominance of Orthodox Christianity among the native people.

The Klondike Gold Rush focused attention on a disputed border between Canada and the Alaska region. The dispute would not finally be resolved until 1903.

Soon after the Pearl Harbor attack of December 7, 1941, concern grew about the defensibility of Alaska. Three days prior to Pearl Harbor, attack submarines of the Imperial Japanese Navy began conducting covert reconnaissance of the Aleutian Islands. Jimmy Doolittle's famous air raid on April 8, 1942, known as the Tokyo Raid, did little physical damage but had a tremendous psychological impact on the Japanese. Needing to secure their homeland from future attacks, the Japanese sought to establish a defensive perimeter far from their home islands. The Aleutians Islands, off the Alaska Peninsula, are closer to Tokyo (about 2,400 miles) than San Francisco. This need for defense compelled the Japanese to attack Midway Island in June 1942. The Japanese Navy's defeat at the Battle of Midway was a turning point of the war in the Pacific.

The Midway campaign was a two-pronged offensive. The major part ended in disaster for the Japanese at Midway. The secondary part, led by Admiral Kakuji Kakuta, was an attack on American forces in the Aleutian Islands. Two Japanese aircraft carriers, *Ryūjō* and *Junyo,* launched an air attack on Dutch Harbor, the principal American military base in the Aleutians on June 3–4, 1942. Only a weak American naval presence containing no aircraft carriers had been allocated to Alaska. A transport ship, *Northwestern*, was sunk, and several buildings were damaged in Dutch Harbor.

In the predawn hours of June 7, 1942, the Japanese began landing about 2,500 troops on the islands of Attu and Kiska. A tiny American garrison was quickly overwhelmed and captured. The Japanese, learning of their naval disaster at Midway, settled in for a long occupation of the remote islands. B-17s from Alaska's Eleventh Air Force were soon bombing Japanese positions on the islands. Combatants on both sides had to contend with the hazards and discomfort of the frigid Aleutian climate.

The capture of American territory by the Japanese was an embarrassment for the US government. Alaska was strategically important to Allied war efforts, partly because military materiels flowed through Alaska on their way to the Soviet Union, as allowed by the Lend-Lease Act of 1941. The Japanese needed to be expelled from American soil.

American naval forces reinforced Alaska while Japanese troops were dramatically reduced after Midway. On March 26, 1943, the Battle of the Komandorski Islands, a surface-fleet engagement lacking carriers, was fought in Alaskan waters. After three and half hours of trading gunfire, Admiral Hosogaya was forced to withdraw. The United States finally had naval supremacy in Alaskan waters, setting the stage for a reinvasion of the Aleutian Islands.

That invasion began on May 11, 1943, when scout battalions launched from American submarines landed on Attu. The American battleships *Idaho* and *Pennsylvania* bombarded Chichagof Harbor. The 7th Division, which had distinguished itself during World War I, soon established its beachhead at Massacre Bay. Three weeks of bloody fighting by 15,000 American troops was required to kill nearly 3,000 Japanese defenders. Colonel Yasuyo Yamasaki, the Japanese commander, was killed while wielding a sword in a desperate banzai attack. Fewer than thirty Japanese prisoners were taken on Attu.

The August 1943 invasion of Japanese-occupied Kiska was widely anticipated to be a repeat of the carnage experienced on Attu. Instead, 35,000 American invaders found the island deserted, but booby-trapped. The Japanese had evacuated via submarine the previous month. Americans suffered over three hundred casualties due mainly to friendly fire, booby traps, and trench foot.

The Japanese had been expelled from Alaska. About two hundred Japanese balloon bombs called Fu-Go would, however, fall harmlessly on the vast Alaskan territory in 1944 and 1945. On April 13, 1945, nine balloons were spotted over Attu and shot down by P-38 fighters from the 11th Air Force.

Alaska became the forty-ninth American state in 1959. Soviet submarines prowled along the Alaskan coastline during the Cold War. In the 1980s, the *Arctic Storm*, a fishing vessel, lost its nets and over $150,000 of equipment in

Alaskan waters. The US Navy denied responsibility, and many suspected a Soviet submarine was responsible for the accident.[1]

The Russians completed construction of a new submarine base in Kamchatka in 2015.


## ALASKA
### MILITARY HISTORY SITES

**Alaska Aviation Museum**
Location: 4721 Aircraft Drive, Anchorage, AK 99502
Web: www.alaskaairmuseum.org

**Alaska State Museum-Juneau**
Location: 395 Whittier Street, Juneau, 99801
Web: museums.alaska.gov

**Aleutian World War II National Historic Area Visitor Center**
Location: Amaknak Island, Unalaska Airport, Unalaska, AK 99685
Web: nps.gov/aleu

**Fort Abercrombie State Park & Kodiak Military History Museum**
Location: 1400 Abercrombie Drive, Kodiak, AK 99615
Web: dnr.alaska.gov/parks/units/kodiak/ftaber.htm
Web: kadiak.org

**Klondike Gold Rush National Historic Park**
Location: 291 Broadway, Skagway, AK 99840
Web: nps.gov/klgo

**Museum of the Aleutians**
Location: 314 Salmon Way, Unalaska, AK 99685
Web: aleutians.org

---

1    Source: August 2016 interview by CRK with *Arctic Storm's* owner, Wally Pereyra.

**ST. MICHAEL'S
RUSSIAN ORTHODOX
CHURCH** (Sitka)
Source: iStock/NNehring

**ALEUTIAN ISLANDS CAMPAIGN 1943** Source: akg-images

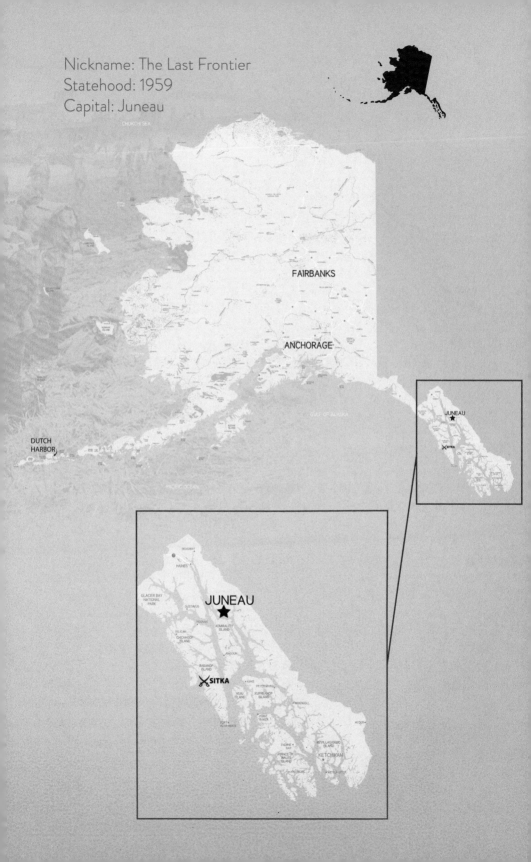

Nickname: The Last Frontier
Statehood: 1959
Capital: Juneau

**Pioneer Park & Pioneer Air Museum**
Location: 2300 Airport Way, Fairbanks, AK 99701
Web: old.fnsb.us/pioneerpark
Web: pioneerairmuseum.org

**Sitka National Historical Park**
Location: Tongass National Forest, 103 Monastery Street, Sitka, AK 99835
Web: nps.gov/sitk

**The Sitka History Museum**
Location: Harrigan Centennial Hall, 330 Harbor Drive, Sitka, AK 99835
Web: sitkahistory.org

# ARIZONA

Native Americans have a long history in what is now known as Arizona. The Hopi town of Oraibi in northeastern Arizona was founded before AD 1100, making it the oldest continuously occupied settlement in the United States. Successive waves of Native Americans migrated to Arizona over the next centuries. The Pueblo dominated the area from the eleventh to the fourteenth centuries. The Apache and Navajo arrived in Arizona from the north (Canada) around AD 1300.

A Spanish priest, Father Marcos de Niza, was the first European to explore Arizona in 1539. The Spanish conquistador Francisco Vázquez de Coronado passed through Arizona in 1540. Coronado did not find gold here, but he did journey along the rim of the Grand Canyon.

Spanish missionaries soon "invaded" Arizona, building nine missions from 1629 until 1768. Attempts were made to convert and enslave the indigenous people. The Pueblo Revolt of 1680 spilled into Arizona, which was part of New Spain at the time (see New Mexico).

And more rebellions were to come. For instance, in 1751 the Pima Revolt, also known as the O'odham Uprising, broke out. A peace deal was eventually negotiated; and in 1752, a presidio, or fort, was established at Tubac to help control the locals.

In 1776, Presidio San Augustin del Tucson was established. It was soon to see action. The fort was attacked a number of times in the next years as part of an ongoing struggle for power between Spanish authorities and Apaches.

Spanish rule over Arizona ended with the Mexican Revolution of 1821. The area became part of the Mexican province of Sonora. Intermittent warfare flared in Sonora between Mexicans and Native Americans. The foot-fighting Apaches were meanwhile driven from the plains to the mesas of Arizona by the horse-mounted Comanche.

In 1829, the Apache leader Geronimo was born near the Upper Gila River in Sonora, along what is now the Arizona-New Mexico border. Throughout his long lifetime, Geronimo led many raids against Mexicans, declaring in his autobiography, "I have killed many Mexicans; I do not know how many, for frequently I did not count them."

Most of what comprises Arizona was added to the United States as a direct result of the Mexican-American War (1846–48). Fighting did not really take place in Arizona during that war. General Stephen Kearny and about a hundred dragoons of the US Army did, however, pass through Arizona on their way to California from New Mexico in 1846 (see California). The town of Kearny, Arizona, in Pinal County was named in his honor. The Treaty of Guadalupe Hidalgo, signed in 1848 at the end of the war, compensated Mexico for lost territory, including Arizona, with $15 million.

The 1850–53 Yuma War, pitting the US Army against the Yuma tribe, mainly took place in California, but Arizona saw some action.

In 1854, the US Senate ratified the Gadsden Purchase from Mexico, which, at a cost of $10 million, added over 29,000 square miles to the United States, including much of southern Arizona.

In 1856, American Dragoons occupied Tucson.

As settlers and miners entered the area, tensions with the Apache rapidly led to clashes.

The New Mexico Territory, including Arizona, had considerable sympathy for the Confederate cause during the US Civil War, and Arizona briefly became Confederate territory.

In 1862, Colonel James Carleton marched east from California with 2,300 Union troops (known as the California Column) to quell Confederate support in the New Mexico Territory. Confederate sympathizers had seized Tucson in February 1862, proclaiming it the capital of the Confederate Arizona Territory. Union and Confederate forces skirmished at the Battle of Picacho Peak near Tucson on April 15, 1862. Carleton may have come to Arizona intending to fight Confederates, but he wound up fighting Apaches. The Battle of Apache

Pass, fought near Fort Bowie on July 15–16, 1862, was a lopsided American victory over Apache warriors. Carleton established a brutal reputation among the Apache, declaring, "All Indian men of that tribe are to be killed whenever and wherever you can find them."

The Arizona Territory was carved out of the New Mexico Territory in 1863.

Colonel Christopher Houston "Kit" Carson, a legendary figure of the American West, led over three hundred troopers of the 1st New Mexico Cavalry against the Navajo. The Battle of Canyon de Chelly was won by Carson in Arizona Territory on January 12–14, 1864. After their defeat, about eight thousand Navajo were forced onto a reservation in New Mexico in what became known as the Long Walk of the Navajo. The site of Canyon de Chelly is today one of the nation's most popular National Monuments.

And tensions with the Apache were about to flare up again. In April 1871, almost 150 Apache were slaughtered in the Camp Grant Massacre. The period of fighting that followed dragged on for years.

Lieutenant Howard Cushing, a veteran of the Civil War, had been posted to the Arizona Territory in 1867. On May 5, 1871, he and his cavalry troop engaged a band of Apache warriors at the Battle of Whetstone Mountains. Cushing later became known as the Custer of Arizona.

Lieutenant Colonel George Crook launched a campaign to track down the Apache and their Yavapai allies and return them to reservations. The campaign saw US victories, such as the Battle of Salt River Canyon and the Battle of Turret Peak.

Geronimo had a long history of fighting the Mexican military, and eventually he clashed with the US military and US settlers as well. In fact, rumors persist that Cushing may have been killed by Geronimo himself. After 1871, Geronimo lived as a man on the run between Mexico and the southwestern United States for many years. In 1886, he finally surrendered to American authorities at Skeleton Canyon, Arizona. Geronimo ultimately converted to Christianity and settled down to a peaceful life. He even joined in Teddy Roosevelt's inaugural parade in 1905. Arizona's most famous warrior died at age eighty in Oklahoma in 1909.

Arizona remained a dangerous territory even after the conclusion of the main Indian Wars. On October 26, 1881, the Gunfight at the O. K. Corral was fought in Tombstone between a gang of outlaws called the Cowboys and lawmen led by Wyatt Earp. Three of the outlaws were slain after a thirty-second exchange of gunfire.

In 1882, the Reverend Endicott Peabody, later the founder of Groton School, "invaded" Tombstone. He arrived just a few months after the Gunfight at the O. K. Corral. Peabody built the first Protestant church in Arizona, even getting lawman Wyatt Earp to help foot the bill for the altar rail.

Arizona was the forty-eighth and final state in the contiguous United States to join the Union, in 1912. The battleship *Arizona*, a Pennsylvania-class dreadnought, was launched the following year in honor of Arizona statehood.

The Battle of Naco was fought in the fall of 1914, mainly between Mexican rival factions. Nevertheless, Buffalo Soldiers under Colonel John Guilfoyle were sent to Naco to guard the border with Mexico. One American soldier was killed in the crossfire.

In January 1917, news of the Zimmerman Telegram, in which Kaiser William II of Germany proposed an alliance with Mexico in the event that America joined the Allied side in World War I, shocked Americans. On April 4, 1917, the Senate voted to declare war on Germany. Before it ended, World War I would come to Arizona.

Border towns on the Arizona-Mexico border were a persistent source of tension and dispute. On August 27, 1918, these tensions erupted into violence in what became known as the Battle of Ambos Nogales. A Mexican carpenter was carrying a large package across the border when a US customs agent told him to halt. A shot was fired. The customs agent was killed, and both sides quickly escalated the violence. A nearby detachment of Buffalo Soldiers was called in. Six Americans and over one hundred and twenty Mexicans were killed, including many civilians. Among the Mexican dead were two Germans who may have been agents provocateurs.

And even in 1918, US forces and Native Americans could still clash. The Battle of Bear Valley in January saw US Cavalry tackle a group of armed Yaqui.

The first aerial bombardment of an American target in the continental United States took place in Arizona. Patrick Murphy, an American pilot, dropped bombs on Naco during the Escobar Rebellion. He was employed as a mercenary at the time. No one was killed in these attacks.

On Sunday December 7, 1941, a Japanese bomb found the magazine of the *Arizona* as it lay at anchor at Pearl Harbor. The subsequent explosion killed 1,177 members of its officers and crew. The submerged fuel tanks of the ship weep drops of oil that are visible to this day at the Arizona Memorial.

During World War II, several hundred Navajo from Arizona were recruited by the US Marine Corps as code talkers. Using code based on their native languages, the code talkers transmitted messages by radio and phone during the war. Their codes were never broken. Today, over one quarter of the state of Arizona is made up of Indian reservations, including the Navajo Nation.

At least two Fu-Go, Japanese balloon bombs, landed in Arizona in 1945. One was at the border town of Nogales, while another landed in Ajo. No one was injured.

In May 2011, US Navy Seals chose to honor Geronimo by using his name as the code word to confirm the identification of Osama bin Laden, killed in their successful raid on Abbottabad, Pakistan.

## ARIZONA
## MILITARY HISTORY SITES

### Arizona Military Museum
Location: 5636 East McDowell Road, Phoenix AZ 85008
Web: dema.az.gov/army-national-guard/papago-park/arizona-military-museum

### Canyon de Chelly National Historic Site & Visitor Center
Location: Canyon de Chelly National Monument, Indian Route 7, Chinle, AZ 86503
Web: nps.gov/cach

### Navajo Code Talkers Museum
Location: Moenave Street, Tuba City, AZ 86045
Web: discovernavajo.com/museums.aspx

**GERONIMO STAMP**
1829-1909
Source: iStock/raciro

**CANYON DE CHELLY**
Battle of Canyon de Chelly,
January 12-14, 1864
Source: iStock/venemama

**WYATT EARP**
1848-1929
Source: akg-images

**USS ARIZONA (BB-39)**
Launched 1915
Source: akg-images/arkivi

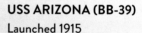

**ENDICOTT PEABODY**
1857-1944
Groton School, Groton MA
Source: Author photo

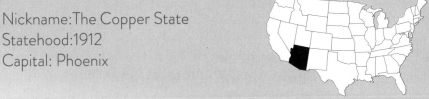

Nickname: The Copper State
Statehood: 1912
Capital: Phoenix

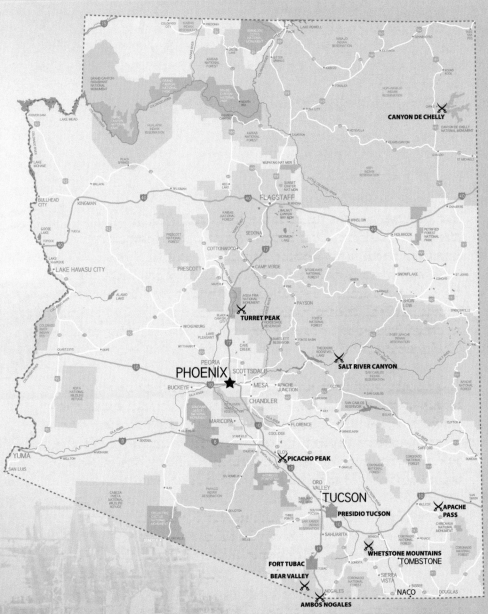

CANYON DE CHELLY

FLAGSTAFF

TURRET PEAK

SALT RIVER CANYON

PHOENIX

PICACHO PEAK

TUCSON

APACHE PASS

PRESIDIO TUCSON

WHETSTONE MOUNTAINS

TOMBSTONE

FORT TUBAC

BEAR VALLEY

AMBOS NOGALES

**Navajo Nation Museum-Hwéeldi Baa Hane' Exhibit**
Location: Highway 264 and Loop Road, Window Rock, AZ 86515
Web: navajonationmuseum.org

**O.K. Corral® Historic Complex**
Location: 326 East Allen Street, Tombstone, AZ 85638
Web: ok-corral.com

**Picacho Peak State Park**
Location: 15520 East Picacho Peak Road, Picacho, AZ 85141
Web: azstateparks.com/picacho

**Pima Air & Space Museum**
Location: 6000 East Valencia Road, Tucson AZ 85756
Web: pimaair.org

**Presidio San Agustín del Tucson**
Location: 196 North Court Avenue, Tucson, AZ 85701
Web: tucsonpresidio.com

**Spanish Colonial Missions-Southwest Travel Itinerary**
Location: Multiple sites across Arizona
Web: nps.gov/subjects/travelspanishmissions/list-of-sites.htm

**Titan Missile Museum**
Location: 1580 West Duval Mine Road, Sahuarita, AZ 85629
Web: titanmissilemuseum.org

**Tombstone National Heritage Museum**
Location: 517 Fremont Street at 6th Street, Tombstone, AZ 85638
Web: thetombstonemuseum.com

**Western Spirit: Scottsdale's Museum of the West**
Location: 3830 North Marshall Way, Scottsdale AZ 85251
Web: scottsdalemuseumwest.org

# ARKANSAS

Humans have inhabited the area we know today as Arkansas for a very long time. The Mississippians built mounds around Arkansas in AD 1300 that are still visible today.

Many Native American tribes made their homes in Arkansas, including the Osage, Caddo, and Quapaw. Arkansas is, in fact, a Siouan word derived from *Acansa*—the name of a Quapaw village in southeastern Arkansas.

The Spanish explorer Hernando de Soto crossed the Mississippi River on June 28, 1541, into what is today Arkansas, searching for gold. His "invasion" of Arkansas lasted about a year and was the first visit to this area by Europeans. De Soto died on the banks of the Mississippi, near or in Arkansas, of natural causes in 1542.

In 1673, coming from the opposite direction, French explorers Father Jacques Marquette and Louis Joliet came south on the Mississippi, getting as far as an area inhabited by Quapaw, near where the Arkansas and Mississippi Rivers meet, before heading north again.

Robert de La Salle explored Arkansas for the French in 1681. In 1686, Henri de Tonti, a Neapolitan serving Louis XIV, established the Arkansas Post. This was an important trading post on the banks of the Arkansas River. A number of forts were constructed around the post to provide security against Native Americans. The French formed an informal alliance with the local Quapaw tribe, supplying them with arms and trading furs.

In 1738, the French, with local allies, launched a campaign against the Chickasaw.

The 1762 Treaty of Fontainebleau gave Spain control of the Louisiana Territory, including Arkansas. During the American Revolution, the British and their native allies attempted to seize Arkansas Post from the Spanish. They were defeated on April 17, 1783, at the Battle of Arkansas Post. Spain would control Louisiana until 1800, when it ceded it to Napoleonic France in the Third Treaty of San Ildefonso.

Campo de la Esperanza was established opposite Memphis in 1797. It became a Spanish naval outpost and, again, was used to counter Chickasaw raiders.

In 1803, all of Arkansas was included in the Louisiana Purchase, which consummated the sale of territory by Napoleon to the United States.

And in 1804, American explorers Dr. George Hunter and William Dunbar traveled up the Ouachita River to Hot Springs.

More American settlers would soon arrive, bringing slavery with them. Fort Smith was first established by the US military in 1817.

In 1817, the US government established a Cherokee nation in Arkansas. Many other Arkansas tribes perceived this as an "invasion" of their territory.

Eventually, the familiar process of Native Americans being dispossessed would take place. For instance, in 1824, Quapaw ceded the rest of their land south of the Arkansas River. In 1828, the Cherokees left their northwest Arkansas territory and moved westward.

Arkansas played a role in the Texas Revolution as a base for rebels and a source of volunteers.

The Arkansas Territory joined the Union as the twenty-fifth state in 1836.

Construction of the Arsenal Barracks began in Little Rock in 1840. The Barracks were built mainly to protect settlers and travelers from potential attacks by Native Americans.

On May 6, 1861, Arkansas voted to secede from the Union with other Southern states. Support for the Union remained, however, especially in the Ozark Mountains. Thousands of Arkansans would serve in gray during the Civil War, though some would fight in blue as well. Over 5,000 ex-slaves from Arkansas would fight in the Union Army.

In early 1862, Confederate hopes were high. General Van Dorn, a great-nephew of Andrew Jackson, hoped to advance through Arkansas and seize St. Louis, Missouri.

The Battle of Pea Ridge, fought near Bentonville from March 7–8, 1862, was likely the most important Civil War battle fought in Arkansas. An outnumbered Union force commanded by Major General Samuel Curtis repelled attacks by Confederate forces led by Major General Van Dorn. Confederate ranks were augmented by Native American cavalry that was commanded by Brigadier General Albert Pike, a Little Rock newspaperman. Van Dorn was forced to withdraw his forces across the Mississippi, leaving Arkansas largely undefended.

A second attempt by the Confederates to reestablish control of Arkansas was mounted by Major General Thomas C. Hindman, who moved into the northwest of the state in the autumn of 1862. At the Battle of Prairie Grove on December 7, Hindman was confronted by Union troops under Brigadier General Herron. Although outnumbered three to one, Herron managed to detain Hindman by ordering immediate attacks until reinforcements under Brigadier General Blunt arrived. Hindman was thwarted. Largely due to his weak artillery and poor supply situation, he was forced to withdraw. Although Prairie Grove was on balance a tactical draw, it was a strategic victory for the Union. Never again would the Confederates be able to make a serious attempt to recover control of Arkansas.

In the Battle of Arkansas Post, fought January 9–11, 1863, an overwhelming Union force of around 33,000 led by Major General John McClernand defeated a smaller Confederate force, about 5,000, led by Brigadier General Thomas Churchill. Most of the Confederates, mainly dismounted Texas cavalry, surrendered to the superior Union Army near Fort Hindman.

After the fall of Vicksburg in 1863, the Confederacy was effectively cut in two along the line of the Mississippi River. The western portion of the Confederacy, including Arkansas, was no longer able to supply vital livestock to the South.

Many small-scale engagements were fought in Arkansas throughout the Civil War. The Battle of Helena, fought on the Fourth of July, 1863, secured the eastern half of the state for the Union. Little Rock was captured by the Union in September 1863. A month later, on October 25, Union cavalry skirmished with Confederates at the Battle of Pine Bluff. The 3rd Arkansas

Infantry Regiment would fight with Lee in Virginia until the surrender at Appomattox Courthouse in 1865.

Soon after the Civil War ended, another war hit Arkansas. Well, sort of. The 1874 Brooks-Baxter War saw a close gubernatorial election turn into a literal battle for power as militias supporting each contender clashed. Brook's militia initially ejected Baxter from the Arkansas Capitol building. Militia supporting Baxter counterattacked, and eventually US troops stepped in and restored Baxter to power.

In 1880, Douglas MacArthur was born in the Arsenal Barracks, which had been renamed the Little Rock Barracks in 1873, to a military family. This distinguished graduate of West Point would serve in France in World War I. MacArthur eventually became a five-star US general who famously "returned" to liberate the Philippines in World War II. As Commander of UN forces, he planned and executed the successful invasion of Inchon during the Korean War. MacArthur Park and MacArthur Museum of Arkansas Military History can be found in Little Rock today, near his birthplace.

Arkansas was not, of course, invaded during World War II. However, more than 23,000 German and Italian prisoners of war were held at bases in the state, such as Fort Smith and Camp Robinson.

Titan II missiles were based in Arkansas during the Cold War. On August 9, 1965, fifty-three workers were killed by an accidental fire at an Arkansas launch facility.

## ARKANSAS
## MILITARY HISTORY SITES

### Arkansas Air & Military Museum
Location: 4290 South School Avenue, Fayetteville, AR 72701
Web: arkansasairandmilitary.com

### Arkansas Heritage Trails
(Civil War Trails-Trail of Tears-Butterfield Trail-Southwest Trail)
Location: across Arkansas
Web: arkansasheritagetrails.com

Nickname: The Natural State
Statehood: 1836
Capital: Little Rock

**DOUGLAS MacARTHUR STAMP**
1880-1964 Born on
January 26, 1880, in Little Rock
Source: iStock/traveler1116

**BATTLE OF PEA RIDGE**
March 7-8, 1862
Source: akg-images

**Arkansas Post National Memorial**
Location: 1741 Old Post Road, Gillett, AR 72055
Web: nps.gov/arpo

**Fort Smith National Historic Site**
Location: 301 Parker Avenue, Fort Smith, AR 72901
Web: nps.gov/fosm
Museum of History, National Cemetery, and Air Museum in proximity

**Historic Arkansas Museum**
Location: 200 East Third Street, Little Rock, AR 72201
Web: historicarkansas.org

**MacArthur Museum of Arkansas Military History**
Location: 503 East 9th Street, Little Rock, AR 72202
Web: macarthurparklr.com/military-history-museum

**Museum of Veterans & Military History**
Location: 53 North Mount Olive Road, Vilonia, AR 72173
Web: veteransmuseumvilonia.com

**Pea Ridge National Military Park**
Location: 15930 East Highway 62, Garfield, AR 72732
Web: nps.gov/peri

**William J. Clinton Presidential Library & Museum**
Location: 1200 President Clinton Avenue, Little Rock, AR 72201
Web: clintonlibrary.gov

**WWII Japanese-American Internment Museum**
Location: 100 South Railroad Street, McGehee, AR 71654
Web: rohwer.astate.edu

# CALIFORNIA

The great California writer John Steinbeck noted in his novel *Tortilla Flat* that "Monterey had been invaded many times in two hundred years." Not just Monterey, though, and not just the past two hundred years.

Many waves of European explorers/invaders arrived on the Pacific Coast, disrupting the indigenous people and eventually paving the way for an American conquest. The Spanish were the first Europeans to explore what is now the state of California. For instance, in 1542, Juan Rodriguez Cabrillo stopped at a place he named Bahia de los Pinos, better known today as Monterey Bay.

In 1602, Sebastián Vizcaíno cruised along the southern California coast. He left a major legacy of his efforts by naming San Diego, Santa Catalina Island, Santa Barbara, and Monterey. However, the Spanish were to have little enthusiasm for extending their influence farther in the area until the eighteenth century, when they began to fear other European powers expanding into it.

At that time, the Spanish sought to extend both their religious and military influence, both by sea routes and by land routes. Father Junipero Serra established the first Spanish mission in the area in San Diego in 1769, and Spanish officer Gaspar de Portolà led a military contingent and claimed the region for Spain. The Spanish seized Monterey. In 1775, 240 colonists, led by Juan Bautista de Anza and Father Pedro Font, moved from Sonora to San Francisco harbor.

The Spanish eventually built twenty-one missions in Alta and attempted to convert the natives to Catholicism. Diseases such as measles devastated the indigenous population, and the Spanish enslavement of native people generated some opposition. An uprising in 1775 in San Diego, for example, led to the deaths of three Spaniards. The Spanish tightened their grip on California by building presidios, or forts, in Monterey, San Francisco, Santa Barbara, and San Diego. The Spanish explorer Juan Francisco de la Bodega y Quadra charted the waters near Bodega Bay in 1775. The first major European fortification built in California was at the Presidio of San Francisco, which was constructed by the Spanish in 1776.

The Spanish would soon be followed by the British. Sir Francis Drake, the famous Elizabethan pirate, arrived off the shores of California in 1579, hoping to capture Spanish treasure ships. Accounts vary as to whether he stopped in Drake's Bay, California, the Oregon coast, or even possibly British Columbia. Other Englishmen followed. A fur trader by the name of James Hanna traveled there in 1785; George Vancouver, an officer in the Royal Navy, arrived in Spanish California in 1792. Vancouver, observing the weak defenses of the Dons, noted that an invasion of California would be "an event which is by no means improbable." The Hudson's Bay Company engaged in fur trapping along the west coast.

In 1837, rumors swirled that Mexico might cede California to Britain in exchange for repayment of debt. American fears of a renewed British presence in California helped spur the call for Manifest Destiny.

Many Englishmen have followed in the footsteps of Drake and Vancouver, smitten by the California sun and the lure of economic opportunity. Charlie Chaplin, Basil Rathbone, Alfred Hitchcock, and John Cleese are just a few Englishmen that have launched personal and peaceful "invasions" of California. Hollywood would be hard-pressed to make movies without the help of English villains! Among the many English actresses that have "invaded" California are Julie Andrews and Angela Lansbury.

The French also were attracted to California. In 1786, Jean-François de Galaup La Pérouse of the French Navy arrived in Monterey to assess the territory with a view to expanding opportunities for trade and commerce. Abel du Petit-Thouars returned in 1837 to scout for whaling opportunities. Captain Cyrille Laplace arrived with the *L'Artémise* in 1839 and became friendly with Governor Alvarado. He even warned Alvarado about the avaricious intentions of the Americans, and suggested the formation of a French protectorate.

Many Frenchmen would beat a path to California, some attracted by the state's winemaking potential. George de Latour would found Beaulieu Vineyard in 1900. A bubbly "invasion" of California was launched in 1973 with the introduction of méthode champenoise by Domaine Chandon.

Czarist Russia made a serious bid for California, which left a legacy that endures to the present. In 1806, officials of the Russian-American Company first visited San Francisco. They sought mainly a source of food to supply their colony in Russian Alaska. In 1812, the same year that Napoleon invaded Russia, the Russians "invaded" northern California, establishing Fort Ross in what is today Sonoma County. The Russians already had an important colony established in Alaska, where the harsh climate made agriculture problematic. Eighty Aleuts and twenty-five Russians helped build a stockade. The cannons of Fort Ross were never fired in anger. Today Fort Ross is a California state park.

The Russians traded with the native Kashaya people who had inhabited the land around Fort Ross for thousands of years. Some Russian colonists intermarried with Kashaya women. The Russians and their Aleut allies pursued sea otters and planted orchards, growing peaches, apples, and pears. They built a Russian Orthodox church. An outbreak of smallpox in 1837 decimated the indigenous people, and by the 1830s, the sea otter population had been greatly diminished (only about 2,500 otters remain in the twenty-first century). The Russians opted in 1841 to sell Fort Ross to Captain John Sutter, a Mexican citizen of Swiss extraction, who later became famous for igniting the California Gold Rush of 1849.

The Russian departure from Fort Ross in 1842 did not mean the end of Russian influence on California. A Russian Orthodox cathedral was built in San Francisco in 1881. The Russian River, popular with kayakers, cuts through Sonoma County. Fictional Russians would return to Northern California (doubling for Massachusetts) in 1966 to film *The Russians Are Coming, the Russians Are Coming* near Fort Bragg. In 2016's *Hail Caesar*, a Soviet submarine is met off the California coast by a boatload of leftist Hollywood screenwriters.

The Spanish did not perceive the Russian presence at Fort Ross as much of a threat to their empire. In fact, Spanish sovereignty over California was repeatedly tested and weakened. In 1808, Napoleonic France invaded Spain, providing a catalyst for the Mexican Revolution. Hippolyte Bouchard, a French Argentine, commanded two ships that cruised against the Spanish in 1818. In December of that year, Bouchard's pirates seized and subsequently burned much of San Juan Capistrano. A revolution that swept aside Madrid's power in the New World would begin in 1810 and culminate with Mexican independence in 1821.

During the Mexican period, Father Eugene Macnamara from County Clare led a brief Irish "invasion" of the San Joaquin Valley. A stream of American immigrants also began to flow into Mexican California.

In 1844, James Polk, an aggressive expansionist, was elected president of the United States. During the campaign, he had threatened British Canada with the slogan "Fifty-four forty or fight!" (Oregon's northern boundary is 54 degrees, 40 minutes.) After his inauguration, however, he focused his attention southward, toward Mexico. In 1845, he annexed Texas and prepared for war with Mexico. In June of 1845, Brevet Captain John C. Frémont set out from St Louis on an expedition to explore and map the source of the Arkansas River. Included in Frémont's command were the frontiersman Kit Carson and a band of Delaware Indian scouts. Frémont, known as the Pathfinder, wound up in Sacramento in January 1846. After being confronted by the Mexican General Castro at Gavilan Peak, Frémont withdrew north into Oregon.

By April 27, 1846, hostilities in the Mexican-American War began. A three-pronged invasion would conquer Mexican California on behalf of the Americans: Captain Frémont marched his group of filibusters south from Oregon, Commodore John Sloat of the US Navy's Pacific squadron led a naval offensive, and Brigadier General Stephen Kearny invaded southern California.

In June, Frémont captured towns in Sonoma. On July 1, he was ferried across the San Francisco Bay and spiked ten Mexican cannon. On July 4, 1846, the Bear Flag Republic was proclaimed, and Frémont became the head of the California Army.

General Kearny, a veteran of the War of 1812, was appointed to command the Army of the West in 1846. He set out with a force of nearly 1,700 men from Fort Leavenworth, Kansas, in June of that year. After capturing Santa Fe (see New Mexico), Kearny led his much-reduced force into Mexican California. Kearny and his men soon occupied San Diego. Frémont captured San Luis Obispo that same month.

Prior to the war, Commodore John Sloat had been instructed to seize San Francisco in the event of hostilities between the United States and Mexico. On July 7, 1846, Sloat captured Monterey with a force of three ships and fewer than three hundred sailors and marines without a shot being fired. Sloat immediately announced the annexation of California. By the end of July, the sixty-eight-year-old Sloat was replaced in command of the Pacific squadron by "Fighting Bob" Stockton. Commodore Stockton ferried Frémont's men south, where they captured San Diego and Los Angeles.

On August 9, 1846, General Castro of the Californio forces called for "Death to the Invaders," but promptly fled south to Mexico. All seemed to be going remarkably smoothly for the Americans, who were now in charge of all significant towns in California, but not for long. Archibald Gillespie, left in charge of Los Angeles with a force of forty-eight men, began to impose a harsh and unpopular martial law. Californio resistance coalesced under the leadership of Andrés Pico, a ranchero who owned the oldest building in the San Fernando Valley, which still stands today.

The bloodiest battle of the American invasion of California was fought on December 6, 1846, at San Pasqual, between General Kearny's forces and the Californios, led by Pico. Nineteen Americans were killed in the fifteen-minute-long engagement, most pierced by the willow lances of the mounted Californios, who were excellent horsemen. Kearny himself was wounded, but his regulars forced the Californios to withdraw. Casualties among the Californios are unknown. The intervention of naval and marine forces would quickly overwhelm the resistance of the Californio forces. Frémont and Pico negotiated the Treaty of Cahuenga, which ended the fighting in California. Pico Boulevard in Los Angeles honors the family of the Californio leader.

Victory by American forces in the Mexican-American War led finally to the Treaty of Guadalupe Hidalgo in 1848, which ceded California to the United States. California was admitted to the Union in 1850, and Frémont became one of the state's first two senators.

The discovery of gold near Sutter's Fort in the Sacramento Valley in 1849 spurred a Gold Rush that brought a flood of new settlers to California. The Gold Rush was followed by waves of immigrants from Europe, Asia, and other parts of the United States.

The continual flow of settlers created intense competition for land, and the Native American population often suffered severe brutality from US forces and settlers. A series of clashes and minor wars occurred. For instance, in 1850, 130 Pomo men, women, and children were killed by US forces on an island in Clear Lake. The Mariposa War of 1851 saw Native American resistance crushed in the Sierra Nevada. The Yuma fought US forces over control of the Yuma crossing of the Colorado River. Overall, a huge percentage of the Native American population in California was wiped out during the nineteenth century.

Gold from California played a significant role in funding the Union during the Civil War. Ulysses S. Grant wrote, "I do not know what we would do in this great national emergency were it not for the gold sent from California."

Some smaller units made up of Californians would fight on the Union side in the Civil War. The California battalion formed part of the Second Massachusetts Cavalry and fought in over fifty engagements, mainly in Virginia. The California brigade suffered high casualties at Antietam in 1862 and at Gettysburg in 1863. A California Column was used to drive Confederate sympathizers out of Arizona and New Mexico.

Fort Mason was built in 1864 during the Civil War on property owned by Frémont. It was intended to protect San Francisco from Confederate raiders. The previous year, a group of Confederate sympathizers had outfitted a schooner, the *J. M. Chapman,* to serve as a privateer operating out of San Francisco Bay. Most Californians, however, remained loyal to the Union.

The 1860s and 1870s saw a number of clashes between US forces and Native Americans in Northern California, during the so-called Snake War of 1864–1868 and the Modoc War of 1872–1873.

When the War of the Pacific was fought (1879–1883) between Chile on one side against Peru and Bolivia, the Chilean Navy was considered superior to the US Navy's Pacific fleet, and America did not intervene.

As Pacific powers such as Russia and Japan expanded their respective navies, the security of California's long coastline became of heightened concern. Forts Baker, Barry, and McDowell were built to defend San Francisco from feared invasions between 1876 and 1905. In 1917, Fort MacArthur (named after Chester MacArthur) was built in San Pedro during World War I. More California forts would be built during World War II.

On December 7, 1941, the battleship *California,* moored near the southern edge of Ford Island at Pearl Harbor, was struck on her port side by two Japanese torpedoes. The Tennessee-class battleship sank (and was later refloated), and one hundred members of her crew were killed. After the Pearl Harbor attack, submarines of the Imperial Japanese Navy prowled offshore of California, and fear gripped the West Coast. The Rose Bowl scheduled for New Year's Day 1942 in Pasadena was initially cancelled due to fears of further Japanese attacks. Ultimately the game was played in Durham, North Carolina, where Oregon State beat Duke, 20 to 16.

On December 23, 1941, the Imperial Japanese Navy's *I-21* under Commander Matsumura torpedoed and sank the oil tanker *Montebello* off the California coast, near Cambria. The surfaced sub also used its machine guns to shoot crew members that were attempting to use the ship's lifeboats. Poor visibility allowed the crew to escape. In 1996, the wreck of the *Montebello* was discovered. Eight of its ten oil storage tanks are an on-going environmental concern as they rust in coastal California waters.

On February 23, 1942, *I-17* surfaced near Santa Barbara. The Japanese sub used her 140mm deck guns to shell the Ellwood oil refinery with sixteen to twenty-four rounds. Damage was minimal and no one was killed or injured in the attack, but Radio Tokyo crowed, "Sensible Americans know that the submarine shelling of the Pacific coast was a warning to the nation that the Paradise created by George Washington is on the verge of destruction."

In the early morning hours of February 25, 1942, the air-raid sirens of Los Angeles sounded after an unknown aircraft triggered a blip on the radar. Anti-aircraft guns fired over ten tons of ordnance into the night sky. Eight citizens died during the "raid," mostly due to heart attacks. The phantom raid had involved no Japanese planes. Panic had swept the West Coast. This incident later inspired Stephen Spielberg's movie *1941*.

The US Navy's decisive victory at the Battle of Midway in June of 1942 largely eliminated the threat of Japanese invasion to California and the West Coast. In November of 1944, the first of at least twenty Japanese balloon bombs to land in California was spotted off the coast of San Pedro, near Fort MacArthur, by a US auxiliary ship.

Philip K. Dick's 1962 science-fiction novel *The Man in the High Castle* (and the subsequent TV series) posited an Axis victory of World War II and a Japanese occupation of California and the West Coast.

The small rocky island at the heart of San Francisco Bay known as Alcatraz has been subject to many invasions over time. In the 1850s, it was fortified by the US Army Corps of Engineers. During the Civil War, it was used to defend against Confederate privateers on the Pacific Coast and to house Confederate prisoners of war. It would later evolve from a military prison into a federal maximum-security prison, housing the likes of Al Capone and "Machine Gun" Kelly. The prison was finally closed in 1963. In 1969, Native Americans "invaded" the island and occupied it as a protest for two years. Today Alcatraz is "invaded" daily by masses of tourists eager to hear tales of "The Rock."

On December 2, 2015, fourteen Americans were killed in a terrorist attack in San Bernardino, launched by an American citizen and his Pakistani-born wife.

## CALIFORNIA
### MILITARY HISTORY SITES

**Fort MacArthur Museum—Battery Osgood-Farley Historic Site**
Location: 3601 S. Gaffey Street, San Pedro, CA 90731
Web: www.ftmac.org/

**Fort Ross State Historic Park**
Location: 19005 Coast Highway One, Jenner, CA 95450
Web: www.fortross.org

**Golden Gate National Recreation Area—San Francisco County**
(Alcatraz Island, Battery Chamberlin, Crissy Airfield & Field Center, Fort Mason, Fort Point, Presidio of San Francisco) Location: South of Golden Gate Bridge
Web: www.nps.gov/goga

**Japanese American National Museum**
Location: 100 North Central Avenue, Los Angeles, CA 90012
Web: www.janm.org

**Mission Dolores (Mission San Francisco de Asís)**
Location: 3321 16th St, San Francisco, CA 94114
Web: www.missiondolores.org/old-mission/visitor.html

**Nixon Presidential Library & Museum**
Location: 18001 Yorba Linda Boulevard, Yorba Linda, CA 92886
Web: www.nixonlibrary.gov

**Pacific Battleship Center (USS Iowa)**
Location: 250 South Harbor Boulevard, Los Angeles, CA 90731
Web: www.pacificbattleship.com

**Ronald Reagan Presidential Library & Museum**
Location: 40 Presidential Drive, Simi Valley, CA 93065
Web: www.reaganfoundation.org

**San Francisco National Maritime Historic Park
(USS Pampanito, SS Jeremiah O'Brien)**
Location: Pier 45 Fisherman's Wharf, San Francisco, CA 94133
Web: www.maritime.org
Web: www.ssjeremiahobrien.org

**San Pasqual Battlefield State Historic Park**
Location: 15808 San Pasqual Valley Road, Escondido, CA 92027
Web: www.parks.ca.gov

**Sutter's Fort State Historic Park**
Location: 2701 L Street, Sacramento, CA 95816
Web: www.suttersfort.org

**USS Hornet Sea, Air, & Space Museum**
Location: 707 W Hornet Avenue, Pier 3, Alameda, CA 94501
Web: www.uss-hornet.org

**USS Midway Museum**
Location: 910 North Harbor Drive, San Diego, California, 92101
Web: www.midway.org/

# America Invaded: CALIFORNIA

CALIFORNIA REPUBLIC

FORT BRAGG

THE RUSSIAN RIVER

FORT ROSS

★ SUTTER'S FORT
**SACRAMENTO**

FORT BAKER

FORT BARRY
FORT McDOWELL
•ALCATRAZ
FORT PRESIDIO
FORT MASON

SAN
FRANCISCO / YERBA BUENA

• ALCATRAZ

• STOCKTON

CALIFORNIA

• MONTEREY

**FORT ROSS STATE
HISTORIC PARK**
A Russian fort
from 1812-1842
Source: Author photos

SANTA BARBARA
**BATTLE OF ELLWOOD** ⚔

**MISSION DOLORES**
San Francisco, founded 1776
Source: Oona Kelly

Nickname: The Golden State
Statehood: 1850
Capital: Sacramento

### JUNÍPERO SERRA
**1713-1794, Mission Dolores**
San Francisco
Source: Oona Kelly

### JOHN C. FRÉMONT
**The Pathfinder, 1813-1890**
Source: iStock/wynnter

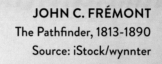

### ALCATRAZ
Alcatraz Island
Source: akg-images/
De Agostini/W. Buss

LOS
ANGELES •

FORT MacARTHUR

PACIFIC
OCEAN

SAN PASCUAL

• SAN DIEGO

# COLORADO

ong before the Europeans came to what is now Colorado, a number of Native American peoples made it their home. But the Europeans were definitely coming.

In 1682, French explorer Robert de La Salle claimed what is now Colorado east of the Rockies in the name of France. Later, French explorers like the Mallet brothers, Pierre and Paul, would explore parts of eastern Colorado.

Meanwhile, the Spanish too were taking an interest in Colorado territory.

The Spanish may have reached parts of what is now Colorado as early as the sixteenth century. In 1706, Juan de Ulibarrí entered southeastern Colorado; and in the eighteenth century, a number of Spanish attempts to explore the region took place. For instance, in 1765, an expedition under Juan Maria Rivera headed into the San Juan and Sangre de Cristo Mountains looking for precious metals. In 1776, Escalante and Dominguez explored the west of what is now Colorado. In 1779, Juan Bautista de Anza, then governor of New Mexico, attacked a Comanche village on Fountain Creek. In 1787, he set up a short-lived settlement near what is now Pueblo.

The Spanish even sent a military expedition onto the plains of eastern Colorado in 1720, but the attempt turned into a disaster (from the Spanish point of view) when the column was ambushed by Native Americans in what is now Nebraska.

In 1803, though, the French sold their claims on eastern Colorado to the United States under the Louisiana Purchase, and soon the expanding power of the United States would come into contact with the Spanish in the area.

In 1806, Lieutenant Zebulon M. Pike was dispatched with a small reconnaissance party to investigate this new land that the United States had purchased. A year later, he went a bit too far (from the Spanish point of view). He crossed the Sangre de Cristo Mountains into the San Luis Valley. The Spanish arrested him and took him to Santa Fe, but they later let both him and his men go.

Further US expeditions into the area were to come. For instance, in 1820, Major Stephen H. Long, while investigating the southwest limits of what the United States had bought, advanced up the South Platte River. And in 1842, Lieutenant John C. Frémont began a series of five expeditions into the Rocky Mountains. His last would be in 1853.

Meanwhile, American traders and trappers were moving into the area. Soon the United States would take over Spanish claims in what is now Colorado.

In 1846, during the Mexican-American War, the Army of the West under General Kearney advanced through southeastern Colorado and eventually took New Mexico. And in 1848, under the peace deal that ended the war, Mexico handed over to the United States its claims to a big chunk of Colorado. Then in 1850, the US government bought from Texas its claims on Colorado territory.

The US government might assert that it owned all the land of what is now Colorado, but not everybody agreed. In 1851, a new permanent settlement was established at Conejos in the San Luis Valley, and Fort Massachusetts was set up to protect the settlers from local Native American resentful of the newcomers taking land.

In 1854, Utes and Apaches, led by Ute leader Tierra Blanca, attacked Fort Pueblo, killing all fifteen inside. Following that, Ute warriors entered the San Luis Valley and attacked more settlers. In April 1855, the American cavalry won a victory at the Battle of Poncha Pass, and the fighting came to a temporary end.

Gold was found in the area in the 1850s, and the Pike's Peak gold rush reached its height in 1859 as miners flooded into the area.

Other changes were coming. Also in 1859, American settlers established Jefferson Territory on what was self-administering US territory, even though it was never recognized by the US government. In 1861, a large portion of Jefferson Territory was renamed Colorado Territory.

Colorado was not exactly a focus of the Civil War. Perhaps the closest to an actual Civil War battle in Colorado was the 1862 Battle of Glorieta Pass, when Confederate forces intending to invade Colorado and smash Union control in the West were defeated in New Mexico by Union forces, including troops from Colorado. However, some in Colorado did have Confederate sympathies, and Confederate partisans probably did operate there, although there was a perhaps inevitable tendency during the war to attribute crimes committed by nonpolitical criminals to roving bands of desperate Confederates.

In August 1864, twenty alleged Confederate partisans who had been attacking trains and stagecoaches were captured by Colorado troops. En route to Fort Lyon, they were all killed, allegedly during an escape attempt, though some suspect a deliberate massacre.

Certainly one massacre would happen soon after, though it was a massacre of Native Americans, not of Confederates.

Tensions had been rising for years as miners advanced farther into Colorado in search of gold, pushing Cheyenne and Arapaho out of some of their territory. Attempts were made by the US government to force the Cheyenne and Arapaho onto a small reservation. In April 1864, American forces attacked a group of Cheyenne at Fremont's Orchard. Native Americans retaliated, attacking settlers and mail stations. By autumn, extensive damage had been done, and Denver was cut off by the attacks.

Volunteer American units reacted with brutality. Colonel John Chivington's men had already been involved in the deaths of the twenty Confederate partisans. In November, he ordered the 3rd Colorado Volunteers to attack a peaceful Cheyenne camp at Sand Creek. Cheyenne chief Black Kettle had both a US flag and a white flag flying to show his peaceful intentions toward US forces. Nevertheless, the seven-hundred-man attacking force, equipped with four howitzers, slaughtered between two and three hundred men, women, and children, often with particular brutality. Chivington's actions provoked public outrage and were severely condemned by later enquiries into the massacre.

Native Americans responded with more attacks into 1865, including attacking Julesburg in January and February. In September 1868, at the Battle of Beecher Island, a small group of US scouts trailing raiders were attacked by a much larger Native American force, and they only just managed to hold out until relief parties arrived. But American military might ruthlessly applied was having an impact. In November, Black Kettle was killed by forces under Lieutenant Colonel George Armstrong Custer at the Washita River. Custer's forces, in an action described by some as a battle and by others as a massacre, launched a surprise attack on a village, killing, wounding, and capturing a number of fighters and civilians. The 1869 fighting at Summit Springs, in which US cavalry and Pawnee scouts attacked a Cheyenne band led by Tall Bull, marked an end to major fighting in the east of the region.

In 1876, Colorado became a state of the Union. Some more fighting, though, was still to come.

In 1879, Utes rebelled against attempts to turn them into settled farmers, leading to the White River War, or Ute War. US Indian Agent Nathanial Cook Meeker, who had been leading the attempts to resettle the Utes, was killed in the so-called Meeker Massacre, and a column of troops sent to his aid clashed with Ute fighters at Milk Creek. The US forces suffered heavy losses in the initial fighting, and were only saved by relief columns rushing to their aid.

When the fighting was over, the Ute were forced off most of their lands in Colorado and expelled to Utah.

Native American resistance would not last forever. In 1888, the brief so-called Colorow's War erupted from a dispute over an alleged incident of horse theft. Mistrust and misunderstandings led to a clash between Utes from Utah and Colorado National Guardsman. Comparatively small though the incident was, it was also, in a sense, the end of an era. Colorow, a Native American leader who was also involved in the much more serious Milk Creek fighting, would die later the same year.

Other incidents of violence would follow, including the Ludlow Massacre of April 10, 1914, as the Colorado National Guard and camp guards of the Colorado Fuel & Iron Company were sent in against striking miners. Stability, however, was coming to Colorado. And Colorado has, of course, played a major role since then in military matters. For instance, by hosting the headquarters for the North American Aerospace Defense Command (NORAD) and the Cheyenne Mountain Complex. And Coloradans, including, for example, Admiral Arleigh Burke—who fought in World War II and the Korean War, and eventually served as Chief of Naval Operation—have gone on to fight in other wars, just not within the borders of Colorado. In 1955, construction began on the United States Air Force Academy in Colorado Springs.

# America Invaded: **COLORADO**

Nickname: The Centennial State
Statehood: 1876
Capital: Denver

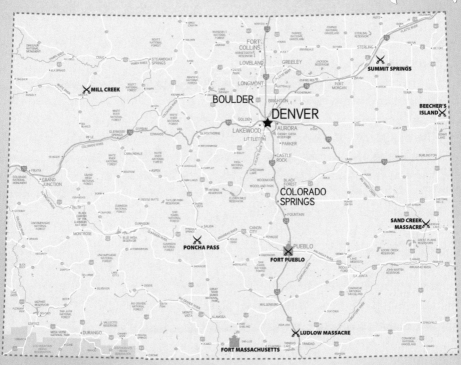

**US AIR FORCE ACADEMY**
Colorado Springs
Founded 1954
Source: iStock/mtcurado

The end of the nineteenth century did not, however, mean Colorado had seen its last attack from abroad. During World War II, Colorado was subject to attack from a number of Japanese balloon bombs, though they did little damage.

## COLORADO
## MILITARY HISTORY SITES

**Fort Collins Museum of Discovery**
Location: 408 Mason Court, Fort Collins, CO 80524
web: fcmod.org

**History Colorado Center**
Location: 1200 Broadway, Denver, CO 80203
Web: historycoloradocenter.org

**National Museum of World War II Aviation**
Location: 755 Aviation Way, Colorado Springs, CO 80916
Web: worldwariiaviation.org

**Peterson Air & Space Museum**
Location: 150 East Ent Avenue, West Gate Entry, Peterson AFB, CO 80914
Web: petemuseum.org

**Sand Creek Massacre National Historic Site**
Location: 910 Wansted, POB 249, Eads, CO 81036
Web: nps.gov/sand

**United States Air Force Academy**
Location: 2304 Cadet Drive, Colorado Springs, CO 80840
Web: usafa.af.mil

**Wings Over the Rockies Air & Space Museum**
Location: 7711 East Academy Boulevard, Denver, CO 80230
Web: wingsmuseum.org

# CONNECTICUT

When Europeans arrived in the area, they found it inhabited by Algonquian peoples like the Pequot, Mohegan, and Nipmuc. The name *Connecticut* comes from a Mohegan word, *Quinnehtukqut*, referring to a long river.

The Dutch were the first Europeans to explore the area. In 1614, Adriaen Block actually sailed up the Connecticut River, and soon the Dutch were trading along its banks. And in 1633, they established a fort and called it the House of Hope. However, if the Dutch were hopeful of controlling the area long-term, they were in for a disappointment.

Already in 1631, the Earl of Warwick had issued the Warwick Patent, granting land rights in what is now southeastern Connecticut. And in 1633, the same year that the Dutch were setting up the House of Hope, William Holmes established a trading post that became the town of Windsor. In 1634, Captain John Oldham started a settlement that became the town of Wethersfield. Fort Saybrook was established in 1635; and in 1636, Thomas Hooker founded Hartford.

Things weren't looking good for the Dutch, but the situation was looking even worse for the local Native American population. They had already suffered heavily from smallpox caught from the European settlers, and now a battle for control of the region would lead to bitter fighting. In cooperation with the Dutch, the Pequot had attempted to establish control over trade and over the other native peoples in the area. The expansion of English power and attempts by other tribes to destroy Pequot dominance produced a tense and dangerous situation. The deaths of two English traders at the hands of the Pequot ignited the Pequot War. The Pequot and their local allies were up against not just the English, but also other Native Americans, including the Narragansett and the Mohegan.

In the spring of 1637, the Pequot besieged Fort Saybrook and launched raids against the Connecticut English. English forces struck back brutally. On May 26, 1637, English forces under Captain John Mason and John Underhill, along with Native American allies, surrounded a palisaded Pequot village near what is now Groton. What followed was the Mystic Massacre, as the English forces first set light to the village and then killed anyone who escaped the flames. Hundreds died. The massacre and subsequent defeat of the Pequots in the rest of the war left the tribe broken and almost exterminated.

Another devastating war would strike New England a few decades later. King Philip's War saw the English and native allies (including the Mohegan and some Pequots) fight the Wampanoag under their leader, Metacom, and their Native American allies. Militiamen from Connecticut were heavily involved in the fighting. A lot of the action took place outside Connecticut, but some combat also took place there. For instance, Nipmucs attacked Groton on March 13, 1676, and Simsbury was attacked on March 26 by Metacom's forces. English forces carried out reprisals against Native American settlements in Connecticut, and significant numbers of natives were taken out of Connecticut as slaves. By the end of the war, Metacom was dead and the Wampanoag, Nipmuc, and Narragansett had been almost wiped out.

A number of wars followed that involved Native Americans and the French to the north, but on the whole, Connecticut's role in these was restricted to sending men to fight. The action took place elsewhere.

A large white oak tree grew in Hartford. It was the Charter Oak since, according to legend, it concealed a copy of Connecticut's Royal Charter in its hollows. The white oak became a symbol of American independence.

When the American Revolution erupted, Connecticut was back in the firing line. It became known as the Provision State because of all the supplies it sent to the revolutionary cause, and Connecticut militiamen served at key battles, such as Bunker Hill. But Connecticut also saw a number of raids. One of the more dramatic was the one on Danbury. British forces under Major

General William Tryon landed on the coast in April 1777 and marched to Danbury, where they destroyed buildings and stores.

In retaliation, in May of the same year, Colonel Return Jonathan Meigs launched a raid on Long Island using thirteen whaleboats. After destroying ships and stores, the attackers returned with ninety-six prisoners. Whaleboats armed as privateers and operating out of Stamford scored a number of successes against British targets.

However, perhaps the most historically significant action in Connecticut during the war was a raid led by a Connecticut man. Yes, Benedict Arnold was born in Norwich. And on September 6, 1781, by then fighting for the British, he led an attack on New London and Groton. The attack on New London was a success. Fort Trumbull fell quickly, and the British destroyed stored provisions in the town. However, taking Fort Griswold at Groton was considerably harder. British casualties were high, and when the fort fell, a large number of the defenders were killed in the confusion, even as they were trying to surrender.

Ultimately, though, the day's events did British forces little good. The decisive American victory at Yorktown came just a few weeks later.

The end of the War of Independence was not entirely the end of conflict for Connecticut. A dispute over its border with New York had been settled finally in 1683. A dispute over its border with Pennsylvania proved rather harder to solve.

Connecticut claimed land that now represents a third of Pennsylvania. And settlers from Connecticut established themselves there. Pennsylvania objected, and intermittent violence accompanied the dispute. The British government ruled in favor of Connecticut, but after the Revolution, a commission ruled in favor of Pennsylvania. Connecticut eventually gave in, but it did get its claim to land farther west, the Connecticut Western Reserve, ratified. In the end, though, Connecticut sold that land.

The War of 1812 was widely unpopular in Connecticut, as it was elsewhere in the region. At the Hartford Convention, there was even some talk of secession and forming a separate New England Confederation. Nevertheless, despite its lack of enthusiasm for the war, Connecticut did not entirely escape its effects. Privateers, for example, operated out of Connecticut ports during the war.

The British Navy blockaded Captain Stephen Decatur and his ships in

New London, amidst talk that somebody on shore was warning the British ships about Decatur's movements by lighting blue lights.

An attack was attempted on HMS *Ramillies* as it lay off New London on June 26, 1813, using an early form of torpedo—a schooner made into a bomb that exploded near the warship, killing eleven men.

On April 8, 1814, in retaliation the British raided what is now called Essex, rowing up the Connecticut River to burn privateer ships in a devastating raid. And in August 1814, they attacked Stonington, demanding its surrender and, when that was refused, bombarding it for days. The Stonington Battle Flag remains a treasure of early American history, stored at the Stonington Historical Society, Woolworth Library.

One person from the state who played a major role in the war was Captain Isaac Hull, born in Derby. Hull was in command of the USS *Constitution* when, on August 19, 1812, it encountered and defeated HMS *Guerriere.*

In the Civil War, Connecticut sent soldiers (including the 14th Connecticut Infantry, which fought to hold Cemetery Ridge at Gettysburg) and munitions, but the fighting was elsewhere.

During World War I, New London did get a visit from *Deutschland,* a German submarine. But, bizarre as it may seem now, that visit was before the entry of the United States into the war, and the submarine was there to trade with Americans, not to attack them. The *Deutschland* would later be taken over by the German Navy, but in November 1916, when it arrived in New London, it was actually a merchant submarine built to beat the Allied naval blockade. It brought gems, medicines, and other goods to sell, and it returned with silver on board. While in New London, it did actually manage to sink an American ship, though unintentionally. It collided with a tugboat and sank it, and the submarine had to be repaired in New London before it finally set off on its return journey to Germany.

At one stage, a World War II U-boat was actually based at New London. OK, it's not quite as much of a shock as it seems, because this was in 1947 and the U-boat in question was being operated by the US Navy. *U-2513* was one of the revolutionary Type XXI submarines developed by the Germans late in the war. It was captured intact at the end of the war, and the US Navy operated it for a few years so as to evaluate fully all its advanced technical features.

And submarines were to play a major role in Connecticut's Cold War history. USS *Nautilus*, the first operational nuclear-powered submarine, was built at Groton. The submarine is now the official state ship of Connecticut and is on display near the New London submarine base. The USS *Triton*, the first submarine to complete a submerged round-the-world voyage, set out on its record-breaking mission, Operation Sandblast, from New London in 1960.

## CONNECTICUT
## MILITARY HISTORY SITES

### Connecticut Air & Space Center
Location: 550 Main Street, Stratford, CT 06615
Web: cascstratford.wordpress.com

### Fort Griswold Battlefield State Park & Monument Museum House
Location: 57 Fort Street, Groton, CT 06340
Web: fortgriswold.org

### Museum of Connecticut History
Location: Connecticut State Library Building, 231 Capitol Avenue, Hartford, CT 06106
Web: museumofcthistory.org

### Mystic Seaport
Location: 75 Greenmanville Avenue, Mystic, CT 06355
Web: mysticseaport.org

### Nathan Hale Homestead
Location: 2299 South Street, Coventry, CT 06238
Web: ctlandmarks.org

### National Coast Guard Museum
Location: 15 Mohegan Avenue Parkway, New London, CT 06320
Web: coastguardmuseum.org

**New England Air Museum**
Location: Bradley International Airport, 36 Perimeter Road, Windsor Locks, CT 06096
Web: neam.org

**New England Civil War Museum & Library**
Location: 14 Park Place, Rockville, CT 06066
Web: newenglandcivilwarmuseum.com

**Putnam Cottage**
Location: 243 East Putnam Avenue, Greenwich, CT 06830
Web: putnamcottage.org

**R.W. Woolworth Library-Stonington Historical Society**
Location: 40 Palmer Street, Stonington, CT 06378
Web: stoningtonhistory.org

**Submarine Base Museum (USS *Nautilus*)**
Location: One Crystal Lake Road, Groton, CT 06340
Web: ussnautilus.org

Nickname: The Constitution State
Statehood: 1788
Capital: Hartford

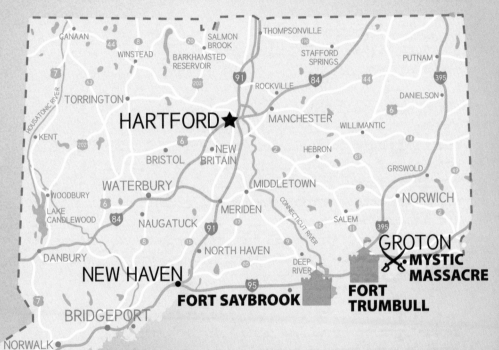

CANAAN
44
WINSTEAD
7
53
TORRINGTON
KENT
202
WOODBURY
LAKE
CANDLEWOOD
6
84
NAUGATUCK
8
DANBURY
7
NORWALK
95
15
BRIDGEPORT
**NEW HAVEN**
NORTH HAVEN
30
95
**FORT SAYBROOK**
15
91
MERIDEN
17
**HARTFORD** ★
6
BRISTOL
**NEW BRITAIN**
WATERBURY
SALMON BROOK
BARKHAMSTED RESERVOIR
20
91
202
ROCKVILLE
THOMPSONVILLE
190
STAFFORD SPRINGS
84
MANCHESTER
2
HEBRON
87
MIDDLETOWN
CONNECTICUT RIVER
82
DEEP RIVER
9
11
SALEM
PUTNAM
395
DANIELSON
6
WILLIMANTIC
14
GRISWOLD
49
**NORWICH**
2
395
**GROTON**
⚔ **MYSTIC MASSACRE**
**FORT TRUMBULL**
HOUSATONIC RIVER

**BENEDICT ARNOLD**
1741-1801
Stained Glass Window
St Mary's Church, London, UK
Source: Author photo

# DELAWARE

The territory of what is now Delaware had already seen conflict before the arrival of Europeans. For example, the Minqua, or Susquehannock, had regularly clashed with Eastern Algonquian tribes like the Lenni-Lenape.

Italian explorer (with English backing) John Cabot (looking at it from an English point of view), or Giovanni Caboto (from the Italian), was already cruising around the area in the late fifteenth century.

In the first part of the seventeenth century, however, the Europeans were moving in on the scene seriously. The name *Delaware* itself is a souvenir of early attention from across the Atlantic. It was named after one Thomas West, who also was known by the rather more imposing name of Baron De La Warr, which, if you run it all together becomes, yes, *Delaware*. De Le Warr was appointed governor and captain general of Virginia for life in 1610. Though in this case, that wasn't going to be quite as long as it might have been, since in 1618, when on his way back to America from England, he died.

In any event, it was going to be other Europeans, not the English, who would make the first serious invasions of what is now Delaware. In 1631, the Dutch set up a colony at Lewes, which at that stage went by the considerably more Dutch name of Zwaanendael. It wasn't a great start, not for the Dutch anyway. After about two years, the locals destroyed the settlement. But the Europeans kept on coming, and eventually pushed out the indigenous people of the area.

Next it was Sweden's turn to have a go. Swedes were encouraged to emigrate by a former director of New Netherland, Peter Minuit, who had fallen out with his former colleagues. The Swedes imaginatively called their colony New Sweden. In 1638, they set up a trading post at Fort Christina, which was imaginatively named after their queen who was called, yes, Christina. There were also Finns involved in this venture, though since many had taken Swedish names, finding them in the historical record hasn't always been easy. Although it is not hugely surprising to find that Finns Point had some Finns involved with its founding.

The Dutch, however, despite suffering a setback over Zwaanendael, were not out of the game yet, not by a long way. In 1651, Peter Stuyvesant established Fort Casimir. Three years later, the Swedes thought it would be a good idea to seize Fort Casimir. It wasn't a good idea, not for the Swedish anyway. Dutch commander Stuyvesant hit back, effectively terminating New Sweden. During their brief tenure, the Swedish had renamed Fort Casimir Fort Trinity, because they'd taken it on Trinity Sunday. Now that the Dutch were back in control, they renamed it New Amstel. Luckily, this was in the days before road signs.

And then, finally, it was the turn of the English. In September 1664, they took New Amstel and moved in on the area along the Delaware. The Dutch, however, didn't give up without a fight—though it wasn't a huge fight. After killing three Dutch soldiers, the attackers, as attackers often did in those days, looted New Amstel. New Amstel was renamed (yet again) with the much more English-sounding name of New Castle, and the new owners split up Delaware into three counties that couldn't sound more English: New Castle, Kent, and Sussex. Delaware's Lewes is in Delaware's Sussex County, just as England's Lewes is in the English county of East Sussex. And Delaware's Dover is in Delaware's Kent County, just as England's Dover is in the English county of Kent.

However, not everybody was entirely happy with the new arrangements. In 1669, "Long Finn" Marcus Jacobson had a go at leading a Swedish and Finnish rebellion against England. The English weren't pleased about this when they found out, and they exiled him from the colony.

And it wasn't long before Dutch ships struck back. By 1672, the Dutch and the English were at war yet again. This time, it was a Dutch fleet that sailed into New York, took that, and moved in on Delaware. However, almost before they'd got used to being Dutch again, the inhabitants suddenly found they were English once more. By the Treaty of Westminster in 1674 that ended the third Anglo-Dutch War, the English got New Netherland and the Dutch got Suriname.

Meanwhile, things had been getting a little tense between Delaware and an enemy located even closer to home—Maryland.

The problem was all due to competing historical land claims. Already by 1669, Maryland was claiming land in Delaware. And in 1672, armed Marylanders attacked Lewes. Two years later, they were on the attack again. Charles II of England attempted to arrange a compromise but failed, and Lord Baltimore and William Penn and their successors had a long run of conflict ahead of them. Cresap's War broke out in the 1730s (see Maryland and Pennsylvania), and the regional dispute was only finally settled by the Mason-Dixon Line in 1767.

And just to show that this was a time when you didn't have to be a big player to launch an invasion, in 1698, French pirates attacked Lewes as well.

By the time the Mason-Dixon Line was drawn, though, another and rather more major conflict was about to erupt.

In June 1776, the Delaware assembly suspended royal authority and, shortly afterwards, joined the revolution. Caesar Rodney rode through the night to Philadelphia in July 1776 to ensure that Delaware supported the resolution on independence.

A few Delawareans—including, for instance, Thomas Robinson—did remain actively loyal to the crown; and the Black Camp Rebellion in the summer of 1780 briefly saw some take up arms against the revolution.

In 1777, a British army invaded Delaware. In late August, a British fleet sailed into Delaware Bay, and a British army disembarked at Turkey Point, Maryland, with Philadelphia as its eventual target. Americans harried the British, but the attacking forces were far more powerful than the defenders. On September 3, advancing British and Hessian troops under the command of General William Howe reached Iron Hill near Newark, Delaware, where they clashed with the American Corps of Light Infantry under General William Maxwell, which was stationed at Cooch's Mill. The resulting Battle of Cooch's Bridge wasn't the biggest battle in history, but both forces suffered casualties as American troops desperately fought to hold back repeated attacks by the advancing British forces. According to a popular, but now rather controversial, legend, this skirmish was the first time the Stars and Stripes were flown in battle.

Eventually, the defenders were forced to retreat. Howe advanced into Pennsylvania, and on September 11 defeated Washington's forces in the biggest battle of the revolution, at Brandywine Creek.

In 1783, though, at the Treaty of Paris, Britain acknowledged the United States' independence.

But that did not mean Delaware had seen the last of British invaders.

The War of 1812 brought British warships back to the area. The British declared a blockade of Delaware Bay, and on April 6, 1813, after being refused provisions, the delightfully named Commodore John Poo Beresford ordered his sailors to bombard Lewes. The slight problem from the British point of view was that they couldn't actually see their target because of trees. The ensuing twenty-two-hour bombardment managed to kill no people at all. However, one chicken was killed, and a pig's leg was broken. Worse was to come for the British as the locals found that the British cannonballs fitted some of their own guns. They promptly gathered up expended British balls and returned them, forcefully, to their source.

A British cannonball from HMS *Poictiers* is still located in the foundation of the aptly named Cannonball House, which now is a museum.

The war also resulted in a number of small British raids in the region, including an attack on Reedy Island.

Delawareans had somewhat divided loyalties during the Civil War, but the majority remained loyal to the Union. Men from Delaware served on both sides, but the numbers fighting for the Union were in their thousands, whereas the numbers fighting for the Confederacy were only in the hundreds. The fighting was elsewhere, but Du Pont's gunpowder factory at Wilmington supplied huge amounts to Union forces, and Fort Delaware on Pea Patch Island became a major prisoner-of-war camp.

And the Civil War was not the end of conflicts in the region.

Invaders from across the Atlantic would again put in an appearance off the shores of Delaware in the twentieth century.

Yes, it's U-boat time.

And it wasn't just World War II. Already in World War I, comparatively primitive German submarines had made it all the way across the Atlantic. In spring 1918, *U-151* terrorized ships off the US coast and laid mines in Delaware Bay.

But in World War II, things got much busier on the submarine front.

In the early days of the war, while US naval defenses were comparatively inexperienced and unprepared, the Germans sent submarines that caused havoc off America's East Coast. A number of U-boats carried out operations in the vicinity of the Delaware coast in 1942 and 1943. For instance, on March 10, 1942, *U-94*, which had been waiting off Fenwick Island, fired two torpedoes into the Norwegian freighter *Hvosleff* and sank it. Five of the crew were killed. And on June 11, 1942, *U-373* was spotted laying mines off Lewes. However, the efficiency of US countermeasures improved rapidly, and the U-boats would never find the waters off Delaware and the rest of the East Coast so inviting again.

In the last days of the war, the Germans attempted to repeat the success of their early operations off the American coast. But times had changed drastically, and the operation had little effect. One of the submarines involved was *U-858*. On May 8, 1945, VE Day in Europe, *U-858* surfaced off the US coast to surrender. The submarine was escorted to a point off Cape May, and its crew was taken to Fort Miles near Lewes. The US Navy operated a submarine listening post at Fort Miles on the Delaware coast from 1963 until 1981.

## DELAWARE
## MILITARY HISTORY SITES

### 1812 MEMORIAL (CANNONBALL) PARK
Location: corner of Savannah Road and Front Street, Lewes, DE 19958
Web: ci.lewes.de.us/index.cfm?ref=12200&ref2=5

### Air Mobility Command Museum
Location: 1301 Heritage Road, Dover Air Force Base, Dover, DE 19902
Web: amcmuseum.org

### DiscoverSea Shipwreck Museum
Location: 708 Coastal Highway, Fenwick Island, DE 19944
Web: discoversea.com

### First State National Historic Park (Fort Christina)
Location: 1110 East 7th Street, Wilmington, DE 19801
Web: nps.gov/frst/planyourvisit/fort-christina.htm

**Fort Miles Museum and Historical Area**
Location: Cape Henlopen State Park,
15099 Cape Henlopen Drive, Lewes, DE 19958
Web: destateparks.com/attractions/fort-miles

**John Dickinson Plantation**
Location: 340 Kitts Hummock Road, Dover, DE 19901
Web: history.delaware.gov/museums/jdp/jdp_main.shtml

**Lewes Historical Society Properties**
Location: 110 Shipcarpenter Street, Lewes, DE 19958

**Cannonball House; Maritime Museum**
Location: 118 Front Street, Lewes, DE 19958

**Ryves Holt House**
Location: 218 2nd Street, Lewes, DE 19958
Web: historiclewes.org/visit/society-properties

**Pencader Heritage Museum (Battle of Cooch's Bridge)**
Location: 2029 Sunset Lake Road, Newark, DE 19702
Web: pencaderheritage.org

# America Invaded: DELAWARE

Nickname: The First State
Statehood: 1787
Capital: Dover

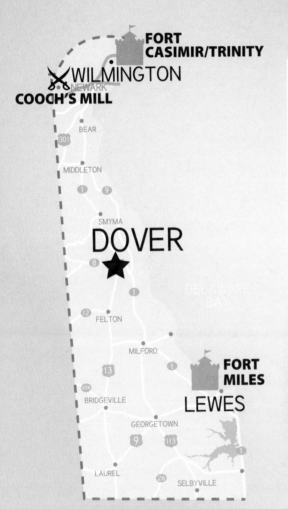

**GEORGE WASHINGTON**
1732-1799
Statue, Boston Common, MA
Source: Author photo

# FLORIDA

ong before the arrival of Europeans, Native Americans developed sophisticated cultures in what is now Florida, producing complex and impressive sites like the Crystal River Mounds. By the time of the first European contact, a wide variety of tribal groupings occupied the area, including Apalachee, Timucuans, Calusa, and Tequesta.

Hard now to know whether Juan Ponce de León was actually the first European ever to set foot in what is now Florida, but he's the first that we definitely know about. Sometime in early April 1513, he landed somewhere in northeast Florida and, in fact, named it La Florida, after the *Pascua Florida*, the Feast of Flowers. In 1521, he returned with a couple hundred colonists, fifty horses, and other kit. Ponce de León was back, and this time it was serious. Serious for Ponce de León, that is. The Calusa weren't keen on the idea of being colonized. Not keen at all, in fact. They attacked, and the colonists and a wounded Ponce de León made for Cuba, where he died.

It hadn't been a great start from the Spanish point of view, and things wouldn't improve much for them anytime soon.

In 1528, Pánfilo de Narváez turned up unexpectedly on Florida's west coast and took a look at the Tampa and Tallahassee areas. He marched inland a bit looking for gold, didn't find any, alienated the local population, got attacked, tried to use rafts to escape, and failed to do so. Only four of his men managed to escape in the end. As disastrous expeditions go, it doesn't get much worse than that.

Another Spanish disaster occurred in 1539. Hernando de Soto arrived in Florida also looking for gold. After four years of wandering around, slaughtering, and stealing from the locals, he died somewhere near the Mississippi, still not having found any gold.

You'd think it could only get better for the Spanish, but you'd only be half right. Next came another disaster, but in some senses, not quite as comprehensive a one. In 1559, Tristán de Luna y Arellano arrived with settlers in Pensacola Bay. They weren't, however, to remain settled for very long, as a combination of bad weather and logistical and personnel problems rapidly brought the venture to an end.

Then, when it seemed like things couldn't get worse for the Spanish in Florida, suddenly they did. In 1562, Frenchman Jean Ribaullt turned up looking for a site for a French Huguenot colony; and in 1564, Frenchman René Goulaine de Laudonnière founded Fort Caroline, near what is now Jacksonville.

But the situation for the Spanish in Florida was finally about to take a turn for the better. And the situation for the French was about to take a turn, very much so, for the worse. In 1565, Pedro Menéndez de Avilés established San Augustine, a permanent settlement that, as St. Augustine is still permanent, is in fact the first permanent European settlement in the territory that became the United States. Not content with that, however, he then went on to turn Fort Caroline into San Mateo after slaughtering a bunch of French. The French returned the compliment two years later, when Dominique de Gourgue slaughtered a bunch of Spanish. But Spain had made its mark, and Spanish control would soon expand substantially. Catholic missionaries started getting active.

However, another European power was about to take a serious interest in Florida. Yes, it's England. Already in 1586, Sir Francis Drake was dropping in on St. Augustine, not for a bit of sightseeing, but for a bit of burning and stealing. It was the first of a number of English attacks on the town. Gradually, the English colonists farther north expanded their area of control southward. Queen Anne's War of 1702–1713 saw extensive fighting between the English forces in Carolina and Spanish forces in Florida, with assorted expeditions headed in both directions. In 1702, for instance, English forces under James Moore, governor of colonial Carolina, burned the town of St. Augustine but failed to take the fort.

The local Native American population had already been having a tough time. A number of rebellions against the Spanish had been crushed; and now with the arrival of extensive land warfare between two European powers, they were dragged into that as well, both as fighters and as victims. Since the late seventeenth century, the English had been trading with and arming some Native Americans, particularly the Creek, who used their weapons against Spanish missions. In 1704, Moore launched another raid, with his own and Creek forces targeting Spanish missions and killing or displacing a large number of Apalachees.

Meanwhile, approaching from the west was yet another European competitor for power, the French. For instance, in 1698 they tried to enter Pensacola, and Spanish ships had to prevent them. In 1719, though, they took the town and held it until 1722, when they abandoned it.

Between 1727 and 1729, Britain and Spain were at war again, and there was more fighting in the region.

Britain and Spain went to war yet again in 1739, in, yes, the War of Jenkins' Ear. An unusual name for a war, and one that refers to a certain British merchant captain who claimed to have lost his ear in an encounter with a Spanish coast guard prior to the war.

This time it was the British governor of Georgia, James Oglethorpe, who marched on Florida. Again, St. Augustine was attacked. At Fort Mose, the northern defense of St. Augustine, the British came up against free African militiamen, many of them slaves who had escaped from Carolina, and were defeated at the Battle of Bloody Mose on June 26, 1740. Eventually, the British forces gave up and retreated. Spanish forces then invaded Georgia, but they were defeated.

Not long after, another round of hostilities took place between Britain and Spain, but this one ended more decisively. In the 1763 peace deal, Spain handed over Florida to Britain.

Though, to be fair, *decisively* might be too strong a word, since yet another war was coming. When Spain handed over Florida, it largely evacuated its people from there, and the new settlers who came in under British rule stayed mainly loyal to the British Crown. During the American Revolution, American forces made a number of attempts to invade Florida, but without much success. A 1777 attempt ended with an ambush and disaster for the American forces at the Battle of Thomas Creek; and the 1778 attempt led to the Battle of Alligator Bridge, which wasn't exactly a success for the American forces either.

However, things weren't going so well for Britain elsewhere in the war. The Spanish got involved on the American side and took Pensacola from the British in 1781 after bitter and prolonged fighting. The siege lasted just under two months and was the longest siege of the American Revolution. The city of Galveston in Texas was later named in honor of the Spanish commander at Pensacola—Bernardo de Gálvez.

In 1784, as part of the peace deal that ended the War of Independence, the Spanish got Florida back—although they did have to hand over some territory elsewhere in exchange, and they did have to sort out a border dispute with the new United States.

The Count of Aranda, a Spanish minister, declared soon after the peace was signed that "the day will come when it [the United States] will grow into a giant, even a fearsome colossus in the hemisphere. Then it will forget the assistance it received from [us] and will think only of its own exaltation. The first step of this power … will be to seize upon the Floridas, in order to dominate the Gulf of Mexico."[2]

The count's prediction would come true, but the initial conflict would be with the Native Americans. In the last decades of the eighteenth century, a new tribe developed, formed by Creek Native Americans who had moved south into Florida and other groups. They became known as Seminoles.

The British, by now, had a long tradition of working with the Creek, and with the start of the War of 1812, they saw an opportunity to use their Creek and Seminole contacts against the United States. They even sent troops back into Florida to help develop this mission and a fort that was known, reasonably enough, as the British Post on the Apalachicola River at Prospect Bluff. Here they recruited Native Americans and escaped slaves to fight the United States. The war ended before the British mission could achieve very much. What it did, however, was point to a coming conflict between the United States and forces in Florida that were beyond the control of the Spanish authorities who were, in theory, supposed to be in charge. And the disappearance, largely, of the British from the equation did not end the tensions in the region.

---

2      James Cusick, *The Other War of 1812: The Patriot War and the American Invasion of Spanish East Florida* (Athens, GA: The University of Georgia Press, 2007), 17.

In 1817, in what came to be known as the First Seminole War, General Andrew Jackson invaded Spanish Florida and pushed the Seminoles farther south. By 1819, Spain had had enough of the declining situation in Florida and signed the Adams-Onís Treaty. Under the terms of the treaty, Spain pulled out of Florida in 1821, handing power to the United States. More violence between the United States and the Seminoles was to come.

Under a controversial 1832 treaty, the United States reckoned that the Seminoles had agreed to abandon their lands in Florida and move to Oklahoma. A lot of the Seminoles reckoned that they had not. In 1835, US troops arrived and attempted to enforce the deportation of the Seminoles. What followed was a bitter war, in which Seminoles skilfully fought a guerrilla war of determined resistance against far larger US forces. A few incidents that were large enough to be called battles did occur. For instance, the Battle of Wahoo Swamp took place in 1836, as about 2,500 Tennessee volunteers, US artillerymen, and Florida militiamen, supported by hundreds of Creek, were held up by Seminole fire. And in 1837, the Battle of Lake Okeechobee saw US troops launch an assault against Seminole fighters holding prepared positions. The US forces compelled the Seminoles to retreat, but at a cost, and most of the defenders slipped away unharmed.

The war cost the Unites States more than $20 million and killed 1,500 American troops. In the end, the United States was reduced to desperate measures to try to win, including seizing and imprisoning Seminole leader Osceola when he turned up for negotiations under a flag of truce. The war dragged on until 1842, but ultimately the Seminoles could not resist the sheer military might of the United States. By the end of the war, most Seminoles were either dead or deported.

In 1855, yet more fighting broke out. By the end of it, the Seminoles had been virtually wiped out in Florida.

During the American Civil War, Florida was part of the Confederacy. Union troops, though, remained at locations within its borders throughout the war. It was generally regarded as a strategic backwater; and as the war progressed, many Confederate troops stationed there were redeployed to more critical locations. Despite this, a significant number of clashes and raids did take place in Florida.

Early in the war, fighting took place around Santa Rosa Island at Pensacola, which held the Union-controlled Fort Pickens. In September

1864, Union cavalry launched a devastating raid from Fort Barrancas near Pensacola that culminated in something of a Union victory at the Battle of Marianna.

The Union Navy conducted a blockade of much of Florida's coast, and even ran patrols on some of its rivers. In early 1864, a powerful Union force landed at Jacksonville and advanced inland. However, after defeat at the Battle of Olustee, it retreated again to Jacksonville. And in March 1865, another Union force landed near St. Marks Lighthouse and again advanced inland. Again it was stopped by a Confederate force, this time at the Battle of Natural Bridge, and was forced to withdraw to the coast. Elsewhere though, the Confederacy was on the brink of defeat. It was on May 10, 1865, that Union Brigadier General Edward McCook entered Tallahassee, and on May 20, the United States flag was raised over the state capitol.

World War II would once again bring conflict to the seas off Florida. For instance, on the night of April 10, 1942, crowds in Jacksonville watched aghast as the steamer *Gulfamerica*, just five miles off shore, was first torpedoed and then finished off with surface fire by Reinhard Hardegen's *U–123*. The waters of the region were particularly dangerous in the months soon after America's entry into the war, before it had time to adapt to the realities of World War II U-boat warfare.

And later that year, in June 1942, *U–584* landed four German saboteurs near Ponte Vedra Beach. They cached explosives and kits in the sand and then headed for New York and Chicago. All were caught and executed.

During the Cold War, with Cuba so close, Florida was in some sense on the front line again. After the Cuban Missile Crisis of 1962, Che Guevara admitted to a reporter that, had his fingers been on the trigger (instead of the Soviets'), missiles would have been launched, presumably targeting Florida.

On June 12, 2016, the most deadly terrorist attack since 9/11 took place at the Pulse nightclub in Orlando. Forty-nine people were killed by Omar Mateen, an American citizen of Afghan descent.

## FLORIDA
## MILITARY HISTORY SITES

**Air Force Armament Museum**
Location: 100 Museum Drive, Eglin Air Force Base, Fort Walton Beach, FL 32542
Web: www.afarmamentmuseum.com

**Castillo de San Marcos National Monument**
Location: 1 South Castillo Drive, St. Augustine, FL 32084
Web: www.nps.gov/casa

**Fort Mose Historic State Park**
Location: 15 Fort Mose Trail, St. Augustine, FL 32084
Web: www.floridastateparks.org/park/Fort-Mose

**Harry S. Truman Little White House**
Location: 111 Front Street, Key West, FL 33040
Web: www.trumanlittlewhitehouse.com

**Kennedy Space Center Visitor Complex**
Location: Kennedy Space Center, SR 405, Titusville, FL 32899
Web: www.kennedyspacecenter.com

**National Naval Aviation Museum**
Location: 1750 Radford Boulevard, NAS Pensacola, FL 32508
Web: www.navalaviationmuseum.org

**Natural Bridge Battlefield Historic State Park**
Location: 7502 Natural Bridge Road, Tallahassee, FL 32305
Web: www.floridastateparks.org/park/Natural-Bridge

**Navy Seal Museum**
Location: 3300 North Highway A1A, Fort Pierce, FL 34949
Web: www.navysealmuseum.org

**NATIONAL NAVAL
AIR MUSUEM**
(background photo)
Pensacola
Source: Author photo

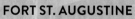

**FORT ST. AUGUSTINE**
Castillo de San Marcos
St. Augustine founded in 1565
Source: Author photos

Nickname: The Sunshine State
Statehood: 1845
Capital: Tallahassee

**THOMAS CREEK**

**FORT CAROLINE**

**JACKSONVILLE**

**OLUSTEE**

**TALLAHASSEE**

**NATURAL BRIDGE**

**FORT MOSE**

**FORT ST. AUGUSTINE**

GAINESVILLE

OCALA

**WAHOO SWAMP**

ORLANDO

**TAMPA**

**LAKE OKEECHOBEE**

**MIAMI**

**US NAVY BLUE ANGELS**
Based in Pensacola
Source: Author photo

**Okeechobee Battlefield Historic State Park**
Location: 3500 SE 38th Avenue, Okeechobee, FL 34974
Web: www.okeechobeebattlefield.com

**Olustee Battlefield Site and Reenactment**
Location: 5815 Battlefield Trail Road, Sanderson, FL 32087
Web: www.battleofolustee.org

**Ponce de Leon's Fountain of Youth Archaeological Park**
Location: 11 Magnolia Avenue, St. Augustine, FL 32084
Web: www.fountainofyouthflorida.com

**U.S. Coast Guard Cutter Ingham Maritime Museum**
Location: Truman Waterfront, Foot of Southard Street by Fort Taylor, Key West, FL 33040
Web: www.uscgcingham.org

# GEORGIA

The Mississippian culture built pyramid-shaped mounds in the area we now know as Georgia from around AD 700 to 1600. The Creek and Cherokee dominated Georgia when Europeans first arrived in the fifteenth century.

One of the first European "invaders" of Georgia may have been Italian. Giovanni Caboto, who was, strictly speaking, Genoese, seems to have explored the coast of Georgia in 1498.

A Spanish explorer, Lucas Vázquez de Ayllón, is likely to have established in 1526 the first European colony in Georgia. There were problems with the indigenous people, and the colony only survived for three months. De Ayllón died that year in the colony, which was located near Sapelo Island.

Spain began to explore more of the area and to settle colonies on the sea islands of Georgia. They claimed Jekyll Island as early as 1510. A number of missions were founded, and attempts were made to convert the nearby Gaule people to Catholicism.

Soon the French too would take an interest in the region, and then the English. In 1680, the English launched an attack on the Spanish mission on St. Catherine's Island. Eventually, all the Spanish missions were wiped out, and English clashes with local Native Americans created the possibility of English colonization.

James Oglethorpe was the founder of the English colony of Georgia, the last of the original thirteen. Oglethorpe was granted a charter for the colony in

1732. He conceived the notion of founding it as a refuge for those were confined in debtor's prison. Oglethorpe named the colony in honor of King George II.

Spain would soon clash with Britain over Georgia, during the War of Jenkins' Ear (1739–48). In 1740, Oglethorpe launched an invasion of Florida before withdrawing. Subsequently, Spain launched a full-scale invasion of Georgia. An army of 2,000 to 5,000 men led by Governor Manuel de Montiano y Luyando sailed from St. Augustine on July 1, 1742. James Oglethorpe assumed command of the Georgia Rangers, who were augmented by Chickasaw and Creek warriors. Oglethorpe prevailed in a skirmish that is known as the Battle of Bloody Marsh on July 18, 1742, on St. Simons Island. The Spaniards burned Fort St. Andrews before retreating back to Florida. Spaniards would never again invade Georgia.

The French and Indian War came and went, and the Creek gradually ceded more land to Georgia.

Many Georgians were sympathetic to the ideals of the American Revolution from its start. A branch of the Sons of Liberty, for example, broke into the magazine at Savannah and stole its gunpowder in 1775.

A fleet of the Royal Navy arrived in Savannah harbor in January 1776. In March of that year, Royal Marines in Savannah seized some merchant ships in what became known as the Battle of the Rice Boats.

In 1778, the British chose to employ a Southern strategy in order to subdue the rebellious colonies. A 3,000 man British Army led by Lieutenant Colonel Archibald Campbell landed in the swamps near Savannah on December 28. His forces quickly seized Savannah. More British troops landed, led by Swiss-born general Augustine Prévost, who assumed command. Campbell and his reinforced army marched to Augusta in January in order to recruit more Tory support.

Benjamin Lincoln was the local Patriot commander, with about 1,500 Continental troops. On September 12, 1779, Lincoln's troops were reinforced by 3,500 French troops commanded by Admiral d'Estaing, who "invaded" Georgia and began laying siege to Prévost in Savannah. On October 9, the Franco-American forces assaulted the city. By that time, hundreds of slaves had fortified Savannah. The Battle of Savannah was one of the bloodiest of the American Revolution, with 244 killed. Polish General Pulaski, known as the Father of the American Cavalry, was killed in the engagement. D'Estaing lifted the siege and withdrew his forces to the West Indies. Lincoln retreated to South Carolina.

In the period after the Revolution, more and more of Georgia's boundaries would become fixed. Still, the exact course of its border in some locations would be causing controversy long afterwards.

During the War of 1812, members of the Georgia militia were engaged in the Creek War in other Southern states. Savannah was subject to a British blockade. On January 10, 1815, Admiral George Cockburn launched an invasion of Georgia, landing Royal Marines on Cumberland Island. These were reinforced with the arrival of more troops led by Major Edward Nicolls, who commanded a force of British regulars, Native Americans, and some freed black slaves. Nicolls occupied the nearby town of St. Marys. News of the Treaty of Ghent that ended the war, signed on December 24, 1814, forced a British withdrawal from Georgia.

On January 19, 1861, delegates convening at the Georgia state capital of Milledgeville voted in favor of secession from the Union. Over 133,000 Georgians would serve in the Confederate military in the Civil War. Around 5,000 Georgians would also serve in the Union Army, in units such as the 1st Georgia Infantry Battalion.

In September 1863, Union Major General William Rosecrans advanced from Tennessee into Georgia. On September 19–20, he led his 66,000 man army against General Braxton Bragg's Army of Tennessee at the Battle of Chickamauga. "The two armies came together like two wild beasts," one eyewitness recounted. Chickamauga in Georgia would prove to be the second bloodiest battle of the entire war, exceeded only by Gettysburg. Over 34,000 Americans were killed at Chickamauga. Rosecrans withdrew his army back to Chattanooga after the battle.

In 1864, it would be Sherman's turn to invade Georgia.

William Tecumseh Sherman, an Ohioan, was, after Grant, the greatest Union commander of the US Civil War. Sherman, who famously declared that "War is hell," became an apostle of the concept of total war, which would become all too familiar in the twentieth century. In his postwar memoirs, Sherman explained, "we are not only fighting hostile armies, but a hostile people, and must make old and young, rich and poor, feel the hard hand of war, as well as the organized armies." Sherman had distinguished himself as a division commander under Grant at the Battle of Shiloh in Tennessee, and he established a close friendship with Grant. Though despised in the South, Sherman was revered by most of his men, who nicknamed him Uncle Billy.

Many years later, Sherman would become Commanding General of the United States Army under President Grant, and apply some of the same principles of war to the Indian Wars in the American plains.

In May of 1864, Sherman, commanding the Military Division of the Mississippi, led an invasion of Georgia with 112,000 men from his base in Chattanooga, Tennessee. The mountainous area of northern Georgia was defended by Joseph Johnston, whose Army of Tennessee was made up of about 62,000 men. In May, Sherman and Johnston would clash at the battles of Rocky Face Ridge, Resaca, New Hope Church, Pickett's Mill, and Dallas. At the Battle of Kennesaw Mountain on June 27, 1864, Sherman launched a costly frontal assault against the fortified positions of the Confederates. Three thousand Union casualties were the result, four times more than those suffered by the Confederates.

On July 20, 1864, Sherman won the Battle of Peachtree Creek against John Hood, who had replaced Johnston. This time, Confederate losses exceeded Union loses by more than two to one. Hood withdrew into Atlanta, where he was soon besieged by Union forces. He launched a sortie from the city on July 22 in the Battle of Atlanta, which, after some initial success, proved to be a damaging failure. Union Major General James McPherson was killed that day. Union artillery began shelling the city to devastating effect. Union troops severed the Confederate supply lines by seizing and destroying the railways that fed the city. Hood was forced to abandon Atlanta on September 2, 1864.

Sherman left Atlanta on November 16, 1864, on his March to the Sea. He had telegraphed Grant: "I can make this march, and I will make Georgia howl!" His troops were encouraged to lay waste to the infrastructure of the South, destroying factories, public buildings and bridges. Twisted railways became known as Sherman's Neckties.

In May of 1865, Sherman's forces liberated the notorious Andersonville Prison in Georgia. Nearly 50,000 Americans died because of the appalling conditions that existed in Confederate and Federal prisoner-of-war camps during the Civil War. Andersonville's commandant, Captain Henry Wirz, was tried and executed after the war—the only Confederate war criminal. Today one can visit the National Prisoner of War Museum in Andersonville, which commemorates prisoners' experience from all American wars.

Sherman's March led his forces from Atlanta through Macon and Milledgeville, finally reaching Savannah. On December 13, 1864, Union troops assaulted the redoubts that surrounded the city. Confederate forces abandoned Savannah on December 20, allowing Sherman to present it "as a Christmas gift" to President Lincoln.

In early 1865, Sherman left Georgia and advanced north through the Carolinas. It was not, however, the end of fighting in Georgia. For instance, the Battle of Columbus on April 16, 1865, is regarded by some as the last battle of the war.

In 1924, Franklin Delano Roosevelt first came to Warm Springs, Georgia, to recuperate from the polio that would plague the rest of his life. President FDR would die in Warm Springs in April 1945.

During World War II, the Georgia coast was subject to numerous attacks by German U-boats. In April of 1942, Lieutenant Commander Reinhard Hardegen of *U-123* sank three merchant ships off the Georgia coast. After being decorated personally by Hitler, Hardegen boldly criticized the Führer, saying, "You make the mistake of looking only to the east, while the war will be won or lost in the west—at sea."[3]

In 2015, a Russian intelligence gathering ship was spotted off King's Bay, home to a US Navy ballistic submarine base.

## GEORGIA
## MILITARY HISTORY SITES

### Andersonville National Historic Site and National Prisoner of War Museum
Location: 496 Cemetery Road, Andersonville, GA 31711
Web: www.nps.gov/ande

### Chickamauga & Chattanooga National Military Park
Location: 3370 LaFayette Road, Fort Oglethorpe, GA 30742
Web: www.nps.gov/chch

### Currahee Military Museum
Location: 160 Alexander Street, Toccoa, GA 30577
Web: www.toccoahistory.com

---

3     Michael Gannon, *Operation Drumbeat: The Dramatic True Story of Germany's First U-Boat Attacks Along the American Coast in World War II* (Annapolis MD: Naval Institute Press, 2009), 407.

**WILLIAM TECUMSEH SHERMAN**
1820-1891
Source: iStock/ivan-96

**BATTLE OF ATLANTA**
July 1864
Source: akg-images/Universal Images Group/
Universal History Archive

Nickname: The Peach State
Statehood: 1788
Capital: Atlanta

FORT OGLETHORPE
✕ CHICKAMAUGA
DALTON
✕ ROCKY FACE RIDGE
LAFAYETTE
CHATTAHOOCHEE NATIONAL FOREST
OSCO
BLUE RIDGE
BLAIRSVILLE
CLAYTON
LAKE BURTON
CHATTAHOOCHEE NATIONAL FOREST
CARTERS LAKE
CLARKESVILLE
SUMMERVILLE
JASPER
DAHLONEGA
TOCCOA
LAVONIA
HARWELL LAKE
FAIRMOUNT
LAKE SIDNEY LANIER
ROME
CANTON
GAINESVILLE
COMMERCE
ELBERTON
RUSSELL LAKE
CARTERSVILLE
ALLATOONA LAKE
NEW HOPE CHURCH ✕
✕ KENNESAW MOUNTAIN
MARIETTA
LAWRENCEVILLE
ATHENS
WATKINSVILLE
LEXINGTON
LAKE STROM THURMOND
PICKETT'S MILL ✕
MABLETON
✕ PEACHTREE CREEK
WASHINGTON
OCONEE NATIONAL FOREST
LAKE OCONEE
TALLAPOOSA
★ ATLANTA
MADISON
UNION POINT
MARTINEZ
CARROLLTON
UNION CITY
STOCKBRIDGE
AUGUSTA
PEACHTREE CITY
JACKSON
MONTICELLO
SPARTA
ATHENS
BLYTHE
NEWNAN
JACKSON LAKE
LAKE SINCLAIR
WAYNESBORO
FRANKLIN
GRIFFIN
OCONEE NATIONAL FOREST
WEST POINT LAKE
BENOIA
ZEBULON
GRAY
MILLEDGEVILLE
LA GRANGE
FORSYTH
TENNILLE
WADLEY
MILLEN
SYLVANIA
THOMASTON
HAMILTON
MACON
MCINTYRE
JEFFERSONVILLE
WRIGHTSVILLE
SWAINSBORO
STATESBORO
FORTSON
TALBOTTON
ROBERTA
DUBLIN
SPRINGFIELD
✕ COLUMBUS
BUTLER
FORT VALLEY
WARNER ROBINS
COCHRAN
RENTZ
SOPERTON
LYONS
CLAXTON
POOLER
RICE BOATS ✕
CUSSETA
ELLAVILLE
MONTEZUMA
HAWKINSVILLE
EASTMAN
MCRAE
SAVANNAH ✕
TYBEE ISLAND
RICHLAND
AMERICUS
LAKE BLACKSHEAR
CORDELE
ABBEVILLE
HAZELHURST
HINESVILLE
GEORGETOWN
CUTHBERT
DAWSON
FITZGERALD
BAXLEY
JESUP
WALTER F GEORGE RESERVOIR
ALBANY
LEARY
TIFTON
DOUGLAS
ALMA
FORT GAINES
BLAKELY
CAMILLA
ADEL
HOMERVILLE
WOODBINE
NAHUNTA
BRUNSWICK
✕ BLOODY MARSH
JEKYLL ISLAND
COLQUITT
MOULTRIE
LAKELAND
WAYCROSS
DONALDSONVILLE
BAINBRIDGE
THOMASVILLE
VALDOSTA
OKEFENOKEE NATIONAL WILDLIFE REFUGE
FOLKSTON
ST MARYS
FORT ST. ANDREWS
LAKE SEMINOLE
QUITMAN
FARGO

ATLANTIC OCEAN

**Fort McAllister State Park**
Location: 3894 Fort McAllister Road, Richmond Hill, GA 31324
Web: www.gastateparks.org/FortMcAllister

**Fort Pulaski National Monument**
Location: Cockspur Island, US-80, Savannah, GA 31410
Web: www.nps.gov/fopu

**Jimmy Carter Library & Museum**
Location: 441 Freedom Parkway NE, Atlanta, GA 30307
Web: www.jimmycarterlibrary.gov

**Kennesaw Mountain National Battlefield Park**
Location: 900 Kennesaw Mountain Drive NW, Kennesaw, GA 30152
Web: www.nps.gov/kemo

**Museum of Aviation**
Location: 1942 Heritage Boulevard, Robins Air Force Base, Warner Robins, GA 31098
Web: www.museumofaviation.org

**National Civil War Naval Museum**
Location: 1002 Victory Drive, Columbus, GA 31901
Web: www.portcolumbus.org

**National Infantry Museum & Soldier Center**
Location: 1775 Legacy Way, Columbus, GA 31903
Web: www.nationalinfantrymuseum.org

**Savannah History Museum—Battlefield Memorial Park**
Location: 303 Martin Luther King, Jr. Boulevard, Savannah, GA 31401
Web: www.chsgeorgia.org/SHM

**Southern Museum of Civil War and Locomotive History**
Location: 2829 Cherokee Street NW, Kennesaw, GA 30144
Web: www.southernmuseum.org

# HAWAII

The beautiful islands of Hawaii are a popular modern-day tourist destination, where mainlanders go to escape stress, sip mai tais, and find a slice of paradise under the sun. But these islands have seen their share of fighting and invasions.

Around 1,500 years ago, Polynesian people first arrived in the Hawaiian Islands. These hardy souls had journeyed 2,000 miles in outrigger canoes from other Pacific islands.

The Hawaiian culture was feudal and warlike. The Hawaiian word for warrior is *koa*. Koa, lacking metallurgy, armed themselves with stone, wood, and even shark's teeth. Their principal weapon was the *pololu*—a long wooden spear that a warrior also used to vault forward. Warfare was highly ritualized process. Being a successful warrior enhanced a koa's prestige or *manu*.

Interisland and civil wars flared up in the Hawaiian Islands almost continuously during the eighteenth century. The Kona-Hilo war, for example, was fought between 1700 –1720 on the big island of Hawaii until it was resolved by a political marriage. During 1776, the year America declared her independence from Britain, the third Hawaii-Maui war was being fought. This conflict featured an unsuccessful invasion of Maui by natives of the Big Island.

In 1778, with the arrival of Captain Cook at Waimea Bay on the island of Kauai, two warrior cultures collided in mutual misunderstanding. Captain

Cook of Britain's Royal Navy was on his third voyage of exploration. His preferred technique for dealing with native populations was a combination of bluff, hostage taking, and firepower.

In his Journals, Cook explicitly described how his exploration method could be construed or misconstrued as an invasion:

> We attempt to land in a peaceable manner, if this succeeds its well, if not we land nevertheless and maintain the footing we thus got by the Superiority of our fire arms, in what other light can they than at first look upon us but as invaders of their Country; time and some acquaintance with us can only convince them of their mistake.

At first the Hawaiians regarded Cook with reverence. Many prostrated themselves at his feet, and some may have taken him for the god Lono. Some of the women were eager to trade sex for nails. His two ships were restocked with fresh water, fruits, and vegetables. Cook christened Hawaii the Sandwich Islands in honor of his patron, the Earl of Sandwich.

Cook departed the islands to voyage north to Alaska, but returned to Kealakekua on the Big Island in February of 1779. His ship, the *Resolution*, had a broken mast that needed repairing. Cook described the native Hawaiians in glowing terms: "These people trade with the least suspicion of any Indians I ever met … It is also remarkable that they have never once attempted to cheat us in exchanges or once to commit a theft."

The death of Cook on February 14, 1779, in Hawaii remains something of a mystery to this day. His crew had earlier taken some sacred wooden palings from the Hawaiians for use as firewood. This distressed the native people. Cook's attempt to seize a local priest misfired badly. A mob of Hawaiians gathered. Cook fired his two pistols. He was stabbed with an iron dagger, which must have been procured or stolen from one of his ships. Four royal marines were also killed in the skirmish. Cook's body was seized by the Hawaiians, mutilated, and partially devoured. Today, a white obelisk commemorates the spot near where Cook fell.

After Cook's death, Hawaii's greatest king rose to power. From 1783 to 1796, King Kamehameha led his people in the thirteen-year war of

Unification. This war was fought with muskets and gunpowder, and the king employed Westerners to help train his army.

The first threats to the independence of the Hawaiian kingdom did not come from Britain or America. Astonishingly, they came from the Russians and the French. Georg Anton Schäffer, a German doctor working for the Russian-American Company, led an attempted invasion of Hawaii in 1816. Schäffer ordered the crew of the *Myrtle,* a Russian vessel, to build a fort near Honolulu Harbor. He also built Fort Hipo on Kauai. King Kamehameha had Schäffer and the Russians evicted from Hawaii in 1817. The ruins of Fort Hipo are visible on Kauai today.

King Kamehameha died in 1819. The following year, American missionaries began arriving in Hawaii. They softened some of the warlike ways of the Hawaiians. Boxing, for example, was banned, though less on account of the violence than due to the gambling the sport engendered.

Protestant missionaries also managed to convince the Queen Regent Ka'ahumanu to have Catholicism made illegal. This led directly to a brief French "invasion," or rather, extortion of Hawaii. In 1839, Captain Cyrille Laplace of the French Navy's *L'Artémise* arrived in Honolulu. Laplace insisted that the Hawaiian kingdom pay reparations of $20,000 for their affront to French Catholic interests, or his frigate would bombard their coast. Lacking a modern navy, the kingdom paid the ransom. In 1839, King Kamehameha III passed laws granting religious tolerance.

In 1843, the British captain of the *Carysfort*, Lord George Paulet, arrived in Honolulu and made a series of demands on the Hawaiian crown. The Hawaiian flag was lowered and the Union Jack was raised over Oahu. Later that year, Rear Admiral Richard Thomas arrived in Honolulu and declared that Paulet had exceeded his authority. The British impact on Hawaii (or the Sandwich Islands) persists to this day, however, with the presence of the Union Jack in one quadrant of its state flag.

American sugar planters arrived in the islands soon after the missionaries. American influence also spread from the West Coast of North America to the shores of Hawaii.

The US Civil War meant an economic boom for Hawaii, which supplied sugar, beef, salt, and more to the Union Army. King Kamehameha IV remained officially neutral during the war.

Native Hawaiians, however, served on both sides during the war. About thirty veterans of the Union Army are buried in Oahu Cemetery. Twelve Hawaiians served on board the CSS *Shenandoah*, a merchant raider that terrorized Union ships in the Pacific.

The late nineteenth century saw a period of increasing political turmoil in the Hawaiian kingdom. In a series of rebellions, political and commercial interests clashed over the future of the kingdom. Then, in 1893, a rebel militia called the Honolulu Rifles and led by Lorrin A. Thurston, a grandson of American missionaries, launched a coup d'état against Queen Liliuokalani. A landing party of marines and sailors from the USS *Boston* came ashore, ostensibly to protect US lives and property. It took no active part in the coup, but was perceived by many as a sign of support for it. Finally, in order to prevent bloodshed, the queen ordered her forces to surrender, and Hawaii was declared a republic. In 1993, in the centenary year of the coup, Congress passed a resolution apologizing for US involvement in it.

The start of the Spanish American War in 1898 dramatized the strategic importance of Hawaii. US Navy ships passed through Pearl Harbor to re-coal on their way to the war in the Philippines. Admiral Dewey defeated the Spanish fleet at the Battle of Manila Bay. When the Philippines became an American colony, the critical, strategic need for Pearl Harbor was evident.

Finally in 1898, President McKinley annexed the Hawaiian Islands, which became an American territory. On August 12, 1898, soldiers of the First New York Volunteer Infantry Regiment arrived on Oahu.

Hawaii kept the flame of its monarchical past alive even after annexation. In 1916, the 32nd Infantry Regiment, also known as the Queen's Own, was mustered at Schofield Barracks. The only royal regiment in the US Army marched on parade before the former queen.

From 1925 until 1927 George Patton served as an officer at the Schofield Barracks in Honolulu. Based on his Hawaiian experience, Patton authored a 1937 report in which he prophesied, "The unheralded arrival during a period of profound peace of a Japanese expeditionary force within 200 miles of Oahu during darkness; this force to be preceded by submarines who will be in the immediate vicinity of Pearl Harbor.… An air attack by [Japanese] navy fighters and carrier borne bombers on air stations and the submarine base using either gas or incendiary bombs."

On December 7, 1941, Patton's prediction came true. Two-man midget submarines of the Imperial Japanese Navy managed to penetrate Pearl Harbor undetected. One was sunk by the USS *Ward*, an antiquated World War I US Navy destroyer. The flotilla of midget subs did no real damage, and Ensign Kazuo Sakamaki, the only survivor, washed up on shore at Waimanalo Beach, where he became the first Japanese prisoner of war captured by the Americans in World War II.

Shortly after 7:00 a.m. on the "Day of Infamy," a large concentration of aircraft was detected by Oahu radar stations that were monitored by the Army Signal Corps. Misinterpreted as the B-17s scheduled to arrive that day at Hickam Field from California, the aircraft were not seen as a threat and no warning was sounded. Admiral Nagumo's flight of torpedo planes and bombers escorted by Zeros began their attack on Battleship Row. The *Arizona* blew up after a hit near turret II and sank to her final resting place. Four battleships in all were sunk, and many more ships were damaged. Of the American planes on the ground, 188 were destroyed. Over 2,400 Americans were killed in Hawaii that day.

Fortunately, no US aircraft carriers were in Pearl Harbor. Admiral Nagumo, fearing for the safety of the six carriers in Operation Z, declined to order a second air attack. As a result, the vital fuel tanks on Oahu were not destroyed.

Admiral Yamamoto's bold plan to strike at Hawaii had scored a devastating blow against the United States. The Imperial Japanese forces would "run wild in Pacific for the next six months," just as Yamamoto had predicted. But Japan had awakened a sleeping giant that was finally united and bent on swift vengeance. "Remember Pearl Harbor" became the rallying cry across all of America.

After December 7, Hawaii lived in fear of an imminent invasion that never really happened. Unlike the West Coast of the United States, however, the territory of Hawaii did not imprison its population of Japanese Americans, many of whom served loyally in US forces.

Nonetheless, although many know about December 7, 1941, few realize that there was a second Japanese attack on Hawaii during the war.

On March 1, 1942, the Japanese launched a second, much smaller air attack on Pearl Harbor. It involved coordination between the air and submarine arms of the Imperial Navy. A pair of Kawasaki H8K1 flying boats flew from Wotje Atoll in the Marshall Islands to rendezvous with two large Japanese submarines at French Frigate Shoals. This time, American radar detected the incoming aircraft and sounded the alert. Curtiss P-40 Warhawk fighter planes were scrambled. One Japanese plane dropped its ordinance harmlessly on Mount Tantalus near Honolulu. The other dropped its payload in the ocean miles from any target. The boldly conceived Japanese plan was well executed, but it also lacked proper intelligence and was ineffective.

The loss of four Japanese aircraft carriers at the Battle of Midway on June 7, 1942 (with an American loss of only one carrier), was a turning point in the war in the Pacific. Never again during the war would the Japanese credibly menace Hawaii.

In 1959, Hawaii became the fiftieth and, thus far, final state to be admitted to the Union.

During the Cold War, Soviet submarines would prowl off the coast of Hawaii. On March 6, 1968, the Soviet Navy's *K-129*, a diesel submarine equipped with ballistic missiles, sank with all hands about 1,500 miles from Oahu.

## HAWAII
## MILITARY HISTORY SITES

**Battleship *Missouri* Memorial**
Location: 63 Cowpens Street, Honolulu, Oahu, HI 96818
Web: https://ussmissouri.org

**Iolani Palace**
Location: 364 South King Street, Honolulu, Oahu, HI 96813
Web: www.iolanipalace.org

**Kealakekua Bay State Historical Park (Captain Cook)**
Location: 82-6099 Puuhonua Beach Road, Kealakekua, HI 96750
Web: hawaiistateparks.org/parks/hawaii/kealakekua-bay-state-historical-park

**National Memorial Cemetery of the Pacific**
Location: 2177 Puowaina Drive, Honolulu, Oahu, HI 96813
Web: www.cem.va.gov/CEMs/nchp/nmcp.asp

**Pacific Aviation Museum Pearl Harbor**
Location: 319 Lexington Boulevard, Historic Ford Island, Honolulu, Oahu, HI 96818
Web: www.pacificaviationmuseum.org

**Pearl Harbor—WW II Valor in the Pacific National Monument**
Location: 1 Arizona Memorial Place, Honolulu, Oahu, HI 96818
Web: www.nps.gov/valr

**Russian Fort Elizabeth State Historical Park (Fort Hipo)**
Location: Highway 50, Waimea, Kauai, HI 96796
Web: https://hawaiistateparks.org/parks/kauai/russian-fort-eliza-beth-state-historical-park
Web: www.nps.gov/nr/travel/Asian_American_and_Pacific_Islander_Heritage/Russian-Fort.htm

**U.S. Army Museum of Hawaii**
Location: 2131 Kalia Road, Honolulu, Oahu, HI 96815
Web: hiarmymuseumsoc.org

**USS *Bowfin* Submarine Museum & Park**
Location: 11 Arizona Memorial Drive, Honolulu, Oahu, HI 96818
Web: bowfin.org

# America Invaded: HAWAII

FORT HIPO

NIIHAU

PUUWAI

KAUAI

KILAUEA
ANAHOLA
KAPAA
KEKAHA
HANAMAULU
KALAHEO

## OAHU

PUPUKEA
HAUULA
WAHIAWA
WAIANAE
KAHALUU
KAILUA
EWA BEACH
WAIMANA
HONOLULU

## OAHU

KAHUKU POINT
PUPUKEA
KAHUKU
LAIE
HAUULA
WAIALUA BAY
HALEIWA
KAENA POINT
MOKULEIA
KAAAWA
SCHOFIELD BARRACKS
WAHIAWA
WAIKANE
MAKAHA
AHUIMANU
WAIANAE
PEARL CITY
WAIPAHU
KANEOHE
MARINE CORPS BASE HAWAII
NANAKULI
KAILUA
MAKAKILO CITY
EWA BEACH
PEARL HARBOR
MANANA ISLAND
BARBERS POINT
HONOLULU
MAMALA BAY
DIAMOND HEAD
KOKO HEAD

### KING KAMEHAMEHA I
c. 1736-1819
Honolulu
Source: iStock/
compassandcamera

### USS ARIZONA MEMORIAL
Pearl Harbor
Source: iStock/HaizhanZheng

Nickname: The Aloha State
Statehood: 1959
Capital: Honolulu

## CAPTAIN JAMES COOK
### 1728-1779
#### Killed in Hawaii on February 14, 1779
Source: iStock/GeorgiosArt

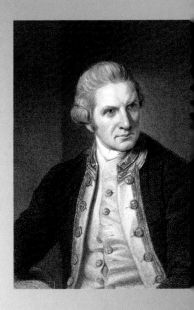

MAUI

MAUNALOA
KAULAPUU
HALAWA
KAUNAKAKAI
KAHAKULOA
PAUWELA
LAHAINA
KAHULUI
LANAI CITY
MAKAWAO
KIHEI
HANA
HALEAKALA NATIONAL PARK
KIPAHULU

HAWAII

KAPAUU
HONOKAA
WAIMEA
PUAKO
PEPEEKEO
HILO
KAILUA KONA
KEAAU
CAPTAIN COOK
PAHOA
HAWAII VOLCANOES NATIONAL PARK
KALAPANA
MILOLII
PAHALA
NAALEHU

## CAPTAIN COOK MEMORIAL
Westminster Abbey, London
Source: Author photo

# IDAHO

daho is more famous for her potatoes than for invasions, but fighting has taken place within her borders.

Humans have inhabited the area we know today as Idaho for thousands and thousands of years. The Nez Perce and Coeur d'Alene tribes were established in the region long before the arrival of Europeans. Idaho's rugged mountain terrain and lack of a coastline delayed the arrival of Europeans until the nineteenth century.

In 1803, David Thompson, a British fur trader with the Hudson's Bay Company, arrived in what is now Idaho. Fort Boise was established in 1834 on the Snake River by the Hudson's Bay Company.

Not long after Thompson, Lewis and Clark's Corps of Discovery made its way through Idaho. In August 1805, Lewis described what he saw along what is today the Idaho-Montana border: "We proceeded on to the top of the dividing ridge from which I discovered immense ranges of high mountains still to the West of us with their tops partially covered with snow." Later, Lewis and Clark camped near the present site of Lewiston. Lewis and Clark State College can be found in Lewiston today.

Andrew Henry, an American fur trader, explored Idaho and founded Fort Henry around 1810. This was the first fur-trading post west of the Mississippi River.

A man who would feature large in the early history of Idaho, and who would exemplify the competition for power in the region, was Donald

Mackenzie. He was born in Scotland and was working for the Canadian North West Company when he arrived in the area. He eventually signed up with the American Pacific Fur Company. However, during the War of 1812, American fur-trading operations in the area were curtailed due to fear of British actions. Mackenzie rejoined the North West Company and did more exploring in their service.

And in the period after the war, Britons and Americans continued to compete in the area. In the 1820s, American fur traders and explorers William H. Ashley and Jedediah Smith arrived in Idaho.

The Battle of Pierre's Hole in 1832 saw a group of American trappers with Native American allies clash with a party of Gros Ventre, another Native American tribe.

French Canadians may have played a role in naming Idaho's capital city of Boise, exclaiming *"Les bois, les bois"* on seeing its tree-lined riverbank in the 1820s. French fur traders named the Indians they encountered *Nez Perce* or "Pierced Nose," although it remains a matter of dispute whether they did actually pierce their noses. The name of the Coeur d'Alene tribe (and also an Idaho city) is French and means "Heart of an Awl," and was given by French Canadian fur traders.

Idaho was part of the Oregon Country that was claimed by both Britain and the United States. The Oregon Treaty of 1846 established the American claim on Idaho.

As settlers increasingly moved into the area, occasional clashes with local Native Americans erupted. For instance, in 1851, the so-called Clark Massacre saw Shoshone attack a wagon train, killing some of its members and seizing horses.

Gold was first discovered in the Idaho territory in 1860 along Clearwater River. A gold rush was ignited, bringing more American settlers to the territory. This led directly to more encroachment onto lands that belonged to Native Americans.

The largest battle recorded in the state was the Bear River Massacre, which took place during the US Civil War on January 29, 1863, in southeastern Idaho. Colonel Patrick Connor, a native of Ireland, led US Army forces against the Shoshone tribe in response to attacks on American miners. Twenty-one American soldiers, mostly from California, were killed, along with at least ten times as many Shoshone, including many women and children. Bear Hunter, the Shoshone chief, was among those killed that day.

A second Fort Boise was built in Boise by the Union Army in 1863 to help secure the Oregon Trail. The facility was closed in 1912. Gold from Idaho helped to finance the Union cause during the Civil War. Idaho was part of the Territory of Washington until the Idaho Territory was formed in 1863.

Idaho would see some action during the so-called Snake War of 1864–1868. As tensions between Native Americans and miners continued, a series of clashes erupted. At first, volunteers and then, increasingly after the end of the Civil War, US troops tried to counter occasional Native American raids.

The Nez Perce tribe had welcomed Lewis and Clark when they passed through Idaho in 1805, providing food and materiel support for their journey. In their journals, Clark described Twisted Hair, a Nez Perce chief, as being "A Chearfull man with apparent Siencerity." An 1855 treaty between the US government and the Nez Perce tribe seemed to guarantee the preservation of their homelands. Gold fever, however, would alter the arrangement. A revised 1863 treaty reduced the Nez Perce lands by 90 percent. Chief Joseph of the Nez Perce was a voice counseling patience and moderation. Violence, however, flared up on June 14, 1877, when Nez Perce warriors killed four settlers. American soldiers responded quickly.

The Battle of White Bird Canyon, fought on June 17, 1877, during the Nez Perce War, was a rare defeat for American forces during the Indian wars. Thirty-four soldiers under Captain David Perry were killed while only three men of the Nez Perce were wounded. US forces would once again suffer at the hands of the Nez Perce at the Battle of Camas Creek in southeastern Idaho on August 20, 1877. The Nez Perce were later defeated at the Battle of Big Hole (see Montana), and many fled into Canada. Chief Joseph was resettled onto a reservation in Colville, Washington.

In 1890, Idaho became the forty-third state to join the Union.

The USS *Idaho* was a New Mexico-class battleship that served in both world wars and was nicknamed Big Spud. United States Army Air Force crews began training in Mountain Home in 1943.

A Japanese balloon bomb, or Fu-Go, landed in Boise in February 1945, along with more than half a dozen throughout the state. Little damage was done.

## IDAHO
## MILITARY HISTORY SITES

**Experimental Breeder Reactor No. 1 (EBR-I) Atomic Museum**
Location: Highway 20-26, Arco, ID 83213
Web: www4vip.inl.gov/ebr/

**Fort Hall Replica**
Location: 3002 Alvord Loop, Upper Level Ross Park, Pocatello, ID 83201
Web: www.forthall.net

**Idaho State Historical Museum**
Location: Bureau of Reclamation Building, 214 South Broadway Avenue (temporary location), Boise, ID 83702
Web: https://history.idaho.gov/idaho-state-historical-museum

**Idaho Military History Museum**
Location: 4692 West Harvard Street, Boise, ID 83705
Web: https://museum.mil.idaho.gov

**Legacy Flight Museum**
Location: 400 Airport Road, Rexburg, ID 83440
Web: rexburg.org/pages/lfm-legacy-flight-museum

**Lewis and Clark Discovery Center**
Location: 4832 Hells Gate Road, Hellsgate State Park, ID 83501
Web: http://visitlcvalley.com/directory/hells-gate-state-park-lewis-and-clark-discovery-center/

**Sacagawea Interpretive, Cultural, & Education Center**
Location: 2700 Main Street (Highway 28), Salmon, ID 83467
Web: www.sacajaweacenter.org

**Warhawk Air Museum**
Location: 201 Municipal Drive, Nampa, ID 83687
Web: warhawkairmuseum.org

# America Invaded: IDAHO

Nickname: The Gem State
Statehood: 1890
Capital: Boise

**LEWIS AND CLARK EXPEDITION STAMP, 1954**
Source: iStock/traveler1116

**SACAGAWEA**
Born in what is today Idaho
1788-1812 (or 1884)

# ILLINOIS

Illinois was home to Cahokia and the spectacular civilization that flourished there long before the arrival of Europeans. When they finally did arrive, they found a land populated by a number of Algonquian-speaking peoples.

And it would be the French who would first bring European influences into the area. In 1673, French explorers Jacques Marquette and Louis Jolliet entered the region; and in 1675, Marquette established a mission near present-day Utica. By 1680, Robert de La Salle and Henri de Tonti were building Fort Crèvecoeur near what is now Peoria.

It wasn't, however, just the French who were on the move. The Iroquois had been battling for some time to control the lucrative fur trade created by European expansion. Their westward drive brought them into conflict with tribes in the Illinois region; and that same year, 1680, they destroyed the Great Village of the Illinois. In the winter of 1682–3, de La Salle built Fort Saint Louis du Rocher opposite the Great Village of the Illinois. It too was attacked by the Iroquois, and Henri de Tonti had to abandon the fort in 1691.

Fighting with the Iroquois went on in the region until the Great Peace of Montreal brought a respite from hostilities.

The early eighteenth century saw significant expansion of French influence in the area. In 1717, Illinois was removed from Canadian control and instead incorporated into the French province of Louisiana. Work began on building

Fort Chartres in 1718, and in 1730, it became the capital of the French Illinois Country. In 1721, they built a fort at Kaskaskia.

But the expansion of French control would not occur without conflict. The French, for instance, clashed repeatedly with the Fox/Meskwaki. The Second Fox War saw a massacre in 1730 in east-central Illinois of Fox/Meskwaki by the French and their Native American allies.

The future of Illinois was not going to be French, however. Another European power was exerting increasing influence in the region. Yes, Britain.

Under the 1763 peace deal that ended the French and Indian War, the territory that is now the state of Illinois became British.

However, as the British took control of the region, resistance to the new authorities broke out almost immediately, caused by changes in trade policies and the arrival of fresh settlers.

The focus of Pontiac's War (1763–1766) was to the east, but it delayed British control of Illinois and sucked in local tribes, including the Illinois. Pontiac himself was killed in or near Cahokia by a member of the Peoria tribe.

And another war was coming, one that would dramatically change the future of Illinois. Even territory this far west was to see major action during the War of Independence.

For instance, in July 1778, George Rogers Clark, leading a column of Virginian troops, marched into Illinois—which had been left lightly defended by Britain—and seized a number of settlements, including Kaskaskia and Cahokia. Many of the local French welcomed the American arrival and swore an oath of allegiance to Virginia and the United States. But this was not to be the last fighting in the region during the War of Independence. In 1780, a combined force of British and Native Americans commanded by Emanuel Hesse attacked St. Louis and Cahokia, but failed to achieve very much. Some of the British attempted to escape along the Illinois River. A force consisting of American, French, and Spanish troops went after them, but got involved in attacking a Sauk and Fox/Meskwaki settlement. In 1781, a Spanish expedition passed through the area, en route to attacking Fort St. Joseph.

When peace came in 1783, what is now the state of Illinois was confirmed as being under American control.

In 1784, Virginia gave up its claim to Illinois; and in 1787, under the Northwest Ordinance, it became part of the Northwest Territory. Soon the process of opening up the area to American settlements began. In 1803, the

Kaskaskia gave up almost all their land in Illinois to the United States. More settlers arrived. In 1804, in a disputed agreement in St. Louis, the United States thought it had bought the lands of the Sauk and Meswkaki east of the Mississippi.

In 1799, African-American pioneer Jean-Baptist-Point Du Sable founded the first settlement on the site of what is now Chicago. In 1803, the US Army established Fort Dearborn. And the young United States was already beginning to look far to the west of Illinois. In 1804, William Clark (brother of George Rogers Clark, who had taken Kaskaskia and Cahokia in 1778) and his troops departed from Camp Dubois to join up with Meriwether Lewis and head west.

Some might have thought that the process of establishing American domination of Illinois would from then on be a smooth one. If so, they would have been wrong.

Early in the War of 1812, in August 1812, American troops were ordered to withdraw from Fort Dearborn in the belief it would be impossible to defend. During the ensuing Battle of Fort Dearborn, the American military withdrew, and military and civilians were attacked and captured by Potawatomis. In turn, American forces attacked Potawatomi and Kickapoo villages in the Peoria area; and in 1813, they built Fort Clark in Peoria. Other clashes occurred in what is now Illinois. For instance, in April 1813, American rangers were ambushed by Kickapoo warriors at the so-called Battle of Africa Point. Later in the war, in 1814, American troops suffered a defeat at the Battle of Rock Island Rapids on what is now Campbell Island.

The peace deal that ended the war, however, left the area under American control, and the following decades would see Native Americans squeezed out and even more settlers flowing in.

Already, for example, soon after the war, veterans settled in Illinois. In 1819, the year after Illinois became a state, most of the Kickapoo moved west of the Mississippi. In 1829, by an agreement at Prairie du Chien, Chippewa, Ottawa, and Potawatomi ceded territory in northern Illinois. However, some would resist the American government's attempt to remove all Native Americans from Illinois. In the decades after the disputed St. Louis agreement of 1804, many Sauk and Meskwaki had moved west across the Mississippi, but not all were willing to stay there.

In 1830 and 1831, Black Hawk, a chief of the Sauk and Meskwaki who had fought alongside the British in the War of 1812, returned to his ancestral lands in Saukenuk, Illinois. He returned again in 1832, with hundreds of men, women, and children who formed what became known as the British Band, because of their habit of using the British flag to defy US sovereignty and to stress their British connections. Armed American militiamen met Black Hawk and his supporters, and when Black Hawk tried to negotiate a truce, fighting broke out. The result was a defeat for the American forces, known as the Battle of Stillman's Run. What followed was a series of minor clashes and raids on settlers—some involving Black Hawk's British Band, some involving other Native Americans who had been inspired by his actions—that stretched across large parts of Illinois and Wisconsin. The short war culminated in a massacre of Black Hawk's followers in the Battle of Bad Axe River (see Wisconsin).

In 1833, an agreement at Chicago included provision for the ceding and settling of the last remaining Native American lands in Illinois.

In 1839, expelled Cherokee on the Trail of Tears trekked through southern Illinois.

When the Civil War came, Illinois, a very important state in Abraham Lincoln's life (he had even served as a captain in the Illinois militia in the war against Black Hawk), stayed with the Union, despite Confederate sympathies in some parts of southern Illinois, known as Little Egypt.

The state played a major part in the successful Union river campaign. In 1861, Commodore John Rodgers, commanding the Union river flotilla, chose Cairo, located where the Mississippi and Ohio Rivers meet, as a major operations base. Confederate raiders did occasionally cross into Illinois. For instance, on August 19, 1864, a small number of Confederate raiders seized goods at Bayfield, near present-day Bay City. And in March 1864, the Charleston Riot saw Union troops clash with Copperheads (Democrats who opposed the war), and nine people died.

That's pretty much the end of combat in Illinois. Occasional violence would follow, like the Haymarket Affair bombings of 1886; and during World War II, Herbert Haupt was arrested in Chicago for espionage. Haupt, born in Stettin in 1919 to German parents, had grown up in Chicago. In 1941, he left the United States on a world tour, winding up in Nazi Germany, where was recruited for a sabotage mission. A member of Operation Pastorius (see Florida and New York), he was dropped off by a German U-boat near Jacksonville, Florida, and made his way by train back to Chicago, where he was reunited with his parents. After being informed on by another German saboteur, he was arrested, tried, and executed in 1942 at the age of twenty-two.

Al Capone of Brooklyn, New York, "invaded" Chicago in the 1920s to lead the Chicago mob, but that is another story....

## ILLINOIS
## MILITARY HISTORY SITES

### Abraham Lincoln Presidential Library and Museum
Location: 212 North Sixth Street, Springfield, IL 62701
Web: www.illinois.gov/alplm

### Battle of Fort Dearborn Park
Location: 1801 South Calumet Avenue, Chicago, IL 60616
Web: www.chicagoparkdistrict.com/parks/Battle-of-Fort-Dearborn-Park/

### Cahokia Mounds State Historic Site
Location: 30 RameyStreet, Collinsville, IL 62234
Web: cahokiamounds.org

### Chicago History Museum
Location: 1601 North Clark Street, Chicago, IL 60614
Web: www.chicagohistory.org

### Fort de Chartres State Historic Site
Location: 1350 State Route 155, Prairie du Rocher, IL 62277
Web: www.fortdechartres.us

### Fort Kaskaskia State Historic Site
Location: 4372 Park Road, Ellis Grove, IL 62241
Web: www2.illinois.gov/ihpa/Experience/Sites/Southwest/Pages/Fort-Kas-kaskia.aspx

**Oak Ridge Cemetery—Lincoln's Tomb, War Memorials**
Location: 1441 Monument Avenue, Springfield, IL 62702
Web: www.oakridgecemetery.org
Web: lincolntomb.org

**Pritzker Military Museum & Library**
Location: 104 South Michigan Avenue, Chicago, IL 60603
Web: www.pritzkermilitary.org

**Ronald Reagan Boyhood Home & Visitors Center**
Location: 816 South Hennepin Avenue, Dixon, IL 61021
Web: https://reaganhome.org

**Russell Military Museum**
Location: 43363 North US Highway 41, Zion, IL 60099
Web: www.russellmilitarymuseum.com

**Ulysses S. Grant Home**
Location: 500 Bouthillier Street, Galena, IL 61036
Web: www.granthome.com

# America Invaded: **ILLINOIS**

ILLINOIS

Nickname: Land of Lincoln
Statehood: 1818
Capital: Springfield

**ABRAHAM LINCOLN**
1809-1865
Source: iStock/wynnter

# INDIANA

The Hoosier state derives its name from being a *Land of Indians*. Native Americans resided in the area for thousands of years before Europeans came.

Even before Europeans arrived in significant numbers in what is now Indiana, their activities farther east would have a knock-on effect in the area. The competition among Native Americans to supply valuable furs to European traders and receive firearms from those same traders helped ignite the so-called Beaver Wars, or Iroquois Wars. Iroquois attacked Algonquian tribes.

In 1679, French explorer Robert de La Salle arrived in what is now Indiana and camped at what became South Bend. By 1681, he had negotiated a deal with the Miami and Illinois people, and the French started allowing them to buy guns. With France increasingly involved in fighting the Iroquois and aiding their Native American enemies, peace was finally on the way. The Great Peace of Montreal in 1701 brought an end to the fighting.

In the period after, French influence and trade in the area began to expand. The French founded the settlement at Vincennes, and built forts like Fort Miami at what is now Fort Wayne, and Fort Ouiatenon at what is now West Lafayette.

However, British influence was starting to spread into the area as well. French officer Celoron de Bienville (or Blainville) led French attempts in the region both to deter British traders and to dissuade Native Americans from trading with them, but the end of French power in the area was not far off. Fort Miami had already been attacked during King George's War. During the French and Indian War, the North American part of the Seven Years' War, British forces again advanced into the area and seized Fort Miami and Fort Ouiatenon. Through the peace deal that ended the war in 1763, the French passed their claims on the area to the British. This did not, however, take into account the fact that many of the local tribes were not eager about accepting British rule and new settlers. In a war that became known as Pontiac's War, after one of the Native American leaders, tribes across the area attacked British targets, and Britain lost control again of Fort Miami and Fort Ouiatenon.

After Pontiac's War finally ground to a halt, Britain began to expand its control in the area, but there was more conflict ahead. In 1773, the British made the area part of the Province of Quebec, which hugely upset those colonists that had been hoping for their own chance to expand into the territory. Soon another battle to control the area had begun.

The War of Independence saw a number of military operations within what is now the state of Indiana.

In 1778, George Rogers Clark, having advanced from Virginia, seized a number of locations in the region, including Vincennes. The British recaptured it, but in February 1779, Clark retook it, establishing a strong US presence in southern Indiana. In late 1780, a militia force raised from the French community and led by Augustin de la Balme attempted to seize Fort Detroit, but instead ended up ambushed and defeated by forces under Chief Little Turtle near what is now Columbia City.

After attacking Fort St. Joseph, at what is now Niles, Michigan, a raiding party under Jean Baptiste Hamelin and Lieutenant Thomas Brady suffered a similar fate at about the same time in the Battle of Petit Fort on the Indiana shore of Lake Michigan. In February 1781, however, a Spanish and Native American force under Captain Don Eugenio Pouré passed through Indiana and captured Fort St. Joseph. The fort was plundered, and then Pouré's troops safely withdrew to the south again.

In August 1781, another American attempt to capture Fort Detroit again ended in defeat. A force of Pennsylvania militiamen under Archibald Lochry was destroyed by Mohawk leader Joseph Brant near what is now Aurora.

Nevertheless, in 1783, in the peace deal that ended the war, Britain passed all its claims to the area to the young United States. This was not, however, the end of fighting. The United States might think it controlled the territory, but a lot of the local Native Americans were less than keen on the idea. A lot less than keen.

The tribes combined to resist the arrival of American settlers and to combat American military expeditions sent into the area. In 1791, Little Turtle and Blue Jacket, leading fighters from fourteen tribes, scored a significant victory in the Battle of the Wabash, destroying an American force under Major General Arthur St. Clair. For the price of a few of fighters killed and wounded, the Native American forces killed 623 Americans and wounded 258. It was a stunning defeat for the newly established United States.

In response, Congress commanded Major General "Mad Anthony" Wayne to build a bigger and better military force, the Legion of the United States. The Native Americans hoped for aid from the British, who still occupied Fort Miami, but it did not come. The decisive battle was, in the end, fought in 1794 near Fort Miami, at a place where a tornado had hit recently. The battle became known as the Battle of Fallen Timbers. It was a crushing defeat for the Native American confederation, and they were forced to accept peace terms under the Treaty of Greenville in 1795, which allowed American settlement in some parts of southeastern Indiana.

But more war was to come. In 1808, by the Treaty of Fort Wayne, the Delaware and the Potawatomi agreed to sell three million acres in the Indiana Territory to the United States. A Shawnee leader, Tecumseh, and his brother Tenskwatawa, a spiritual leader, united a number of tribes to resist. Tecumseh said that the land was shared by other tribes as well, and demanded that Governor William Henry Harrison—who would be elected president of the United States in 1840—agree not to implement the treaty. In 1811, Harrison marched a military force toward Prophetstown. On November 7, Tenskwatawa led an attack on Harrison's forces at what is now Battle Ground, Indiana. In what became known as the Battle of Tippecanoe, casualties were about equal on both sides, but eventually American cavalry managed to force back the Native Americans.

And fighting in the region was still not finished. The War of 1812 broke out. Tecumseh allied himself with the British against the United States, and many of the tribes rose in resistance against US forces. In 1812, Fort Harrison and Fort Wayne came under heavy attack, but both managed to hold out. Settlers were also targeted in incidents like the Pigeon Roost Massacre. An American punitive expedition launched against Miami villages in retaliation for the violence against settlers was set upon in December at the Battle of Mississinewa, but managed to hold off its attackers with the use of cavalry. In 1813, Kickapoo warriors clashed with Indiana Rangers at the Battle of Tipton's Island. However, in 1814, the war came to an end, and the Native Americans were left to face the United States without British assistance.

In 1816, Indiana became the nineteenth state of the Union. A new capital was established at Indianapolis in 1821. In the decades following, the American settler presence expanded, and the areas still controlled by Native Americans diminished. Successive treaties took blocks of land away from the Native Americans. Gradually, most of the tribes were forced out until few Native Americans remained in the state. In 1838, the notorious Potawatomi Trail of Death saw hundreds of members of the Potawatomi tribe forcibly expelled from their lands in Indiana and compelled to march to Kansas. Many, particularly children, died on the way.

Indiana was a Union state during the Civil War and sent substantial numbers of troops to fight in it. The fighting itself, though, only visited Indiana occasionally.

In particular, on July 18, 1862, Confederate Colonel Adam Johnson crossed the Ohio River and captured the Indiana town of Newburgh, with the help of two fake artillery pieces, constructed out of stovepipes, logs, and wheels from a wagon. After briefly holding the town and seizing provisions, the raiders withdrew to Kentucky. And on July 9 of the following year, Morgan's Raid erupted onto Indiana territory. Morgan's force, consisting of Confederate cavalry, brushed aside the Indiana Legion at the Battle of Corydon. As concern grew that he would attack the capital, Morgan instead led his men eastward into Ohio, spending only a few days actually in Indiana.

It's worth mentioning one last thing about Indiana and the Civil War. General Ambrose Burnside, who was born in Liberty, Indiana, had facial hair that left a lasting legacy. Whiskers along the side of the face are called sideburns after him. Burnside later served as a senator from Rhode Island and as the first president of the National Rifle Association.

And that was pretty much the end of military operations in Indiana. From then on, the wars would be elsewhere, though, Indiana would, of course, still send people to fight. Samuel Woodfill, for instance, born in Jefferson County, was called by General Pershing America's most outstanding soldier of World War I. Also, General Walter Bedell Smith, born in Indianapolis, would become Chief of Staff to Eisenhower in World War II.

## INDIANA
## MILITARY HISTORY SITES

### Benjamin Harrison Presidential Site
Location: 1230 North Delaware Street, Indianapolis, IN 46202
Web: www.presidentbenjaminharrison.org

### Fort Harrison State Park
Location: 6000 North Post Road, Indianapolis, IN 46216
Web: www.in.gov/dnr/parklake/2982.htm

### Fort Ouiatenon Blockhouse Museum
Location: 3129 South River Road, West Lafayette, IN 47906
Web: www.tippecanoehistory.org/our-sites/blockhouse-museum/

### Grouseland (William Henry Harrison Mansion)
Location: 3 West Scott Street, Vincennes, IN 47591
Web: www.grouselandfoundation.org

### Old Fort Wayne
Location: 1201 Spy Run Avenue, Fort Wayne, IN 46805
Web: https://oldfortwayne.org

### Indiana Military Museum
Location: 715 South 6th Street, Vincennes, IN 47591
Web: https://indymilitary.com/

### Indiana War Memorial Museum
Location: 51 East Michigan Street, Indianapolis, IN 46204
Web: www.in.gov/iwm/2333.htm

**Mississinewa Battlefield**
Location: 6000 North 300 W27, La Fontaine, IN 46940
Web: www.mississinewa1812.com

**Tippecanoe Battlefield & Museum**
Location: 200 Battle Ground Avenue, Battle Ground, IN 47920
Web: www.tippecanoehistory.org

**USS *Indianapolis* Memorial**
Location: 692 Ellsworth Street, On the Canal, Indianapolis, IN 46202
Web: www.ussindianapolis.org

**Veterans Memorial Museum of Terre Haute**
Location: 1129 Wabash Avenue, Terre Haute, IN 47807
Web: terrehaute.com/veterans-memorial-museum-of-terre-haute

# America Invaded: INDIANA

Nickname: The Hoosier State
Statehood: 1816
Capital: Indianapolis

**WILLIAM HENRY
HARRISON**
1773-1841
Source: iStock/traveler1116

# IOWA

The impact of French invasions on Iowa is discernible today in city names such as Des Moines, Lafayette, and even tiny Bonaparte. So it is not surprising that the first Europeans to enter what is now Iowa were Frenchmen—Louis Jolliet and Father Jacques Marquette in 1673. In 1682, another Frenchman, Robert de la Salle, claimed a vast chunk of land in the Mississippi River Valley in the name of the French throne.

It didn't make a lot of immediate difference to the large majority of people living in the territory, who were Native Americans belonging to a variety of tribes. What would make a difference, though, as the eighteenth century progressed, was the movement into Iowa of other Native American peoples, displaced during the process of European expansion westward into North America.

In 1762, French defeat in the Seven Years' War led to the largely theoretical French control of the area becoming the largely theoretical Spanish control of the area. The Spanish period did see some increase in activity by Europeans, including, in 1788, the establishment by Julien Dubuque of the first European settlement. In 1800, the French regained their largely theoretical control of the territory; and then in 1803, they sold their claims to the newly formed United States as part of the Louisiana Purchase.

The year 1804 saw the Lewis and Clark expedition arrive in Iowa. It also saw the United States purchase land off Sauk and Meskwaki representatives, led by Quashquame, in a disputed deal that many on the Native American side rejected as invalid.

In 1808, Fort Bellevue was built; its name would soon change to Fort Madison.

The focus of the War of 1812 was, of course, far to the east, but the war did add to Iowa's history some of the comparatively few incidents that can actually be called battles.

Sauk leader Black Hawk rejected Quashquame's 1804 agreement with the United States and allied himself with the British. His first success was to besiege Fort Madison and force US troops to abandon it. Late in the war, he fought alongside British forces at the Battle of Credit Island, in what is now Davenport.

During the first half of the nineteenth century, Native Americans ceded their lands in Iowa in stages. Some, like the Sauk and Meskwaki, had already been forced to move into Iowa by settler expansion into lands farther east. Now they would move again. A series of deals, ending with the Sioux giving up their Iowa territory in 1851, meant basically the end of Native American peoples controlling territory in Iowa. However, some Meskwaki did return and were allowed to purchase land. The Meskwaki Settlement in Tama County still exists today.

However, the process of settling the land would not come without violence. Black Hawk would, in 1832, again fight US troops, though this time the fighting would be in Illinois and Wisconsin. In 1857, in the Spirit Lake Massacre in northwestern Iowa, Sioux warriors led by Inkpaduta killed men, women, and children.

And there was some tension between settlers. In 1839, the Honey War broke out. OK, the Honey War wasn't exactly a war, but it is a fun name, and it's one of those quirky little stories about the creation of state borders that are always of interest. While Missouri and Iowa were arguing over the location of the border between their two states, an attempt was made to seize honey in lieu of taxes. Hence, the name of the "war." Militias were turned out by both sides before an agreement was reached.

But an infinitely more serious war than the Honey War was coming.

In 1846, Iowa became the twenty-ninth state in the Union. When the American Civil War broke out, it remained in the Union, sending significant numbers of men to fight for the cause of the Union. However, there were some

Confederate sympathizers in the state, particularly in the southern section, and small numbers of Confederate guerrillas and raiders were sometimes active within the state's borders. For instance, on October 12, 1864, twelve Confederate Missouri Partisan Rangers, led by Lieutenant James "Bill" Jackson and disguised in Union uniforms, invaded Iowa and rode as far as Bloomfield on their raid before withdrawing to Missouri.

And on one occasion, a Civil War battle was fought on Iowan soil. Or at least, a battle mainly fought on Missouri soil spilled over the state border. During the Battle of Athens on August 5, 1861, Missouri State Guards managed to shell the depot at Croton. Militiamen from the Keokuk Rifles returned fire.

But Iowa was to suffer one last foreign invasion. During World War II, Iowa proved to be within reach of Japanese balloon bombs, which landed near towns such as Pocahontas, Laurens, and Holstein, but did little damage.

## IOWA
## MILITARY HISTORY SITES

### Fort Des Moines Museum and Education Center
Location: 75 East Army Post Road, Des Moines, IA 50315
Web: www.fortdesmoinesmuseum.org/

### Herbert Hoover Presidential Library & Museum
Location: 210 Parkside Drive, West Branch, IA 52358
Web: www.hoover.archives.gov

### Iowa Aviation Museum
Location: 2251 Airport Road, Greenfield, IA 50849
Web: www.flyingmuseum.com

### Iowa Gold Star Military Museum
Location: 7105 Northwest 70th Avenue, Johnston, IA 50131
Web: www.goldstarmuseum.iowa.gov

**Iowa Great Lakes Maritime Museum**
Location: 243 West Broadway Street, Arnolds Park, IA 51360
Web: www.okobojimuseum.org/

**Soldiers' and Sailors' Monument**
Location: 1305 East Walnut Street, Des Moines, IA 50319
Web: www.iowacivilwarmonuments.com/cgi-bin/gaarddetails.
pl?1210273429~2

**State Historical Museum of Iowa**
Location: 600 East Locust Street, Des Moines, IA 50319
Web: www.iowaculture.gov/history/museum

# America Invaded: IOWA

Nickname: The Hawkeye State
Statehood: 1846
Capital: Des Moines

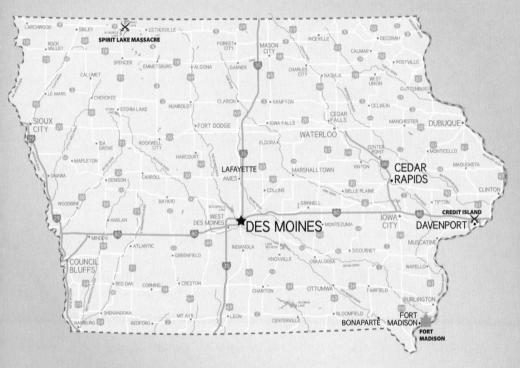

**FORT MADISON**
Founded 1808
Source: akg-images

# KANSAS

B leeding Kansas" has seen its share of fighting and invasions.
A number of Native American tribes have occupied Kansas, including the Kansa, Pawnee, Comanche, and Kiowa.

A Spanish explorer, Francisco Vázquez de Coronado, was the first European to enter Kansas in 1541. He had heard rumors of a wealthy civilization on the plains called the Quivira. Coronado did not find gold, but he did find masses of buffalo (or technically, bison). An estimated 60,000,000 buffalo in pre-Colonial North America made the plains black and provided nearly everything to sustain the indigenous people. As late as 1871, a herd of four million buffalo was spotted tramping through southern Kansas.

Fifteen hundred horses accompanied Coronado's expedition, or "invasion," of Kansas. Some of these found their way into Indian hands, utterly transforming the culture of the Plains Indians. The Comanche quickly became the preeminent cavalrymen of the Plains, including Kansas. Organized around war, they proceeded to terrorize their fellow indigenous people.

In the eighteenth century, a number of European explorers would venture into Kansas. For instance, in 1724, Frenchman Etienne de Bourgmont arrived in search of trading opportunities. In 1792, Pedro Vial set out from Santa Fe to establish a route to St. Louis, Missouri. En route, he passed through Kansas.

In 1806, Facundo Malgares, tasked with resisting American encroachment in areas of interest to Spain, also led an expedition through Kansas.

Most of Kansas was included in the Louisiana Purchase, negotiated between Napoleon and the Jefferson administration in 1803. Settlers would soon begin moving into Kansas, but Americans would not be the first to battle Indians there.

The first recorded battle fought in Kansas seems to have been the Battle of Chouteau's Island in the spring of 1816. Auguste Chouteau, leading a group of French fur traders, was attacked by several hundred Pawnee. This was the first time the Pawnee had encountered firearms. Seven Pawnee and one trader were killed. Chouteau survived the battle and later helped found St. Louis.

In 1827, Fort Leavenworth was constructed. Originally, Kansas was a destination for Native Americans removed from their lands to the east, but eventually in Kansas too the familiar process of increasing land cessions by Native Americans and increasing influxes of settlers would apply.

During the Mexican-American War (1846–48), American forces skirmished with Comanche and Kiowa at the Battles of Love's Defeat and Coon Creek in the Kansas territory.

In 1853, the US Army established Fort Riley in order to protect settlers on the Oregon and Santa Fe Trails.

The Kansas Nebraska Act in 1854 proposed the admission of Kansas as a slave state and Nebraska as a free state. Southerners saw it as a reasonable compromise while abolitionists denounced it as a betrayal. Kansas bordered Missouri, which was a slave state. The Kansas Territory was filled with proponents of both Northern Free Staters and Southern border ruffians, which soon led to violence in Kansas. The Free Staters also became known as Jayhawkers.

The "bleeding" in Kansas began on May 21, 1856, with the Sacking of Lawrence. The town had been founded by abolitionists from New England. Proslavery agitators attacked the town's printing office, killing one.

On May 25–26, 1856, the abolitionist John Brown (later executed after Harper's Ferry, see Virginia) led free-state forces at the Pottawatomie massacre, which killed five proslavery settlers. He was retaliating for the Lawrence incident.

On August 30, 1854, Border Ruffians avenged themselves on John Brown's followers, killing five of the Free Staters at the Battle of Osawatomie.

This period also saw a number of clashes between US forces and Native Americans. For example, in 1859, US cavalry clashed with Comanche warriors at the Battle of Crooked Creek and defeated them.

In January of 1861, Kansas was admitted to the Union as a free state, becoming the thirty-fourth state. Kansas would become much bloodier when the Civil War was ignited in April 1861. Over 20,000 Kansans would serve in the Union forces during the war, about 1,000 with the Confederacy. Two regiments of black soldiers from Kansas would serve in the Union Army.

The bloodiest day ever recorded in Kansas was the Lawrence Massacre, which took place on August 21, 1863. Irregular Confederate forces led by William Quantrill torched the town and began murdering men and even boys. Over 150 were killed that day. Jayhawkers would retaliate by laying waste to much of Missouri.

Quantrill struck again in October 1863 at the Battle of Baxter Springs in southeastern Kansas. This time he engaged Union regulars, killing over a hundred in this bloody raid. Quantrill and his forces retreated to Texas after the engagement. Quantrill, aged twenty-seven, was killed in a Union ambush in Kentucky in 1865.

In October 1864, the battles of Marais des Cygnes and Mine Creek, followed by the Battle of Marmiton River, marked the end of the unsuccessful Confederate cavalry raid known as Price's Raid. The Confederate commander was Major General Sterling Price. The Battle of Mine Creek was one of the biggest cavalry battles of the war.

After the war ended, General Sherman was dispatched west to assist in clearing a path for the railroads. By 1866, the Kansas Pacific had reached Manhattan, Kansas. That same year, the Civil War veteran George Armstrong Custer arrived at Fort Riley to assume command of the 7th Cavalry. In 1867, Custer left his wife Libbie behind at Fort Riley to set out on the Kansas campaign against the Sioux and Cheyenne. Lieutenant Kidder led a small party of twelve men who failed to rendezvous with Custer, and they were overwhelmed at Beaver Creek. All of Kidder's men were killed; some were tortured before they died. Custer, catching a rumor of cholera at Fort Riley, abandoned his command during this campaign to return to his wife. Custer was court-martialed and found guilty on five of eleven counts.

More skirmishes between Americans and Indians were fought in Kansas. The Battle of Saline River, for example, was fought between Cheyenne and African-American Buffalo Soldiers in Kansas in August 1867.

On September 11, 1874, Cheyenne near Fort Wallace in western Kansas massacred most of the John German family. Four young girls were taken prisoner.

The last battle fought in Kansas between Indians and Americans was the Battle of Punished Woman Fork, fought on September 27, 1878. There was one fatality.

In 1890, Dwight David Eisenhower was born in Denison, Texas. He grew up, however, in a very religious, antiwar family on the wrong side of the tracks in Abilene, Kansas. This West Point graduate would lead the greatest American (and Allied) invasion of all time as commander of Operation Overlord—the D-Day landings of June 6, 1944. He is buried at his presidential library in Abilene.

On February 23, 1945, a Japanese Fu-Go balloon bomb was recovered in Bigelow. It did no damage and was the only device known to have landed in the state in World War II.

Fort Riley remains today the home of the "Big Red One"—the 1st Infantry Division. The US Cavalry Museum can be found in a building that once served as Custer's headquarters.

## KANSAS
## MILITARY HISTORY SITES

**Combat Air Museum**
Location: Topeka Regional Airport/Forbes Field, 7016 SE Forbes Avenue, Topeka, KS 66619
Web: www.combatairmuseum.org

**Dwight D. Eisenhower Presidential Library, Museum and Boyhood Home**
Location: 200 Southeast Fourth Street, Abilene, KS 67410
Web: eisenhower.archives.gov/index.html

**Fort Hays State Historic Site**
Location: 1472 US Highway 183 Alternate, Hays, KS 67601
Web: www.kshs.org/fort_hays

# America Invaded: KANSAS

Nickname: The Sunflower State
Statehood: 1861
Capital: Topeka

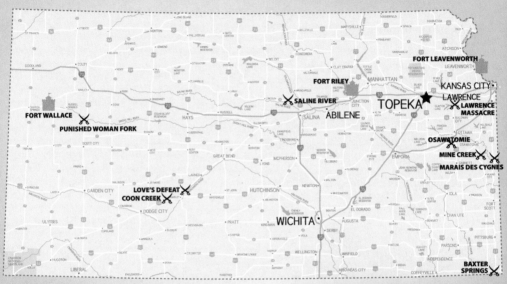

**DWIGHT DAVID EISENHOWER**
1890-1969
Statue, Grosvenor Square, London
Source: Author photo

**AMERICAN BISON**
Source: iStock/CarbonBrain

**Fort Larned National Historic Site**
Location: 1767 Kansas Highway 156, Larned, KS 67550
Web: www.nps.gov/fols/index.htm

**Fort Riley**
Location: 885 Henry Drive, Henry Gate, Fort Riley, KS 66449
Web: www.riley.army.mil

**Frontier Army Museum**
Location: 100 Reynolds Avenue, Fort Leavenworth, KS 66027
Web: usacac.army.mil/organizations/cace/csi/frontier-museum

**Holley Museum of Military History**
Location: Ramada Topeka, 420 SE 6th Avenue, Topeka, KS 66607
Web: www.topekaramada.com/hmmh/

**Kansas Museum of Military History**
Location: 135 Walnut Street, Augusta, KS 67010
Web: www.kansastravel.org/kansasmilitarymuseum.htm

**Mine Creek Civil War Battlefield**
Location: 20485 Kansas 52 Scenic, Pleasanton, KS 66075
Web: www.kshs.org/p/mine-creek-civil-war-battlefield/19567

**United States Cavalry Museum**
Location: 205 Henry Avenue, Fort Riley, KS 66442
Web: www.fortrileyhistoricalsociety.org/us-cavalry-museum.html

# KENTUCKY

Kentucky is perhaps better known for horse racing and bourbon, but it has seen its share of invasions and fighting over the years.

The first humans in Kentucky arrived many thousands of years ago. The Mississippian culture built mounds at numerous Kentucky locations, including Wickliffe Mounds.

Kentucky's rugged Appalachian Mountains and the absence of a coastline made it more difficult for Europeans to reach initially. The Shawnee and Cherokee were significant tribal units in the area, which was known to them as Kantucqui.

Robert de La Salle, the French explorer, seems to have been the first European to visit Kentucky. His expeditions in 1669 and 1670 passed through Kentucky territory, claiming the area on behalf of Louis XIV. The Joliet-Marquette expedition seems to have voyaged through Kentucky in 1673.

Other explorers would follow. For instance, in 1693, the governor of New York sent Arnout Viele, a Dutchman, to explore the Kentucky frontier and engage with the Indian tribes.

In the eighteenth century, pioneers from Virginia, such as John Howard (1742), and other American colonies began arriving on the western frontier.

The first European woman to have seen Kentucky seems to have been Mary Draper Ingles, who was taken hostage by Shawnee warriors after the Draper's Meadow Massacre in Virginia in 1755. She later managed to escape and return to Virginia, where she lived until her death in 1815.

George Croghan, a Dubliner and a fur trader, was among the first Europeans to explore Kentucky. Croghan negotiated many treaties with the Indians and fought in the Seven Years' War.

In 1774, Harrod's Town was founded as the first permanent colonial settlement in Kentucky.

Daniel Boone, a founding hero of Kentucky, was born in 1734 in Pennsylvania. Boone first explored Kentucky in 1769, and he founded Boonesborough in 1775. The frontiersman was captured by Shawnee, but managed to escape. Boone served in the Kentucky militia during the American Revolution, leading the Patriot forces at the Siege of Boonesborough in September of 1778. Squire Boone Jr., Daniel's brother, was wounded in the shoulder during the siege. The British-supported Shawnees assaulted Boonesborough on September 17, but were repelled after suffering heavy losses (thirty-seven were killed during the siege). Boone would later move to Missouri, where he died in 1820.

British Captain Henry Bird led an invading force into Kentucky that was composed of about a thousand Native American warriors and around 150 English regulars and Loyalist militia, in June of 1780. Bird's force captured around three hundred American settlers at engagements such as Ruddle's station before withdrawing back over the Ohio River.

On September 13, 1781, the Long Run Massacre occurred near what is today Floyd's Fork. Shawnee warriors killed around fifteen settlers.

Even after the surrender of Lord Cornwallis at Yorktown in October 1781, resistance to the Patriot cause continued in Kentucky. On August 19, 1782, the Shawnees managed to ambush a Patriot force at the Battle of Blue Licks. Daniel Boone had tried to sound a warning, but was disregarded. Seventy-two Kentucky militiamen were killed in one of the final British victories in the American Revolution.

Kentucky became the fifteenth state to join the Union in 1792.

During the War of 1812, Kentucky militia served with distinction in the Creek War (see Alabama) and under Andrew Jackson at the Battle of New Orleans (see Louisiana). A Kentucky rifleman killed British Major Whitaker from nearly three hundred yards at the Battle of New Orleans in January 1815.

In 1818, the Jackson Purchase saw the Chickasaw cede their rights to a large area of land in southwestern Kentucky.

In 1836, many sharpshooting Kentuckians would fight and die at the

Alamo in the Texas Revolution. James L. Allen of Kentucky fought at the Alamo, but lived. He was the last courier to flee the Alamo on March 5, 1836—one day prior to Santa Anna's final assault.

In 1808, Jefferson Davis, the future president of the Confederate States, was born in Fairview, Kentucky. In 1809, Abraham Lincoln was born in Hodgenville, Kentucky.

Bloody Monday occurred in 1855, as supporters of the anti-immigrant Know-Nothing Party attacked immigrant neighborhoods.

Kentucky was a border state in the US Civil War, with many sympathizers for both the North and South. Initially, Kentucky declared its neutrality in the coming war. Though it was a slave state, it did not secede from the Union. Ultimately, though, Kentuckians fought on both sides. The First Kentucky, or Orphan, Brigade fought on the Confederate side at the Battle of Shiloh (see Tennessee) and elsewhere. The Union's 10th Regiment Kentucky Volunteer Cavalry, on the other hand, skirmished near Florence, Kentucky, and helped defend Cincinnati from rebel raiders.

Confederate Major General Leonidas Polk violated Kentucky's neutrality by ordering the occupation of Columbus in September 1861. Ulysses S. Grant responded by launching a Union invasion of Kentucky, seizing Paducah in one of his first actions of the war. In his memoirs he wrote, "I never after saw such consternation depicted on the faces of the people. Men, women and children came out of their doors looking pale and frightened at the presence of the invader. They were expecting rebel troops that day."

The first major Union victory of the war was fought and won in Kentucky at the Battle of Mill Springs on January 19, 1862.

In the summer of 1862, Confederate General Braxton Bragg launched a full-scale invasion of Kentucky. Don Carlos Buell, a cautious Ohioan, led the Army of Ohio against Bragg's Army of Mississippi. They met for the decisive battle of the Kentucky campaign on October 8, 1862, at Perryville in Boyle County. Bragg inflicted more casualties (about 4,200 versus around 3,400), but he withdrew from the field and the state. Buell, slow to pursue, would be relieved of his command after scoring his victory. The Union controlled Kentucky for the war's duration, but further clashes would follow. Morgan's thousand-mile raid passed through Kentucky on its way from Tennessee to Ohio in the summer of 1863. In September 1863, the Battle of Cumberland Gap was a bloodless victory for Union forces. And a number of other

Confederate raids targeted Kentucky in 1864.

Fortifications were constructed near the present site of Fort Knox beginning in 1861, during the Civil War. Fort Knox continues to be an active duty Army base and the United States Bullion Depository, storing much of America's gold reserve. Auric Goldfinger and Pussy Galore would attempt to launch a fictional invasion of Fort Knox in the 1964 James Bond film *Goldfinger*.

In 1917, Camp Taylor was opened as a training facility in Kentucky during World War I. Over 80,000 Kentuckians would serve in the military during the Great War.

Admiral Husband Kimmel of Kentucky was commander in chief of the US Navy in the Pacific at Pearl Harbor on December 7, 1941. Over 300,000 Kentuckians served in the Second World War, and more than 100,000 jeeps were built at the Ford plant in Louisville.

Axis forces did not, of course, invade Kentucky during World War II, but thousands of Axis prisoners were held as POWs in the state at Fort Knox, Fort Campbell, and other locations. In February of 1945, a German paratrooper escaped from Fort Knox and made it all the way to Nashville via bus before turning himself in to authorities.

Fort Campbell, built in 1941, is the home of the 101st Airborne Division, known as the Screaming Eagles.

## KENTUCKY
## MILITARY HISTORY SITES

### Abraham Lincoln Birthplace National Historical Park
Location: 2995 Lincoln Farm Road, Hodgenville, KY 42748
Web: www.nps.gov/abli/index.htm

### Camp Wildcat Battlefield
Location: Old Wilderness Road, Daniel Boone National Forest, London, KY 40391
Web: www.fs.usda.gov/detail/dbnf/learning/history-culture/?cid=fsb-dev3_032547

**Cumberland Gap National Historic Park**
Location: 91 Bartlett Park Road, Middlesboro, KY 40965
Web: www.nps.gov/cuga/index.htm

**Daniel Boone's Grave**
Location: Frankfort Cemetery, 215 East Main Street, Frankfort, KY 40601
Web: www.kentuckytourism.com/daniel-boones-grave-frankfort-cemetery/1498/

**Fort Boonesborough State Park**
Location: 4375 Boonesborough Road, Richmond, KY 40475
Web: www.fortboonesboroughlivinghistory.org

**General George Patton Museum**
Location: Fort Knox, 4554 Fayette Avenue, Fort Knox, KY 40121
Web: www.generalpatton.org

**Kentucky Military History Museum**
Location: 125 East Main Street, Frankfort, KY 40601
Web: history.ky.gov/visit/kentucky-military-history-museum/

**The Lincoln Museum**
Location: 66 Lincoln Square, Hodgenville, KY 42748
Web: www.lincolnmuseum-ky.org

**Mill Springs Battlefield & Museum**
Location: 9020 West Highway 80, Nancy, KY 42544
Web: www.millsprings.net

**Perryville Battlefield State Historic Site**
Location: 1825 Battlefield Road, Perryville, KY 40468
Web: www.perryvillebattlefield.org

FORT KNOX
RADCLIFF
HENDERSON
OWENSBORO
ELIZABETHTOW
WAVERLY
FORDSVILLE
OHIO RIVER
STURGIS
CALHOUN
ROUGH
RIVER
LAKE
LEITCHFIELD
NOLIN
LAKE
PROVIDENCE
BEAVER
DAM
GREEN RIVER
MARION
MADISONVILLE
BROWNSVILLE
GREENVILLE
MORGANTOWN
OHIO RIVER
CROFTON
BOWLING
GREEN
PADUCAH
BENTON
HOPKINSVILLE
RUSSELVILLE
MAYFIELD
FAIRVIEW
FRANKLIN
SCOTSVILLE
KENTUCKY
LAKE
LAKE
BARKLEY
MURRAY
OAK GROVE
FORT CAMPBELL

**DANIEL BOONE**
1734-1820
Source: iStock/
traveler1116

Nickname: The Bluegrass State
Statehood: 1792
Capital: Frankfort

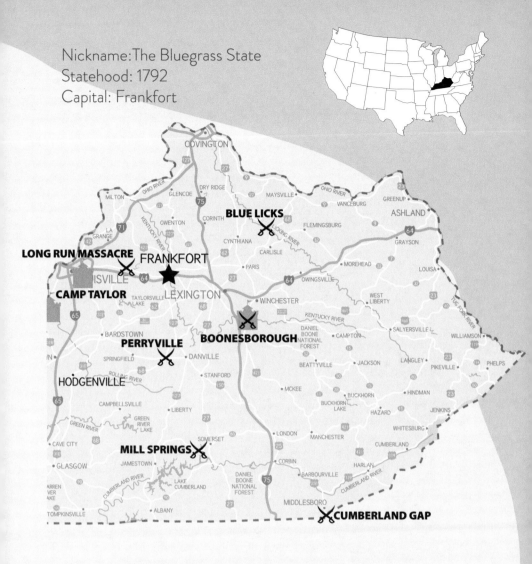

**TANKS AT FORT KNOX**
Site first fortified in 1861. Source: akg-images/IAM

# LOUISIANA

Today New Orleans is invaded on a daily basis by an army of tourists and conventioneers that cruise along Bourbon Street hoping to *Laissez les bons temps roulez* (Let the good times roll). But nomads first came to the area known as Louisiana thousands of years ago. Humans living near Poverty Point built mounds two thousand years before the birth of Christ. Many tribes, such as the Natchez and the Choctaw, inhabited the Gulf Coast region when the Spanish explorers first began arriving in the sixteenth century.

In 1519, the Spanish explorer and cartographer Álvarez de Pineda seems to have arrived at the mouth of the Mississippi River. He encountered a substantial Native American population. Other Spanish explorers were to follow, including, in 1528, Pánfilo de Narváez. Hernando de Soto, the Spanish conquistador, explored the Mississippi River in 1541 and died, possibly in Louisiana, in 1542.

Spanish colonial interest, however, soon focused elsewhere, and it was the French who initially became the dominant colonial power in the area. In 1682, Robert de La Salle named a large area of America, including the present-day state, *Louisiana*, in honor of Louis XIV—the Sun King. In 1718, Jean-Baptiste Le Moyne, Sieur de Bienville, a French Canadian, founded Nouvelle Orleans.

However, after the French defeat in North America in the Seven Years' War, Louisiana became a part of New Spain until 1800. This vast territory stretched north from New Orleans up the Mississippi into the Midwest.

Not everybody was happy about the new management. In 1768, the Louisiana Rebellion erupted around New Orleans. The new Spanish governor of Louisiana, Antonio de Ulloa, was forced to return to Spain, but the rebellion was, in the end, crushed. Alejandro O'Reilly, a Spanish Marshal who had been born in Dublin, became governor of Louisiana, earning the nickname Bloody O'Reilly for his execution of a number of Creole citizens. Canary Islanders were recruited to populate the new colony.

The Third Treaty of San Ildefonso signed in 1800 assigned Louisiana from Spain back to Napoleonic France. The Napoleonic Code was imposed on Louisiana's legal system, where it had an enduring impact. Napoleon attempted to reinforce his hold on Louisiana by dispatching General Charles Leclerc, his brother-in-law, with an army of 40,000 men to the New World. Their mission was to crush the Haitian rebellion and then to proceed to and reinforce New Orleans. Toussaint L'Ouverture, the great Haitian leader of history's most successful slave rebellion, had other plans. Leclerc and many of his men were killed by Yellow Fever and never made it to Louisiana.

In 1803, Napoleon, unable to defend his New World holdings and strapped for cash, sold the Louisiana Territory to the United States for the sum of $15 million. By the stroke of a pen, Thomas Jefferson had doubled the size of the United States.

Louisiana saw a number of slave rebellions over the decades; and in 1811, it experienced the German Coast Rebellion. Charles Deslondes led a force of rebels that managed to seize some guns and ammunition, and then marched on New Orleans, intending to capture it. After serious fighting, US soldiers and militiamen managed to halt the rebels about twenty miles from New Orleans. Many of the rebels who surrendered were executed.

The most consequential invasion of Louisiana was surely launched by the British in 1814 during the War of 1812.

In the summer of 1812, James Madison induced Congress to declare war on Britain. The war did not go well at first, with Britain repulsing a series of invasions into Canada, as well as burning the White House and Capitol Building in 1814. New England, never happy about Mr. Madison's War, threatened to secede from the Union at the Hartford Convention.

It was at this point that Britain dispatched a fleet and army to invade Louisiana.

Since Nelson's decisive victory at the Battle of Trafalgar in 1805, Britain was indisputably the greatest naval power in the world. This meant that Britain could effectively land troops on any coastline across the globe. A British army led by the Duke of Wellington had, by 1814, driven Napoleon's forces from Portugal and Spain. British infantry were widely thought to be the finest in the world.

So, in 1814, Britain chose to invade Louisiana. Their fleet was led by the able Lord Cochrane, who had distinguished himself in numerous sea battles. Cochrane expected to earn massive prize money for seizing the "beauty and booty" that the rich commercial entrepôt of New Orleans offered. The land forces would be led by Sir Edward Pakenham, the Duke of Wellington's brother-in-law. The duke's appraisal of his brother-in-law was that "Pakenham may not be the brightest genius, but my partiality for him does not lead me astray when I tell you he is one of the best we have."

Pakenham ultimately had at his disposal an army of over 10,000 soldiers, supplemented by 1,500 Royal Marines. The British outnumbered the ragtag bunch of Americans that were hoping to defend New Orleans. Most of the American defenders were not regular soldiers, but rather a mix of state militia and other groups. There were more Tennessee volunteers than any other state. A group of 2,368 sharpshooting Kentuckian riflemen arrived on January 3, 1815, just five days before the Battle of New Orleans. These militia were augmented by forces from Louisiana: Baratarian privateers led by Jean Laffite, free black soldiers, and even Choctaw Indians. The British never foresaw that General Andrew Jackson would manage to weld this diverse group into a devastatingly effective fighting force.

Jackson was a veteran of the American Revolution, and by 1814, he had also led many successful campaigns against Native American tribes. As a young man, he had served with British forces, acquiring a powerful Anglophobia. After not polishing a British officer's boots correctly, he was slashed at with a sword, which left a scar on his face and on his soul. At New Orleans, he would take his long-awaited revenge.

The British invasion force landed at Lake Borgne on December 14, 1814. By Christmas Eve, it had proceeded to within seven miles of New Orleans, to the Villere's Plantation. When Jackson learned of the British approach, he immediately ordered a daring nighttime counterattack. He was forced to withdraw, but British casualties exceeded those of the Americans.

The American schooner *Carolina* attacked the British troops with grapeshot until it was finally set on fire by heated "red hot shot." On December 16, Jackson declared martial law in Louisiana, placing himself in total control of the population.

Jackson established a defensive line that ran about eight hundred yards along the Rodrigez Canal, from the Mississippi River to a swamp. Along the Jackson line, strong breastworks were established. Some of the thirteen American cannon along the line were manned by Baratarian privateers led by Laffite and his brother. The night before the Battle of New Orleans, Jackson shared a cup of coffee with Laffite's comrade Dominique You, joking that their supply of coffee was so good that it must have been smuggled.[4]

On January 8, 1815, the British launched a frontal assault against the Jackson line. The Chalmette Plantation, offering no cover, became a deadly killing ground. Three British generals were killed that day, including Pakenham. The battle was a one-sided American victory with thirteen Americans killed against hundreds of British dead and almost 1,300 wounded. A truce was arranged for burial of the dead, and soon after, the British withdrew to their waiting ships.

The Battle of New Orleans was fought after the Treaty of Ghent was signed in Belgium on December 24, 1814, ending the War of 1812. Some have argued that it was, therefore, a "pointless" battle. The treaty, however, would not be ratified by the US Senate until February. Had the British succeeded in capturing New Orleans, it is not clear they would have surrendered it, despite the provisions of the treaty. The Americans' unexpected victory at the Battle of New Orleans led to a surge of national pride throughout the country, and the January 8 victory was celebrated throughout America for half a century. Moreover, the battle launched the political career of Andrew Jackson, which eventually catapulted him into the White House.

Louisianans plotted in the 1820s to bring one of history's greatest invaders to their shores. A conspiracy was formed to rescue the exiled Napoleon from his British captors on the rocky island of St. Helena in the South Atlantic. Ships were obtained, crews were formed. A house was built to suit the emperor for his sojourn in the New World. From this house, future Napoleonic invasions directed against the possessions of the dying Spanish Empire in Central

---

4　　　Jackson said, "That smells like better coffee than we can get. Where did you get such fine coffee? Maybe you smuggled it in?" Winston Groom, *Patriotic Fire: Andrew Jackson and Jean Laffite at the Battle of New Orleans* (New York: Vintage Books, 2007), 187.

and South America might be hatched. Today, the Napoleon House in New Orleans remains a watering hole for thirsty tourists, who can savor its grilled alligator po-boys while enjoying its historic atmosphere. Napoleon himself foiled the conspiracy by dying, most likely of stomach cancer, in 1821, prior to the execution of the plot.

Louisiana joined the Confederacy in 1861, shortly after the secession of South Carolina in December 1860. Louisiana was a slave state, but she was also the most diverse Southern state, with a substantial population of free blacks. In May of 1861, a regiment of Free Men of Color began forming among these men in support of the Confederate cause. Italian Americans from New Orleans also raised a Garibaldi Legion that served in Confederate gray.

The state would see a number of campaigns, battles, and clashes during the war as both sides sought to control key areas and key communications routes.

Recognizing that New Orleans was the largest city in the South and its most important port, General Winfield Scott of the Union Army proposed the Anaconda Plan, which would strangle the rebellious Southern states by seizing New Orleans and denying access to the Mississippi. Not all of this plan was adopted, but a blockade of the South became a keystone of Union strategy in the war. In April of 1862, David Farragut of the US Navy led a squadron of seventeen ships that would invade New Orleans with far more success than Lord Cochrane's efforts during the War of 1812. The Confederates had two forts—Jackson and St. Philip—defending the approach to the city. They also stretched a chain across the water in order to block the entrance to the Mississippi River. By April 19, the Union Navy broke through the Confederate barriers and began battering the Confederate forts with guns and mortars. Lacking a leader approaching the calibre of Old Hickory, the Confederates surrendered Fort Jackson on April 28. Major General Butler led approximately 15,000 Union troops that occupied the city on May 1, 1862. His harsh treatment of the Louisianans earned him the nickname Beast Butler, but the Confederacy would never regain New Orleans.

On May 29, Farragut landed forces that would capture the Louisiana state capital at Baton Rouge. On August 5, Union forces would win the Battle of Baton Rouge and maintain their control of the city. Eighty-four men were killed on each side that day.

October of the same year saw a Union victory at the Battle of Georgia Landing, as Union forces targeted Confederate forces in the Laforche area.

Both sides recognized that control of the Mississippi was key. April 1863 saw a series of clashes as Confederate forces tried to resist the advance of Union soldiers under Nathaniel Banks, who were advancing toward Alexandra and Port Hudson. The Union advance ended in a lengthy siege before Port Hudson finally surrendered.

Meanwhile, General Grant's operations against Vicksburg also resulted in a number of clashes in Louisiana as Confederate forces attempted to disrupt Grant's campaign. These included the Battle of Miliken's Bend and the Battle of Goodrich's Landing, both in June 1863.

That summer, Confederate forces were also repulsed at the Battle of La Fourche Crossing and at the second Battle of Donaldsville.

And in 1864 came the Red River Campaign, a Union operation along the Red River aimed at capturing Shreveport and destroying the Confederate army of Richard Taylor. On April 8, Union forces suffered a serious defeat at the Battle of Mansfield. And the Battle of Pleasant Hill on April 9, while in some sense a Union victory, was also followed by a Union retreat. In the end, the Red River Campaign was a serious failure for Union forces, but it did not change the ultimate outcome of the war.

After the Civil War ended, Louisiana would be subject to Reconstruction, imposed by the Union victory. It was a period that saw some significant violence in the state.

In the summer of 1940, around 400,000 troops participated in the Louisiana Maneuvers training exercises. Participants included Eisenhower, Patton, and Omar Bradley. More maneuvers took place in Louisiana in 1941.

During World War II, Louisiana played its part in American invasions of other countries through the production of landing craft and … Tabasco sauce. Thousands of wooden Higgins boats played a crucial role in the D-Day invasion of Normandy, and many other American invasions, and they were manufactured in New Orleans. Eisenhower even described Andrew Higgins as "the man who won the war for us." Walter Stauffer McIlhenny, known as Tabasco Jack, served as a brigadier general in the US Marine Corps at Guadalcanal. This native of Avery Island became the CEO of the Tabasco company after the war, and introduced the zesty sauce to the K-rations of generations of marines.

World War II saw extensive operations by U-boats in the Gulf of Mexico. For instance, on July 30, 1942, a German submarine, *U-166*, that had earlier sunk four merchant ships in the Gulf, was herself sunk by a US Navy Patrol boat off the coast of Houma, Louisiana. The sub's wreck was discovered in 2001.

## LOUISIANA
## MILITARY HISTORY SITES

**Chalmette Battlefield and Chalmette National Cemetery**
Location: Jean Lafitte National Historical Park and Reserve, 8606 West St. Bernard Highway, Chalmette, LA 70043
Web: www.nps.gov/jela/chalmette-battlefield.htm

**Chennault Aviation and Military Museum**
Location: 701 Kansas Lane, Monroe, LA 71203
Web: www.chennaultmuseum.org

**Jackson Square**
Location: Bound by Chartres Street & St. Ann Street, Decatur Street & St. Peter Street, New Orleans, LA 70116
Web: www.nola.gov/parks-and-parkways/parks-squares/jackson-square/

**Louisiana Maneuvers and  Military Museum (Camp Beauregard)**
Location: 623 G Street, Pineville, LA 71360
Web: www.geauxguardmuseums.com/about-the-museums

**Confederate Memorial Hall Museum**
Location: 929 Camp Street, New Orleans, LA 70130
Web: www.confederatemuseum.com

**Napoleon House**
Location: 500 Chartres Street, New Orleans, LA 70130
Web: www.napoleonhouse.com

**ANDREW JACKSON**
1767-1845
Statue, Jackson Square, New Orleans
Source: Author photo

**CANNON, JACKSON LINE**
Chalmette Battlefield
New Orleans
Source: Author photo

**NAPOLEON HOUSE**
New Orleans
Source: Author Photo

Nickname: Bayou State
Statehood: 1812
Capital: Baton Rouge

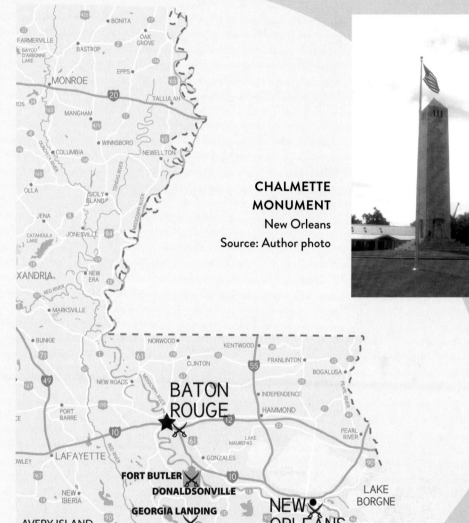

**CHALMETTE
MONUMENT**
New Orleans
Source: Author photo

FARMERVILLE
BAYOU
D'ARBONNE
LAKE
BASTROP
BONITA
OAK
GROVE
EPPS
MONROE
TALLULAH
MANGHAM
WINNSBORO
NEWELLTON
COLUMBIA
OUACHITA RIVER
OLLA
JENA
SICILY
ISLAND
JONESVILLE
CATAHOULA
LAKE
TENSAS RIVER
MISSISSIPPI RIVER
XANDRIA
NEW
ERA
RED RIVER
MARKSVILLE
BUNKIE
NORWOOD
KENTWOOD
CLINTON
FRANLINTON
BOGALUSA
NEW ROADS
**BATON
ROUGE**
INDEPENDENCE
HAMMOND
PEARL RIVER
PORT
BARRE
LAFAYETTE
RED RIVER
LAKE
MAUREPAS
PEARL
RIVER
GONZALES
**FORT BUTLER**
**DONALDSONVILLE**
**GEORGIA LANDING**
NEW
IBERIA
AVERY ISLAND
BALDWIN
THIBODAUX
**LA FOURCHE CROSSING**
MORGAN
CITY
HOUMA
CHAUVIN
**NEW
ORLEANS**
LAKE
BORGNE
CHANDELEUR
SOUND
**FORT
ST. PHILIP**
**FORT
JACKSON**
VENICE

**National WWII Museum—New Orleans**
Location: 945 Magazine Street, New Orleans, LA 70130
Web: www.nationalww2museum.org

**Poverty Point National Monument**
Location: 6859 Louisiana Highway 577, Pioneer, LA 71266
Web: www.nps.gov/popo/index.htm

**Tabasco Museum & Visitors Center and Pepper Sauce Factory**
Location: Highway 329 Avery Island Road, Avery Island, LA 70513
Web: www.tabasco.com/avery-island/visitor-information/

**USS *Kidd* Veterans Museum**
Location: 305 South River Road, Baton Rouge, LA 70802
Web: www.usskidd.com

# MAINE

Maine may have been the place in what is now the United States where Europeans first encountered Native Americans. That is, if Vikings from Newfoundland sailed that far south, hugging the Atlantic coastline. Certainly by the late fifteenth century, and increasingly through the sixteenth century, Europeans became more familiar with the area; and in the early seventeenth century, they started attempting permanent settlements. They were drawn to the area by the rich fishing, with the added benefit of the state's famous and plentiful lobsters.

They encountered a territory occupied mainly by Abenaki, with Mi'kmaq in the east.

In 1604, the French briefly established a settlement on Saint Croix Island before giving up and moving elsewhere. In 1607, the English briefly established a settlement, the Popham Colony, at what is now Phippsburg, before giving up and going home. It wasn't a great start for either the French or the English, but it was an indication of what was to come. French and English fought for control of the area, and the Native Americans suffered from the conflicts and the diseases brought from Europe.

In 1613, the French tried again, this time establishing a permanent settlement at Pentagouet, at what is now Castine. Assorted English efforts to the south gradually led to a permanent English presence as well, linked to Massachusetts. Competition between the Europeans for control of the area and its natural resources began early. In 1613, two French Jesuit missionaries attempted to establish a colony on Mount Desert Island, but it was wiped out by Samuel Argall from Jamestown just a few weeks later. In 1625, New Englanders took Pentagouet, only for it to be returned to French control in 1635. The Dutch briefly interrupted the Anglo-French competition for control by seizing the area around Castine in 1674 and declaring it New Holland, but then gave it back to the French in 1678 in a peace deal that ended the war between the two countries.

Meanwhile, from 1675, the English settlers in the area had another war to worry about: King Philip's War. Much of the fighting in this war took place to the south, and it is covered in the relevant chapters for Connecticut, Massachusetts, New Hampshire, and Rhode Island. In Maine, the fighting consisted of Native Americans, with French encouragement, raiding English settlements, and the English attacking with ruthlessness and as much firepower as they could muster. The English denied the Native Americans guns (a ban that was one of the causes of the war), but the French supplied them. English colonists suffered some serious losses in the fighting, including the destruction of Scarborough. English settlers were forced out of a long bit of coastline east of Casco Bay. The war settled little in Maine, but it did set a pattern of fighting and conflict that would, in some senses, continue until 1763.

The next upsurge of fighting came with King William's War of 1688–1697. In April 1688, English forces attacked what is now Castine. In this war, French and Native Americans again teamed up against the English settlers, clearing them out of their settlements east of Falmouth. In August 1689, French and Abenaki fighters destroyed Fort Charles at Pemaquid; and fierce fighting took place at the Back Cove settlements in September 1689, as English rein-forcements drove off a determined Native American attack. In 1690, New England forces launched campaigns deep into French-held territory. French and Abenaki fighters besieged Pemaquid and took Fort William Henry in August 1696, before England and France signed a peace deal in 1697 and the Wabenaki made peace with England that same year.

But the next war came along pretty soon.

Queen Anne's War, 1702–1713, again saw fierce fighting in Maine and elsewhere. In 1703, English settlements along the coast between Wells and Casco Bay suffered terribly when attacked by French troops and fighters from the Wabenaki Confederacy. The New Englanders hit back with raids into French territory. In the end, in the peace deal that finished the war, the

French gave up French Acadia and Newfoundland. That set the scene for even more conflict between New Englanders and Native Americans in the region.

It was not long before another war broke out—Father Rale's War, also known as Dummer's War, 1722–1725. More and more settlers had been moving into territory east of the Kennebec River. Again, Native Americans with French encouragement raided the settlements; and again, the New Englanders attacked with as much force as they could muster. Father Rale himself, a Jesuit priest blamed by the New Englanders for inciting Native Americans against them, was killed in August 1724. Many Abenaki, including women and children, also died at the Abenaki village at Norridgewock. As a result of the war, the Native American presence, particularly in western Maine, was eroded even further.

And, yes, there was more war to come. King George's War lasted from 1744–1748. Again, both sides launched raids against each other with their Native American allies. In June 1745, the New Englanders captured Louisbourg on Cape Breton Island. In retaliation, forces of the Wabenaki Confederacy crossed the Kennebec River and attacked settlements on the other side in a series of raids.

The last war in the region that matched Britain against France was the French and Indian War of 1754–1763. That war, in the end, saw the near total victory of Britain over France in North America, north of the Caribbean.

However, it was not a victory that Britain was going to be able to enjoy in peace for long.

As the American Revolution erupted, Maine quickly became involved. In April 1775, Samuel Thompson and militiamen seized Captain Mowat, commander of HMS *Canceaux*. And in June 1775, HMS *Margaretta* was captured in Machias.

On October 17, in retaliation for acts like these, British ships bombarded Falmouth, seriously damaging much of the town.

Privateers from Maine were soon operating against British shipping, and Maine also became the base for a number of major American military operations. The Penobscot Expedition was a particular disaster for American forces. In 1779, Massachusetts sent a large naval expedition to attack British forces at Fort George on Penobscot Bay. The attacking forces besieged but failed to take Fort George. When a British naval force arrived to relieve the defenders, the American naval force was trapped, and its ships were either captured or destroyed. Before the end of the War of Independence finally came, some areas of eastern Maine had been forced to consider neutrality.

And there was yet more war to come in Maine. Another invasion, in fact. During the War of 1812, Britain started off by sending ships to the seas off Maine to attack US shipping and to at least partially blockade Maine's ports. In September 1813, USS *Enterprise* came across HMS *Boxer* off Pemaquid Point and defeated it. In 1814, however, Britain invaded Maine and occupied half of it. The peace deal that ended the war returned the territory to the United States, but the last British troops did not leave until 1818.

And the end of the War of 1812 did not mean the end of disputes between the United States and Canada.

The failure of the United States to protect Maine effectively during the war gave a huge boost to the idea of Maine separating from Massachusetts and becoming its own independent American state. In 1820, it did so. But the border of the new state was not always exactly clear.

In some places, the precise line of the border between the United States and British/Canadian control was ambiguous. In 1827, an American settler named John Baker, after initially attempting to persuade Maine to annex a chunk of disputed territory, instead raised the American flag over it. The British authorities did not see the funny side of the situation and sentenced him to two months in jail and a $25 fine. The Americans may have gotten the last laugh as the area is now known as Baker Brook, New Brunswick.

Then came the Aroostook War of 1838–39. OK, it wasn't exactly a war, but it could have been. Militiamen and eventually some regular troops were turned out to support competing claims over the border, a few prisoners were briefly taken, and the Battle of Caribou (which involved lumberjacks from both sides) ensued, before a compromise deal was finally reached in the Webster-Ashburton Treaty of 1842.

The fighting in the Civil War would, of course, mainly be elsewhere, but Maine played a valuable role in sending troops and munitions, as it would in subsequent conflicts. For example, Colonel Joshua L. Chamberlain from Maine played a vital role at the Battle of Gettysburg, defending Little Round Top, as did the 20th Maine Volunteer Infantry Regiment. Chamberlain later served as president of Bowdoin College and governor of Maine.

And it is worth including here at least one Civil War action, the Battle of Portland Harbor. In June 1863, the Civil War came to Portland. Well, sort of.

Confederate raiders seized a revenue cutter, the *Caleb Cushing*, and were then pursued out to sea by troops and irate armed townsfolk on commandeered steamers. The Confederates were forced to surrender.

The casus belli of the Spanish American War was the violent explosion and sinking of the battle cruiser *Maine* in Havana Harbor on the night of February 15, 1898. Over 250 American sailors aboard the *Maine* were killed that night. Many of the sleeping sailors ended up entombed beneath the sea line, suffocating to death in a manner that eerily foreshadowed the fate of sailors aboard the USS *Arizona* on December 7, 1941. The subsequent battle cry of the Spanish American War, allegedly coined by William Randolph Hearst, became "Remember the *Maine*, to Hell with Spain!" The cause of the explosion that sank the *Maine* has been investigated at least four times but remains one of history's great unsolved mysteries.

War would once again come close to Maine after 1917. When the United States joined the First World War, suddenly its ships were targets for German U-boats. For instance, in 1918, *U-156* attacked and sank over twenty US fishing vessels in the Gulf of Maine.

Canada had at one stage, between the world wars, its Defence Scheme No. 1, which envisaged, in the event of an America invasion, Canadian troops seizing Maine, among other targets. But that scheme was never implemented.

Maine did, though, play a crucial role during World War II. Casco Bay was conveniently located close to convoy routes and served as a major naval base; and the Portsmouth Naval Shipyard in Kittery became the largest US submarine base on the Atlantic coast. Inevitably, proximity to the convoy routes drew U-boats to the area.

But not all U-boat activity in the waters off Maine consisted of attempts to sink enemy ships. In November 1944, *U-1230* landed two spies, American defector William Colepaugh and German agent Erich Gimpel, on the Maine coast in Operation Magpie (*Unternehmen Elster*). They traveled from there to New York, where Colepaugh, disillusioned with his mission, contacted the FBI, and both were arrested.

At the end of the war with Germany, four U-boats surrendered at the Portsmouth Naval Shipyard.

But while the fighting is over, the competition for control of territory in and around Maine isn't. That's right. Despite all the fighting that has gone on around the area over the centuries, Maine's borders are still not 100 percent agreed on by everybody. Three unpopulated islands situated between Maine and Nova Scotia, the biggest of them being Seal Island, are *still* disputed between Canada and the United States. The islands themselves may not be hugely exciting, but there's valuable fishing around.

## MAINE
## MILITARY HISTORY SITES

### Fort Edgecomb State Historic Site
Location: 66 Fort Road, Edgecomb, ME 04556
Web: www.maine.gov/cgi-bin/online/doc/parksearch/details.pl?park_id=32

### Fort Knox State Historic Site
Location: 740 Fort Knox Road, Fort Knox, ME 04981
Web: fortknox.maineguide.com

### Fort McClary Memorial & State Historic Site
Location: Route 103, Kittery Point, Kittery, ME 03905
Web: www.fortmcclary.org

### Fort Williams Park
Location: 1000 Shore Road, Cape Elizabeth, ME 04107
Web: fortwilliams.org

### Joshua L. Chamberlain Museum
Location: 226 Maine Street, Brunswick, ME 04011
Web: pejepscothistorical.org/chamberlain

### Maine Maritime Museum
Location: 243 Washington Street, Bath, ME 04530
Web: www.mainemaritimemuseum.org

### Maine Military Historical Society Museum
Location: 194 Winthrop Street, Augusta, ME 04330
Web: www.mainemilmuseum.org

# America Invaded: MAINE

Nickname: The Pine Tree State
Statehood: 1820
Capital: Augusta

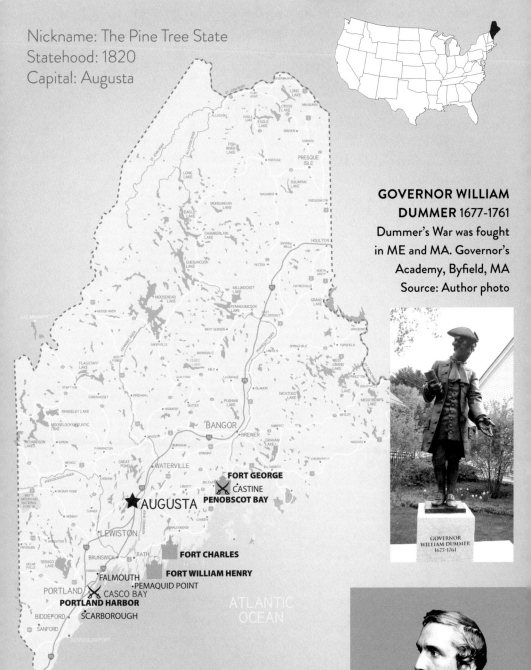

**GOVERNOR WILLIAM DUMMER** 1677-1761
Dummer's War was fought in ME and MA. Governor's Academy, Byfield, MA
Source: Author photo

GOVERNOR
WILLIAM DUMMER
1677-1761

FORT GEORGE
CASTINE
PENOBSCOT BAY

AUGUSTA

LEWISTON

FORT CHARLES
BRUNSWICK    BATH

FORT WILLIAM HENRY
FALMOUTH
PEMAQUID POINT
PORTLAND    CASCO BAY
PORTLAND HARBOR
SCARBOROUGH

BANGOR
BREWER

WATERVILLE

ATLANTIC
OCEAN

**JOSHUA CHAMBERLAIN**
1828-1914
Source: akg-images/John Parrot/Stocktrek Images

**Maine Military Museum and Learning Center**
Location: 50 Peary Terrace, South Portland, ME 04106
Web: www.mainemilitarymuseum.info/

**Old Fort Western**
Location: 16 Cony Street, Augusta, ME 04330
Web: www.oldfortwestern.org

**Penobscot Marine Museum**
Location: 5 Church Street, Searsport, ME 04974
Web: www.penobscotmarinemuseum.org

# MARYLAND

European explorers, including Giovanni da Verrazano, reached the vicinity of present-day Maryland in the sixteenth century. And in 1608, Captain John Smith entered Chesapeake Bay and mapped it. Cecil Calvert, 2nd Baron Baltimore, was granted a charter in 1632 for what would become the Province of Maryland. Calvert was Catholic, and one of the motivations for the founding of the colony was to allow English Catholics freedom of worship without some of the restrictions they faced in England at the time. The colony was named after Henrietta Maria, the French Catholic wife of Charles I of England.

In 1633, English settlers aboard the *Ark* and the *Dove* set off from Cowes, England. On March 25, 1634, the settlers landed at St. Clement's Island. Later, land would be purchased from local natives, and the Fort at St. Mary's City would be built.

The new colonists entered an area largely occupied by various Algonquian-speaking tribes, but to the north were also the Iroquoian-speaking Susquehannock.

The early colony went to war with the Susquehannock. However, a peace deal was reached in 1652.

Much of the early conflict in Maryland was internal. The political and religious disputes that caused the English Civil War across the Atlantic were, to some extent, reflected in Maryland, with the addition of border disputes with Virginia. Figures like Claiborne and Ingle were prominent in a period of clashes and raids known as the Plundering Time, which saw Puritan and Parliamentary privateers at odds with forces loyal to Leonard Calvert. By 1646, Calvert had managed to reassert his control, but in 1647 he died and was succeeded by his son, another Cecil Calvert, Lord Baltimore.

In 1649, Charles I was executed in London, and England became a republic, the Commonwealth. And so in Maryland in the 1650s, further tensions played out between different pro-Commonwealth factions and the Catholic Lord Baltimore. The 1655 Battle of the Severn saw forces loyal to William Stone, who had originally been appointed governor by Cecil Calvert, clash with Puritan forces defending Providence. Stability was only fully restored in Maryland after the restoration of Charles II to the English throne in 1660.

However, later in the seventeenth century, political and religious conflict in England was once again reflected in Maryland. In 1688, the Catholic King James II was toppled in a revolution. In 1689, Maryland underwent an anti-Catholic revolution led by Colonel John Coode, which seized power and installed a Puritan government that banned Catholicism. Coode's government didn't last long, but discrimination against Catholics remained until the American Revolution.

Maryland was not a key area for fighting during much of the long struggle between Britain and France for colonial power in North America. Most of the land action took place farther north. Maryland's shipping did, however, sometimes get caught up in the fighting. For instance, during Queen Anne's War, French privateers had a huge impact on Maryland's merchant fleet.

However, in the 1730s, Maryland was to find an enemy rather close to home. Right next door, in fact. Geographical uncertainties in the early years of settlement led to uncertainty over the exact course of the border between Pennsylvania and Maryland. Eventually, as settlers from both sides moved into the disputed border zone, conflict ensued. It is often known as Cresap's War, because a Marylander called Thomas Cresap played a key role in starting the "war" and keeping it going. The "war" tended to consist of minor marauding, pilfering, and attempts to impose authority on one side or the other; and it only ended after Thomas Cresap was captured by Pennsylvania, and the British Crown stepped in to impose a border. The border in question, when properly surveyed, became, yes, the Mason-Dixon Line.

In 1754, war with France broke out yet again in North America, and this conflict would be decisive. That same year, Fort Cumberland was built.

General Braddock used it as a base in his campaign against Fort Duquesne (in what is now Pittsburgh). This campaign was not a great success. In fact, it wasn't a success at all. Braddock's force, including the young George Washington, was ambushed on July 9, 1755, by French forces and their Native American allies, and was defeated in the Battle of the Monongahela, or Battle of the Wilderness (see Pennsylvania). Braddock himself was killed, and Washington helped rally the troops and ensure some kind of orderly withdrawal. The war saw raids by French and their Native American allies into the area around Fort Cumberland and farther east, toward Frederick and Winchester. In the end, however, the British managed to capture Fort Duquesne in 1758, and France lost the war. By the 1763 treaty that ended the Seven Years' War, France gave up basically all its claims to American territory north of the Caribbean.

But another war was coming fast. In 1765, in one of the first acts of violence in the chain of events that would lead to the American Revolution, the Stamp Tax collector for Maryland, Zachariah Hood, was attacked by a mob and forced to flee to New York. In 1774, in the Annapolis Tea Party, a Maryland cargo ship, the *Peggy Stewart*, was attacked by a mob and burned because its captain had broken the boycott on tea imports. In 1776, Maryland declared independence from Britain.

Maryland would play a key role in the American Revolution, more through the troops and help it supplied than as a site of combat, but Maryland did see some campaign activity. For instance, in August 1777, Sir William Howe landed his Anglo-German army on the Elk River before advancing to Head of Elk (now Ellkton), and then pressing on to defeat Washington at the Battle of Brandywine in Pennsylvania. Howe then took Philadelphia.

From November 26, 1783, to June 3, 1784, Annapolis served as the capital of confederation of the United States of America, and it was there on January 14, 1784, that the Confederation Congress ratified the Treaty of Paris that ended the war.

However, another war with Britain was coming, and this time Maryland would see plenty of action.

In the War of 1812, the British launched raids on targets in Chesapeake Bay, including Havre de Grace. Joshua Barney's Chesapeake Flotilla tried to counter the British Navy's efforts in the area, but in the end had to be scuttled to avoid capture by the British.

In August 1814, the British fleet sailed up the Patuxent River and landed troops at Benedict. At the Battle of Bladensburg on August 24, despite the bravery of Joshua Barney and his now ship-less sailors and marines, the British brushed aside the American defenders before capturing Washington DC and burning the Capitol and other major buildings. President James Madison was forced to flee the victorious British. On August 31, though, a British landing party was ambushed in the Battle of Caulk's Field. And even worse for the British, on September 12, their attempt to take Baltimore was repulsed at the Battle of North Point. The next day saw the British fruitlessly bombard Fort McHenry with cannon and Congreve rockets, an event that inspired Francis Scott Key to write a poem that would eventually become the lyrics for the United States' national anthem, "The Star-Spangled Banner." In October, the British fleet withdrew from Chesapeake Bay; and in December 1814, the peace deal that would end the war was agreed. However, before it could be ratified by the US Senate, Marylanders were to fight one last battle, the Battle of the Ice Mound. On February 7, 1815, Maryland militiamen came across a British raiding party—and the sheep they had captured—in a small boat, stationary in ice and unable to return to the HMS *Dauntless*. After two hours of being shot at, the British crew surrendered.

Several decades later, 1856 saw a sort of mini-war in Baltimore. In the Know-Nothing Riot of that year, street gangs battled each other in the city when Thomas Swan, the candidate of the anti-immigrant American Party, known to many as the Know-Nothing Party, was elected mayor. Shots were fired, people died, and at one stage even artillery was involved.

But a much, much bigger war was about to erupt.

Maryland was a border state, and Marylanders were deeply divided at the start of the Civil War. Its citizens would serve in both the Confederate and Union armies. At the Battle of Front Royal in Virginia in May 1862, Marylanders fought Marylanders.

The first bloodshed of the war took place in April 1861, when troops from Massachusetts were attacked by a mob in Baltimore, prompting the soldiers to open fire. Twelve of the crowd and four soldiers died in the fighting.

In the end, firm use of military force prevented any attempt by the many Confederate sympathizers in Maryland to take the state out of the Union. In May, General Benjamin F. Butler positioned artillery on Federal Hill with orders to bombard Baltimore if necessary, as he occupied the city and declared martial law. In the following months, many influential figures suspected of having Confederate sympathies were arrested.

In September 1862, Confederate General Robert E. Lee struck north into Maryland. After a Union victory at the Battle of South Mountain on September 14, McClellan's Army of the Potomac clashed with Lee's Army of Northern Virginia at the Battle of Antietam on September 17, the bloodiest day ever for American military forces. Over 3,500 Americans were killed that day, and more than 17,000 were wounded. The result was not a conclusive victory for either side, but it meant Lee calling an end to his offensive, and it was a significant step on the path to ultimate Union victory in the war.

October 1862 saw Confederate General J. E. B. Stuart's cavalry raiders ride through Maryland.

And in the summer of 1863, Lee returned to Maryland. This time his forces were headed for Gettysburg. After the battle they were again in Maryland, but now in retreat.

It was not, however, the last time Maryland would see Confederate forces. In July 1864, General Jubal Early held Hagerstown and Frederick for ransom, and his Confederate forces defeated General Lew Wallace at the Battle of Monocacy.

On April 14, 1865, Marylander John Wilkes Booth assassinated President Lincoln at Ford's Theatre in Washington and fled to Maryland to escape detection. Dr. Samuel Mudd ("You're name is Mudd!") set his injured leg near Waldorf. Booth was killed by Union soldiers at Garrett's farm in neighboring Virginia on April 26.

The end of the Civil War marked pretty much the end of combat in Maryland. From then on, Marylanders would fight their battles elsewhere.

However, the twentieth century would see war in the waves off Maryland. U-boats operated in those waters. For instance, on the night of April 2, 1942, *U-552* intercepted the SS *David H. Atwater* between Cape Charles and Cape Henlopen. The submarine surfaced and sank the cargo ship with gunfire.

## MARYLAND
## MILITARY HISTORY SITES

### Antietam National Battlefield
Location: 5831 Dunker Church Road, Sharpsburg, MD 21782
Web: www.nps.gov/anti/index.htm

### Baltimore Civil War Museum
Location: 601 President Street, Baltimore, MD 21202
Web: baltimore.org/listings/historic-sites/baltimore-civil-war-museum-president-street-station

### Fort McHenry National Monument and Historic Shrine
Location: 2400 East Fort Avenue, Baltimore, MD 21230
Web: www.nps.gov/fomc/index.htm

### George Washington's Headquarters
Location: Riverside Park, Greene Street, Cumberland, MD 21502
Web: www.dar.org/national-society/historic-sites-and-properties/old-fort-cumberland-and-george-washington's

### Historic Ships in Baltimore
Location: Pier 1, 301 East Pratt Street, Baltimore, MD 21202
Web: www.historicships.org/index.html

### Monocacy National Battlefield
Location: 5201 Urbana Pike, Frederick, MD 21704
Web: www.nps.gov/mono/index.htm

### South Mountain State Battlefield
Location: 6620 Zittlestown Road, Middletown, MD 21769
Web: dnr2.maryland.gov/publiclands/Pages/western/southmountainbattlefield.aspx

### The Dr. Samuel A. Mudd House Museum
Location: 3725 Doctor Samuel Mudd Road, Waldorf, MD 20601
Web: drmudd.org

# America Invaded: MARYLAND

Nickname: Old Line State
Statehood: 1788
Capital: Annapolis

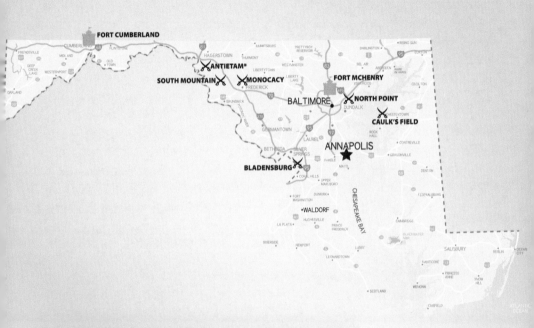

**FORT McHENRY**
Source: iStock/EyeJoy

**The Star-Spangled Banner Flag House**
Location: 844 East Pratt Street, Baltimore, MD 21202
Web: www.flaghouse.org

**United States Naval Academy**
Location: 121 Blake Road, Annapolis, MD 21402
Web: www.usna.edu/homepage.php

# MASSACHUSETTS

Massachusetts is famous for its Minutemen and, of course, for its patriotism.

Long before the arrival of Europeans, the area was home to a number of Algonquian people, including the Massachusett people themselves. It's possible the Vikings may have made it as far south as Cape Cod. Basque fishermen are likely to have cruised the waters off the coast of Massachusetts, searching for cod and stopping for water and supplies. (Later explorers encountered Basque-speaking Native Americans.) Certainly, by the early seventeenth century, assorted Europeans were taking a serious interest in the area.

The distinctively named Englishman Bartholomew Gosnold explored the area in 1602, and is said to have named Cape Cod. Frenchman Samuel de Champlain did a bit of mapping in the area in 1605, and Englishmen John Smith and Henry Hudson weren't far behind.

And not far behind them, of course, the *Mayflower* brought the Pilgrim Fathers in 1620. William Bradford, the founder of Plymouth and subsequent governor of Massachusetts, described the New World as "a hideous and desolate wilderness, full of wild beasts and wild men." The first Thanksgiving seems to have been celebrated between the Pilgrim newcomers and the Wampanoag in 1621, after they had agreed on a mutual defense treaty. Thanksgiving commemorates a period of peace, but this peace would not last.

Soon after 1620, English settlers began to spread inland from the coast, founding the Massachusetts Bay Colony. In 1636, what is now Springfield was founded by a group of settlers under William Pynchon.

The Massachusetts Bay Colony took part in the Pequot War, even though the focus of the fighting was elsewhere. The Pequot were almost wiped out in that war.

However, Massachusetts would not get off so lightly in the next war.

By now, under increasing pressure from the expansion of the settlements, the views of the Wampanoag leadership had changed. A new leader, Metacom, known to the English as Philip, started building alliances with other Native American peoples in the region, including the Nipmucs, the Penacook, and, eventually, after the war had already started, the Narragansett. In July 1675, a group of Wampanoag attacked Swansea, and King Philip's War started. The governments of New England combined to fight the war, but English forces suffered a number of disasters early in the conflict, including the Battle of Bloody Brook. Captain Lathrop and about sixty men died in September of that year, during the process of evacuating Deerfield. English settlements across Massachusetts were attacked, and in October, Springfield suffered a major attack in which many of its building were burned to the ground.

In the end, though, English forces ruthlessly crushed their Native American opponents and, as a result of the war and reprisals, the Wampanoag, Nipmuc, and Narragansett peoples were almost eradicated.

Massachusetts was to be affected by a number of other conflicts in the years to come. What is now the state of Maine, but was then part of Massachusetts, often saw even heavier action, but we deal with that in the Maine chapter.

During King William's War of 1689–1697, New England sent forces north to attack the French and their Native American allies in Acadia; and the French and their Native American allies launched various raids into Massachusetts. In March 1697, French forces with Abenaki allies attacked Haverhill, burning homes, capturing some settlers, and killing others. Among their captives was Hannah Duston, who later became famous for accounts of her time in captivity and for how she eventually escaped, killing in their sleep a number of those holding her prisoner (see New Hampshire). In Queen Anne's War of 1702–1713, once again, forces from New England went north to attack the French and their Native American allies in Acadia; and once again the French and their Native American allies launched raids into Massachusetts.

In 1704, Deerfield was attacked, with many inhabitants killed or captured, and much of the settlement destroyed (though some fortified houses did remain standing). In 1708, another raid was launched on Haverhill. Although the attackers did much damage again, Massachusetts militiamen pursued the retreating raiders, killing some of them and rescuing some of their captives.

In Father Rale's War of 1722–1725, also called Dummer's War, New Englanders again headed north, and again Massachusetts was raided. Abenaki raider Grey Lock launched a succession of raids on places like Northfield and Deerfield. In response, the Province of Massachusetts Bay militia pushed the area of British colonial control farther north by building Fort Dummer in what is now Vermont.

In King George's War of 1744–1748, the governor of the Province of Massachusetts Bay, William Shirley, launched an expedition that captured the mighty French fortress of Louisbourg on Cape Breton Island, Nova Scotia. And, yes, Massachusetts got raided again. For instance, in August 1746, French forces with Native American allies besieged and captured Fort Massachusetts, at what is now North Adams.

In the French and Indian War of 1754–1763, William Shirley, who was once again governor of the Province of Massachusetts Bay, played a significant role in the early stages of the war, strengthening the fortifications of Fort Oswego and building Fort George and Fort Ontario. However, he was eventually forced out of his command due to disagreements with others within the British colonial administration. The end of the war saw the end of French power north of the Caribbean (except for St. Pierre and Miquelon). But very soon Massachusetts would be deeply involved in another conflict.

Crispus Attucks, of African and Wampanoag heritage, is widely acknowledged as the first casualty of the American Revolution when he was killed in the Boston Massacre on March 5, 1770. Nearly 5 percent of Patriot soldiers who served during the American Revolution were of African heritage.[5] While numerous tribes fought for the Loyalist cause, many Native Americans, and notably those of the Stockbridge, Oneida, and Tuscarora tribes, joined the Patriot ranks.

Massachusetts is, of course, famous for being the site of some of the most significant events linked to the American Revolution. There were, for instance,

---

5        4.6 percent of the Continental Army was black according to Michael Stephenson's *Patriot Battles: How the War of Independence Was Fought* (New York: Harper Perennial, 2007), 186.

the Boston Tea Party—during which Americans disguised themselves as Mohawk "invaders" to dump crates of tea into Boston Harbor; the Boston Massacre of 1770; Paul Revere's ride to Lexington to warn of the approach by sea of British troops. It saw the Battles of Lexington and Concord that marked the start of the war, with the famous "shot heard round the world." The Battle of Bunker Hill was a victory for the British, but it was won at a heavy cost; and there was the evacuation of British forces from Boston on March 17, 1776, after Washington installed heavy artillery on Dorchester Heights. In one of the most remarkable feats of the American Revolution, these cannon had been dragged by men and oxen about three hundred and fifty miles from Fort Ticonderoga in New York under the leadership of Henry Knox, a Boston bookseller. Dorchester Heights then and now has a commanding view of Boston Harbor, and the Patriot guns directly threatened ships of the Royal Navy. This was a hugely significant early victory for the revolutionary forces, and Evacuation Day is celebrated every March 17 in Suffolk County. It was not, however, the final action on the soil of Massachusetts. In May 1778, local militia drove off a British raiding party in the Battle of Freetown. Later, British raids hit New Bedford and Martha's Vineyard. In 1779, the Penobscot Expedition turned into a major disaster for the naval forces of Massachusetts in Maine, one of the worst naval disasters ever suffered by American forces (see Maine).

The War of Independence was not the last eighteenth-century conflict to hit Massachusetts. In 1786, Shays' Rebellion broke out. Unrest linked to it spread to other states, but its focus was Massachusetts. The rebellion sprang from anger about debt and taxes in the economically difficult period after the end of the Revolutionary War. Armed groups forced some courts to close, and Daniel Shays, who had been a captain in the Continental Army, helped lead a rebel force of about 1,500 men that attempted to seize the arsenal at Springfield in January 1787. The attack was repulsed, and a hastily raised militia under General Benjamin Lincoln scattered the rebel force when they attacked the rebels' camp in early February. The final battle of the rebellion came at Sheffield on February 27, in which a small rebel group was crushed, with many wounded on both sides. The rebellion was over. Some efforts were made by the Massachusetts legislature to help debtors, and Shays' Rebellion and the fears it had inspired among politicians had an impact on subsequent debates about the Constitution.

The War of 1812 was widely unpopular in Massachusetts, as it was elsewhere in New England, and even led to talk at one stage of New England seceding. Governor Strong of Massachusetts went so far as to send a representative up to Nova Scotia to explore the possibility of negotiating a separate peace. Massachusetts farmers sold food and cattle to ships of the Royal Navy during the war. Captain William Bainbridge of the US Navy at one stage had to make it clear that if Boston surrendered to British forces without a fight, then he would bombard the city. The local lack of enthusiasm for the war did not, however, mean that Massachusetts entirely escaped the war.

Privateers operated out of Boston and other locations in Massachusetts, and there was marine combat in the area between the two navies. For instance, in June 1813, off Boston, HMS *Shannon* fought USS *Chesapeake*. The American ship was badly damaged by gunfire, and then boarded and captured by the British. After serving with the Royal Navy, the *Chesapeake* was eventually broken up in Britain. Some of its timbers were used to build the Chesapeake Mill at Wickham, which still stands today.

The USS *Constitution*, which won significant battles over the British in the War of 1812, is today docked in the Charlestown Navy Yard.

In 1814, the British Navy blockaded the Massachusetts coast and began attacking towns along it. On January 28, HMS *Nimrod* anchored off Falmouth and demanded that the town surrender its cannon. The demand was refused, and *Nimrod* proceeded to bombard the town. The local militia rallied to oppose an invasion, and eventually the *Nimrod* gave up and sailed off. And the somewhat grandly named Battle of Rock Harbor, fought in December 1814, saw a British landing party clash briefly with local militiamen before departing. Nantucket wasn't so lucky. Starved by the British blockade, it was finally forced to negotiate a deal with British forces and declare itself neutral in return for access to food.

In 1835, conflict broke out in Boston again. The so-called Gentleman's Riot saw an anti-abolition mob attack abolitionist William Lloyd Garrison. It was a taste of things to come.

The Civil War was not fought in Massachusetts, but the state sent plenty of men and munitions to fight it, including the well-known 54th Massachusetts Infantry, the first Union army regiment consisting of African-American soldiers (with white officers.) The 1989 movie *Glory* was based on their exploits.

Colonel Robert Gould Shaw, commemorated on Boston Common, died while leading the 54th into battle in South Carolina.

During the First World War, the US Navy and other Allied ships battled U-boats for supremacy in the cold waters of the Atlantic, but on July 21, 1918, the war came rather closer to Massachusetts. In fact, suddenly Massachusetts was in the firing line. *U-156* surfaced and attacked a tugboat and the barges it was towing. Some of its shells fell on Nauset Beach at Orleans. American planes eventually turned up and tried to bomb the submarine. They missed, but the *U-156* had had enough. It departed hastily after the only direct enemy attack on the US mainland during World War I.

U-boats would again operate off the coast of Massachusetts during World War II, but they would never shell it as *U-156* did.

Massachusetts was ready to defend itself, and help defend the United States, if the Cold War ever turned hot, but fortunately it never did. In the 1966 film *The Russians Are Coming, the Russians Are Coming*, a submarine full of Russian sailors lands on the fictional Gloucester Island in Massachusetts, proving the comedic value of fictional invasions.

On the morning of September 11, 2001, ten terrorists affiliated with Al Qaeda boarded two commercial airliners flying out of Boston's Logan Airport. An American Airlines jet and a United Airlines jet were hijacked and flown into the World Trade Center in New York City in the worst terrorist incident in American history.

On April 15, 2013, the Boston Marathon was targeted by two Chechen-American brothers. Two bombs detonated near the finish line, killing three and injuring many more. After being identified by CCTV cameras, the Tsarnaev brothers killed an MIT policeman and hijacked a vehicle. One terrorist was killed. The other was arrested and remains in prison.

## MASSACHUSETTS
## MILITARY HISTORY SITES

**Boston Common**
Location: 139 Tremont Street, Boston, MA 02111
Web: www.boston.gov/parks/boston-common

**Boston Tea Party Ships & Museum**
Location: 306 Congress Street, Boston, MA 02210
Web: www.bostonteapartyship.com

**Bunker Hill Monument & Museum**
Location: Boston National Historical Park, 43 Monument Square, Charlestown, MA 02129
Web: www.nps.gov/bost/learn/historyculture/bhmuseum.htm

**Freedom Trail**
Location: Boston, MA
Web: www.thefreedomtrail.org

**John F. Kennedy Presidential Library and Museum**
Location: Columbia Point, Boston, MA 02125
Web: www.jfklibrary.org

**Lexington Battle Green**
Location: Bedford Street, Lexington, MA 02173
Web: www.tourlexington.us/attractions#anchor_battlegreen

**Minute Man National Historical Park**
Location: 174 Liberty Street, Concord, MA 01742
Web: www.nps.gov/mima/index.htm

**Old North Church**
Location: Boston National Historic Park, 193 Salem Street, Boston, MA 02113
Web: oldnorth.com

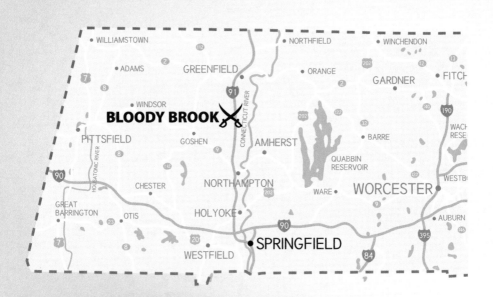

### SITE OF THE BOSTON MASSACRE
March 5, 1770
Boston
Source: Author photo

### MINUTE MAN STATU
Old North Bridge
Minute Man National
Historic Park
Concord
Source: Author photo

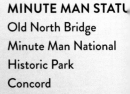

### PAUL REVERE
### & OLD NORTH
### CHURCH
Boston
Source: Author
photo

Nickname: The Bay State
Statehood: 1788
Capital: Boston

ATLANTIC OCEAN

NEWBURYPORT
HAVERHILL
PLUM ISLAND
LAWRENCE
MERRIMACK RIVER
GROTON
IBURG
LOWELL
GLOUCESTER
SALEM
LEXINGTON
CONCORD
MASSACHUSETTS
HUSETT RVOIR
MARLBOROUGH
BUNKER HILL
BOSTON
FORT MASSACHUSETTS
DORCHESTER HEIGHTS
OROUGH
QUINCY
NORWOOD
MARSHFIELD
MILFORD
FOXBOROUGH
BROCKTON
PLYMOUTH
CAPE COD
BRIDGEWATER
ROCK HARBOR
ATTLEBORO
NAUSET BEACH (ORLEANS)
TAUNTON
SWANSEA
ASSAWOMPSET POND
SANDWICH
CHATHAM
NEW BEDFORD
BARNSTABLE
FALMOUTH

DORCHESTER HEIGHTS
March 1776
Boston

MARTHA'S VINEYARD

NANTUCKET

CAPTAIN JOHN PARKER
1729-1775
Lexington Battle Green
Source: Author photos

**Plymouth Rock**
Location: Pilgrim Memorial State Park, 79 Water Street, Plymouth, MA 02360
Web: www.seeplymouth.com/things-to-do/plymouth-rock

**USS *Constitution***
Location: Boston National Historic Park, Charlestown Navy Yard, Boston, MA 02129
Web: www.navy.mil/local/constitution/

# MICHIGAN

Even before Europeans reached what is now Michigan, their arrival farther east had had something of an impact on the Native American people of the area.

When Europeans first entered Michigan, they found a land inhabited by a range of Native American peoples, particularly the peoples that formed part of the Algonquian-language group, like the Ottawa, the Ojibwa, the Potawatomi, and the Miami, but also people from the Iroquoian-language group, like the Wyandot.

When Europeans did arrive in the area, it was the French who played the leading role.

In the early seventeenth century, Étienne Brulé explored some of the region; and soon, other French missionaries, explorers, and traders followed. In 1668, Father Jacques Marquette founded the first permanent European settlement in what is now Michigan at Sault Ste. Marie. And in 1671, Simon François, Sieur de St. Lusson arrived at the Sault and claimed a vast chunk of western America for France. A number of French forts were established; and in 1701, Detroit itself was founded.

But the French were beginning to encounter serious opposition from both local Native American peoples and another European power, Britain.

By the late seventeenth century, parts of Michigan had already been affected by the Iroquois Wars, as the Iroquois sought to establish control over the lucrative fur trade with the Europeans. And in the early eighteenth century, competition for land and trade led to clashes, as the Fox tribe fought the French and their Native American allies. The result was great suffering for the Fox and the Sauk.

And indeed, French power in Michigan did not have long left. The French and Indian War saw the collapse of French power throughout North America. In 1760, the British accepted the surrender of Detroit.

But almost as soon as the British had taken control of the area, they faced major opposition to their rule from Native Americans. Unhappy with the new British rule and the arrival of more settlers from the east, a variety of peoples combined to attack British targets. Prominent among those leading the effort was an Ottawa leader, Pontiac, and the conflict has consequently become known as Pontiac's War. It didn't start well for the British in Michigan. Not well at all.

Fort Detroit managed to avoid being captured by a surprise attack, but it then came under siege. Elsewhere in Michigan, the British faced near disaster. Fort St. Joseph and Fort Michilimackinac would both be captured, and British troops suffered defeat on the battlefield as well. In May 1763, fifty-six out of ninety-six men from a British supply unit were killed at Point Pelee. And in July of that same year, an attempt by British forces from Detroit to attack Pontiac led to defeat and the deaths of twenty British soldiers at the Bloody Run. Settlers were attacked as well.

However, Detroit did not fall, and the Native American forces were defeated elsewhere too. Gradually, the Native American alliance fell apart as separate peace deals were negotiated with the British. The British administration also attempted to deal with one of the main local grievances by restricting the arrival of settlers into the region. Pontiac himself finally made peace with the British in 1766.

But another war was coming. During the American Revolution, the British used Detroit as a base to launch raids against American targets farther south. Detroit also saw the arrival of Daniel Boone as a prisoner, and the construction of Fort Lemoult.

And in one dramatic venture, Spain invaded Michigan. Briefly. In 1780, American forces had attacked Fort St. Joseph, located in what is now Niles. In 1781, it was the turn of the Spanish. The Spanish commandant of St. Louis sent an expedition that launched a surprise attack on the fort on February 12,

1781, crossing ice to take the target. The Spanish briefly raised the Spanish flag, looted the fort, and then returned to safety in St. Louis.

Ultimately, the result of the War of Independence would be determined by actions farther to the east; and in the 1783 peace deal that ended the war, Michigan became American. Except that it didn't exactly. Britain, for instance, remained in control of Detroit, and elections were even held there in 1792 for representatives to the provincial assembly of Upper Canada.

The situation was a headache for the United States government. Not only did it see Britain, via Detroit and other locations, assisting Native American resistance to the United States' attempts to impose its rule on the region, but it also had to deal with competing claims to the Michigan territory from existing states. In the end, it was determined that existing states would not have control of the territory; and in 1795, after the defeat of Native Americans at the 1794 Battle of Fallen Timbers, the British finally agreed to withdraw from all Northwest Territory lands. In 1796, they left Detroit.

But not for the last time. Another war was coming, and soon British forces would return to Detroit.

In 1805, most of what is now Michigan was defined by the United States as Michigan Territory. In 1807, the United States signed a deal in Detroit with the Ottawa, Chippewa, Wyandot, and Potawatomi, under which these peoples ceded lands. It would be the first of a number of deals in which Native Americans gave away their land rights in Michigan.

The War of 1812 didn't start well for America in Michigan. In July 1812, Mackinac Island fell without a shot to the British, because the British in the area had been told they were at war and the Americans in the area hadn't. And the situation wasn't going to get any better for the Michigan authorities anytime soon. In August, Detroit surrendered to the British. And January 1813 saw a major American defeat by British and Native American forces at the Battle of Frenchtown, also known as the Battle of the River Raisin. However, events in the region were about to take a major turn in America's favor. Victory for Olive Hazard Perry in the Battle of Lake Erie was followed by a significant British defeat at the Battle of the Thames. In September, the British withdrew from Detroit, this time for the final time. In the summer of 1814, Americans attempted but failed to retake Mackinac Island, but the war came to an end in February 1815. In July, British forces withdrew from Mackinac Island. Small changes to the border between the United States and Canada would still be made decades after the war.

The end of the War of 1812 was not the last fighting in Michigan. Another war was coming. Well, sort of.

In 1835–1836, a sort of war broke out between Michigan and Ohio, or as it is also known, the Toledo War. Confused surveying had left control of a strip of land stretching west from Toledo in dispute. When applying for statehood in 1835, Michigan claimed it. Ohio wasn't very happy about that. In fact, it wasn't happy at all. Both Michigan and Ohio sent militias to the area. Tensions ran high, and some shots were fired at the so-called Battle of Phillips Corner, as Ohio's surveyors ran into Michigan militiamen. In the end, though, the only actual casualty was a Michigan sheriff who got stabbed, but not killed, while attempting to arrest an Ohioan. In the end, a compromise was found. Ohio got the Toledo strip, and the new state of Michigan, recognized in 1837, ended up with most of the Upper Peninsula. Michigan wasn't very happy about the deal at the time, but became a lot happier when it realized how much valuable natural resources its new territory contained.

And that's almost the end of combat in Michigan. The state sent people and supplies to the fighting in the Civil War, but the battles took place elsewhere.

In the early twentieth century, the United States still had a war plan for the invasion of Canada, which would have involved thrusts from Michigan across the border. It was never needed. Similarly, Canada had at one stage, between the world wars, its Defence Scheme No. 1, which envisaged, in the event of an America invasion, Canadian troops seizing Detroit, among other targets. But that was never needed either.

Over 600,000 Michiganders served in the armed forces in World War II. The state's automotive industry became an arsenal of Democracy, producing thousands of tanks, jeeps, and other vehicles. Almost 5,000 German and Italian POWs were held in camps in Michigan, such as Fort Custer. But one last foreign attack on Michigan was still to come. During the Japanese balloon-bomb campaign of the Second World War, some Fu-Go balloon bombs did make it as far as Michigan, with one landing near Grand Rapids.

## MICHIGAN
## MILITARY HISTORY SITES

**Fort Michilimackinac**
Location: 113 Straits Avenue, Mackinaw City, MI 49701
Web: www.mackinacparks.com

**Fort Wayne**
Location: 6325 West Jefferson Avenue, Detroit, MI 48209
Web: www.historicfortwaynecoalition.com/

**Gerald R. Ford Presidential Library & Museum**
Location: 1000 Beal Avenue, Ann Arbor, MI 48109
Web: www.fordlibrarymuseum.gov

**Michigan's Military and Space Heroes Museum**
Location: 1250 Weiss Street, Frankenmuth, MI 48734
Web: www.michigansmilitarymuseum.com/

**Michigan Military Heritage Museum**
Location: 153 North Union Street, Grass Lake, MI 49240
Web: https://glahc.com/

**Michigan Military Technical & Historical Society**
Location: 16600 Stephens Road, Eastpointe, MI 48021
Web:  www.mimths.org

**River Raisin National Battlefield Park**
Location: 1403 East Elm Avenue, Monroe, MI 48162
Web: www.nps.gov/rira

**Saginaw Valley Naval Ship Museum**
Location: 1680 Martin Street, Bay City, MI 48706
Web: www.ussedson.org

**USS Silversides Submarine Museum**
Location: 1346 Bluff Street, Muskegon, MI 49441
Web: www.silversidesmuseum.org

**World War II Glider and Military Museum**
Location: 302 Kent Street, Iron Mountain, MI 49801
Web: www.menomineemuseum.com

**White Chapel Memorial Park Cemetery**
Location: 621 West Long Lake Road, Troy, MI 48098
Web: www.whitechapelcemetery.com

Nickname: The Great Lake(s) State
Statehood: 1837
Capital: Lansing

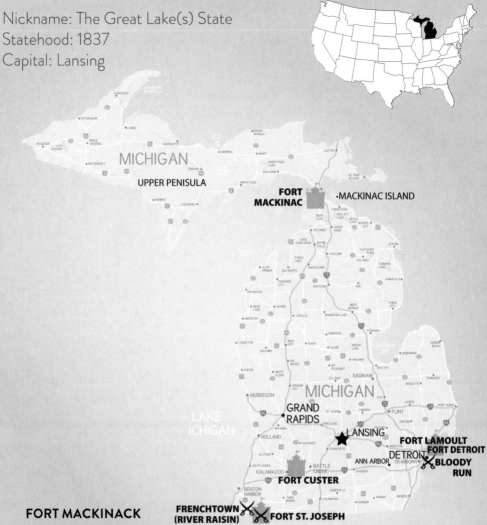

**FORT MACKINACK**
Mackinack Island
Source: Mike and Mark E. Grobbel

# MINNESOTA

The Kensington Runestone, currently located in Alexandria, Minnesota, is claimed by some to be proof that Norseman "invaded" Minnesota in the fourteenth century. However, many others claim that the stone is a much later creation and does not prove that at all.

When the French arrived in the area in the seventeenth century, they found a land inhabited by a number of Native American peoples. These include the Dakota and, increasingly, the Ojibwe. With weapons bought from the French and with European colonies expanding to the east, the Ojibwe pushed deeper into Minnesota, forcing the Dakota to withdraw westward.

The first French into the region included explorers, fur traders, and missionaries. In 1679, Daniel Greysolon, Sieur DuLhut raised the flag of France in a local settlement on what is now known as Mille Lacs Lake. An English version of *DuLhut* would later give Duluth its name.

Pierre Gaultier de Varennes et de La Vérendrye in 1732 built Fort St. Charles in what is now Minnesota's Northwest Angle. In 1736, an expedition from the fort that included his son was attacked and destroyed by Native Americans.

In 1727, a French expedition under René Boucher de La Perrière built Fort Beauharnois on the shore of Lake Pepin. It took its name from Charles de Beauharnois, then governor of New France. Occasional occupation of the post followed, but the French abandoned it for the last time in 1756 as the

French and Indian Wars raged to the east. Defeat in that war meant that in 1763, France's claims to the area passed to Britain.

The British period saw increased development of the Grand Portage route by fur traders; and in 1778, the North West Company built a trading post on Lake Superior northeast of Duluth. Grand Portage National Monument now features a reconstructed version of this.

British defeat in the War of Independence meant new claimants to what is now the state of Minnesota. While the young United States claimed the eastern portion of the area, the part of the state that is southwest of the Mississippi became part of Spanish territory. Britain still hung on to parts of the north. In 1800, however, France briefly reclaimed control from Spain, but in 1803, it sold its claim to the United States under the Louisiana Purchase. It would, however, take quite a lot longer until the current border between Minnesota and Canada was finally established and fully accepted by both sides.

The focus of the War of 1812 was far to the east of Minnesota, but the war did have major implications for the future of Minnesota. During the war, Britain was the major colonial power in the area. However, the indecisive nature of the war meant it failed to establish its presence in the area on a long-term basis. Despite British claims to the Red River Colony area, the 1818 Anglo-American Convention established the 49th parallel as the border west of the Lake of the Woods. Well, except for the little anomaly known as the Northwest Angle, that small bit of Minnesota that can only be reached on land by passing through Canada. It came about due to the confusion of early geographers over the exact lay of the land; and despite occasional attempts to make the Northwest Angle Canadian, it remains Minnesotan today. The Webster-Ashburton Treaty of 1842 mainly sorted out the border east of the Lake of the Woods. Some Minnesotans hoped to push the border farther north into the area then known as Rupert's Land to capitalize on transportation routes that led from Minnesota into the area, but in 1870, Canada set up Manitoba as a province and sent troops to Winnipeg.

After the War of 1812, the United States' problems with Britain in Minnesota were largely at an end. Canada did, even as late as the 1920s, have its Defence Scheme No. 1, which envisaged, in the event of an America invasion, Canadian troops seizing Minneapolis and Saint Paul, but that was never executed.

However, the United States' problems with the local population, who were mainly Native Americans, were not at an end.

In 1819, the United States established Fort Snelling. Part of its function was to police potential hostilities between the Ojibwe and Dakota peoples. It would also become instrumental in the founding of Minneapolis and Saint Paul, the Twin Cities.

As American settlers expanded into the area, Native Americans were increasingly pressured to cede their lands. For instance, in 1837, the Ojibwe gave up some territory, and a series of further cessions would follow. The Dakota too gradually relinquished land in a series of agreements. In particular, the Treaty of Traverse des Sioux in July 1851 and the Mendota Treaty of August 1851 saw the Dakota cede vast territories in Minnesota.

In 1858, Minnesota became the Union's thirty-second state. Minnesota then played a central role in some of the events leading up to the Civil War. Many Minnesotans fought on the side of the Union, but the fighting took place elsewhere.

However, war did come to Minnesota during the Civil War years.

In 1862, the Dakota War or Sioux Rebellion erupted. Crop failures, hunger, and a delay in annuity payments created an explosive situation. On August 17, 1862, four young warriors killed five settlers. Little Crow, leader of the Santee, a part of the Sioux nation, reluctantly agreed to lead his men in a campaign aimed at both settlers and the official US presence.

On the next day, he led the attack on the Redwood Agency. Buildings were burned, and in the Battle of Redwood Ferry, twenty-four soldiers were killed. As the Santee widened their campaign, they attacked many settlements, and hundreds of settlers were killed. Little Crow attacked Fort Ridgely, but had no answer to the defenders' howitzers. On August 23, Santees attacked the village of New Ulm, but after heavy fighting in which both sides suffered many casualties, the defenders managed to drive off the attackers. On September 2, a US Army detachment came under attack and suffered serious casualties in the Battle of Birch Coulee.

The chaos and carnage eventually forced the US government to pay attention to the situation, despite the Civil War raging elsewhere. Major reinforcements arrived under the command of Colonel Henry Sibley. The Santee attacked at the Battle of Wood Lake on September 23, but were heavily defeated. The war was over. The Santee surrendered or fled westward, pursued by punitive expeditions (see North Dakota). A military commission sentenced 303 Santee to death. Lincoln reduced that number to thirty-eight. Numerous Santee faced imprisonment in conditions so dreadful, many died. After the Dakota War, countless Native Americans were forced to leave large tracts of Minnesota. The 1889 Nelson Act allowed the United States to take even more land.

And that's pretty much it for conflicts within the borders of Minnesota. Minnesotans, including those of Native American, European, and other heritages, would do all their military combat outside the state's borders from then on.

It's a matter of some controversy as to whether the Japanese balloon-bomb campaign ever managed to hit Minnesota. Most accounts of the campaign mention no bombing in Minnesota. However, some evidence suggests that a Japanese incendiary balloon bomb landed in northern Minnesota in March 1945.

## MINNESOTA
## MILITARY HISTORY SITES

### Birch Coulee Battlefield
Location: Junction of Renville County Highway 2 and Highway 18, Morton, MN 56270
Web: sites.mnhs.org/historic-sites/birch-coulee-battlefield

### Fort Ridgely State Park
Location: 72158 County Road 30, Fairfax, MN 55332
Web: www.dnr.state.mn.us/state_parks/fort_ridgely/index.html

### Fort Snelling State Park
Location: 101 Snelling Lake Road, Saint Paul, MN 55111
Web: www.dnr.state.mn.us/state_parks/fort_snelling/index.html

### Fort St. Charles
Location: Magnuson's Island, Angle Inlet, MN 56711
Web: www.fortstcharles.com

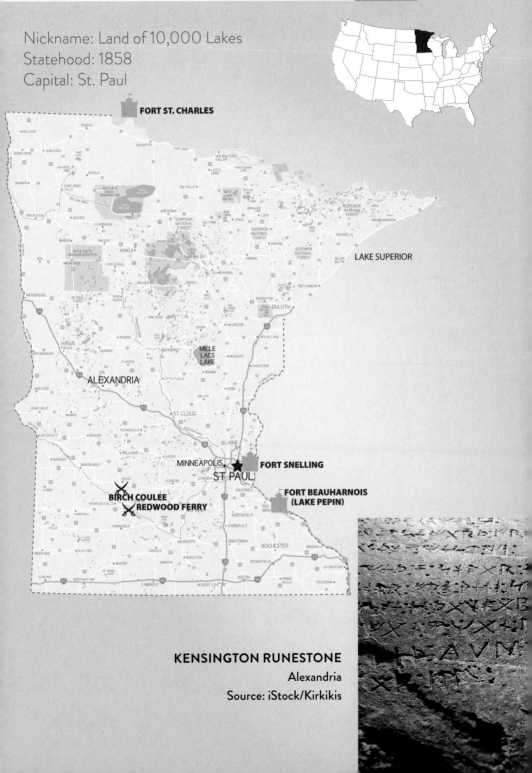

# America Invaded: MINNESOTA

Nickname: Land of 10,000 Lakes
Statehood: 1858
Capital: St. Paul

**FORT ST. CHARLES**

**LAKE SUPERIOR**

ALEXANDRIA

MINNEAPOLIS. **FORT SNELLING**
ST. PAUL

**FORT BEAUHARNOIS
(LAKE PEPIN)**

**BIRCH COULEE**
**REDWOOD FERRY**

### KENSINGTON RUNESTONE
Alexandria
Source: iStock/Kirkikis

**Herreid Military Museum**
Location: 213 East Luverne Street, Luverne, MN 56156
Web: www.luvernechamber.com/m/listing/view/user304

**Historic Fort Snelling**
Location: 200 Tower Avenue, Saint Paul, MN 55111
Web: www.historicfortsnelling.org

**Minnesota History Center**
Location: 345 West Kellogg Boulevard, Saint Paul, MN 55102
Web: www.minnesotahistorycenter.org

**Minnesota Military Museum**
Location: Camp Ripley, 15000 Highway 115, Little Falls, MN 56345
Web: www.mnmilitarymuseum.org

**Runestone Museum**
Location: 206 Broadway Street, Alexandria, MN 56308
Web: www.runestonemuseum.org/runestone

# MISSISSIPPI

The Mississippian culture, which extended through many southeastern states, built mounds from around AD 800 to 1600.

Hernando de Soto, a Spanish explorer, was the first European to arrive in Mississippi in 1540. De Soto died on the banks of the Mississippi River in either Arkansas or Louisiana in 1542.

The French, however, were the first Europeans to begin colonization of Mississippi. Robert de La Salle claimed Mississippi for France in 1682. Pierre Iberville built the first French fort in Mississippi at Fort de Maurepas on Biloxi Bay. The French also introduced African slaves to Mississippi.

The French colonists did have various conflicts with local Native Americans.

For instance, they clashed with the Natchez on a number of occasions. In 1736, after a dispute over land, the Natchez attacked and destroyed the French post at Fort Rosalie. The French, with local Native American allies, launched a war against the Natchez that forced them from their homes and scattered them.

They also clashed with the Chickasaw, though not always successfully from the French point of view. For example, in 1736, the French suffered defeats at both the Battle of Ackia and the Battle of Ogoula Tchetoka.

French rule in Mississippi came to an end in 1763 with their defeat in the Seven Years' War. King George III's proclamation of 1763 banned migration to the Mississippi territory in order to maintain peace with Native Americans tribes, such as the Choctaw.

Settlers seeking good farming land made their way west regardless of George III, and this accelerated with the American Revolution.

In 1779, the Spanish, sympathetic to the American cause, declared war on Britain and captured Natchez. And in 1791, Fort Nogales was built near what is now Vicksburg to counter American expansion in the region. However, in 1795, Spain relinquished control of territory north of the 31st parallel to the United States. In 1798, Spain evacuated Natchez.

The Louisiana Purchase of 1803 secured Mississippi's western border. The southern coast of Mississippi, however, remained under Spanish control until 1812.

As happened elsewhere, Native Americans were bribed and pressured to yield control of their land. For instance, in 1801, the Choctaw ceded over two million acres; and in 1805, they relinquished another four million acres.

Most of the struggles between Americans and indigenous people in the Mississippi Territory took place during the Creek War of 1813–1814 in present-day Alabama (see Alabama).

Fort Massachusetts was built on West Ship Island after the War of 1812. It would be seized by Union forces in 1862 with Admiral Farragut's capture of nearby New Orleans.

Mississippi joined the Union as the twentieth state in 1817.

In the period following, most Native Americans were removed from the state and relocated to the west.

Mississippi, a cotton-growing slave state, was among the first to join the Confederacy in 1861. Abraham Lincoln had not even been on the ballot in Mississippi in the election of 1860. Around 80,000 Mississippians would serve in Confederate gray during the war. Over 17,000 freed slaves from Mississippi would eventually serve in Union blue.

After the Union victory at the Battle of Shiloh in April 1862 (see Tennessee), Grant's Army of Tennessee advanced south into Mississippi. The Battle of Iuka was fought in Mississippi September 19–20, 1862. An unusual "acoustic shadow" prevented Grant from hearing about the battle being fought by Rosecrans against Price. An opportunity for a decisive Union victor was thereby squandered.

On May 30, 1862, Major General Henry Halleck captured Corinth after a month-long siege. Corinth would become a major Union supply base from which the struggle for Vicksburg was launched.

On October 3–4, 1862, the Confederates struck back in Mississippi at the bloody Second Battle of Corinth. Union Major General Rosecrans fought Van Dorn with evenly matched forces, and around 5,000 men were killed, with both sides suffering similar losses. The Confederates withdrew.

Ulysses S. Grant identified the critical nature of the fortress city of Vicksburg in his memoirs:

> Vicksburg is important to the enemy because it occupied the first high ground coming close to the river below Memphis. From there a railroad runs east, connecting with other roads leading to all points of the Southern States. A railroad also starts from the opposite side of the river, extending west as far as Shreveport, Louisiana. Vicksburg was the only channel … connecting the parts of the Confederacy divided by the Mississippi. So long as it was held by the enemy, the free navigation of the river was prevented.

Vicksburg, therefore, became a major strategic target for Union forces. David Farragut, the Union admiral from Virginia, had been the first to attempt to storm "the Confederate Gibraltar" in June of 1862. Farragut even tried to build a canal in the river bend south of Vicksburg to avoid having Union ships shelled from the bluff-top batteries. Farragut's fleet passed by under the guns of Vicksburg on June 28 with minimal damage, but the admiral recognized that the Union could not hope to capture it without ground troops.

In the fall of 1862, Ulysses S. Grant with the Army of Tennessee and Admiral Porter of the Union Navy mounted a combined-arms siege of Vicksburg. The city was defended by 40,000 troops of the Army of Mississippi, commanded by John Pemberton. The Confederate Cavalry general, Nathan Bedford Forrest, would attempt to interdict Grant's long line of supply back to Kentucky. General Sherman also skirmished with Confederate forces at the Battle of Chickasaw Bayou about six miles from Vicksburg in late December of 1862. Admiral Porter's fleet engaged Confederate shore defenses on April

29, 1863, in the Battle of Grand Gulf. The Union fleet ferried Grant's Army safely across the Mississippi.

The siege of Vicksburg intensified from the spring of 1863 into the summer. On May 16, Grant won the Battle of Champion Hill, forcing the Confederate forces back into the rapidly closing trap of Vicksburg. On July 4, Pemberton finally surrendered a Confederate Army of nearly 30,000 men in Vicksburg. The Confederacy has effectively been cut in two along the line of the Mississippi River. Lincoln exulted, "The Father of Waters again goes unvexed to the sea."

Jackson, the state capital, fell to Union forces. Natchez was also occupied in 1863.

In 1864, more battles were fought in Mississippi.

In February 1864, Sherman took Meridian, but Union cavalry forces that were supposed to meet him there before a push into Alabama were repulsed at the Okolona.

And in the summer of 1864, Confederate forces defeated a Union force at Brice's Cross Roads as they attempted to attack Union supply lines. The reinforced Confederates subsequently suffered defeat at the Battle of Tupelo.

America's bloodiest war finally ended in April of 1865 with Lee's surrender at Appomattox Courthouse.

When the United States entered World War I in April 1917, Mississippi was divided. One senator voted in support of Wilson's declaration of war while one opposed it. Desertion rates in the state ran at 12 percent, and two deserters were killed in Tippah County.

On May 12, 1942, *U-507* sank the SS *Virginian* at the mouth of the Mississippi River. Many German submarines operated in the Gulf of Mexico in 1942 and 1943. A number of airfields were built in the state in order to enable the US Army Air Force to fly air combat patrols in the nearby gulf.

## MISSISSIPPI
## MILITARY HISTORY SITES

**Beauvoir**
Location: 2244 Beach Boulevard, Biloxi, MS 39531
Web: www.visitbeauvoir.org

**Brices Cross Roads National Battlefield Site**
Location: 128 Highway 370, Baldwyn, MS 38824
Web: www.nps.gov/brcr/index.htm

**Camp Van Dorn World War II Museum**
Location: 138 East Main, Centreville, MS 39631
Web: www.vandornmuseum.org

**Corinth Civil War Interpretive Center**
Location: 501 West Linden Street, Corinth, MS 38834
Web: www.nps.gov/shil/learn/historyculture/corinth.htm

**Fort Massachusetts**
Location: Gulf Islands National Seashore, Ship Island, MS 38626
Web: www.nps.gov/guis/learn/historyculture/fort-massachusetts.htm

**G. I. Museum**
Location: 5796 Ritcher Road, Ocean Springs, MS 39564
Web: www.gimuseum.com

**Natchez National Historical Park**
Location: 210 State Street, Natchez, MS 39120
Web: www.nps.gov/natc/index.htm

**Rosemont Plantation: Home of Jefferson Davis**
Location: Just off US 61 on Mississippi 24, Woodville, MS 39669
Web: www.rosemontplantation1810.com

**Tupelo National Battlefield**
Location: 2005 Main Street, Tupelo, MS 38801
Web: www.nps.gov/tupe/index.htm

**USS *Cairo* Gunboat and Museum**
Location: 3201 Clay Street, Vicksburg National Military Park, Vicksburg, MS 39183
Web: www.nps.gov/vick/u-s-s-cairo-gunboat.htm

**Vicksburg National Cemetery**
Location: Vicksburg National Military Park, Vicksburg, MS 39183
Web: www.nps.gov/vick/learn/historyculture/cemhistory.htm

**Vicksburg National Military Park**
Location: 3201 Clay Street, Vicksburg, MS 39183
Web: www.nps.gov/vick/index.htm

# America Invaded: MISSISSIPPI

Nickname: The Magnolia State
Statehood: 1817
Capital: Jackson

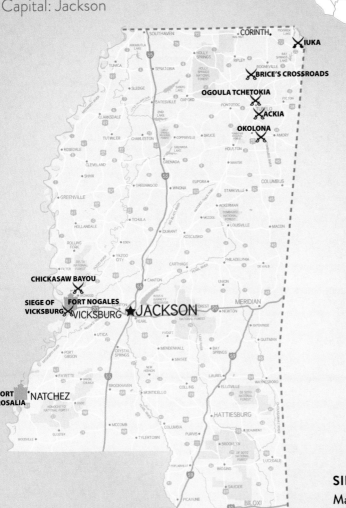

**SIEGE OF VICKSBURG**
May-July 1863
Source: iStock/traveler1116

# MISSOURI

The land that is now Missouri had already had a long period of human habitation before Europeans arrived. For instance, the Mississippian Culture flourished in the area, and one of its major sites, as well as the largest prehistoric city, is Cahokia Mounds, Illinois, just across the Mississippi River from St. Louis.

Native American occupation of the area developed something of a cultural divide between the native peoples of the east, like the Missouria, who had links to the Northeast group of indigenous peoples, and the people of the west, like the Quapaw and Osage, who had links to the Plains groups.

Hernando de Soto seems to have led the first European expedition to Missouri in 1541. The city of De Soto in Jefferson County was named after him.

It would be the French, however, who first opened up the area to European expansion.

In 1673, Jacques Marquette, a French Jesuit priest, and Louis Jolliet, a French trader, traveled along the Mississippi through territory that now forms part of Missouri and, apart from anything else, introduced the name *Missouri* (for the people and the river) to Europeans.

More French were to follow, eventually carving out a corridor that linked French-controlled territory in Canada to the north with the Gulf of Mexico in the south, and also conveniently (from the French point of view, but increasingly inconveniently from the British point of view) prevented British expansion westward.

Robert de La Salle cruised down the Mississippi in 1682. Upon reaching the Gulf of Mexico, he claimed the entire Mississippi basin for France, giving it the thoroughly French name (at that time anyway) of Louisiana. Not, of course, that La Salle proclaiming it French actually made it French, but it was a start. And La Salle might have spent more time in Missouri except that, in 1684, some of his men got tired of wandering around America's vast spaces looking for the mouth of the Mississippi and killed him.

So far, the French hadn't actually achieved much in the way of demonstrating that the Mississippi part of what is now Missouri was in fact French. In 1700, French priest Pierre Gabriel Marest established a settlement at the mouth of the River des Peres, with a group of Kaskaskia who were moving because of fear of attack by the Iroquois. It could have been the start of something major and French in Missouri. It wasn't. After just three years, the Kaskaskia decided they'd be better off on the east side of the Mississippi, and Marest went with them.

However, the French weren't giving up. In the early eighteenth century, Étienne de Veniard, Sieur de Bourgmont was getting to know the Missouri (people and river) very well. So well, in fact, that he married the daughter of a Missouri chief and they had a son in 1714. In 1723, as commander of a French expedition to explore and protect developing French trade in the area, he built Fort D'Orleans near what is now Brunswick. He returned to France in 1725 with a party of Native Americans from the area, who were royally entertained and then sent home to Missouri carrying lavish gifts. His Missouri wife was even baptized in France. Fort Orleans could have been the start of something major and French in Missouri. It wasn't. A few years after it was built, the French abandoned Fort Orleans.

However, a permanent French settlement in what is now Missouri was finally about to arrive. Some time after Fort Orleans was abandoned, the French settlement of Sainte Genevieve was established on the banks of the Mississippi, and it has been there ever since. Well, sort of. It actually moved a couple of miles after some disastrous floods in the late eighteenth century, but it has been there, or thereabouts, ever since.

This too could have been the start of something major and French in Missouri. It wasn't. In 1754, the French and Indian War broke out. It was disastrous, at least for the French. For the British, it was a huge victory that ended French control of all territory (except St. Pierre and Miquelon, which are so small they hardly count) north of the Caribbean. However, rather than the British taking control of Louisiana west of the Mississippi, as part of the reshuffling of colonial territories at the end of the Seven Years' War, Britain allowed Spain to take control while it focused on land east of the Mississippi, French Canada, and what had previously been Spanish Florida. Somewhere in the midst of all this confusion, in 1764 Pierre Laclède and Auguste Chouteau, both fur traders, managed to found St. Louis (at that time, still a thoroughly French name) before the Spanish took full control.

Shortly after the Spanish took control, the American Revolution broke out, and Missouri was about to face an invasion from yet another European power. Spain started sending supplies to the American revolutionaries; and by 1779, Spain was openly at war with Britain. Which meant that Spanish territory in Missouri was now a target for Britain. In late May 1780, a combined British and Native American force attacked St. Louis. The assault resulted in considerable casualties in the outlying, undefended parts of the settlement before cannon fire and a force that mainly consisted of militiamen under the command of Fernando de Leyba drove off the attackers. It wasn't exactly the biggest battle in history, but it was significant in hindering British attempts to control the Mississippi River.

British defeat in the War of Independence brought a sort of peace to the area, but it also brought a new player on the scene—the United States. The settlement of New Madrid, a thoroughly Spanish name, became a particular focus for American settlers looking for new land.

But the peace wasn't to last. By 1796, as war engulfed Europe, Spain and Britain were enemies again, which made Missouri a potential target for British forces in Canada. Increasing numbers of Americans were allowed to settle west of the Mississippi, including a certain Daniel Boone.

And at this point, France was back on the scene. Yes, in 1800, with Spain under pressure from Napoleonic France, it was time to declare Missouri French again. They would have needed new French Republic flags, not just the old French royal flags from the last time France ruled the area. As it turned out, any investment in new French flags would hardly have been worth it, because in 1803, as part of the Louisiana Purchase, France sold its interests in the area to the United States.

Three Flags Day (March 9 and 10, 1804) is commemorated in St. Louis to remember the days when the Spanish turned control over to the French who, in turn, handed it to the Americans, formalizing the Louisiana Purchase.

These were bad times for the Missouria people. In the eighteenth and early nineteenth century, they came under attack a number of times by other Native American peoples, including the Osage.

But some of these other peoples were facing problems of their own. In 1804, the Sauk and Fox signed the Treaty of St. Louis at Portage des Sioux, which gave up land in Missouri and elsewhere in return for an annual payment. In 1808, William Clark (of Lewis and Clark fame) established Fort Osage; and it was there that the Osage people signed away their rights to vast amounts of south Missouri. Further treaties would follow.

Britain, though, was to have one last attempt at getting militarily involved in the area. Or at least, Britain's allies were. The War of 1812 officially ended in February 1815, but terminating hostilities over a wide area in a period before electronic communication was easier said than done. US and British Navy ships were still clashing in late March, and then on May 24 came the final land battle of the war. And it was in Missouri. Sauk fighters ambushed Missouri Rangers in the Battle of the Sink Hole. The Sauk were led by Black Hawk, who had been unhappy about how the United States had dealt with his people. The British had commissioned Black Hawk as a brevet brigadier general, and the Sauk's campaign against US forces in the area had had some success. This final battle of the war, though, was somewhat indecisive. So, a bit like the whole war, really.

Other clashes between the forces of indigenous Americans and American settlers were to follow. Growth in the number of settlers and the expansion of their farming activities had long been putting pressure on Native Americans.

In 1829, the slightly farcical Big Neck War took place, in which a group of Iowa were on the move, led by Chief Big Neck, and clashed with settlers at The Cabins in Adair County. Generally speaking, mutual misunderstanding and suspicion, rather than any determined offensive intention, seems to have caused the clash, which was over almost before it had begun. A few people did die, and eventually some of the Iowa were tried in a US court for murder. They were acquitted.

But as well as farce, some significant events were taking place. The 1836 Platte Purchase resulted in yet more land being bought from Native Americans.

In 1838 and 1839, large numbers of Cherokee were forced westward through Missouri. Today, the Trail of Tears State Park commemorates their suffering.

However, it wasn't just Native Americans and settlers clashing in Missouri. There was, in 1838, the Missouri Mormon War. In 1831, Mormonism's founder, Joseph Smith, announced that western Missouri was where Zion would be built. Consequently, the area rapidly became a focus for Mormon settlement and expansion. Friction built in the region, culminating in the Mormon War.

The so-called Gallatin Election Day Battle in August, which was more of a brawl, was followed by more serious violence in October. In the Battle of Crooked River, a brief but sharp clash, Mormon forces defeated Missouri militiamen. In response, Missouri Governor Lilburn Boggs commanded that the Mormons be expelled from Missouri, or exterminated. On October 30, the Haun's Mill Massacre resulted in eighteen Mormon men and boys killed. Soon after, thousands of Mormons became refugees, fleeing to Illinois.

The 1839 Honey War was less serious. A lot less serious. As Missouri and Iowa squabbled over the location of the border between the two states, a Missouri tax collector, according to legend, attempted to seize honey in lieu of taxes. Militias were turned out by both sides, but it wasn't exactly a war.

But as the issue of slavery began to tear the United States apart, a low-level border war, sometimes called Bleeding Kansas, erupted in the 1850s along the border between Missouri and Kansas, sparked by the question of whether slavery should be legal in Kansas. Antislavery groups based in Kansas clashed with proslavery groups in Missouri. It set the scene for the vicious fighting that would erupt as the main Civil War exploded into action.

Missouri was a border state, and Missourians were deeply divided in their loyalties. Claiborne Jackson, the governor, was pro-Confederacy. On April 20, 1861, secessionists seized the Liberty Arsenal in Kansas City. As the political climate deteriorated, General Nathaniel Lyon organized pro-Union volunteers to serve alongside regular Union forces; and the Missouri State Guard was formed, which would fight alongside Confederate forces. On June 15, Lyon's men took Jefferson City, securing the state capital and seat of government for a pro-Union administration. On June 17, in the First Battle of Boonville—the first battle of the war in Missouri—Union forces under Lyon brushed aside the Missouri State Guard under Jackson. However, the Union forces were not going to have it all their own way. As the fighting spread, pro-Union forces were defeated by the Missouri State Guard at the Battle of Carthage in July;

and pro-Confederate forces, including the Missouri State Guard, were victorious at the Battle of Wilson's Creek in August 1861, in which Lyon himself was killed. Pro-Confederate forces followed this up by advancing northward and securing another victory at the first Battle of Lexington in September. In October 1861, his confidence boosted by these victories, Jackson called a rebel assembly at Neosho, which unofficially declared Missouri free of the Union. Shortly after that, it was announced that Missouri was joining the Confederacy.

However, a string of Union victories followed. In February 1862, Brigadier General Samuel Curtis took Springfield before advancing into Arkansas and achieving a major victory over Sterling Price's Missouri State Guard and local allies at the Battle of Pea Ridge. In the same month on the other side of Missouri, Union forces were victorious at the Battle of Island No. 10, which proved vital in opening up the Mississippi for the Union. With their hopes of seizing Missouri militarily dashed, the Confederates increasingly turned to guerrilla tactics and raids, relying on bases in Arkansas, and they scored a number of successes with this new approach.

The war also became increasingly bitter and brutal. On August 21, 1863, William Quantrill and his pro-Confederate Missourian guerrilla group launched an attack on Lawrence, Kansas, in revenge for actions by Union forces. They killed 150 men and boys and looted the town. In response to the massacre, Union General Thomas Ewing Jr. ordered that the population of much of four western Missouri counties be expelled. Twenty thousand refugees were forced to flee, and Union forces set fire to abandoned property.

In September 1864, General Sterling Price launched what was to be the last Confederate incursion into Missouri. The Confederate forces had a number of successes, including victory at the Battle of Pilot Knob on September 27. Ultimately though, they failed to achieve anything huge; and after defeat at the Battle of Westport in October, they abandoned Missouri. In January 1865, the Emancipation Ordinance of Missouri was passed, and later in the year, the war ended. Some Confederate forces fled the state rather than surrender. Former Confederate guerrilla Jesse James would find notoriety after the war, and was killed at St. Joseph, Missouri, in 1882.

The end of the Civil War also saw the end of major military action in Missouri.

The state would, of course, send people (including John Pershing, Omar Bradley, and Maxwell D. Taylor) and munitions to many other wars. And the USS *Missouri*, the last US battleship completed, would famously be the site of the Japanese surrender in 1945, and is now a museum ship at Pearl Harbor. But after the Civil War, the fighting would not be in Missouri.

## MISSOURI
## MILITARY HISTORY SITES

### Battle of Carthage State Historic Site
Location: 111 West Chestnut Street, Carthage, MO 64836
Web: **www.mostateparks.com/park/battle-carthage-state-historic-site**

### Battle of Lexington State Historic Site
Location: 1101 Delaware Street, Lexington, MO 64067
Web: www.mostateparks.com/park/battle-lexington-state-historic-site

### Battle of Westport Visitor Center
Location: 6601 Swope Parkway, Kansas City, MO 64132
Web: www.battleofwestport.org/

### Fort Osage National Historic Landmark
Location: 107 Osage Street, Sibley, MO 64088
Web: www.fortosagenhs.com/

### Harry S. Truman Library and Museum
Location: 500 West US Highway 24, Independence, Missouri 64050
Web: www.trumanlibrary.org

### Museum of Missouri Military History
Location: 2405 Logistics Road, Jefferson City, MO 65101
Web: https://www.visitmo.com/museum-of-missouri-military-history.aspx

**Missouri History Museum**
Location: 5700 Lindell, St. Louis MO, 63112
Web: www.mohistory.org/

**National Churchill Museum**
Location: 501 Westminster Avenue, Fulton, MO 65251
Web: www.nationalchurchillmuseum.org/

**National World War I Museum and Memorial**
Location: 2 Memorial Drive, Kansas City, MO 64108
Web: www.theworldwar.org

**Wilson's Creek National Battlefield**
Location: 6424 West Farm Road 182, Republic, MO 65738
Web: www.nps.gov/wicr/

# America Invaded: MISSOURI

Nickname: The Show Me State
Statehood: 1821
Capital: Jefferson City

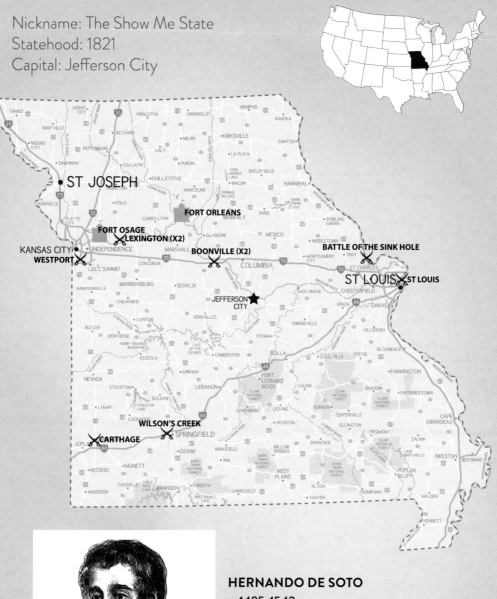

**HERNANDO DE SOTO**
c. 1495-1542
Source: akg-images

# MONTANA

Today, Montana is known as Big Sky Country. The state is noteworthy for being the site of one of the greatest United States military disasters of all time—the Battle of Little Bighorn.

Humans first arrived in what is now Montana thousands of years ago. Significant tribes in Montana include the Crow, Blackfeet, and Lakota Sioux.

Spanish explorers bestowed the name *Montaña del norte* to the mountainous area at the extreme northern end of their New World Empire. The Spaniards, though, did not have much direct impact on Montana.

French explorers too would make early visits to what is now the state of Montana.

Spain traded her New World Empire to France in 1800 with the Third Treaty of San Ildefonso, and Napoleon sold the territory to the United States. Most of Montana was included in the Louisiana Purchase of 1803, which was negotiated by the Jefferson administration with Napoleon. Shortly thereafter, Jefferson eagerly dispatched Lewis and Clark on a voyage of discovery to the Pacific. In 1805, the Lewis and Clark Expedition made its way through Montana. On the return journey in 1806, they passed the place that later became the town of Missoula.

In the years that followed, fur traders would exploit the resources of the area and build infrastructure. In 1828, the Fort Union Trading Post was established.

The discovery of gold in Montana in 1862–3 brought an influx of miners to the Montana territory, which led to an escalating series of conflicts between Americans and indigenous people. The most direct route to the gold fields lay along the Bozeman Trail, which was in the heart of Cheyenne country. John Bozeman of Georgia led a party of 2,000 settlers along this route in 1864. In 1867, while traveling along the Yellowstone River, Bozeman was murdered by Blackfeet Indians, or, perhaps, by his business partner Tom Cover.

Confederate forces never approached the Montana Territory in the Civil War. Some Confederate sympathizers in southwestern Montana did, however, propose naming their town *Varina* in honor of Varina Davis, the First Lady of the Confederate States. Ultimately, it was named, and remains, Virginia City. Gold from the Montana Territory was used by both sides to finance their respective war efforts.

In 1865, General Patrick Edward Connor led over 2,000 American troops on a punitive expedition targeting Native Americans in the Montana Territory. The Powder River invasion culminated with the Battle of Alkali Creek in September 1865. The redoubtable Chief Red Cloud of the Oglala Sioux led the opposition to the American expedition, which resulted in the deaths of over thirty Americans and over one hundred Indians. Connor withdrew his forces back to Fort Laramie. The costly campaign resulted in the adoption of a peace policy by the US government. After negotiating peace, Red Cloud would play no part in the Great Sioux War of 1876–77.

As the number of settlers and the process of pushing Native Americans off their lands proceeded, violence flared regularly.

In the Marias Massacre of January 1870, US troops attacked a Piegan Blackfeet encampment and killed hundreds, mostly old men, women, and children.

Crazy Horse of the Lakota Sioux fought the inconclusive Battle of Rosebud against Brigadier General Crook on June 17, 1876. Thirty-two American soldiers were killed, and twenty-one were wounded.

Historians and writers slow down to observe the phenomenon of Custer's defeat at Little Bighorn in much the same way motorists tap the brakes to observe a smoking wreck on the interstate. Little Bighorn, which was fought during the Great Sioux War, was the deadliest battle in Montana's recorded history.

George Armstrong Custer was a body in motion that stayed in motion until he finally came to rest at the Battle of Little Bighorn in Montana on June 25, 1876. After graduating thirty-fourth out of a class of thirty-four at West Point in 1861, Custer was immediately swept up in the conflagration of the Civil War. Custer disdained the slow-moving infantry; he was a horseman and a natural cavalryman. He fought for his country as a dashing Union cavalry officer, serving at the First Battle of Bull Run and the Battle of Gettysburg, and was present at Lee's surrender at Appomattox. Custer, a lifelong Democrat from Ohio, was said to have held presidential aspirations.

His long blond hair and swagger attracted the attention of Elizabeth "Libbie" Bacon, whom he married. In 1867, military discipline could not prevent the uxorious Custer from going AWOL to reunite with Libbie—for which he was court-martialed on eight counts, the most egregious charge being abandonment of his command.

During the 1873 Yellowstone Expedition, at the Battle of Honsinger Bluff, Custer encountered opponents he would meet again—the forces of Sitting Bull and Crazy Horse. This time Custer and most of his men managed to live through the experience.

Prior to Little Bighorn, Custer was advised to equip his unit with the latest in killing technology: Gatling guns. He refused as their transportation might slow him down. Custer also made the fatal mistake of dividing his command.

Chief Crazy Horse had assembled approximately 1,800 warriors, who outnumbered Custer's 7th Cavalry by about three to one. Many of the Sioux warriors were armed with Winchester repeating rifles that were superior to the Springfield rifles Americans carried. Of course, not all Indians opposed Custer. Many Crow Indians served as scouts with the 7th Cavalry.

Some of the American soldiers that served with Custer were foreign born. Many were Irish or English. Giovanni Martini, Custer's bugler, was a veteran of the Italian Army. Martini carried Custer's last message to Captain Frederick Benteen, urging him to "Be quick. Bring packs." As a result, Martini survived the battle and died in Brooklyn in 1922 after being struck by a beer truck!

After Custer's death at Little Bighorn, along with 268 of his men, many tried to adapt the Custer legend to their own purposes. His widow Libbie wrote three books that unconvincingly attempted to exonerate her husband by blaming Major Marcus Reno for the debacle. Buffalo Bill Cody exploited the Custer legend by staging reenactments of the battle, sometimes using Indians who had participated in the actual battle. Anheuser Busch transformed

Custer's apotheosis at Little Bighorn into a poster that adorned thousands of saloons across America.

In 1877, Crazy Horse was captured and held at Fort Robinson in Nebraska. He was killed by a bayonet-wielding guard that same year. Sioux resistance weakened after the death of their charismatic leader.

Other tribes, however, took up arms against the Americans. US forces clashed with the Nez Perce at the Battle of the Clearwater in Montana in July 1877. After the battle, the Nez Perce retreated eastward, pursued by the US military. Other clashes followed. On August 9–10, 1877, the Battle of the Big Hole was fought between the US Army and the Nez Perce. It proved to be the second deadliest battle on record ever fought in Montana, costing over 110 lives, including women and children. Many of the Nez Perce surrendered to US forces after the Battle of Bear Paw Mountains later the same year. Others escaped north into Canada.

On November 5, 1887, the final battle between American and Native American forces was fought at the Crow Agency in southern Montana. Sword Bearer, a Crow medicine man who claimed to have supernatural powers, was shot and killed.

Montana was admitted to the Union as the forty-first state in 1889.

In 1877, Fort Missoula was built during the Grant administration in order to protect settlers from Indian raids. Fort Missoula became the headquarters for the 25th Infantry Bicycle Corps in 1897. This African-American unit trekked 1,900 miles to St. Louis the same year. The following year, the unit was shipped to fight in the Philippines in the Spanish-American War.

The Oregon Treaty of 1846 established the northern border of the Montana Territory (and the United States) at the 49th parallel. Canadians may not have "invaded" south into Montana, but hundreds of them did train alongside Americans during World War II at Fort William Henry Harrison near Helena. They formed the First Special Service Force, but are more commonly known as the Devil's Brigade. So, Canadian bagpipers played reveille in Big Sky Country. This extraordinary unit distinguished itself in World War II, fighting on fronts that included the Aleutians, Anzio, and Operation Dragoon, which invaded the south of France.

Fort Missoula became a prisoner-of-war camp in World War II. The crew of the Italian ship SS *Conte Biancamano*, which had been seized in Panama, was transported to Missoula and held prisoner in Fort Missoula.

Japanese-American men were also detained at Fort Missoula. The Italian POWs called the area Bella Vista, and many wound up settling in Montana after the war. So this would qualify as an Italian detention rather than an invasion. There was, however, one violent incident—the Olive Oil Riot. An Italian cook became indignant when told that he must use beef fat for cooking rather than his beloved olive oil. A guard shot himself in the foot during the ensuing disturbance!

In December of 1944, a mysterious device was discovered near Kalispell. Yoshi Sakhara, an American citizen of Japanese ancestry from Whitefish, used the markings on the device to identify it as Japanese in origin. At least thirty Fu-Go balloon bombs landed in the state in the course of the war.

## MONTANA
## MILITARY HISTORY SITES

### Bear Paw Battlefield
Location: Highway 240, Chinook, MT 59523
Web: www.nps.gov/nepe/planyourvisit/bear-paw-battlefield.htm

### Big Hole National Battlefield
Location: 16425 Highway 43 West, Wisdom, MT 59761
Web: www.nps.gov/biho/index.htm

### Camp Disappointment
Location: Blackfeet Indian Reservation, 12 miles northeast of Browning, MT 59417
Web: www.visitmt.com/listings/general/national-historic-site/camp-disappointment.html

### Custer Battlefield Museum
Location: I-90 Exit 514, Town Hall, Garryowen, MT 59031
Web: www.custermuseum.org/index.htm

**CRAZY HORSE STAMP**
c. 1842-1877
Source: iStock/traveler1116

**GEORGE ARMSTRONG CUSTER**
1839-1876, Source: iStock/Andrew_Howe

Nickname: Big Sky Country
Statehood: 1889
Capital: Helena

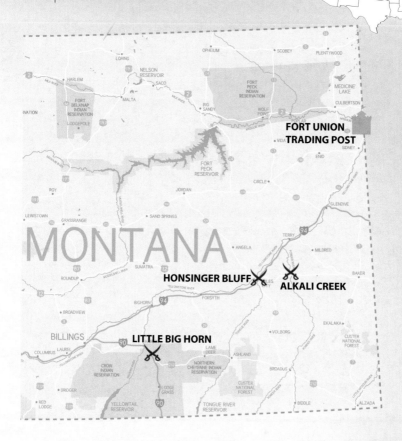

**GIOVANNI MARTINI**
1852-1922
Source: Denver Public Library

**DEVIL'S BRIGADE**
1st Special Service Force
Source: Vincent Driano

**Fort Benton Museums & Heritage Complex**
Location: Old Fort Park, Fort Benton, MT 59442
Web: www.fortbentonmuseums.com

**Historical Museum and Fort Missoula**
Location: 3400 Captain Rawn Way, Missoula, MT 59804
Web: www.fortmissoulamuseum.org

**Fort William Henry Harrison**
Location: 3 miles west of Helena, MT 59602
Web: www.helenahistory.org/fort_harrison.htm

**Little Bighorn Battlefield National Monument**
Location: 756 Battlefield Tour Road, Crow Agency, MT 59022
Web: www.nps.gov/libi/index.htm

**Rosebud Battlefield State Park**
Location: HC 42, Busby, MT 59016
Web: www.stateparks.mt.gov/rosebud-battlefield

**The History Museum**
Location: 422 2nd Street South, Great Falls, MT 59405
Web: www.thehistorymuseumgreatfalls.com

# NEBRASKA

I n the early years of European colonization of North America, European interest in what is now the state of Nebraska came from two main directions: Spain and France.

The first Europeans to come close to the area were probably those in the Spanish Coronado expedition, which set off north from Mexico in search of gold. The expedition finally reached a place they called Quivira where a guide had told them they would find gold. They didn't find any gold, so Coronado had the guide strangled and then went home gold-less. The exact location of Quivira is not known. Some have suggested it was in Nebraska, but it is more likely that it was just to the south, in Kansas.

The Spanish may not actually have been to Nebraska, but they claimed land in the region in the name of the Spanish throne nonetheless.

But soon other Europeans would approach Nebraska from a different direction. In 1682, Frenchman René-Robert Cavelier, Sieur de La Salle claimed for France the whole Mississippi river basin. He too had not actually been to Nebraska.

The fact that two mighty European empires were now expressing an interest in their territory made basically zero difference to the various Native American peoples who were actually living in what is now Nebraska. However, during the eighteenth century, that would change.

French explorers actually entered the area. In 1714, Étienne de Bourgmont journeyed from the mouth of the Missouri River to the mouth of the Platte River, which he referred to as the Nebraskier River.

Meanwhile, the Spanish were getting worried about what the French might be up to in the area, so they decided to act. In 1720, they sent a military expedition north from Santa Fe that eventually reached Nebraska. The expedition wasn't a great success, however. In fact, from a Spanish point of view, it was pretty much a total disaster. Lieutenant-General Pedro de Villasur was in command of the expedition, which consisted of forty-five soldiers, sixty Pueblo Indians, a priest, and an interpreter. Somewhere near what is now Columbus, Pawnee warriors attacked Villasur's overnight encampment. Villasur and most of the soldiers were killed, and what was left of the Spanish party headed for home as fast as it could.

The expedition was a pointless waste in more than one sense since the French, as it turned out, were not in a huge hurry to expand into Nebraska. French-Canadian explorers Pierre and Paul Mallet did turn up at the mouth of the Platte River in 1739. However, by 1763, France had lost the Seven Years' War, and all their claims in the area had been handed over to the Spanish.

The Spanish, in turn, took a relaxed approach to exploring and exploiting Nebraska, and another war was needed to energize the situation. The American Revolution created a new, aggressive colonizing power to the east and left Britain, still in control of Canada, keen to exert its influence where it still could.

With the enthusiastic support of the Spanish authorities in St. Louis, the Company of Explorers of the Upper Missouri was formed in 1793. In the end, it did not achieve a huge amount, but an expedition under the Scottish John McKay did at one point establish an outpost called Fort Charles somewhere near what is now Dakota City. The days of the fairly limited Spanish power in the area were almost at an end. Soon after, France reasserted its claims to the land and then rapidly sold the land to the young United States in the Louisiana Purchase.

The United States, in turn, moved rapidly to explore its new purchases. Lewis and Clark's Corps of Discovery Expedition headed west in 1804, managing to avoid ambush by Spanish forces sent to Nebraska to intercept them.

The War of 1812 saw another flaring of the battle for influence in North America between Britain and the United States. Neither side had much of a presence in Nebraska at that time, but Manuel Lisa, a Spanish-American fur trader from New Orleans, had established Fort Lisa near the Council Bluff. His widespread commercial and social contacts with the local tribes helped prevent British influence from spreading.

The disastrous Yellowstone Expedition of 1819 did at least reach the Council Bluff site. However, the men then suffered a terrible winter in which many of them died. In the spring of 1820, they built Fort Atkinson.

Gradually, more traders and eventually settlers followed, and the process began of the Native American tribes in Nebraska being pressured and bribed to give up their lands.

In 1854, the Kansas-Nebraska Act created Nebraska Territory (which included much more land than the current state of Nebraska). By its provisions, the act allowed the settlers in Kansas to decide whether Kansas would be a state allowing slavery or not. This led to the period known as Bleeding Kansas, as pro- and antislavery gangs clashed. Some of this chaos and carnage spilled over into Nebraska.

However, it was not slavery that would soon see the US Army campaigning on the soils of what is now Nebraska.

There was the Battle of Ash Hollow in 1855, though *battle* is perhaps a rather grand name for what happened. After the so-called Grattan Massacre (see Wyoming), Brigadier General Willliam S. Harney was dispatched with a column of troops to conduct punitive operations and find those who had killed Grattan's men. In September 1855, Harney found a Sioux encampment. After he failed to convince the Sioux to hand over the men he was after, Harney attacked. Many of the Sioux, including women and children, were killed.

By contrast, the Pawnee War of 1859 ended without bloodshed after only a few days. After hearing reports of Pawnee raids on settlers of Elk Horn Valley in July of that year, militia and US dragoons prepared to attack a large Pawnee village. The Pawnee promptly surrendered, and the "war" came to an end.

When the Civil War began, soldiers from what is now Nebraska served in the Union army. No battles were fought there. However, some of the widespread lawlessness (some of it political, some of it criminal) that often emerges in war zones did spill over into Nebraska. Jayhawking and bushwhacking were persistent problems for the authorities. For instance, in October 1861, Missouri bushwhackers briefly descended on Falls City and told the inhabitants they were prisoners of war. In October 1863, Felix Von Eaton Jr., US marshal of

Fremont County, Ohio, was killed near Nebraska City when in pursuit of alleged Missouri bushwhackers.

The Civil War would not see extensive combat against Confederates in Nebraska, but there was an upsurge of clashes with Native Americans.

In August 1864, Cheyenne launched several raids along the Overland Trail. Ranches along the Little Blue River were attacked. Wagons were attacked. At Elk Creek on August 16, a column of soldiers from Fort Kearny was attacked by Cheyenne and forced to make a hasty escape.

Fighting continued in 1865. In early February, US troops under Colonel William O. Collins clashed with a group of Cheyenne, Lakota Sioux, and Arapaho in the Battle of Mud Springs. It wasn't a big victory for either side, and casualties were light. Collins subsequently pursued his enemy and engaged them again a few days later in the Battle of Rush Creek. After another inconclusive encounter, Collins broke off his pursuit.

In 1867, Nebraska became the thirty-seventh state.

In 1873, Sioux attacked Pawnee in the Massacre Canyon Battle.

And in 1876, during the turmoil after Custer's defeat at the Battle of Little Bighorn, a party of Cheyenne skirmished with US troops in the Battle of Warbonnet Creek. During the action, Buffalo Bill Cody killed and scalped a Cheyenne warrior called Yellow Hair.

Nebraska was to see one last military invasion. In World War II, it was attacked by Fu-Go, Japanese balloon bombs. A plaque on a wall in the Dundee neighborhood of Omaha records the aerial explosion of a Japanese balloon-delivered incendiary device on April 18, 1945. Johnny Carson, who attended the University of Nebraska, served in the US Navy during World War II.


## NEBRASKA
## MILITARY HISTORY SITES

### Andrew Jackson Higgins National Memorial
Location: 2001 Higgins Drive, West Pawnee Park, Columbus, NE 68601
Web: www.higginsmemorial.com

# America Invaded: NEBRASKA

Nickname: Cornhusker State
Statehood: 1867
Capital: Lincoln

**FORT KEARNY STAMP**
Source: iStock/clu

**Civil War Veterans Museum**
Location: 910 First Corso, Nebraska City, NE 68410
Web: www.civilwarmuseumnc.org

**Durham Museum**
Location: 801 South 10th Street, Omaha, NE 68108
Web: www.durhammuseum.org

**Fort Kearney**
Location: 1020 V Road, Kearney, NE 68845
Web: www.nps.gov/oreg/planyourvisit/site4.htm

**Fort Omaha**
Location: 5730 North 30th Street, Omaha, NE 68111
Web: www.omahahistory.org/fort_omaha.htm

**Fu-Go Bomb Plaque**
Location: 50th and Underwood, Omaha, NE 68132
Web: www.wwiiomaha.com/dundee/april.html#

**Heartland Museum of Military Vehicles**
Location: 606 Heartland Road, Lexington, NE 68850
Web: www.heartlandmuseum.com/index.php

**Homestead National Monument of America**
Location: 8523 West State Highway 4, Beatrice, NE 68310
Web: www.nps.gov/home/index.htm

**Sallows Military Museum**
Location: 1101 Niobrara Avenue, Alliance, NE 69301
Web: www.sallowsmilitarymuseum.com

**Strategic Air Command & Aerospace Museum**
Location: 28210 West Park Highway, Ashland, NE 68003
Web: www.sacmuseum.org

# NEVADA

Nevada, though known as the Battle Born State, has been the site of relatively little fighting compared to many other American states.

Father Francisco Garcés was the first European to see Nevada. He was killed in California in 1781 by Native Americans during the Yuma uprising. Nevada at first was part of New Spain, but when Mexico gained its independence from Spain in 1821, Nevada became part of Alta California.

American victory in the Mexican-American War led to the Treaty of Guadalupe Hidalgo, which made Nevada an American territory in 1848.

In 1860, the Paiute War was fought in the Nevada territory between settlers aided by US Army units and several Indian tribes. The Paiutes were responding to encroachments on their land by miners and the American settlers. At the First Battle of Pyramid Lake on May 12, 1860, a group of Paiute warriors nearly wiped out a force of Nevada militia and vigilantes and killed its leader William Ormsby—the founder of Carson City. In the Second Battle of Pyramid Lake, fought in June 1860, militia and American regulars defeated the Paiute, ending the war.

Nevada was admitted to the Union in the fall of 1864 (hence the nickname *Battle Born State*) in order to participate in the election of that year and assure Abraham Lincoln an additional three electoral votes. The entire state constitution was telegraphed at great expense in order to make the looming deadline. One thousand two hundred Nevadans would fight with Union forces in the Civil War, and $400 million worth of silver from the Comstock Lode helped pay for the Union war effort. Nevada is also, of course, known as the Silver State.

The town of Reno was named in honor of Jesse L. Reno, a Virginian who served in the Union Army. Reno was killed by friendly fire at the Battle of South Mountain in Maryland in 1862.

The so-called Snake War of 1864–1868 took place in northern Nevada.

Nevada would see one last battle—the Battle of Kelley Creek, also known as the Last Massacre. In 1911, in the mountains of Nevada, a small group of Shoshone, led by a man known as Shoshone Mike, clashed over cattle with ranchers. The Shoshone had butchered some cattle for food. When four cattlemen investigated the rustling, the Shoshone killed them. A posse pursued the Shoshone through the winter snow. After a two-hundred-mile pursuit, the Shoshone were surrounded at Kelley Creek. Shoshone Mike put on his war bonnet. The incident lasted three hours and left one of the pursuers dead and one wounded. Eight of the Shoshone, including Shoshone Mike, were killed and the rest captured. This skirmish in Nevada marked the end of the era of fighting between Native Americans and Americans.

Nevada's wide open spaces and attractive climate made it an ideal location for military bases. Ellis Air Force Base near Las Vegas, for example, was named in honor of Lieutenant William Ellis, a US fighter ace who was killed during the Battle of the Bulge. Churchill Flight Strip, built by the US Army Air Force in 1942, is known as Silver Springs Airport today.

The battleship *Nevada* was a dreadnought-class ship that served in both world wars. She was present at Pearl Harbor on December 7, 1941, when she was struck by one torpedo and several bombs. The ship was beached and later repaired, serving until 1946.

In June of 1945, a rancher near Yerington (not far from Reno) reported the arrival of a strange silk balloon on his property the previous November, making it one of the first Japanese Fu-Go to strike the continental United States. At least seven Japanese balloon bombs were reported to have landed in Nevada during the war.

## NEVADA
## MILITARY HISTORY SITES

### Battlefield Vegas
Location: 2771 Sammy Davis Junior Drive, Las Vegas, NV 89109
Web: www.battlefieldvegas.com

### Bonnie Springs Ranch
Location: 16395 Bonnie Springs Road, Las Vegas, NV 89124
Web: bonniesprings.com

### Comstock Gold Mill
Location: F Street, By Virginia City Arena and Fairgrounds, Virginia City, NV 89440
Web: www.visitvirginiacitynv.com/attractions/virginia-city-museums/ list-of-museums.html#comstock

### Fort Churchill State Historic Park
Location: 10000 Highway 95A, Silver Springs, NV 89429
Web: parks.nv.gov/parks/fort-churchill

### Hawthorne Ordnance Museum
Location: 925 East Street, Hawthorne, NV 89415
Web: www.hawthorneordnancemuseum.com

### Mackay Mansion Museum
Location: 291 South D Street, Virginia City, NV 89440
Web: www.uniquitiesmackaymansion.com

### National Atomic Testing Museum
Location: 755 East Flamingo Road, Las Vegas, NV 89119
Web: www.nationalatomictestingmuseum.org

**Nevada State Capitol Building**
Location: 101 North Carson Street, Carson City, NV 89701
Web: www.nps.gov/nr/travel/nevada/nev.htm

**Old Las Vegas Mormon Fort**
Location: 500 East Washington Avenue, Las Vegas, NV 89101
Web:parks.nv.gov/parks/old-las-vegas-mormon-fort

**United States Air Force Thunderbirds**
Location: 4445 Tyndall Avenue, Nellis Air Force Base, NV 89191
Web: www.afthunderbirds.com/site

# America Invaded: NEVADA

Nickname: Battle Born State/Silver State
Statehood: 1864
Capital: Carson City

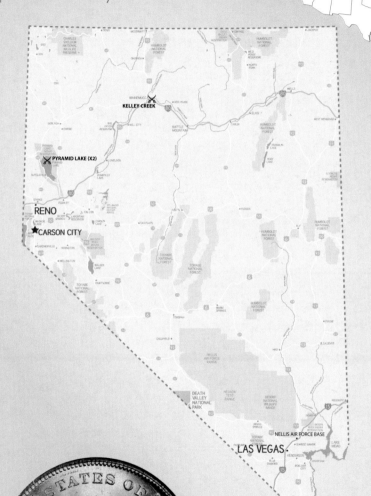

**CARSON CITY SILVER DOLLAR**
Source: Stack's Bowers Galleries

# NEW HAMPSHIRE

Europeian explorers doubtlessly cruised off the short coastline of New Hampshire. It is conceivable the Vikings reached this far south, and certainly expeditions like that of Italian Giovanni da Verrazano's were exploring the area in the sixteenth century. Basque fishermen likely caught cod off the New Hampshire coast in the fifteenth century. But it was in the early seventeenth century that English settlers started living permanently in the coastal regions.

In the 1620s, operating under a grant of land from the English crown, John Mason started settling territory near the mouth of the Piscataqua River with a view, among other things, to exploit fishing opportunities in the region. The area became known as New Hampshire, with a port at Portsmouth, just as Hampshire in Britain has a port at Portsmouth.

At the time, the dominant local power in what is now central and southern New Hampshire was the Pennacook people. Their leader, Passaconaway, seems to have decided to offer no armed resistance to the expansion of English settlement in his territory.

However, violence would find the Pennacook. In 1670, Mohawks attacked them. In 1675, King Philip's War broke out. Although the main fighting would be elsewhere, some violence did occur in what is now New Hampshire. The Native American camp at Ossipee was burned. Wanalancet, son of Passaconaway, tried to maintain his father's approach. He remained neutral despite English forces burning the settlement at Penacook when they found it abandoned. After the English and local allies gained victory in King Philip's War, Wanalancet and many of the Pennacook headed north toward Canada, leaving the path clear for further expansion of English control.

In 1697, during King William's War, a Massachusetts woman named Hannah Duston was captured by Abenaki Indians and brought north into New Hampshire. In the dead of night, while near Penacook, she turned on her sleeping abductors and killed and scalped ten of them, including several children. Her actions made her a New England folk legend, and a statue of Duston can be found in Penacook today. Nathaniel Hawthorne would later describe her as a "raging tigress."

In 1741, Benning Wentworth became the governor of the province of New Hampshire, paving the way for its separation from Massachusetts.

This expansion, though, would lead to a bitter dispute with New York over the territory that would later become Vermont; and, more seriously and violently, repeated clashes both with the French and their Native American allies.

But before all that, all of New Hampshire was thrown into turmoil by Gove's Rebellion. Well, not exactly. By 1683, Governor Cranfield had made himself unpopular for a number of reasons, including taxation. In January of that year, Edward Gove of Hampton decided to do something about it. He rode to Exeter, raised a few armed followers, and returned to Hampton, where they were all promptly arrested. The "rebellion" was over. Gove was sentenced to death for treason, but after three years in prison in the Tower of London, he was set free by King James II.

But more serious events were soon to hit New Hampshire. In June 1689, some of the Penacook returned for revenge. Native women asked to sleep by settlers' fires along the Cocheco River in Dover, then in the night they opened the doors of the settlers' homes to native warriors. Twenty-three colonists were killed and twenty-nine captured. Thus began King William's War of 1689–97, which saw the Eastern Indians ally themselves with the French against the English and their Iroquois allies. Further raids on the colonists followed. Oyster River was attacked by Villieu and a force of Abenaki fighters; and later in the war, Portsmouth suffered repeated attacks.

Queen Anne's War of 1702–1713 saw raids by France's Native American allies into New Hampshire. This time, the defenders had a better grasp of how to intercept the raiders, but some still got through. For instance, in

1703, Hampton was hit; and then in 1704, a force of Penacook and Abenaki attacked Dover.

During Father Rale's War of 1722–1725, colonist forces went on scalping raids in New Hampshire. Captain John Lovewell led his first such raid into New Hampshire's White Mountains in December 1724. In February 1725, he led another raid, launching an attack on an encampment around what is now Wakefield. On his last raid, Lovewell constructed a fort at Ossipee and then led his men into Maine to attack the Pequawket. This time, however, Lovewell and a number of his men were killed in an ambush.

King George's War raged from 1744–1748. Once again, the French and their local allies launched raids southward, and again New Hampshire men took part in ranger operations. John Lovewell's son and at least two of the men who escaped the ambush that killed Lovewell served in the New Hampshire Rangers in this war. In 1747, the Fort at No. 4, at what is now Charlestown, held out against an attack by French and Abenaki forces.

The French and Indian War of 1754–1763 brought a threat yet again from the French and their Native American allies. And once again, the Fort at No. 4 along the Connecticut River (now the border between New Hampshire and Vermont) stood guard against raiders; and once again, New Hampshire men served with distinction, for instance, in the New Hampshire Provincial Regiment. This time, however, decisive British victory would change the face of North America forever, as France lost all its territory north of the Caribbean— except for the not exactly huge Saint Pierre and Miquelon.

The Pine Tree Riot erupted with the woodsmen of New Hampshire in 1772, after the British made it illegal to harvest pine trees in order to preserve them for use by the Royal Navy.

In contrast to its somewhat hectic military history before 1776, after 1776, New Hampshire had peaceful years ahead of it. It would send soldiers and munitions to fight elsewhere, but it would never again be the location of extensive military combat, as it had been in the past.

No battles took place in New Hampshire during the War of Independence. New Hampshire was largely supportive of the Revolution, and British forces would eventually abandon it to concentrate on other areas. The most significant action that took place was, however, to have a substantial impact on the course of the Revolution and of American history. On December 14, 1774, a crowd of locals led by John Langdon rushed Fort William and Mary in New Castle, overwhelming its six defenders and stealing gunpowder. Then, on the night of December 15, more Americans, this time led by John Sullivan, stormed the fort again. This time they took weapons and supplies, including sixteen cannon. After the war, Fort William and Mary was renamed Fort Constitution.

John Stark, the Patriot hero of the Battle of Bennington (fought in New York, commemorated in Vermont), wrote in 1809 a famous missive to those who sought to commemorate his victory. He ended his note with a postscript: "I will give you my volunteer toast—Live free or die: Death is not the worst of evils." New Hampshire adopted the immortal words of the Londonderry native as the state's motto.

New Hampshire did not play the biggest part in the history of the War of 1812. There was plenty of opposition to the war in the area. Militia occasionally turned out to defend Portsmouth from a British invasion that never came, and privateers from Portsmouth had both victories and losses against British targets at sea.

In 1832, though, part of what is now New Hampshire was taken over by a different country (well, sort of) that almost led to war (well, sort of). In that year, the Republic of Indian Stream was declared on territory that was claimed by both Canada and New Hampshire after some locals, not surprisingly, got tired of paying taxes to both. In 1836, a dispute over an unpaid bill led to New Hampshire sending in militiamen. Britain was not at all happy, and the dispute could have escalated. Fortunately, both sides took measures to avoid that happening, and an 1842 agreement between the two sides eventually allotted the territory to New Hampshire.

In the Civil War, New Hampshire again sent many men (including the famous 5th New Hampshire Volunteer Infantry) and plenty of munitions to the fight, but the fighting itself was elsewhere.

At the end of World War I, a captured German U-boat was transported to Portsmouth and analyzed.

And the Second World War brought more enemies to the coast of New Hampshire. U-boats operated there during the war, and countermeasures included an antisubmarine net to keep the enemy out of the Portsmouth port, and lines of mines and another net that guarded the main route into the Piscataqua River.

Even with the end of the war in Europe, it wasn't quite all over in New

Hampshire. In all, nine surrendered U-boats ended up at Portsmouth. On May 15, 1945, a week after the end of the war, surrendering *U-805* was towed into Portsmouth Harbor. Shortly after, *U-873* was brought in, and then *U-1228*. And then, on May 19, came an even more major prize: *U-234*, which had been on its way to Japan with a secret cargo.

As Nazi Germany died, the *U-234* had been sent on a desperate mission to transfer Nazi technological advances and knowledge to Japan to boost the war effort there. Two Japanese scientists who had been on board had already committed suicide. Two German scientists and three Luftwaffe generals were on board, and among the cargo were radar parts, a disassembled Messerschmitt Me 262 jet fighter, and over a thousand pounds of uranium oxide.

Assorted sites in New Hampshire played a key role in the Cold War, including Pease Air Force Base, home at one stage of B-47 Stratojet bombers of Strategic Air Command.

## NEW HAMPSHIRE
## MILITARY HISTORY SITES

### American Independence Museum
Location: 1 Governors Lane, Exeter, NH 3833
Web: www.independencemuseum.org

### Aviation Museum of New Hampshire
Location: 27 Navigator Road, Londonderry, NH 03053
Web: www.nhahs.org

### Fort Constitution Historic Site
Location: Off NH Route 1B at US Coast Guard Station, 25 Wentworth Road, New Castle, NH 03854
Web: www.nhstateparks.org/visit/historic-sites/fort-constitution-state-historic-site.aspx

**Fort Stark State Historic Site**
Location: 211 Wild Rose Lane, New Castle, NH 03854
Web: www.nhstateparks.org/visit/Historic-Sites/fort-stark-state-historic-site.aspx

**Franklin Pierce Homestead**
Location: 301 2nd NH Turnpike, Hillsborough, NH 03244
Web: www.nps.gov/nr/travel/presidents/franklin_pierce_homestead.html

**Hannah Duston Memorial State Historic Site**
Location: 298 US 4, Boscawen, NH 03303
Web: www.nhstateparks.org/visit/Historic-Sites/hannah-duston-memorial-state-historic-site.aspx

**John Paul Jones House**
Location: 43 Middle Street, Portsmouth, NH 03801
Web: www.portsmouthhistory.org/john-paul-jones-house/

**The Fort at No. 4**
Location: 267 Springfield Road, Charlestown, NH 03603
Web: www.fortat4.org/

**USS *Albacore* Museum**
Location: 600 Market Street, Portsmouth, NH 03801
Web: www.ussalbacore.org

**Wright Museum of World War II**
Location: 77 Center Street, Wolfeboro, NH 03894
Web: wrightmuseum.org/index.html

Nickname: The Granite State
Statehood: 1788
Capital: Concord

PITTSBURG

COLEBROOK

ERROLL

NORTH STRATFORD

WHITE MOUNTAIN NATIONAL FOREST

LANCASTER · BERLIN

MOORE RESERVOIR

GORHAM

LITTLETON

WHITE MOUNTAIN NATIONAL FOREST

WOODSVILLE · GLEN

LINCOLN

WHITE MOUNTAIN NATIONAL FOREST

CONWAY

WENTWORTH

MOULTONBORO

PLYMOUTH

LEBANON

**OSSIPEE** · **FORT OSSIPEE**

LAKE WINNIPESAUKEE

**WAKEFIELD**

LACONIA

DANBURY

ALTON

SUNAPEE LAKE

CLAREMONT

**PENACOOK**

**ROCHESTER** ·

CHARLESTOWN

HENNIKER

CONCORD

**DOVER** ·

**FORT AT NO. 4**

MARLOW

**MANCHESTER** · **PORTSMOUTH**

**FORT WILLIAM AND MARY/ CONSTITUTION**

KEENE

DERRY

PETERBOROUGH

WINCHESTER · **NASHUA**

**HANNAH DUSTON**
1657-1736
Statue, Penacook
Source: Tom Winmill

**JOHN STARK**
1728-1822
Statue, Bennington, VT
Source: Author photo

**HANNAH DUSTON PLAQUE**
Penacook
Source: Tom Winmill

HANNAH DUSTIN
1657-1737
Famous symbol of frontier heroism. A victim of an Indian raid in 1697, on Haverhill, Massachusetts, whence she had been taken to a camp site on the nearby island in the river. After killing and later scalping ten Indians, she and the two other captives, Mary Neff and Samuel Lennardson, escaped down the river to safety.

# NEW JERSEY

t seems entirely appropriate that an Italian was one of the first Europeans to "invade" New Jersey. In 1525, Italian explorer Giovanni de Verrazano anchored off Sandy Hook during his cruise along North America's east coast.

Conflicts had already taken place in what is now New Jersey prior to the arrival of Europeans. Lenape/Delaware legends tell of wars with the Iroquois in that period; and in 1633, David de Vries wrote that Native American refugees reported the Susquehannock killing about ninety Sankhikans.

The situation would turn pretty violent pretty quickly when Europeans attempted to land. In 1609, Henry Hudson, English but working at that time on behalf of the Dutch, sailed in with an expedition and began exploring the area. Near what is now Keansburg, he sent in a small boat with five men to have a look at the region around Kill Van Kull and Newark Bay. Two canoes with Native Americans on board attacked the boat, hitting an Englishman called John Colman in the throat with an arrow and killing him. He was buried on land that became known as Coleman's Point.

Henry Hudson went on to what became New Amsterdam before eventually becoming New York.

The Dutch exploration of the area continued, and they soon attempted to establish settlements. Fort Wilhelmus was set up. Captain Cornelius Jacobsen May established Fort Nassau on Big Timber Creek in what is now Gloucester County. The process was not, however, always a success, from the Dutch point of view. In the winter of 1630–31, David de Vries found Fort Nassau in ruins, abandoned by Europeans. In 1635, English settlers from the Virginia Colony seized the fort, though the Dutch eventually expelled them. Meanwhile, to the south, Swedish and Finnish and some Dutch colonists were establishing the colony of New Sweden, which included part of what is now southwestern New Jersey.

In 1643, a series of misunderstandings between settlers and Native Americans, and actions by the director of New Netherland, Willem Kieft, led to Kieft's War. Brutal actions like the Pavonia Massacre, in which Dutch soldiers killed men, women, and children at Communipaw, united the tribes against New Netherland. Fighting dragged on until 1645, when a truce was finally agreed. Kieft was removed and replaced by Peter Stuyvesant.

But more trouble was coming. In 1654, the forces of New Sweden and New Netherland clashed. At first, New Sweden had the upper hand, but in 1655, a squadron of Dutch ships took control of New Sweden. The fighting was not over, though. The Susquehannock had been trading partners with New Sweden, and they weren't happy about the arrival of new Dutch authorities. They weren't happy at all. The so-called Peach Tree War (a reference to a dispute over a stolen peach) erupted. The Susquehannock attacked New Netherland, taking hostages. Stuyvesant was forced to ransom the hostages, renegotiate Dutch land rights in the area, and refortify the region with new block houses.

However, it was neither the Dutch nor the Swedish who would become the dominant colonial power in the region. In 1664, during the Second Anglo-Dutch War, British forces seized control of New Netherland. And so New Jersey acquired its new name, from the island of Jersey in the English Channel.

To the north of New Jersey, bitter fighting would drag on for much of the eighteenth century, as Britain and France competed for control. Occasionally, Native American allies of the French would make raids into the northwestern border region of the colony. During the French and Indian War, a defensive line consisting of a string of blockhouses linked by the Military Road was organized in order to counter such raids.

But New Jersey itself had another enemy rather closer to home—New York.

Disputes over the border between New Jersey and New York led to the New York-New Jersey Line War, which dragged on for much of the eighteenth century, with occasional violence erupting. It wasn't that much of a real war, of course. Finally, in 1769, the British appointed commissioners to determine the border officially, and both states accepted the agreed-upon line just before another war broke out. A war in which New Jersey would become the Crossroads of the Revolution.

Support for the American Revolution in New Jersey was by no means unanimous. In fact, plenty there actively opposed it. The New Jersey Volunteers were a Loyalist unit led by Attorney General Cortlandt Skinner. In the end, more battles of the American Revolution would be fought in New Jersey (over one hundred, plus other minor clashes) than in any other state; and some of the key actions of the war took place in New Jersey. William Franklin, Benjamin's illegitimate son, became the Loyalist governor of the state, permanently estranging father and son.

In particular, New Jersey was the site of a number of important battles in late 1776 and early 1777 that came after a series of reversals for American forces.

On the night of December 25–26, Washington led the Continental Army across the Delaware River and crushed a surprised Hessian force in the Battle of Trenton. Legend suggests that that the Hessians had been overcelebrating the Christmas season the night before. A further British defeat followed in the second battle of Trenton on January 2; and on January 3, Washington once again surprised British forces and defeated them at the Battle of Princeton. The defeats forced British to withdraw from most of New Jersey and gave a significant boost to the morale of the Revolutionary forces.

Further significant engagements in New Jersey were to follow, including the Battle of Monmouth on June 28, 1777. That engagement was fought in sweltering heat and produced the legend of Molly Pitcher, taking the place of her injured husband in a gun crew. Recent scholarship suggests that Pitcher may have been based on a composite of several women who were Patriot camp followers.[6]

As the war approached its last stages, the British made two attempts to invade New Jersey. On June 7, 1780, British forces under Lieutenant General Wilhelm von Knyphausen, which had crossed by ferry from Staten Island to Elizabeth, New Jersey, withdrew after being frustrated in their advance at the Battle of Connecticut Farms. On June 23, a second invasion attempt by Knyphausen was once again frustrated at the Battle of Springfield. The surrender by British General Cornwallis at Yorktown followed in October 1781, and the war came to an end in 1783.

The Revolutionary War alliance between the Americans and the French would not last. The slightly strange quasi war that developed between the United

---

6    Michael Stephenson, *Patriot Battles: How the War of Independence Was Fought* (New York: Harper Perennial, 2007), 179.

States and France in the late eighteenth century saw a number of actions off the US coast, including the capture, by the US Navy sloop *Delaware*, of the French privateer *La Croyable*. *La Croyable* was renamed the *Retaliation*, and the French then promptly retaliated and retook the vessel.

New Jersey was divided over the declaration of the War of 1812, and the state wasn't exactly the main focus of the fighting. Still, New Jersey troops took park in combat beyond the state's borders, and British forces did carry out some operations in and around New Jersey. For example, British raiders entered Barnegat Inlet and also seized some coastal trading vessels.

That was much pretty much the end of combat in New Jersey. The state would play a crucial role in the Civil War, not as a host to battles, but in providing manpower and supplies for the Union side. New Jersey would send munitions and people (including General Norman Schwarzkopf, born in Trenton) to other wars, but the fighting would be elsewhere.

In 1872, construction began on Fort Mott to protect against invasions that never materialized. Today it is a state park.

War did come close to New Jersey again in the twentieth century. In both world wars, German U-boats operated off the New Jersey coast; and in 1997, the wreck of one of them lying in the waters off New Jersey was identified as *U-869*.

Today the battleship *New Jersey,* a veteran of World War II, Korea, and Vietnam, lies docked in Camden, not far from the Phildelphia naval shipyard she was launched from in 1942.

## NEW JERSEY
## MILITARY HISTORY SITES

### Air Victory Museum
Location: 68 Stacy Haines Road, Lumberton, NJ 08048
Web: www.airvictorymuseum.com

### Aviation Hall of Fame & Museum of New Jersey
Location: Teterboro Airport, 400 Fred Wehran Drive, Teterboro, NJ 07608
Web: www.njahof.org

# America Invaded: **NEW JERSEY**

Nickname: The Garden State
Statehood: 1787
Capital: Trenton

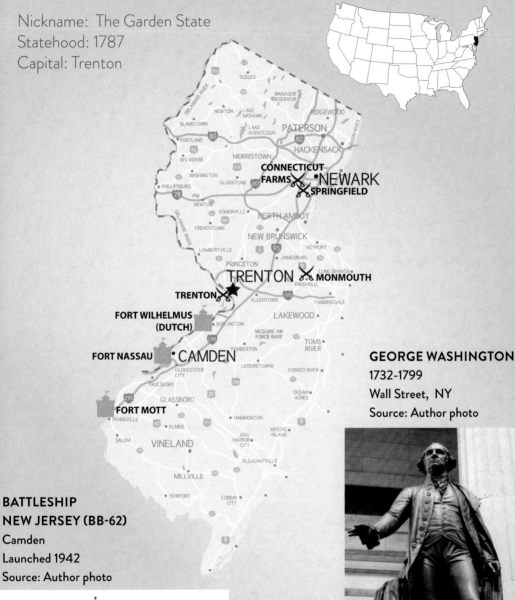

**GEORGE WASHINGTON**
1732-1799
Wall Street, NY
Source: Author photo

**BATTLESHIP
NEW JERSEY (BB-62)**
Camden
Launched 1942
Source: Author photo

**Battleship *New Jersey* Museum and Memorial**
Location: 62 Battleship Place, Camden, NJ 08103
Web: www.battleshipnewjersey.org

**Empty Sky—9/11 Memorial**
Location: Liberty State Park, 1 Audrey Zapp Drive, Jersey City, NJ 07305
Web: nj911memorial.org/empty-sky

**Fort Dix Army Reserve Mobilization Museum**
Location: United Communities, 6501 Pennsylvania Avenue, Fort Dix, NJ 08640
Web: www.dix.army.mil/Services/TMD/Museum.aspx

**Fort Mott State Park**
Location: 454 Fort Mott Road, Pennsville, NJ 08070
Web: www.state.nj.us/dep/parksandforests/parks/fortmott.html

**Monmouth Battlefield State Park**
Location: 16 Business Route 33, Manalapan, NJ 07726
Web: www.state.nj.us/dep/parksandforests/parks/monbat.html

**Old Barracks Museum**
Location: 101 Barrack Street, Trenton, NJ 08608
Web: www.barracks.org

**Princeton Battlefield State Park**
Location: 500 Mercer Road, Princeton, NJ 08540
Web: www.state.nj.us/dep/parksandforests/parks/princeton.html

**Trenton Battle Monument**
Location: 348 North Warren Street, Trenton, NJ 08638
Web: www.state.nj.us/dep/parksandforests/historic/Trentonbattlemonument/index.htm

# NEW MEXICO

New Mexico is a mostly arid and sparsely populated state of great natural beauty. Native Americans have a long history in the area, having established a thriving Pueblo culture. The construction of many of the pueblos, on high, defensible mesas with adobe stone, suggests that warfare was commonplace long before the arrival of the first Europeans.

In 1540, the Spanish conquistador Francisco Vázquez de Coronado sought the fabled seven cities of gold in New Mexico. A war of conquest, the Tiguex War, was fought to subdue the Native American people. The Spanish conquistadors defeated the Zuni at the Battle of Hawikuh.

Further Spanish expeditions would eventually follow after Coronado into New Mexico. The Chamuscado and Rodriguez expedition of 1580–81 may have achieved little in itself, but it was part of the process leading to more sustained Spanish interest in the area.

The Nuevo México Province of Spain was officially declared in 1592 by Philip II of Spain. Philip II, though known as Philip the Prudent, also launched the disastrous attack on England by the Spanish Armada.

In 1598, Juan de Oñate led an expedition of five hundred people and seven thousand head of livestock north into New Mexico. Founding the settlement of San Juan, Oñate began expanding Spanish power across the region. In 1599, after a battle with the Acoma people in which fifteen of his men died, Oñate's forces killed eight hundred Native Americans, enslaved hundreds more, and severed the left foot of all the men over twenty-five still alive.

Santa Fe, founded in 1610, became the capital of Nuevo México.

The Pueblos resented the imposition of Catholicism and the destruction of their native cultures and traditions. They also were angered by the inability of Spanish authorities to protect them from other marauding Indian tribes, such as the Apache. Resistance to the Spanish conquerors simmered until the Pueblo revolt of 1680, which killed four hundred Spanish and drove them from the region for twelve years. In 1692, however, Diego de Vargas launched a largely bloodless reconquest of New Mexico.

It was not, though, the end of resistance. In 1696, a second Pueblo revolt erupted. This time, however, the Spanish authorities quickly crushed it.

The Spanish introduced more than just Catholicism to the Native American people. They also brought horses to the New World. Around 1,500 horses were part of Coronado's sixteenth-century invasion of New Mexico. The horse proved particularly well-suited to the arid plains of New Mexico and Texas. By 1700, all Plains tribes had horses. The nomadic Comanche tribe swiftly adapted, its warriors becoming some of the greatest cavalrymen in military history. Their remarkable horsemanship gave the Comanche the ability to range across Texas, Colorado, Kansas, and New Mexico. By 1706, there were reports of Comanche raids on Taos Pueblo in New Mexico. Similarly, the Apache became proficient horsemen and were raiding Spanish and Pueblo settlements in New Mexico by the 1650s.

The Spaniards built presidios and garrisoned them with soldiers. They also built missions. Around 1706, the Spaniards noticed that Apache raids were diminishing. They did not seem to realize that the wide-ranging Comanche were obliterating the Apache nation. And the war between the Spanish and Comanche was just beginning. The year 1746 featured another major Comanche attack on Taos Pueblo. Horses were like currency to the Comanche, and many more horse-stealing raids would follow.

Don Juan Bautista de Anza, governor of Nuevo México from 1777 to 1787, took a divide-and-conquer approach to the conflicts with the Native Americans. He made peace with the Comanche and Ute tribes, and even recruited them to fight with the Spanish against the Navajo. Santa Fe became a major trade center, where Europeans and indigenous people could gather securely to trade horses and other goods. Inevitably, the two groups intermarried, forming a mestizo (or mixed) culture in New Mexico.

In 1807, the United States began to take a more serious interest in the area. Zebulon Montgomery Pike's expedition advanced into New Mexico—where its members were promptly arrested by the Spanish authorities.

New Spain was succeeded by Mexico after Mexico gained its independence in 1821. The Santa Fe Trail was established in 1822 to facilitate travel and trade through the region, and that led to more contacts between Americans and Mexicans.

In 1837, the Chimayó Rebellion against Governor Pérez led to his death and decapitation. However, a counterrevolution eventually crushed the rebels.

Mirabeau Lamar, the president of Texas, authorized the Texan Santa Fe Expedition in 1841. This Texas "invasion" of New Mexico was aimed at gaining control over the Santa Fe Trail. The expedition was a dismal failure, and its members were captured, force marched to Mexico City, and eventually returned via ship to New Orleans.

In 1844, James K. Polk, a Jacksonian Democrat, was elected president of the United States. Polk's expansionist vision reflected the views of a political party made up largely of land-hungry famers. On April 27, 1846, hostilities in the Mexican-American War began.

General Stephen Kearny, a veteran of the War of 1812, led an invasion from Fort Leavenworth, Kansas, along the Sante Fe Trail into New Mexico with 1,700 soldiers. Santa Fe was occupied on August 18, 1846. The Mexican governor of New Mexico, Manuel Armijo, initially issued a call to arms, but subsequently ordered the state's defenders to go back to their homes. He established a provisional government for New Mexico.

In early 1847, the Taos Rebellion erupted as Spanish and Pueblo allies resisted the American occupation forces in northern New Mexico. The rebellion, however, was swiftly put down.

The Treaty of Guadalupe Hidalgo in 1848 ended the Mexican-American War and ceded New Mexico to the United States.

The proud empire of the Comanche, Comancheria, which dominated much of New Mexico, was decimated in the 1850s and 1860s by smallpox and the hunting to extinction of the buffalo that sustained them.

During the American Civil War, the Confederates hoped to spread Confederate power west from Texas into the New Mexico territory. In 1862, Louisianan Henry Hopkins Sibley, the inventor of the Sibley tent, launched an invasion of New Mexico from Texas. Sibley hoped to capture Fort Craig, which was commanded by Union General Edward Canby, who might have been Sibley's brother-in-law. On February 21–22, 1862, Sibley and his Texas cavalrymen won the Battle of Valverde against a larger Union army, but Sibley abandoned his attempt to capture Fort Craig. He sought instead to capture Albuquerque and Santa Fe before proceeding to California. Sibley's luck ran out on March 26–28, 1862, at the battle of Glorieta Pass. Casualties were roughly even, with just over a hundred killed on both sides. General Canby defeated Confederate forces at Peralta in April, forcing Sibley to withdraw all the way back to San Antonio. It was the final Confederate foray into New Mexico.

Tensions between settlers and the US military on one side, and some groups of Native Americans on the other side, flared up occasionally in the decades after the United States took control of New Mexico.

The Apache-American conflict, which included figures like Geronimo and Cochise, would on occasion spill over into New Mexico.

In 1864, the US military carried out an act of mass expulsion of Native Americans, which led to the tragedy of the Navajo Long Walk.

It's also worth briefly mentioning the Lincoln County War of 1878, a range war that saw two factions battle it out over dry goods and cattle interests. It's largely known these days for the involvement of Billy the Kid.

New Mexico was admitted to the Union as the forty-seventh state in 1912.

It had not, however, seen its last invasion. Violence was not unknown along the border between New Mexico and Mexico, and in March 1916, Pancho Villa launched a cross-border attack on Columbus, New Mexico. He seized supplies and burned the town. In retaliation, President Wilson sent a US force into Mexico to find and capture Villa. It failed to do so.

World War II would transform New Mexico, while weapons developed and tested in New Mexico would transform our world. The sparse population of much of New Mexico made it the ideal location for sites such as the Alamogordo Bombing and Gunnery Range, which was established in December 1941.

In 1943, General Leslie Groves set up a bomb laboratory on a remote mesa in Los Alamos. The first atomic bomb, code-named Trinity, was tested on July 16, 1945, near Socorro, ushering in the atomic age. The device yielded the equivalent of twenty kilotons of TNT. After a bright flash, a mushroom cloud leaped up over the New Mexican desert. Some like Robert Oppenheimer waxed poetic, but Kenneth Bainbridge, the physicist who planned the test, simply remarked, "Now we are all sons of bitches."

The Battleship *New Mexico* was present in Tokyo Bay on September 2, 1945, when the final surrender documents ending World War II were signed.

## NEW MEXICO
## MILITARY HISTORY SITES

### Coronado Historic Site
Location: 485 Kuana Road, Bernalillo, NM 87004
Web: www.nmhistoricsites.org/coronado

### Fort Stanton
Location: 104 Kit Carson Road, Fort Stanton, NM 88323
Web: www.fortstanton.org

### Fort Union National Monument
Location: NM 161, Fort Union, Watrous, NM 87753
Web: www.nps.gov/foun/index.htm

### Indian Pueblo Cultural Center
Location: 2401 12th Street NW, Albuquerque, NM 87104
Web: www.indianpueblo.org

### Kit Carson Home & Museum
Location: 113 Kit Carson Road, Taos, NM 87571
Web: www.kitcarsonmuseum.org

### Pecos National Historic Park
Location: 1 Peach Drive, Pecos, NM 87552
Web: www.nps.gov/peco/index.htm

### The National Museum of Nuclear Science & History
Location: 601 Eubank Boulevard SE, Albuquerque, NM 87123
Web: www.nuclearmuseum.org

**Trinity Site**
Location: White Sands Missile Range, State Road 525, Stallion Gate, Al-amogordo, NM 88002
Web: www.wsmr.army.mil/PAO/Trinity/Pages/Home.aspx

**White Sands Missle Range Museum**
Location: Highway 70, Main Post Gate, Alamogordo, NM 88002
Web: www.wsmr-history.org

# America Invaded: NEW MEXICO

Nickname: Land of Enchantment
Statehood: 1912
Capital: Sante Fe

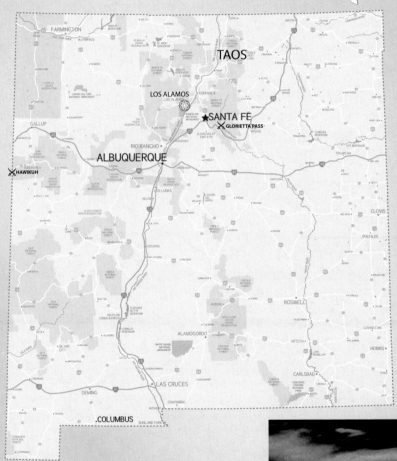

**TRINITY TEST**
July 16, 1945
Source: akg-images

# NEW YORK

The size, wealth, and power of the area known today as New York State have made it a magnet for many invaders and attackers over the course of its history. Its geography makes it particularly vulnerable to invasions. Manhattan, being an island, was the target of many seaborne invasions or attacks, from the Dutch in the seventeenth century to Nazi U-boats in World War II. The unique topography of the Hudson River and Lake Champlain forms a water highway that provides a north-south axis of invasion that has been exploited by many powers.

The wealth that drew the earliest human "invaders," as well as the first Europeans, was New York's bounteous natural environment. The waters around Manhattan were teeming with oysters, which shaped the very landscape of the area. Middens, hills made of discarded oyster shells, were created by the bivalve-loving indigenous peoples of New York. Beavers built their dams in the Mohawk Valley. The governor of New Amsterdam, Adriaen van der Donck, recorded in 1649 the capture of six-foot lobsters! The city of Buffalo seems likely to have gotten its name from the American bison that once ranged through western New York.

The indigenous inhabitants of New York would frequently become caught up in the colonial rivalries between Dutch, French, English, and, finally, American settlers. The many wars they waged amongst themselves prior to the arrival of Europeans are mainly lost to history.

In 1609, Henry Hudson, a Londoner employed by the Dutch East India Company, arrived in what is today New York, seeking a route to the Orient. He did not, of course, find any such thing. Hudson and the crew of the *Half Moon* had mostly peaceful interactions with the Native Americans, but one member of his crew, John Colman, was murdered when an Indian shot an arrow through Colman's neck on September 6, 1609.

Dutch colonizers would follow in Hudson's wake, establishing New Netherlands in 1624. They came in pursuit of the quick profits that could be made from the sale of beaver pelts. Fort Orange was built to protect the early Dutch settlers from the indigenous population. It later became known as Beverwijk and finally, with the arrival of the English, as Albany.

Kiliaen van Rensselaer, my own ancestor (CRK), was a Dutch merchant who purchased vast tracts of land in New York, although he never set foot in the New World. This New York patroon is buried at the Oude Kerk in Amsterdam's red-light district.

Though the Dutch preferred to trade peacefully with the Indians, conflicts did arise. In 1638, Willem Kieft was appointed director by the Dutch West India Company. During his tenure, he reduced the customary annual tribute paid to the indigenous people. The inexperienced Kieft also used the theft of some pigs to start what became known as Kieft's War, which ran from 1643–45. Over a thousand Algonquian people were killed, as well as many Dutch.

The island of Manhattan was famously established by the Dutch not as a conquest, but as a business deal with the native people. Peter Minuit of the Dutch West India Company bought the island of Manhattan for the sum of 60 guilders from the chief of the Carnarsee, though the island was mainly inhabited by Weckquaesgeeks. The Dutch later built a wall along a street to protect Manhattan from the English in Connecticut. Today it is known as Wall Street.

The English invasion of New York began in August 1664, when four British warships led by Richard Nicolls, a subordinate of the Duke of York in the English Civil War, arrived off Manhattan. Peter Stuyvesant, the one-legged director of the Dutch colony, was compelled to surrender. New Amsterdam became New York.

Samuel de Champlain, the French explorer and founder of New France, was the first European to visit the area near the future site of Ticonderoga in the summer of 1609. In late July, Champlain and his Indian allies skirmished with the Iroquois and fired an arquebus loaded with four lead balls. Two Iroquois chieftains fell.

French voyagers and traders settled in New France, north of the British colony of New York. The French built fortifications to prevent encroachment from the more populous British colonies to their south. In 1726, for example, they built Fort Niagara, the heart of which is known today as the French Castle. They also launched occasional raids on British territory.

In the winter of 1690, during the Nine Years' War, a raiding party led by Pierre Le Moyne d'Iberville struck south from New France into New York. The French and their Indian allies came via canoe across Lake Champlain and down the Hudson. Finding Fort Orange (now Albany) too well defended, they pushed on until they reached Schenectady. The town's only guards were two snowmen! A predawn attack on February 9 killed sixty Schenectady residents.

And there was trouble on the home front as well. In England, Catholic King James II was forced from his throne. The next year, in 1689, German-born Jacob Leisler took the opportunity to seize power from Lieutenant Governor Francis Nicholson in New York. Two years later, English soldiers under Major Richard Ingoldesby were ordered to install a new regime to replace Leisler's. Fighting ensued, but Leisler eventually surrendered and was hanged for treason.

There would be plenty of further fighting in the border area as Britain and France continued to compete for colonial dominance in North America.

At the start of the Seven Years' War (known in North America as the French and Indian War) the French, aided by superior generalship, enjoyed some success. Britain would not become dominant in the conflict until late in the war. New York, sharing a long border with New France, saw heavy fighting.

Early in the war, British and Native American forces triumphed over the French at the Battle of Lake George, though that victory did not lead to much. In 1755, the French built Fort Carillon, which later became known as Ticonderoga. This limestone fort gave them a base from which to raid to the south. *Ticonderoga* is an Iroquois word meaning *junction at two waters.*

In 1757, General Montcalm led a force of 1,600 French and Canadian soldiers, along with their Indian allies, and invaded New York, marching south to Lake George. In August, they besieged and sacked Fort William Henry. About fifty prisoners were massacred by the Indians.

On January 21, 1757, the Battle on Snowshoes was fought near Fort Carillon, when an American company of Rangers led by Robert Rogers was ambushed by the French and their Indian allies. Rogers learned from defeat, later writing Rogers Rules of Ranging, which serve even today as a guideline for American Special Forces.

New France had a total population of only 80,000 settlers versus around one and half million in Britain's American colonies. This numerical superiority eventually overwhelmed the defenders of French Canada. Montcalm was killed in 1759 at the siege of Quebec. That same year, the English constructed a new fort at Crown Point. Robert Rogers sortied from Crown Point to launch a punishing raid on the Abenaki village of St. Francis in 1759. That same year, British forces also finally captured Fort Ticonderoga and Fort Niagara.

In 1763, the Treaty of Paris ended the Seven Years' War, with a British annexation of New France that made New York's northern border secure.

The expense of the Seven Years' War had to be paid for, and the British Crown soon started raising taxes on its American colonists, which contributed to the start of the American Revolution.

On May 10, 1775, Ethan Allen and Benedict Arnold captured Fort Ticonderoga in upstate New York. When the British commander asked by whose authority they acted, Arnold thundered, "In the name of the Great Jehovah, and the Continental Congress." Fifty-eight mortar and cannon seized at Ticonderoga would later be dragged by forces led by Henry Knox (a portly Boston bookseller) to Dorchester Heights in Boston, where they would be used to drive the British from that city.

However, the subsequent attempt by the Continental Army to invade north into Quebec was a disastrous failure, and the Fort Ticonderoga area again saw fighting as American forces attempted to resist the advancing British. An American fleet under Benedict Arnold was largely destroyed by British ships in the Battle of Valcour Island.

In June of 1776, a British armada entered lower New York Harbor and began disembarking troops. General William Howe commanded 32,000 men, outnumbering Washington's 19,000 soldiers. A series of engagements were fought, contesting New York. In August, the British landed on Long Island, eventually forcing Washington to evacuate the island. On September 16, the Americans won a sharp engagement at the Battle of Harlem Heights, but soon after Washington was compelled to abandon Manhattan to the British and their Tory supporters. New York, along with New Jersey, was a hotbed of Loyalist support for most of the American Revolution. The King's American

Legion, for example, was made up largely of New Yorkers. At the Battle of White Plains on October 28, American militia were driven from the field, and Continental regulars withdrew from Chatterton's Hill. At the close of 1776, it appeared that New York City had been permanently lost to the British.

The next year, 1777, became known as the year of the hangman due to the similar appearance of the number 7 and a gibbet. This year featured an invasion of New York that was, quite possibly, the most consequential in the area's history. "Gentleman Johnny" Burgoyne, an amateur playwright, led an invading army of over 7,000 troops from Canada that was made up of British, German, Canadian, and Loyalist forces. George III personally ordered the use of Indian forces to supplement his Redcoats, hoping they would terrorize the Americans into submission. British gold subsidized the Native Americans, who were paid an $8 bounty for either live rebel prisoners or their scalps. Burgoyne's aim was to drive south toward British-occupied Manhattan, cutting New England off from the rest of the rebellious colonies.

Burgoyne's complicated plan relied on coordinated British action, with around 1,600 troops led by General St. Leger striking from the St. Lawrence into western New York. Lord Howe, with 16,000 men, would march north from Manhattan to rendezvous with Burgoyne at Albany.

All went well for Burgoyne at first. His forces scouted the crest of Mount Defiance, which looked down upon Fort Ticonderoga. His artilleryman, General Phillips, declared, "Where a goat can go, a man can go; and where a man can go, he can drag a gun." British cannons were dragged to the top of Mount Defiance, and General St. Clair, who commanded around 2,500 outnumbered and outgunned American defenders at Ticonderoga, was compelled to withdraw without a fight. General Phillip Schuyler, St. Clair's superior and the commander of the Northern Department, was subsequently sacked by the Continental Congress and replaced by Horatio Gates. At this point, it seemed America's Founding Fathers truly might be hanged on a gibbet, as Burgoyne and George III intended.

Even before Gates assumed command of the Northern Department, however, the tide began to turn. A reconnaissance into Vermont, led by Lieutenant Colonel Friedrich Baum and his Brunswickers, ended disastrously for the British at the battle of Bennington on August 15. Troops from New Hampshire, led by General John Stark, earned a crucial victory in a battle that was fought in New York but is commemorated today by a large monument in Vermont.

One of the bloodiest battles of the American Revolution was fought in New York on August 6, 1777, when Loyalists and Indians led by Chief Joseph Brant ambushed Colonel Nicholas Herkimer's Tryon County militia at Oriskany. Around 200 Americans and 150 Indians were killed. Oneida Indians fought that day on the Patriot side.

But the most decisive actions of 1777 would be fought in September in the woods near Saratoga. On September 19, Burgoyne's advance toward Albany was halted by American rebels, led by Benedict Arnold and Horatio Gates, at Freeman's Farm on the Hudson River. Burgoyne's forces were repulsed again at Bemis Heights on October 7. Benedict Arnold, under the influence of rum, demonstrated conspicuous courage, and was wounded in the leg that day. Lord Howe, preoccupied with the capture of Philadelphia, had not left Sir Henry Clinton in New York City with enough troops to advance north to Albany. On October 17, 1777, Burgoyne, with many of his troops close to starvation due to their stretched supply lines from Canada, surrendered his army of 5,895. Burgoyne himself was briefly held prisoner at General Schuyler's (another NY ancestor by marriage! [CRK]) mansion in Albany. This decisive American victory was the turning point of the American Revolution, as it gave instant credibility to the rebel movement. Louis XVI's France abandoned its neutrality and joined the war as an American ally directly as a result of the surrender at Saratoga.

Native American forces allied to Britain hit back in the north of New York. In the fall of 1778, Chief Joseph Brant delivered a measure of revenge for Saratoga by leading a massacre at Cherry Valley. This town near Albany had a population of just over three hundred in 1775. On November 11, 1778, fourteen soldiers and thirty civilians were killed by the Iroquois, Among the dead were my ancestors Robert Wells, his wife, and several children, including his teenage daughter Jane (CRK).

As a result, many settlers fled the area, and the Continental Army sent in troops on reprisal operations. In particular, General Sullivan's expedition in 1779 destroyed numerous Native American villages in Pennsylvania and New York.

In the Mohawk Valley and much of New York, the Revolution really came to resemble a civil war with raids and retaliations. The last major battle in the Mohawk Valley that involved regular British soldiers took place in Johnstown in 1781.

In 1780, Benedict Arnold, who had been passed over for promotion by the Continental Congress, conspired to deliver the American fort at West Point to the British. The plot failed, and the unfortunate British Major John André was hanged by the Continental Army for espionage.

On November 25, 1783 (Evacuation Day), British troops finally abandoned New York City. On December 4, Washington bade a tearful farewell to his officers at the Fraunces Tavern on Pearl Street in lower Manhattan.

But another war was coming. In the War of 1812, British and American forces would clash in a number of places along the border between New York and Canada. Numerous raids were also launched across Lake Ontario and the St. Lawrence and Niagara Rivers.

During the war, another one of my ancestors (CRK), General Stephen Van Rensselaer, led an unsuccessful invasion from New York into Canada. Many of the New York militia he commanded saw themselves as a strictly defensive force.

American soldiers in Fort Niagara and British soldiers in Fort George, who had previously enjoyed friendly relations, traded cannon fire across the Niagara River in the summer of 1812. On the evening of December 18, 1813, Colonel John Murray and 550 British soldiers crept toward Fort Niagara. A group of American guards were caught while playing cards and forced to divulge the fort's password. The sleeping garrison was captured at bayonet point. It was to be the last foreign assault on an American military installation on the mainland until the Japanese attack on Fort Stevens in 1942 (see Oregon). On December 30, in retaliation for the American burning of Newark, British troops and Native American allies attacked and burned Buffalo and Black Rock.

In September 1814, one of the decisive naval battles of the war took place at Plattsburgh. The naval elements of a British invasion force were defeated on Lake Champlain by US naval forces under Captain Thomas Macdonough. Realizing that without naval assistance, further progress on land would be hard, British land forces withdrew. The American victory considerably strengthened the hand of the United States in the negotiations to end the war.

During the American Civil War, many New Yorkers would serve in the Union Army. On May 24, 1861, Elmer Ellsworth of Sarasota Springs became the first Union officer to be killed, shot by a Virginia hotelier wielding a shotgun. Moments before, Ellsworth, a Zouave officer, had hauled down the Confederate flag in an Alexandria hotel.

New York has seen a wide array of assorted riots over the centuries, and the Civil War years provided one particularly tragic example. Late in the war, many recent immigrants to New York came to resent conscription into the Union Army. In the summer of 1863, five days of rioting broke out in Manhattan that resulted in over a hundred deaths and the lynching of eleven black men. The historian Samuel Morrison declared that these draft riots were "equivalent to a Confederate victory."

In March of 1899, after the American victory in the Spanish-American War, Kaiser Wilhelm II had plans drawn up for a German invasion of New York City. One hundred thousand troops would land at Sandy Hook in nearby New Jersey and proceed toward Manhattan.

P. G. Wodehouse's 1916 short story "The Military Invasion of America" spoofs invasion fiction that was popular at the time, describing a fictional attack on New York by a German armada, with the Japanese attacking the West Coast. "New York had been bombarded—but fortunately, as it was summer, nobody of any importance was in town."

Allan Stewart Konigsberg was born in the Bronx in 1935. His Jewish grandparents had immigrated from Russia and Austria, and he grew up in Brooklyn speaking German and Yiddish. An imaginative boy, he spent time on the beach looking out for Nazi submarines during World War II. He never actually saw a German U-boat, but he did incorporate his fantasies into the 1987 film *Radio Days.* Konigsberg is, of course, better known to us as Woody Allen.

But Nazi submarines off the coast of New York were no mere fantasy. After the Pearl Harbor attack, the German Navy launched a U-boat campaign against shipping on the Eastern seaboard with Operation Drumbeat. Americans were slow to implement convoy tactics for merchant shipping, and many ships were sunk. U-boat captains such as Captain Reinhard Hardegen used the brightly illuminated skyline of New York City to target ships, to devastating effect. It took many months for blackout laws to go into effect for coastal cities, and for convoy protocol to be adopted.

On June 13, 1942, four German saboteurs were landed from a U-boat near Manhattan. (Four more were later dropped off in Florida.) Two turned themselves in, and the rest were arrested. They had been trained to attack targets such as Penn Station. New York power was quite literally targeted by the saboteurs, who also planned to attack the hydroelectric plant at Niagara Falls. All of the would-be saboteurs were tried by military tribunals, and six were executed (see also Florida and Illinois).

According to Albert Speer, Nazi Germany's Minister of Armaments and War Production, Hitler was obsessed by a vision of New York City in flames. In 1942, the Luftwaffe began plans for a strategic bomber that would have been capable of reaching the Empire State. The Luftwaffe intended to make use of its innovative jet technology. Five prototypes for the Amerika bomber were built, but the plan was never operational.

On September 11, 2001, hijackers belatedly realized Hitler's nightmarish dream by transforming commercial passenger jets into weapons and flying them into the Twin Towers of the World Trade Center. Two thousand six hundred and six people were killed that day by the Al Qaeda attack.

## NEW YORK
## MILITARY HISTORY SITES

### Cherry Valley Museum
Location: 49 Main Street, Cherry Valley, NY 13320
Web: www.thisiscooperstown.com/attractions/cherry-valley-museum

### Destroyer Escort Historical Museum (USS *Slater*)
Location: 1 Quay Street, Albany, NY 12202
Web: www.ussslater.org

### Fort Ticonderoga
Location: 102 Fort Ti Road, Ticonderoga, NY 12888
Web: www.fortticonderoga.org

### Franklin D. Roosevelt Presidential Library & Museum
Location: 4097 Albany Post Road, Hyde Park, NY 12538
Web: www.fdrlibrary.org

### FRENCH CASTLE
Founded 1726

Fort Niagara, Youngstown

Source: Author photo

### FORT TICONDEROGA/FORT CARILLON
Founded 1755

Source: Author photo

### CANNON FROM
### SARATOGA BATTLEFIELD
Battles of Saratoga
fought on
September 19 and
October 7, 1777

Source: Author photo

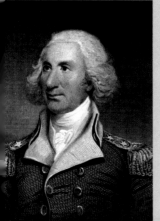

### PHILIP SCHUYLER
1733-1804

Source: iStock/GeorgiosArt

### SCHUYLER MANSION
Albany

Source: Author photo

Nickname: The Empire State
Statehood: 1788
Capital: Albany

CHATEAUGAY
MALONE
MASSENA
WINTHROP
PLATTSBURGH
VALCOUR ISLAND
NICHOLVILLE
OGDENSBURG
CANTON   COLTON
AU SABLE
FORK
LAKE
CHAMPLAIN
HAMMOND
GOUVERNEUR   CRANBERRY
LAKE
LAKE PLACID
TUPPER LAKE
HARRISVILLE
PORT
HENRY
CAPE
VINCENT
CARTHAGE
WATERTOWN
INDIAN
LAKE

**FORT TICONDEROGA**

ADAMS
OLD
FORGE
LOWVILLE

BATTLE ON SNOWSHOES

PULASKI
BOONVILLE
NORTHVILLE
GLENS FALLS
OSWEGO
ONEIDA LAKE
FULTON

ORISKANY
MOHAWK
VALLEY
SARATOGA
SPRINGS
SARATOGA
BENNINGTON

SCOTT
CLYDE
UTICA
SCHENECTADY
SYRACUSE
AUBURN
CHERRY VALLEY

**FORT ORANGE**

ALBANY / BEVERWIJCK

NEW YORK

AURORA
CAYUGA
LAKE
CORTLAND   NORWICH
SENECA
LAKE
ITHACA
ONEONTA
WATKINS
GLEN
BINGHAMTON
ROXBURY
HUDSON
OWEGO
SIDNEY
WALTON
ELMIRA
DEPOSIT
CATSKILL
PARK
KINGSTON
HUDSON RIVER
ROSCOE
LIBERTY
POUGHKEEPSIE
MONTICELLO
NEWBURGH
BEACON
MIDDLETOWN
PEEKSKILL
MONROE
WHITE
PLAINS

HARLEM HEIGHTS
LONG ISLAND
NEW YORK / NEW AMSTERDAM
ATLANTIC
OCEAN

**FRAUNCES TAVERN,**
Lower Manhattan
Source: Author photo

**Fraunces Tavern Museum**
Location: 54 Pearl Street, New York, NY 10004
Web: www.frauncestavernmuseum.org

**Intrepid Sea, Air & Space Museum Complex**
Location: Pier 86, West 46th Street & 12th Avenue, New York, NY 10036
Web: www.intrepidmuseum.org

**The National 9/11 Memorial & Museum**
Location: 180 Greenwich Street, New York, NY 10007
Web: www.911memorial.org

**Old Fort Niagara**
Location: 2 Scott Avenue, Youngstown, NY 14174
Web: www.oldfortniagara.org

**Saratoga National Historical Park**
Location: 648 Route 32, Stillwater, NY 12170
Web: www.nps.gov/sara

**Schuyler Mansion State Historic Site**
Location: 32 Catherine Street, Albany, NY 12202
Web: www.parks.ny.gov/historic-sites/33/details.aspx

**United States Military Academy**
Location: Trophy Point, West Point, NY 10996
Web: www.usma.edu/Visiting/SitePages/Home.aspx

**West Point Museum**
Location: 2110 New South Post Road, West Point, NY 10996
Web: www.westpoint.army.mil/museum.html

# NORTH CAROLINA

The Mississippian culture built mounds around AD 1000. It would eventually be succeeded in the region by the Algonquin people, which included tribes such as the Croatan, Chowanoke, Roanoke, and Weapemeoc. The Tuscarora held much of the interior, while Siouan tribes were concentrated in the southern portion of the state.

The Spanish were the first Europeans to arrive in what is now North Carolina, although the Florentine Giovanni da Verrazano, working for the French, did cruise along the coast in 1524.

In 1526, Lucas Vásquez de Ayllón set up a short-lived colony on the Cape Fear River. Hernando de Soto traveled through the west of the area in 1540 in his search for gold. The explorer Juan Pardo arrived in December 1566 and built Fort San Juan near the present location of Morganton. The Spanish constructed six forts in the interior of North Carolina.

Sir Walter Raleigh attempted to establish a colony on the Outer Banks, on Roanoke Island, in 1585. Virginia Dare, the first English child to be born in the New World, was born on Roanoke Island in 1587. This colony was abandoned in mysterious circumstances, and was perhaps wiped out. Suspicion, in that case, falls on the nearby Croatoan tribe. The fate of Virginia Dare remains a mystery. The capital of North Carolina was named in honor of Raleigh.

Other English explorers gradually arrived in the area.

In 1663, King Charles II granted a royal charter to establish a colony in what would become known as the Carolinas. The colony was named in honor of his late father, Charles I, who had been executed in the English Revolution. Many African slaves were shipped to North Carolina over the next two centuries.

The situation between colonists in the region and Native Americans was not always calm. For instance, in 1675 the Chowanoke attacked settlers in Carolina. And the situation among colonists themselves was not always calm either. In 1677, Culpeper's Rebellion briefly took over control in Albermarle County.

In 1710, Christoph von Graffenried, a native of Bern, led a group of Swiss and German colonists (from Palatine) to North Carolina. Graffenried founded the settlement of New Bern, and was pleased to note that "stags and deer, ducks and geese and turkeys are numerous." But the settlers were soon in conflict with the Iroquoian-speaking Tuscarora people. Graffenried was taken prisoner and, in a surprise attack by the Tuscarora on September 22, 1711, over 120 settlers were killed. Graffenried was eventually released, and he returned to Europe a broken man.

The Tuscarora War would drag on in eastern North Carolina until 1713. The North Carolina House of Burgesses raised £20,000 to make war on the Tuscarora people. In March 1713, Colonel James Moore led an army, which consisted largely of Indians who were friendly to the settler cause, against the Tuscarora at the Battle of Nehucke. Tuscarora power was broken, and the tribe was forced to relocate, with some moving west and others to New York.

After they had been driven out of the Bahamas, pirates became a problem on the Carolina coast. In 1718, Lieutenant Robert Maynard killed Blackbeard in a fight near Ocracoke Inlet.

The eighteenth century would also see a number of clashes in and around North Carolina as Britain battled other European powers. For instance, war broke out between Spain and Britain and other nations in 1717, which led to the Spanish raids on North Carolina.

And again in the 1740s, during the so-called Spanish Alarm, Spanish forces attacked Beaufort and Brunswick.

During the 1754–1763 French and Indian War, there were a number of clashes in the area, with the Cherokee attacking colonists. In early 1760, Cherokee fighters attacked Fort Dobbs and a number of settlements; but in 1761, British troops, American militiamen, and local Native American allies defeated the Cherokee and destroyed a number of their villages.

The next year, Robert Rogers, the leader of the 1758 Battle on Snowshoes (see New York), visited North Carolina. That spring, Rogers, known as the father of the US Rangers, recruited about a hundred men from North Carolina to join him on an expedition to discover the Northwest Passage.

In the late 1760s, the Regulator Movement started emerging among those angry over British taxation and abuses by public officials. Regulators seized the Hillsborough Supreme Court in 1770, but in 1771 they were decisively defeated by militiamen at the Battle of Alamance.

In 1767, Andrew Jackson was born in the Waxhaws settlement on the border between South and North Carolina. He would grow up to become the victor of the Battle of New Orleans and the seventh president of the United States.

North Carolina was one of the original thirteen colonies, and three North Carolinians signed the Declaration of Independence. Many residents would serve in the Continental Army and state militia, while some served with the Tory forces in units such as the Royal North Carolina Regiment. At the age of thirteen, Andrew Jackson joined the North Carolina militia on the Patriot side.

The Battle of Ramsour's Mill was fought in the colony on June 20, 1780, between Loyalist forces led by John Moore and Patriot forces led by Francis Locke. Some of Locke's men seem to have fortified themselves before the battle with a stop at Dellinger's Tavern. Around 150 casualties were suffered by each side, but the Loyalists were driven from the field.

In January of 1781, after his victory at Camden in South Carolina, Lord Cornwallis and several thousand Redcoats marched north to invade North Carolina. On March 15, 1781, the Battle of Guilford Court House was fought near what is today Greensboro. This ninety-minute skirmish pitted Lord Cornwallis and the traitor Benedict Arnold against Nathaniel Greene. North Carolina militia participated in the battle. It was a tactical victory for the British, but their casualties exceeded those of the Patriots. Charles Fox, a British opposition MP, remarked, "Another such victory would ruin the British Army." Nathaniel Greene summed it up from the American perspective: "We fight, get beat, rise, and fight again." In September 1781, attempts to rescue Governor Burke from Loyalist troops under David Fanning led to the Battle of Lindley's Mill. However, in October, Cornwallis would surrender at Yorktown.

The period after the Revolution saw the short-lived state of Franklin; and in 1789, North Carolina ceded lands that would become the state of Tennessee.

During the War of 1812, North Carolina raised seven regiments of state militia. Her ports were blockaded by the Royal Navy. On July 11, 1813, British forces seized Ocracoke and Portsmouth on the coast. The towns were looted before the British withdrew.

North Carolina, as a colony and a state, was a significant source of naval supplies for the British Royal Navy. Turpentine and pitch were substantial exports. North Carolina tar was used to seal the bottom of wooden ships, earning the state its nickname of Tar Heel.

As the nineteenth century progressed, land was continually ceded by local Native Americans. For instance, in 1819, the Cherokee gave up land in what are now Transylvania, Henderson, and Jackson Counties. Despite this, in 1838, about 17,000 Cherokee were forcibly expelled from North Carolina along the Trail of Tears.

North Carolina, among Confederate states, was relatively late to secede, in May of 1861, after the fall of Fort Sumter the previous month. More Confederate troops, about 125,000, were raised from North Carolina than from any other state. Perhaps as many as 10,000 North Carolinians, including freed slaves, fought on the Union side in the war.

Union naval power dominated during the Civil War. In February of 1862, Union troops under General Ambrose Burnside conducted a successful amphibious invasion of Roanoke Island—the site of Raleigh's famous "lost colony." Hatteras Island was captured soon after by Union forces.

North Carolina was on the periphery of most of the fighting in the Civil War. The state's ports, such as Wilmington, were subject to blockade according to the Union's Anaconda Plan, which throttled trade with the Confederacy.

In January 1865, Union forces captured Fort Fisher and shortly afterwards seized Wilmington, the Confederates' last seaport.

Late in the war, the Battle of Bentonville was fought over three days in March of 1865, and was won by the Federal forces. The Confederates were desperately trying to hold off Sherman, who had marched north from Georgia through South Carolina and into the Tar Heel state with an army of 70,000 men. The Confederate general at Bentonville, Joseph Johnston, commanded around 20,000 men. After the battle Johnston acknowledged that, "Sherman's course cannot be hindered by the small force I have. I can do no more than annoy him." After another Confederate defeat at the Battle of Morrisville in April, Johnston surrendered.

Like a number of other formerly Confederate states, North Carolina would see violence in the post-war period as some fought to restore white political control.

In 1903, at Kitty Hawk, the Wright brothers' plane took to the air, inaugurating an era that would change warfare forever.

In 1918, during World War I, German submarines operated off the Outer Banks, destroying six tankers and other smaller ships, including the Diamond Shoals Lightship off Buxton.

In January 1942, shortly after the attack on Pearl Harbor, German U-boats returned to these hunting grounds. Captain Richard Zapp and his boat *U-66* were part of Operation Drumbeat, which attacked merchant shipping on the Atlantic coast. On January 18, *U-66* sent two torpedoes into the *Allan Jackson,* an oil tanker, off the coast of Cape Hatteras, sinking her in minutes. German U-boats would prowl off the Carolina coast from 1942 to the war's end in 1945, sinking an estimated 397 ships in an area that became known as Torpedo Alley. Around 5,000 merchant mariners are estimated to have perished off the Carolina coast.

Not all the victims were, of course, American. On July 14, 1942, *U-576* was sunk by an Allied convoy off Carolina waters with the loss of her crew of forty-five. Her wreck was discovered in 2014.

As noted in our California chapter, the 1942 Rose Bowl between Oregon State and Duke was played in Chapel Hill, due to fears of a Japanese invasion after Pearl Harbor.

Camp Lejeune, established in 1941, is a US Marine base in Jacksonville. Fort Bragg, named after Confederate Commander Braxton Bragg from North Carolina, was founded in 1918. It remains the home to the 82nd Airborne and other units of the US Army.

In 1961, during the Cold War, a B-52 carrying two nuclear bombs broke up in midair near Goldsboro. Fortunately, the bombs did not detonate.

## NORTH CAROLINA
## MILITARY HISTORY SITES

**82nd Airborne Division War Memorial Museum**
Location: Building C-6841, Ardennes Street, Fort Bragg, NC 28310
Web: www.82ndairbornedivisionmuseum.com/

**Airborne & Special Operations Museum**
Location: 100 Bragg Boulevard, Fayetteville, NC 28301
Web: www.asomf.org

**Bennett Place State Historic Site**
Location: 4409 Bennett Memorial Road, Durham, NC 27705
Web: www.bennettplacehistoricsite.com/

**Bentonville Battlefield**
Location: 5466 Harper House Road, Four Oaks, NC 27524
Web: www.nchistoricsites.org/bentonvi/

**Fort Fisher**
Location: 1610 Fort Fisher Boulevard South, Kure Beach, NC 28449
Web: www.nchistoricsites.org/fisher/

**Guilford Courthouse National Military Park**
Location: 2332 New Garden Road, Greensboro, NC 27410
Web: www.nps.gov/guco/

**Kings Mountain Historical Museum**
Location:  100 East Mountain Street, Kings Mountain, NC 28086
Web: www.kingsmountainmuseum.org

**Moores Creek National Battlefield**
Location: 40 Patriots Hall Drive, Currie, NC 28435
Web: www.nps.gov/mocr/

Nickname: Old North State
Statehood: 1789
Capital: Raleigh

**KITTY HAWK**
Source: Ken Curtis

**North Carolina Maritime Museum at Southport**
Location: 204 East Moore Street, Southport, NC 28461
Web: ncmaritimemuseumsouthport.com/

**Wright Brothers National Memorial**
Location: 1000 North Croatan Highway, Kill Devil Hills, NC 27948
Web: https://www.nps.gov/wrbr/index.htm

# NORTH DAKOTA

Humanity has a long history in what is now North Dakota, and Europeans are comparatively recent arrivals.

As Europeans came into increasing contact with the Native Americans of the areas, they encountered peoples like the Lakota, Dakota, the Assiniboine, the Cheyenne, the Mandan, the Hidatsa, and the Arikara. Some of the people were nomadic and had developed a Plains culture focused on herds of bison. Others lived a more settled life.

The European battle to control the area started early, although it was all pretty theoretical at first, and the actual inhabitants of the area would have known nothing about it.

Already by 1610, Henry Hudson was claiming vast areas of North America, including parts of what is now North Dakota, for England. In 1682, Robert de La Salle hit back for France, claiming parts of what is now North Dakota for France. Neither of the individuals had even been to the territory they were claiming, let alone have any control over it, so as far as the inhabitants were concerned, it was all completely irrelevant.

In the eighteenth century, however, actual Europeans did start arriving in the area. In 1738, the French explorer and fur trader Perre de Varennes, sieur de La Vérendrye arrived with a French expedition, making contact with the Mandan and being impressed by the sophistication of their culture. Plenty more fur traders followed.

Elsewhere, major events were about to have a major impact on the development of European power in the region. Things weren't going well for France in the Seven Years' War. In fact, they couldn't have been going much worse. Per two treaties in 1762 and 1763, they handed over almost all their claims and land in America north of the Caribbean to either Britain or Spain.

Soon, as fur traders battled for domination and European powers battled for sovereignty, the situation would get quite confusing.

For instance, the very French Rene Jusseaume would move south from Fort La Souris in 1794 to set up Jusseau's Post at the junction of the Knife and Missouri Rivers; and he would fly the British flag over it, because he represented a company from British-controlled Montreal.

Meanwhile, in 1796, Welshman John Evans, representing Spanish authority in the region, arrived from the south, looking for the descendants of Welsh prince Madoc, who some thought had headed for America in the twelfth century. Evans briefly raised the Spanish flag before being forced out by local Native Americans who were more keen on the British and their trade goods.

Spanish influence in the area, fleeting and largely theoretical, would not last. First they returned the area to French control; and then, in 1803, through the Louisiana Purchase, the United States took over Spanish interests in the area. So, in terms of invading powers, it was going to be a competition between Britain and the young United States.

A number of British posts were established in the region, including Alexander Henry's site at present-day Pembina in 1801, and the Red River Colony in 1811, which included part of what is now North Dakota. But British efforts in the area were hampered by bitter rivalry for control of the fur trade between two British firms—Hudson's Bay Company and the North West Company.

And the United States was beginning to extend its influence in the region.

Captain Meriwether Lewis and Second Lieutenant William Clark turned up in what is now North Dakota, stopping to winter at Fort Mandan on their way to the Pacific coast, and returning on the Missouri River in 1806. American fur trader Manuel Lisa was in the area by 1809, looking for sites for trading posts.

By 1818, Britain was prepared to give up on the region, as part of the terms of the Anglo-American Convention of that year.

After 1818, the United States had no external rival for power in this territory. But just because the United States reckoned it now sort of controlled the area didn't necessarily mean that the Native Americans who lived there agreed.

Over the decades, United States influence in the area expanded, as assorted fur-trading forts were established and assorted expeditions explored the region. In 1857, Fort Abercrombie was constructed. And there was trouble ahead.

In 1862, the Dakota Uprising, or Sioux Uprising, erupted in Minnesota as the Santee there, with a long list of grievances against Americans and facing severe food shortages, rebelled. The fighting soon spilled over into Dakota Territory as American troops pursued rebels and anyone they suspected of being a rebel. Santee and others combined to resist. A succession of clashes took place across the region, as US punitive expeditions advanced.

One such expedition, under Colonel Henry Sibley of the Minnesota militia, fought with and defeated Santee and others at the Battle of Big Mound, the Battle of Dead Buffalo Lake, and the Battle of Stony Lake, all in 1863.

Brigadier General Alfred Sully led other efforts to stamp out resistance at the Battle of Whitestone Hill, also in 1863, and the Battle of Kildeer Mountain and the Battle of the Badlands in 1864.

Ultimately, the local Native American population would not be able to resist US military might so ruthlessly applied. Although one, Lieutenant Colonel George Armstrong Custer, who set off from Fort Abraham Lincoln in 1876, would learn that it was possible to underestimate the military impact of Native Americans.

A series of new US military forts was created in the region. Reservations for Native Americans were established and their land was ceded to the US government. Settlers arrived. In 1872, a new settlement was founded on the Missouri when the North Pacific Railway reached it, and the next year it was named Bismarck in honor of the German chancellor. In 1881, Sitting Bull would surrender at Fort Buford. In 1889, North Dakota was admitted to the union as a state. The same year, the Ghost Dance began spreading across the reservations in that area. In the fallout from that and from land disputes, Sitting Bull was killed in late 1890 during an attempt to arrest him, and his body was taken to Fort Yates.

People from North Dakota, both Native Americans and others, would go on to serve with distinction in the foreign wars of the United States. And in the time since the United States' invasion of North Dakota was complete, the area has seen one more invasion from abroad.

It was not from Canada.

As late as the 1930s, the United States still had plans on what to do in the event of war with Canada, plans in which North Dakota would have played a major part, as US troops thrust northward from the state to capture the strategic rail and communication links at Winnipeg.

Similarly, Canada had at one stage between the world wars its Defence Scheme No. 1, which envisaged, in the event of an America invasion, Canadian troops seizing, among other targets, Fargo. But that was never needed.

In 1932, the International Peace Garden was dedicated, straddling the border between North Dakota and Manitoba, between the United States and Canada. At its heart was a pledge that the two nations would never take up arms against each other.

No, the attack was to come from much farther afield.

Starting in 1944, the Japanese sent balloon bombs riding the air currents across the Pacific to the United States. At least two of these Fu-Go devices landed in North Dakota.

## NORTH DAKOTA
## MILITARY HISTORY SITES

### Battle of the Badlands Interpretive Site
Location: Sentinel Butte, ND 58654
Web: www.fs.usda.gov/recarea/dpg/recreation/recarea/?recid=79473&ac-tid=119

### Fort Abercrombie State Historic Site
Location: County Highway 22, Abercrombie, ND 58001
Web: history.nd.gov/historicsites/Abercrombie
Web: www.ftabercrombie.org

# America Invaded: NORTH DAKOTA

Nickname: Peace Garden State
Statehood: 1889
Capital: Bismarck

**Fort Abraham Lincoln Park and The Custer House**
Location: 4480 Fort Lincoln Road, Mandan, ND 58554
Web: www.parkrec.nd.gov/parks/falsp/falsp.html

**Fort Yates (Sitting Bull Burial Site)**
Location: Sitting Bull Avenue, Fort Yates, ND 58538
Web: www.ndtourism.com/fort-yates/attractions/sitting-bull-burial-site-fort-yates

**Killdeer Mountain Battlefield State Historic Site**
Location: 8.5 miles southwest of Killdeer, ND 58640
Web: history.nd.gov/historicsites/kmb

**Lewis & Clark Interpretive Center (Fort Mandan)**
Location: 2576 Eighth Street SW, Washburn, ND 58577
Web: fortmandan.com

**Ronald Reagan Minuteman Missile State Historic Site**
Location: 555 113 1/2 Avenue NE, Highway 45, Cooperstown, ND 58425
Web: history.nd.gov/historicsites/minutemanmissile

**Theodore Roosevelt National Park**
Location: Multiple Entrances, Medora, ND 58645
Web: www.nps.gov/thro

# OHIO

Ohio had a long and rich Native American history before the arrival of Europeans. The Adena and Hopewell cultures flourished there, and the Great Serpent Mound is a spectacular example of a ceremonial mound.

In the seventeenth century, parts of Ohio were caught up in the Beaver Wars as the Five Nations of the Iroquois, armed with European guns and desperate to secure more hunting grounds for furs for the European market, turned on their neighbors, including the Erie, who were killed or scattered in the onslaught.

The French took an early interest in Ohio. Robert de La Salle, for instance, explored part of it in the seventeenth century, and was the first European to see the Ohio River. Soon the French built Fort Miami near what is now Toledo. The battle for control of Ohio was about to begin. From the east and north came Native Americans, including the Delaware, who had been pushed out of their original lands by the expansion of European settlements. And from the east, also, came people from Virginia and Pennsylvania—and the British.

In 1744, the British made the Treaty of Lancaster with the Iroquois; and in 1748, they made the Treaty of Logtown with the Delaware, Shawnee, and Wyandot. Also in 1748, they formed the Ohio Company. All of which didn't please the French very much. In fact, it didn't please them at all. So in 1752, a force of Ottawa and Ojibwa under Charles de Langlade, who was part Ottawa and part French Canadian, attacked a British trading post at Pickawillany.

Some of the local Miami people who had been trading with the British were killed. Soon open war broke out between Britain and France. By 1763, it was all over. The French had lost and Ohio was British, or so the British thought. Some of the Native Americans had different ideas.

In 1763, resentful of how the new British authorities and settlers dealt with them, a number of different Native American peoples, led by the Ottawa chief Pontiac, attacked a wide range of British targets in the region, including in Ohio. Fort Sandusky and Fort Miami were both captured. In response, a British proclamation was issued that aimed at preventing settlers from encroaching on Native American lands. George III's edict contributed to American dissatisfaction with their colonial masters. In the end, the unity of the different indigenous groups began to fracture, and an expedition led by Colonel Henry Bouquet advanced through Ohio. Fighting eventually petered out, and a peace deal was made.

It was not to last for long. The 1768 Treaty of Fort Stanwix with the Iroquois led to settlers advancing into Shawnee and Delaware lands. The resulting Lord Dunmore's War was focused to the south of the present-day state of Ohio, and it only ended with the 1774 Treaty of Camp Charlotte, after Virginian forces crossed the Ohio.

But another war was coming. Yes, the American Revolution. Ohio was to see extensive fighting. Many Native Americans, including Shawnee and Delaware, sided with the British. The war in Ohio was often bitter and brutal. In the Gnadenhutten Massacre of 1782, American militiamen murdered ninety Native Americans they had captured. A few months later at Sandusky River, a Patriot force battled with a force consisting of Shawnee, Delaware, and Loyalists. Two hundred and fifty Americans were killed either in fighting or after capture. Their commander, Colonel William Crawford, after being captured, was tied to a stake and killed slowly and painfully over a period of two hours. And American victory in the War of Independence would not see the end of fighting in Ohio.

In the period after the American Revolution, the new United States sought to extend its control of territory through a number of controversial treaties. In 1787, Ohio became part of the United States' Northwest Territory, and settlers began to travel there in increasing numbers. New England veterans of the Revolution settled at Marietta on the Ohio in 1788. Settlers from New Jersey arrived near what is now Cincinnati, and the southern part of the territory saw settlers from Kentucky and Virginia too. Tension between the new United States authorities and a number of Native American peoples persisted and frequently flared up.

An attempt was made to form a Native-American confederacy that could resist the expansion of settlements, a confederacy that included Native Americans from a variety of peoples, including the Shawnee, Wyandot, Lenape, and Miami. British forces were still present at a number of locations in the region, and British traders were still supplying guns to the Native Americans. In 1789, the United States constructed Fort Washington and assorted American settlements north of the Ohio River. Native Americans chose to resist and to push the Americans back south of the Ohio.

American forces suffered a number of significant defeats in the subsequent war, but still the Americans constructed a line of forts leading north from Fort Washington, including Fort Hamilton and Fort Jefferson. And in 1792, Major General Anthony Wayne was ordered by Congress to build a bigger and better army, which he did. In late 1793, Wayne with his new command, known as the Legion of the United States, began traveling north into Native-American territory. They constructed two more forts, Fort Greenville and Fort Recovery, to the north of Fort Jefferson. Finally, in August 1794, near what is now Toledo, Wayne's forces decisively defeated Native American forces, which included Shawnee, Delaware, Miami, Wyandot, Ojibwa, and Ottawa, and a detachment of Canadian militiamen at the Battle of Fallen Timbers. The aftermath of the American victory saw final British withdrawal from the area; and with the 1795 Treaty of Greenville, Native Americans ceded more than half of what is now Ohio. More settlers arrived, and in 1803 the State of Ohio was admitted to the Union.

Tecumseh was a Shawnee leader born somewhere near Chillicothe in Ohio. Starting in 1811, he led Native-American military resistance to American expansion in what is now Indiana. But when the War of 1812 started, his campaigns were linked into the wider war between the United States and Britain.

In the spring of 1813, a force consisting of British and Canadian troops under Major-General Henry Proctor and Native Americans led by Tecumseh and Roundhead, a Wyandot leader, attempted to seize Fort Meigs, at what is now Perrysburg. During the ensuing siege, Kentucky reinforcements tried to fight their way through to the fort. Some succeeded. However, a few were captured and killed in the River Raisin Massacre before Tecumseh arrived and put a stop to the slaughter. In the end, though, attempts to take Fort Meigs in 1813 would fail. In September of that year, near Put-in-Bay, United States Navy ships under Commodore Oliver Perry defeated and captured a British Royal Navy force in one of the major US victories in the war. In the aftermath of the British defeat, Procter retreated; and in October 1813, the charismatic Tecumseh was killed at the Battle of the Thames in Canada.

The days of major fighting for control of Ohio were almost at an end, but before they were fully over, there were a few more twists to the story.

In 1835–1836, the Toledo War broke out between Michigan and Ohio. Confused surveying had left control of a strip of land stretching west from Toledo in dispute. When applying for statehood in 1835, Michigan claimed it, but Ohio objected. Both Michigan and Ohio sent militia to the area. In the end, a compromise was found. Ohio got the Toledo strip and Michigan most of the Upper Peninsula.

In 1839, George Armstrong Custer was born in New Rumley.

Ohio wasn't exactly the main focus of the Civil War, but it wasn't entirely quiet in the state either.

For a start, there was the Battle of Fort Fizzle. Fought in June 1863, it wasn't actually much of a battle. In 1863, as the Civil War raged, some conscription officials were attacked in Homes County. When soldiers were sent to restore order and enforce the conscription process, they found hundreds of armed men defying them from a makeshift fort. Some shooting took place, but eventually the resistance fizzled out without too much damage done.

However, the very next month, the situation got a lot more serious. On July 13, Brigadier General John Hunt Morgan's Confederate raiders crossed from Indiana into Ohio. Morgan's famous raid started in Tennessee and stretched over a thousand miles. They headed across southern Ohio, aiming to escape to West Virginia, but were defeated by Union troops and gunboats at the Battle of Buffington Island. Some of Morgan's men would eventually manage to cross the Ohio River, but Morgan himself and most of his men were surrounded and forced to surrender at Salineville. Morgan did manage to escape captivity and returned to the South, but was killed not long afterwards.

The Buckeye State would produce many more well-known military figures, but they would become known for their actions beyond the borders of Ohio, not within them. To select just a few, we have Ulysses S. Grant, William Tecumseh Sherman, Eddie Rickenbacker, Curtis LeMay, and John Glenn.

On May 4, 1970, young Americans in uniform fired on other young Americans who were protesting the bombing of Cambodia and the Nixon administration. Members of the Ohio National Guard killed four unarmed protestors at Kent State University. The tragedy was a watershed event of the Vietnam War.

## OHIO
## MILITARY HISTORY SITES

### Custer Monument
State Route 646 & Chrisman Road, New Rumley, OH 43986

### Fallen Timbers Battlefield and Fort Miamis National Historic Site
Location: Intersection of US 24 and I-475, Maumee, OH 43537
Web: www.nps.gov/fati/

### Fort Meigs
Location: 29100 West River Road, Perrysburg, OH 43551
Web: www.fortmeigs.org

### Miami Valley Military History Museum
Location: 120 Ohio Avenue, Dayton, OH 45428
Web: www.mvmhm.com

### Motts Military Museum
Location: 5075 South Hamilton Road, Groveport, OH 43125
Web: www.mottsmilitarymuseum.org/

**National Museum of the United States Air Force**
Location: 1100 Spaatz Street, Dayton, OH 45433
Web: www.nationalmuseum.af.mil

**Sherman House Museum**
Location: 137 East Main Street, Lancaster, Ohio 43130
Web: www.shermanhouse.org

**Ulysses S. Grant Birthplace**
Location: 1551 OH-232, Moscow, OH 45153
Web: www.usgrantbirthplace.org

**William Henry Harrison Tomb State Memorial**
Location: North Bend, OH 45052

**William McKinley Presidential Library & Museum**
Location: 800 McKinley Monument Drive NW, Canton, OH 44708
Web: www.mckinleymuseum.org

# America Invaded: OHIO

Nickname: The Buckeye State
Statehood: 1803
Capital: Columbus

**GEORGE ARMSTRONG CUSTER**
1839-1876
Source: iStock/Andrew_Howe

**ULYSSES S. GRANT**
1822-1885
Source: akg-images/
Pictures From History

# OKLAHOMA

The Wichita tribe, far less nomadic than other Native Americans, were farming in Oklahoma long before the arrival of Europeans.

The Spanish explorer Hernando de Soto, Oklahoma's first European visitor, came to the region in 1540 searching for gold. The conquistador Coronado arrived the following year.

In 1594 or 1595, two other Spanish explorers, Umana and Leyba, led an expedition into what is Oklahoma today, also searching for gold. Neither would survive. Many years later, an Oklahoma farmer would uncover part of a steel breastplate, presumably from a conquistador.

As the Spanish moved north to Oklahoma, the French moved south from New France. In 1682, Robert de La Salle explored the Mississippi region and claimed this area, including Oklahoma, for the French king. Bérnard de La Harpe led two French expeditions into Oklahoma, in 1719 and 1721. The French trappers left a legacy in Oklahoma in terms of geographic names, such as the Poteau and Grand Rivers.

In 1759, Diego Ortiz Parrilla organized a punitive expedition against Native Americans in Texas and Oklahoma. On October 7, the Battle of the Twin Villages was fought near what is today the Texas-Oklahoma border. The Spanish were defeated by warriors from the Wichita and Comanche tribes.

France regained control (on paper) of the Louisiana territory, including Oklahoma, in 1800 from Spain. In 1803, the Jefferson administration negotiated the Louisiana Purchase from Napoleon for the sum of $15 million. Most of the present state of Oklahoma was included in that deal.

The US Constitution specifically calls out Native Americans, declaring that Congress shall have power "to regulate Commerce … with the Indian Tribes." In 1825, the US government saw the Oklahoma Territory as the solution to their "Indian problem." James Barbour, the Secretary of War, declared the establishment of Indian Country in order that "the future residence of these peoples will be forever undisturbed."

Trying to put all Native Americans into one basket, though, created problems of its own. Numerous wars and skirmishes were fought in Oklahoma among Native Americans. In 1833, for example, the Osage tribe fell upon an undefended group of Kiowa in what became known as the Cutthroat Gap Massacre. Over 150 were killed, including many women and children.

Between the 1830s and 1850s, many of the defeated tribes of the Southeast, such as the Choctaw and Creek, were forcibly relocated to the Indian Territory in Oklahoma. This became known as the Trail of Tears.

In 1842 at Webbers Falls, about twenty-five slaves rebelled in Cherokee territory and headed south toward Mexico. They were joined by more slaves escaping from Creek land. The Cherokee militia were sent after them and recaptured them. Five were executed.

The Treaty of Guadalupe Hidalgo of 1848 that ended the Mexican-American War added the Oklahoma Panhandle, previously claimed by the Republic of Texas, to United States Territory. This land remained an untamed no-man's-land for many years until finally becoming part of Oklahoma.

In 1858, John "Rip" Ford led a party of Texas Rangers across the Red River and into Oklahoma Indian Territory. He earned his nickname during the Mexican-American War, after writing numerous death notifications with the words *Rest in Peace* at the top. His "invasion" was a response to attacks against settlers. Ford's men fought the Battle of Antelope Hills against two separate groups of Comanche on May 12, 1858. The Rangers were armed with .45 caliber six shooters, which outclassed the bows and single-shot muskets of the Comanche. Only two Rangers were killed versus over seventy-five Comanche, with many more Comanche taken prisoner.

In October 1858, troops of the 2nd Cavalry looking for Penateka Comanche chief Buffalo Hump clashed with Comanche warriors at the

Battle of the Wichita Village. The Comanche were defeated, but Buffalo Hump escaped.

But a much bigger war was coming.

During the American Civil War, Native Americans in the Indian territory of Oklahoma at first attempted to remain neutral. Ultimately, Oklahoma fought a mini-Civil War of its own. Four regiments of Indian Home Guard were raised to fight on the Union side. Many Creek warriors from Oklahoma would fight in Union blue. Nearly 8,000 Indians, mainly of the Five Civilized Tribes, would instead fight under the flag of the Stars and Bars.

In the bitter winter of 1861, Unionist Native Americans, under attack from Confederate forces, withdrew to Kansas, fighting a series of engagements en route, including the Battle of Round Mountain and the Battle of Chustenahlah. Among the pursuing forces was Stand Watie.

Stand Watie, a Cherokee leader who was born in Georgia, relocated to the Oklahoma Territory. In August of 1861, he chose to align his tribe with the Confederate cause. He led a force of irregular cavalry that conducted a number of hit-and-run raids on Union targets. Watie rose to become a brigadier general in the Confederate Army. He was, in fact, the last Confederate general to surrender, on June 23, 1865, more than two months after Lee's surrender at Appomattox. After the war, he returned to farming in Delaware County, Oklahoma.

Stand Watie's forces took part in a number of other Civil War clashes in what is now Oklahoma, including the Battle of Old Fort Wayne in October 1862.

The most significant battle of the Civil War fought in Oklahoma was the Battle of Honey Springs on July 17, 1863. Major General James Blunt of Maine, armed with superior artillery, defeated a Confederate force that outnumbered him two to one. The battle was notable for the courageous performance of the 1st Kansas Colored Infantry. This Union victory secured most of the Oklahoma Indian Territory for the duration of the Civil War.

After the Civil War, tensions between American settlers and Native Americans continued. Most of Oklahoma was occupied by the Five Civilized Tribes—Cheyenne, Choctaw, Chickasaw, Creek, and Seminole. Pressure was mounting for the construction of railroads through Indian lands. Perhaps the most notorious battle to ever be fought in Oklahoma took place on November 27, 1868, on the banks of the Washita River. US Army forces led by Lieutenant

Colonel George Armstrong Custer attacked a Cheyenne encampment led by Black Kettle. Black Kettle had been a signatory of the Medicine Lodge Treaties of 1867, which granted money and equipment in exchange for relocation onto two reservations in western Oklahoma and access for the railroad workers.

In the early morning hours of November 27, Custer's 7th Cavalry attacked the sleeping Cheyenne camp from four directions. The engagement remains controversial to this day, with some historians terming it a massacre while others argue that it was a one-sided battle. Twenty-one American soldiers were killed and probably over one hundred Indians, including many women and children. Black Kettle and his wife were among the slain.

Some further clashes between Native Americans and US forces would occur, and 1882 also saw the Green Peach War as Cherokee clashed with Cherokee.

In addition to the land occupied by the Five Civilized Tribes, there was also a section of Oklahoma that was designated Unassigned Territory by the federal government. These areas, including the Panhandle, became subject to a series of land runs starting in 1893. The "Sooners" were the settlers who moved most expeditiously to take advantage of the federal government's largesse.

In 1905, Indian tribes in Oklahoma held a constitutional convention that proposed the admission of an Indian state called Sequoyah. That same year, President Teddy Roosevelt enjoyed a wolf hunt in the Oklahoma Territory with Comanche Chief Quanah Parker (see Texas). In 1907, Oklahoma became the forty-sixth state to join the Union, utilizing the Sequoyah constitution.

In April of 1917, Woodrow Wilson led the United States into World War I on the side of the Allies against the Central Powers. Conscription soon followed. Opposition to conscription broke out in Oklahoma with the Green Corn Rebellion in Pontotoc County. Tenant farmers, along with Creeks, Seminoles, and some African Americans, rioted, and three people were killed. A manifesto issued by the rebels declared that World War I was a "Rich man's war, poor man's fight." This rhetoric could, of course, be applied to many American wars.

Oil was first discovered in Oklahoma in 1859. The state was a crucial producer of oil in both world wars, which brought increased wealth to the state. Today it remains the fifth largest oil-producing state in the United States.

In 1931, the Red River Bridge War erupted. Well, sort of. Briefly. An argument over a bridge jointly built by Texas and Oklahoma led to Texas building barricades on the bridge and Oklahoma tearing them down, and the governor of Oklahoma declaring martial law before the problem was resolved.

The Battleship *Oklahoma*, nicknamed Okie, was torpedoed by Japanese aircraft and sunk on December 7, 1941, at Pearl Harbor. Over 420 of her crew were killed.[7] She was later refloated and repaired, serving in the war until 1944.

Oklahoma, unlike many of its neighboring states, was not apparently struck by Japanese balloon bombs. Astonishingly, Oklahoma did *not* escape bombing during World War II. On July 5, 1943, a B-17 squadron operating out of Dalhart Air Base in Texas accidentally dropped about four practice bombs on Boise City in the Oklahoma Panhandle. One bomb struck the local Baptist church. No one was killed or injured in the only World War II bombing of a city in the continental US. One of the B-17 crewmembers returned after the war and married a woman from Boise City.


## OKLAHOMA
## MILITARY HISTORY SITES

### 45th Infantry Division Museum
Location: 2145 NE 36th Street, Oklahoma City, OK 73111
Web: www.45thdivisionmuseum.com

### Cabin Creek Battlefield
Location: 442370 East 367 Road, Big Cabin, OK 74332
Web: www.okhistory.org/sites/cabincreek

### Confederate Memorial Museum and Cemetery
Location: 258 North US Highway 69, Atoka, OK 74525
Web: www.civilwar.org/visit/heritage-site/confederate-memorial-museum-and-cemetery

### Fort Sill National Historic Landmark & Museum
Location: Fort Sill—Bentley Gate Entrance, 435 Quanah Rd, Lawton, OK 73503
Web: sill-www.army.mil/museum/FSNHLM/aboutus.html

---

7      In all, 429 were either killed or missing.

**Fort Washita Historic Site**
Location: 3348 State Road 199, Durant, OK 74701
Web: www.okhistory.org/sites/fortwashita.php

**Honey Springs Battlefield Historic Site**
Location: 101601 South 4232 Road, Checotah, OK 74426
Web: www.okhistory.org/sites/honeysprings?full

**Stafford Air & Space Museum**
Location: 3000 East Logan Road, Weatherford, OK 73096
Web: www.staffordmuseum.org

**Tulsa Air and Space Museum & Planetarium**
Location: 3624 North 74th East Avenue, Tulsa, OK 74115
Web: www.tulsaairandspacemuseum.com

**Muskogee War Memorial Park (USS *Batfish*)**
Location: 3500 Batfish Road, Muskogee, OK 74403
Web: www.warmemorialpark.org

**Washita Battlefield National Historic Site**
Location: 18555 Highway 47A, Cheyenne, OK 73628
Web: www.nps.gov/waba

# America Invaded: **OKLAHOMA**

Nickname: Sooner State
Statehood: 1907
Capital: Oklahoma City

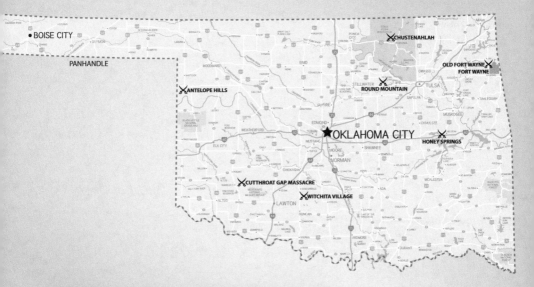

**B-17s BOMBED BOISE CITY**
National World War II Museum, New Orleans, LA
Source: Author photo

# OREGON

Spanish ships had already begun visiting the waters off Oregon in the sixteenth century. For instance, in 1543, Bartolomé Ferrelo may have reached the southwest coast. The trans-Pacific route that Spanish ships took from Mexico to the Philippines passed the area. And the eighteenth century saw a number of Spanish expeditions exploring the region. In 1774, Captain Juan Pérez sailed along the coast. And the following year, Captain Bruno de Heceta "discovered" the Columbia River and named it Rio San Roque.

But the Spanish were not the only Europeans interested in the area.

Some historians suggest that Britain's Sir Francis Drake may actually have landed in Whale Cove, Oregon, rather than in California in 1579.

The French were also advancing toward the region overland from the east.

In 1778, British Captain Cook made landfall at Cape Foulweather on the central coast of Oregon.

An American naval officer, Captain Robert Gray, arrived in Oregon waters in 1792 and "rediscovered" an immense river feeding into the Pacific. He named it Columbia after his ship (*Columbia Rediviva*), which became the first US ship to circumnavigate the globe.

Later that same year, British naval officer William Robert Broughton also took boats up part of the Columbia River.

Russian fur traders are likely to have arrived in the Beaver State a decade before Lewis and Clark. A log cabin in Molalla may have been built by Russians as early as 1795.

On first viewing the wide Pacific in what is now the state of Oregon, William Clark wrote effusively in his journal, "Ocian in view! O! the joy!" Expeditions are not the same as invasions, but there is sometimes a fine line between them. Meriwether Lewis and William Clark were both officers in the US Army on an expedition that had been equipped, and armed, by the US War Department. In 1802, President Jefferson asked a Spanish minister whether his government would "take it badly" if the United States sent an expedition to "explore the course of the Missouri river" through nominally Spanish territory. The minister averred that such an expedition "could not fail to give umbrage to our Government." President Jefferson disregarded the potential for Spanish displeasure and sent Lewis and Clark to explore the west and capture a continent.

After an arduous journey, Lewis and Clark arrived on the northwest coast of Oregon and constructed Fort Clatsop, where they stayed from November 1805 until mid-March 1806. It rained every day. They dined mainly on elk. The expedition interacted with the Clatsop, Chinook, Killamuck, Cathlahmet, and Wahkiakum, whom Lewis wrote were "loquacious and inquisitive." They purchased fish and other items from the Indians. Lewis described the local natives as having "copper brown" complexions and complained that they were "illy shapen." But evidently not all members of the Corps of Discovery agreed or cared about Lewis's judgment. Mercury was used to treat the venereal disease that Private Silas Goodrich picked up from "amorous contact with a Chinnook damsel."

The indigenous population that Lewis and Clark encountered were descended from people who began arriving in present-day Oregon over 10,000 years ago. They were a preliterate people who left no written record of that long precontact period. Lewis and Clark, aided by the Shoshone woman Sacagawea, communicated with them mainly through the use of sign language.

Both British and Americans rapidly became interested in the fur-trading opportunities in the area. In 1811, John Jacob Astor launched a fur-trading settlement in northwest Oregon that would become known as Astoria. The Royal Navy HMS *Raccoon* cruised along the Oregon coast during the War of 1812. Fort Astoria became British and was briefly renamed Fort George.

It was becoming increasingly evident that Britain and America were the two colonial powers that would compete for control of the Oregon territory.

In 1818, the countries agreed to jointly control Oregon. Shortly after that, both Spain and Russia gave up any claims on the area.

By the 1820s, a growing tide of European and American settlers followed the path taken by Lewis and Clark on what became known as the Oregon Trail. The arrival of more settlers brought diseases that shattered the Native American population.

Finally, in 1846, after tensions over control of the area had led to the possibility of war, Britain accepted US control.

US control was not, however, instantly accepted by much of the local Native American population. Decades of clashes would follow as the indigenous people were gradually forced to make land available for settlement.

The first significant discovery of gold near Jacksonville in southwestern Oregon in 1851 attracted more settlers to the Oregon territory.

So it is perhaps not surprising that the early 1850s saw a number of massacres perpetrated against Native Americans in that region. The Chetco, Lower Coquille, and Takelma peoples all suffered attacks.

In 1855–56, the Rogue River War flared up between settlers and Native Americans, also in southwestern Oregon. Governor George Law Curry issued a declaration of war against the Indians. The Battle of Hungry Hill, on Halloween 1855, with around five hundred combatants, was the largest battle of the Rogue River War and a rare victory for the Native Americans. Eventually, the Rogue River Indians were defeated and relocated into reservations in northern Oregon. Curry also got Oregon involved in the Yakima War (see Washington).

Oregon was admitted to the Union as a free state in 1859.

Fort Stevens near the mouth of the wide Columbia was built in 1863 during the Civil War. The earthwork fort was designed to prevent potential Confederate privateers from raiding up and down the Columbia River. The 1st Oregon Volunteer Infantry Regiment was mustered in 1864 to defend the Northwest and replace the US Army regulars who had been transferred east at the start of the war.

Some Confederate sympathizers did, however, exist in Oregon. Confederate supporters raised their flag in Jacksonville, but were then forced to take it down. And 1865 saw the so-called Long Tom Rebellion. After the assassination of Lincoln, Philip Henry Mulkey was arrested by 1st Oregon Volunteer Infantry for shouting pro-Confederate slogans in Eugene. Mulkey had supporters in the Long Tom District ready for a fight, but the infantry removed him from Eugene before further disruption could occur.

From 1864 to 1868, the Snake War was fought by the US Army against a number of tribes located near the Snake River. Some of the skirmishes in this conflict, which claimed nearly 1,800 casualties, were fought in Oregon.

And more clashes were to come in the region. The 1872–1873 Modoc War involved Oregon as well as California. In 1877, the Nez Perce Indian War followed, as the United States attempted to force Nez Perce onto a reservation. A group of Nez Perce led by Chief Joseph, among others, conducted a skilled and lengthy fighting retreat, but they were finally halted in Montana Territory near the Canadian border and forced to surrender. Oregon also saw some fighting in the 1878 Bannock War.

Native American resistance eventually came to an end, but that was not the end of combat for Oregon.

On the evening of June 21, 1942, Commander Tagami of the Imperial Japanese Navy surfaced his *I-25* submarine offshore near Fort Stevens. Seventeen rounds were fired from his 140mm deck gun from around 20,000 yards. No one was killed or injured, and little damage was done in the bombardment. The antiquated fort's 10-inch disappearing guns had a range of only 16,200 yards and could not return fire. The sub slunk off before American Army Air Force planes could respond. It was the first attack on a US Army installation in the continental United States by a foreign power since the War of 1812, when Fort Niagara was attacked by the British (see New York). The attack did help to fuel anti-Japanese hysteria on the West Coast, contributing to the support for internment of Japanese Americans.

In September of 1942, Commander Tagami returned to the Oregon coast to attack by air. Chief Warrant Officer Nobuo Fujita was the first and only officer serving in Axis forces to attack the US mainland from the air. He did so on September 9, 1942, with an E14Y1 reconnaissance floatplane that cruised at eighty-five miles per hour and carried 340 pounds of ordinance. Fujita's goal was to set Oregon forests ablaze with incendiary bombs. Thermite charges were dropped on Mount Emily in the Klamath Mountains near the town of Brookings. Fujita launched a second bombing run near Port Orford on September 29. Recent rain prevented either attack from igniting serious wildfires.

On both attacks, Fujita had brought with him on his seaplane his prized four-hundred-year-old samurai sword. In 1962, amidst some controversy among veterans, Fujita returned to Oregon and apologized for his wartime mission by presenting his samurai sword to the mayor of Brookings in Curry County (named after Governor Curry). Even President Kennedy had been consulted to approve Fujita's visit to the United States. The man who bombed America campaigned for peace and understanding between America and Japan, even helping to endow a scholarship that brought many Oregon students to Japan. His sword, a symbol of war and reconciliation, can be found today in the Chetco Public Library in Brookings.

The most destructive Japanese attack on Oregon, however, was not delivered by a submarine or seaplane. On New Year's Eve 1944, the first of a series of balloon bombs to strike the state landed near Estacada. Thousands of paper balloons made with paste from potatoes had been assembled by Japanese schoolgirls. These bombs, called Fu-Go, were inflated with hydrogen, released into the upper atmosphere, and carried by the jet stream current toward North America. They were the world's first intercontinental weapons.

On May 5, 1945, one of these bombs was discovered and accidentally detonated by children on a weekend outing near Bly. Elsie Mitchell, the pregnant wife of Reverend Archie Mitchell, was killed, along with five children. These were the only fatalities recorded in World War II as a result of the Fu-Go campaign. The Mitchell monument, dedicated in 1950, can be found in a Weyerhaeuser forest on Forest Service 34. The monument is flanked by six cherry trees that were donated by the Japanese government.

Unexploded Fu-Go from World War II doubtless lurk in the vast forests of Oregon and other western states.

## OREGON
## MILITARY HISTORY SITES

### Chetco Community Public Library
Location: 405 Alder Street, Brookings, OR 97415
Web: chetcolibrary.org

**FORT CLATSOP**
Lewis and Clark Expedition Fort (Reconstruction)
Source: Author photo

**RUSSELL BATTERY**
Fort Stevens
Bombarded by Japanese
submarine, June 21, 1942
Source: Author photo

**MITCHELL MONUMENT**
Near Bly
Source: Author photo

Nickname: The Beaver State
Statehood: 1859
Capital: Salem

FORT STEVENS
FORT CLATSOP   FORT ASTORIA / GEORGE

PORTLAND

★ SALEM

EUGENE    BEND    OREGON

ROGUE RIVER

HUNGRY HILL

MEDFORD

BROOKINGS                  BLY

**FUJITA SWORD**
Chetco Community Public Library
Brookings
Source: Author photo

**Columbia River Maritime Museum**
Location: 1792 Marine Drive Astoria, OR 97103
Web: www.crmm.org

**Evergreen Aviation & Space Museum**
Location: 500 NE Captain Michael King Smith Way, McMinnville, OR 97128
Web: www.evergreenmuseum.org

**Fort Stevens State Park**
Location: 100 Peter Iredale Road, Hammond, OR 97121
Web: visitftstevens.com
Web: oregonstateparks.org

**Lewis and Clark National Historical Park/Fort Clatsop**
Location: 92343 Fort Clatsop Road, Astoria, OR 97103
Web: www.nps.gov/lewi

**Mitchell Monument Historic Site**
Location: Weyerhauser Forest Road 34, Bly, OR 97622
Web: www.fs.usda.gov/recarea/fremont-winema/recreation/recarea/?recid=59797&actid=70

# PENNSYLVANIA

European explorers like Giovanni da Verrazano reached the waters off Delaware in the sixteenth century. When Europeans finally arrived in what is now the state of Pennsylvania, they found a land inhabited by a number of Algonquian-speaking tribes, including the Delaware/Lenape and the Shawnee, and a number of Iroquoian-speaking peoples, including the Susquehannock.

Explorers from a number of different European nations navigated the coastline of the area in the early seventeenth century, including Captain John Smith, who explored the Susquehanna River in 1608; Henry Hudson; Captain Samuel Argall; and later, Cornelius Hendrickson and Cornelius Jacobsen May.

In 1643, Johan Printz, governor of New Sweden, set up his base, Fort New Gothenburg, on Tinicum Island. But Pennsylvania was not going to end up under Swedish control. In 1655, Peter Stuyvesant, governor of New Netherland, occupied New Sweden. But Pennsylvania was not going to end up under Dutch control either. In 1664, the English seized it, and although the Dutch briefly took control again in 1673–4, it was Britain that would become the dominant colonial power in Pennsylvania.

Thus on March 4 1681, Charles II, who owed £16,000 on a loan from the late Admiral Sir William Penn, signed the Charter of Pennsylvania for the admiral's son, William Penn. Philadelphia was founded as the capital, land was bought from the local Native Americans, and encouraged by Penn, who was a Quaker, Quakers took a major part in developing the early colony.

Border disputes, including a long-running dispute over the territory that would become the state of Delaware, played a significant role in the early history of Pennsylvania.

In the 1730s, Cresap's War, though it wasn't that much of a war, erupted. The historic Penn-Calvert dispute over the location of the border between Pennsylvania and Maryland produced a situation in which settlers from both sides began to move into the disputed border zone, and conflict ensued. The conflict is often known as Cresap's War because a Marylander called Thomas Cresap played a key role in the war. The "war" was, in fact, mostly minor marauding, and attempts to impose the authority of one side or the other, and ended only after Cresap was captured by Pennsylvania and the British Crown imposed a border. The border in question, when finally properly surveyed became, of course, the Mason-Dixon Line.

But a rather more real war was about to break out, which would finally conclude the long struggle for power between Britain and France in North America. The territory of what is now Pennsylvania included, for much of the early colonial period, land in the west that was controlled by France, and land in the east that was controlled by Britain, with territory in between that was controlled by Native Americans. As such, it was long a frontier zone, but it was in the last war between Britain and France that Pennsylvania saw most action.

In 1739 and 1749, the French sent expeditions into what is now western Pennsylvania, and shortly afterwards they started a program of fort construction in the upper Ohio Valley to cement French control of the area. In 1754, Virginia sent in George Washington, then a lieutenant colonel, to counter the French expansionist moves. After he failed to persuade the French to withdraw peacefully, on May 28, 1754, Washington's forces ambushed French-Canadian forces at the Battle of Jumonville Glen, the opening battle of the French and Indian War. It was a victory for Washington, but after it, fearing an attack on his own forces, he set up Fort Necessity. There he was indeed attacked on July 3, and was forced to surrender and negotiate his withdrawal from the area.

But in 1755, he returned as part of the Braddock Expedition, which was aiming to capture Fort Duquesne. Once again, it turned into a disaster. The expedition was heavily defeated by the French and their Indian allies at the Battle of the Monongahela.

In 1758, though, the Forbes Expedition was to have considerably more success. Washington once again took part. The British managed to persuade much of the local Native American population to support Britain instead of France, and as the expedition's forces approached Fort Duquesne in November, the French blew up the fort and fled.

The 1763 peace deal that ended the war and gave to Britain all of France's claims in the area brought some stability to the area. Or at least it would have done, except that even before the peace, some local Native Americans had risen against Britain, the new colonial power. In Pontiac's War, a Native American alliance captured a number of British forts in the area, including Fort Venango, where they killed the defenders and then tortured the commander to death. Other forts, including Fort Pitt, were attacked but managed to hold out. On August 5, 1763, a British relieving force clashed with Delaware, Shawnee, Wyandot, and Mingo fighters at the Battle of Bushy Run. It was a British victory, but the relieving force suffered heavy casualties. Eventually, the British agreed to restrain the spread of colonial settlers westward; and as the Native American alliance collapsed and smallpox spread, a peace deal was made to end the war.

In 1764, the Black Boys Rebellion, in which settlers seized British military wagons, erupted. The settlers, with faces blackened, were unhappy with British-Indian policy.

With the French no longer a threat and Native American resistance in the area weakening, the stage was set for another of the many conflicts over Pennsylvania's borders. This time the conflict would take place in the Wyoming Valley, as Connecticut settlers competed with Pennsylvania settlers in an area where earlier administrative confusion had produced competing claims.

The Connecticut settlers founded Wilkes-Barre in 1769; and during the so-called Pennamite-Yankee Wars, the Pennsylvania settlers attempted to drive out their competitors. The British crown supported Connecticut's claims in 1771, and the Connecticut side founded Westmoreland as well in 1773. That was not the final chapter in the story, however.

Meanwhile southwestern Pennsylvania was also the subject of conflict. From 1773 until the American Revolution exploded, Lord Dunmore, governor of Virginia, was in control there, basing his claim on yet another anomaly produced by competing land grants.

Pennsylvania was, of course, to play a central role in the American Revolution, including hosting the adoption of the Declaration of Independence in Independence Hall, Philadelphia, in 1776. Later that year, it saw Washington launch his famous Crossing of the Delaware to surprise Hessian troops in Trenton, New Jersey. It was also the site of the hugely significant Philadelphia Campaign. A British landing in Chesapeake Bay led to Washington's defeat at the Battle of Brandywine Creek on September 11, 1777, and the British capture of Philadelphia, seat of the Continental Congress and capital of the Revolution. Another British victory at the Battle of Germantown in October left Philadelphia in British hands and Washington's forces wintering at Valley Forge. In 1778, though, as the French more determinedly entered the war, the British forces in Philadelphia were forced to withdraw to defend New York City.

And there was more fighting to come in the west. In the spring and summer of 1778, Loyalist and Native American forces, including Seneca, Cayuga, and Mohawk leader Joseph Brant, launched a campaign against American settlers and militia in the Wyoming Valley region. Incidents included the Wyoming Valley Massacre, in which 227 militia were killed. As a result, many settlers fled the area, and the Continental Army sent in troops on reprisal operations. In particular, General Sullivan's expedition in 1779 destroyed numerous Native American villages in Pennsylvania and New York.

The years after American victory in the War of Independence would not be totally peaceful ones in Pennsylvania, either.

In 1781, the Pennsylvania troops stationed in New Jersey mutinied, demanding better conditions. In 1783, mutinous soldiers from the Continental Army demanding their pay surrounded Congress in the State House in Philadelphia. When members of the Pennsylvania Executive Council failed to satisfy Congress's demand to protect it, Congress fled from Pennsylvania.

In 1782, the Continental Congress changed the British crown's verdict in the Pennamite-Yankee conflict, giving the land to Pennsylvania instead of Connecticut; and in 1784, conflict flared again.

The Whiskey Rebellion saw occasionally violent resistance, particularly in western Pennsylvania, to a 1791 tax imposed on distilled spirits. The rebellion reached a peak in 1794. In July of that year, rebels attacked General Neville's house at Bower Hill. A number of deaths occurred. In the following weeks, the rebels marched on Pittsburgh. There was even talk of declaring independence and seeking aid from Spain or Britain. Eventually, Washington sent a militia expedition into the area, and the rebellion collapsed.

In 1799, another tax rebellion broke out. This came in response to federal taxes imposed to pay for the quasi war against France. A significant number of the rebels this time were from the German-speaking counties of eastern Pennsylvania, and the rebellion is often known as Fries's Rebellion, after John Fries, son of a German immigrant. The rebellion collapsed after Fries was arrested and sentenced to death for treason. President John Adams later pardoned him.

The Treaty of Fort Stanwix was signed in 1784 between the Americans and the Iroquois League. More settlers flowed into Pennsylvania.

Another major war against Britain, however, was not far off. Pennsylvania was not exactly the main focus of the action in the War of 1812, but Erie did play a particularly important part in the conflict. It became the base for Captain Oliver Hazard Perry's Lake Erie fleet, including the *Niagara*, which became Perry's flagship during his decisive victory over the British at the Battle of Lake Erie on September 10, 1813. The (much restored) *Niagara* is still afloat today and is Pennsylvania's official state ship.

In 1844, muskets and cannons were used on the streets of Philadelphia as anti-immigrant and anti-Catholic Nativist Riots erupted.

But a bigger conflict was about to grip the country, and Philadelphia would play a central role in it: the Civil War.

Pennsylvania was a key state on the Union side during the Civil War, even though a number of prominent antiwar Democrats were from Pennsylvania. The state made a huge contribution to the Union cause in terms of supplying troops and munitions.

It also suffered a number of Confederate raids. In October 1862, J. E. B. Stuart invaded Pennsylvania with a cavalry force in a lightning move, reaching as far as Mercersburg and Chambersburg. And Chambersburg would suffer again in 1864, when General John McCausland reached the town with a Confederate force and demanded a ransom. The ransom was refused, and McCausland set light to the town.

When many people, however, think of Pennsylvania and the Civil War, they tend to think of just one campaign—Gettysburg.

In 1863, Lee launched his second invasion of the north with 75,000 men. Carlisle fell to the invaders, and the campaign culminated in three days of fierce fighting, with terrible casualties on both sides, at Gettysburg. Lee's repeated failure to smash the Union defenses, with multiple assaults ending with Pickett's Charge, forced him to call off the campaign and to order his army to retreat. George Meade commanded the victorious Union forces at Gettysburg. Joshua Chamberlain successfully defended Little Round Top with the 20th Maine Volunteer Infantry Regiment. Waller T. Patton, the great-uncle of General George Patton, was killed while leading Confederate troops in the attack on Cemetery Ridge during Pickett's Charge.

A few months after the battle, President Lincoln visited the Gettysburg Battlefield, where he opened the Gettysburg Address with the line, "Four score and seven years ago our fathers brought forth on this continent, a new nation, conceived in Liberty, and dedicated to the proposition that all men are created equal." Many years later, President Eisenhower would tour foreign dignitaries around the Gettysburg Battlefield in a golf cart near his Pennsylvania home.

The end of the Civil War seemed to mark the end of combat in Pennsylvania. Pennsylvania would see periods of violent industrial unrest, though; for instance, during the Great Railroad Strike of 1877. And it would play a major role in other conflicts. The Philadelphia Naval Shipyard continued to do vital work, particularly during World War II. Combat itself, however, would be elsewhere.

The twenty-first century's war against terrorism began in the airspace over Pennsylvania on September 11, 2001, when combat erupted on United Flight 93. The Boeing 757, on a regularly scheduled flight from Newark to San Francisco, had been seized that morning by four Al Qaeda terrorists. Todd Beamer and other passengers, informed of the attacks on the World Trade Center, voted to storm the cockpit. The plane crashed into the countryside near Shanksville, Pennsylvania, rather than somewhere in the nation's capital. Today it is a National Memorial preserved by the National Park Service.

## PENNSYLVANIA
## MILITARY HISTORY SITES

**Brandywine Battlefield Historic Site**
Location: 1491 Baltimore Pike, Chadds Ford, PA 19317
Web: www.brandywinebattlefield.org

**Bushy Run Battlefield**
Location: 1253 Bushy Run Road, Jeannette, PA 15644
Web: www.bushyrunbattlefield.com

**Eisenhower National Historic Site**
Location: 243 Eisenhower Farm Road, Gettysburg, PA 17325
Web: www.nps.gov/eise/

**Flight 93 National Memorial**
Location: 6424 Lincoln Highway, Stoystown, PA 15563
Web: www.nps.gov/flni/

**Fort Pitt Block House**
Location: Point State Park, Pittsburgh, PA 15222
Web: www.fortpittblockhouse.com

**Fort Pitt Museum**
Location: 601 Commonwealth Pl, Pittsburgh, PA 15222
Web: www.heinzhistorycenter.org/fort-pitt/

**Gettysburg National Military Park**
Location: 1195 Baltimore Street, Gettysburg, PA 17325
Web: www.nps.gov/gett/

**Museum of the American Revolution**
Location: 101 South Third Street, Philadelphia, PA 19106
Web: www.amrevmuseum.org

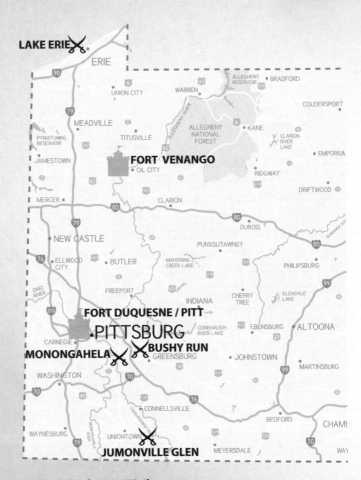

**BARON VON STEUBEN (1730-1794)**
Valley Forge National Historical Park
Source: Author photo

**CABIN (RECONSTRUCTION)**
Valley Forge National Historical Park
Source: Author photo

Nickname: Keystone State
Statehood: 1787
Capital: Harrisburg

SAYRE
MONTROSE
MANSFIELD
TOWANDA
FOREST CITY
GALETON
CANTON
CARBONDALE
SCRANTON
SIEGE OF FORT STANWIX
LAPORTE
MOSCOW
MILFORD
WILLIAMSPORT
WILKES-BARRE
LAKE WALLENPAUPACK
HOWARD
LOCK HAVEN
BLOOMSBURG
MT ROCONO
HAZELTON
BRODHEADSVILLE
STATE COLLEGE
MIFFLINBURG
SUNBURY
EASTON
POTTSVILLE
ALLENTOWN
BETHLEHEM
MT UNION
NEWPORT
LYKENS
LEBANON
READING
DOYLESTOWN
HARRISBURG
LEVITTOWN
CARLISLE
VALLEY FORGE
LANCASTER
GERMANTOWN
YORK
PHILADELPHIA
BERSBURG
GETTYSBURG
BRANDYWINE CREEK
NESBORO
GETTYSBURG

**GEORGE MEADE**
1815-1872
Source: akg-images/ClassicStock
Charles Phelps Cushing

**GEORGE PICKETT**
1825-1875
Source: akg-images

**Pennsylvania Military Museum**
Location: 51 Boal Avenue, Boalsburg, PA 16827
Web: www.pamilmuseum.org

**U.S. Army Heritage & Education Center**
Location: 950 Soldiers Drive, Carlisle, PA 17013
Web: www.ahec.armywarcollege.edu

**Valley Forge National Historical Park**
1400 North Outer Line Drive, King of Prussia, PA 19406
Web: www.nps.gov/vafo/

# RHODE ISLAND

America's smallest state has packed a big historic punch. Native Americans occupied the area for many thousands of years before the arrival of Europeans; and by the sixteenth century a number of different peoples were present in the area—the Wampanoag, the Narragansett, the Nipmuc, and the Niantic.

What is now Rhode Island and Providence Plantations was probably already the scene of occasional conflict before the landings of Europeans, and conflict between Native American groups also occurred in the seventeenth century.

For instance, in the 1620s, the Narragansett expanded their control over land in the area that had previously been held by the Wampanoag. And in the early 1630s, the Pequot took over land previously controlled by the Narragansett.

However, the European invasion was to change the balance of intertribal power in the area, as it was to change pretty much everything else.

That included the area's name. The indigenous name for Rhode Island was Aquidneck. Rhode Island seems to be a European name, though its origins are uncertain. It may have come from a perceived similarity to the island of Rhodes in the Mediterranean, or from a Dutch word meaning *red*.

However, the local population would soon have rather more to worry about than what the newcomers wanted to call the island.

The Italians played a role in Rhode Island right from the outset. Giovanni da Verrazano had already cruised along the coast in 1524, but it was in the 1630s that Europeans began establishing a permanent presence in the area.

In 1636, Anglican clergyman Roger Williams, a believer in religious freedom and the separation of church and state, and who had been banished from the Massachusetts Bay Colony, turned up. He bought land off the locals and established Providence. Other religiously motivated settlers followed.

Fighting flared in the area during the Pequot War of 1636–8, when English settlers allied with locals, including the Narragansett, fought the Pequot. The main action of this war, though, took place in Connecticut, and we deal with it there.

The area, however, was the scene of heavy fighting during King Philip's War of 1675–76. "King Philip" was, in fact, Metacom, leader of the Wampanoag. He fell out with the United Colonies of New England, and even though Rhode Island was not part of that alliance, it would be involved in the fighting.

In the summer of 1675, New England forces clashed with the Wampanoag at Pocasset Swamp. The Narragansett had not been major participants at first, but they were gradually sucked into the slaughter. In December, an invading colonist force, with some local allies that included Pequot fighters, attacked the Narragansett camp near what is now South Kingstown. In a brutal assault, English forces seized and burned the camp. Hundreds of Narragansett fighters and civilians died in the attack, and from cold and hunger afterwards.

The Narragansett now attacked colonist settlements in Rhode Island, including burning Providence in March 1676. In the end, however, the military might and ruthlessness of the settlers proved too much for Metacom His alliances fell apart; and in August 1676, forces of the Plymouth Colony militia and local allies cornered and killed him at Mount Hope. The war caused a huge loss of life to tribes like the Narragansett and Wampanoag, and effectively destroyed indigenous power in Rhode Island.

Rhode Island would occasionally be caught up in the conflicts that raged across America over the next century. For instance, on July 22, 1690, a flotilla of French ships under Pierre le Picard invaded Block Island in retaliation for attacks on Canada, and then threatened Newport before being driven off. A bitter border dispute with Massachusetts also ground on for a long time.

In 1764, Rhode Islanders, upset by the British imposition of the Sugar Act, seized Fort George and opened fire on the HMS *St. John*. Some historians have described these shots as the opening act of the American Revolution.

And there was fierce fighting in the Rhode Island area during the War of Independence. And the violence started early. In 1772, the HMS *Gaspee*, pursuing a packet boat called *Hannah* during a customs-enforcement operation, ran aground in Narragansett Bay. Locals, who were extremely unenthusiastic about such customs enforcement, rowed out, seized the ship, and set light to it.

In 1776, Rhode Island was an early and enthusiastic supporter of independence. British forces occupied Newport, forcing revolutionary forces to evacuate to Bristol. Bristol was bombarded, and the area suffered a number of skirmishes and much damage from foraging. Many of the inhabitants of Newport fled.

With its maritime heritage, Rhode Island rapidly came to play a major role in US naval history. A Rhode Island ship, the *Providence*, became the first ship of the Continental Navy and was John Paul Jones's first command. A replica built for the 1976 bicentennial is now berthed in Providence. And Rhode Islander Esek Hopkins became the Continental Navy's first commander. The US Navy was founded in Rhode Island, and today Newport remains the home of the Naval War College.

In 1778, American and French forces attempted to push out the British. The local militia had been reinforced with thousands of Continental line troops and militiamen in an attempt to break the stalemate on the island. They were also supposed to have French naval support. Unfortunately for the Americans, the French naval force that did turn up confronted an even larger British force. And then, to make matters even worse for the French, they were hit by a hurricane (though to be fair, the British ships suffered from the weather as well). The Americans, hearing that British reinforcements were on their way, decided to abandon the siege of Newport and retreat. At this point, British forces advanced to attack the retreating enemy. On August 29, the two forces clashed in the Battle of Quaker Hill. It was not a hugely decisive battle. The Americans managed to hold off a number of British assaults, but then they withdraw in the night, abandoning Aquidneck Island to the British. The battle is notable for the participation of the 1st Rhode Island Regiment, a locally recruited African-American Regiment.

Colonel William West, from North Kingston, became an ardent Patriot militia leader during the American Revolution. West was one of the signatories of Rhode Island's Declaration of Independence, which preceded that signed by the Continental Congress by about two months.

British control of the colony did not last long. In October 1779, four years before the war ended, British forces withdrew. In July of the next year, about 6,000 French forces arrived at Newport to assist the Revolutionary cause. These troops, under the command of the Count of Rochambeau, later marched to Virginia and played a decisive role in the American victory at Yorktown.

In 1812, Rhode Islander Matthew Perry, later to find a place in history through his involvement in opening up Japan to the west, was on board the USS *President* when it opened fire on HMS *Belvidera* at the start of the War of 1812. The American government's position on the War of 1812 was not hugely popular in Rhode Island. American privateers did, however, operate out of Rhode Island ports, and British forces did burn a number of American ships in Narragansett Bay.

Block Island, as it had done during the Revolutionary War, declared neutrality in the conflict. Nonetheless, the Royal Navy landed there on several occasions. For instance, on May 1, 1813, naval forces under Sir Thomas Hardy not only managed to supply themselves with water and food from Block Island, but they also got their washing done there.

In 1842, Dorr's Rebellion saw an attempt to storm the arsenal in Providence in support of a new constitution. But the rebels gave up after their cannon failed. The leader of the rebellion, Thomas Wilson Dorr, was eventually given a life sentence for treason in 1844, but he was let out of jail a year later.

While Rhode Island and its citizens played a significant role in the Civil War, the fighting took place elsewhere. The USS *Rhode Island* did take the war to the Confederacy with its attacks on blockade runners and its participation in the assault on Fort Fisher in North Carolina.

Rhode Island was clearly not the center of action in World War I either, but at least one incident from the war is worth recounting, and seems somewhat extraordinary now. On October 7, 1916, before America entered the war, German submarine *U-53*—which had been on a war patrol in the Atlantic—sailed boldly into Narragansett Bay. It anchored at Newport, and its commander, Hans Rose, went ashore, making visits as demanded by etiquette to two senior US naval officers. Rose then left the harbor and proceeded to sink Allied and neutral merchant ships. The sinkings took place in international waters, and the US Navy did not intervene.

During World War II, enemy forces once again invaded the waters off Rhode Island. The conflict saw an assortment of U-boat activity. One of the last naval actions involving US and German forces was the Battle of Point Judith.

On May 5, 1945, with Hitler already dead and the end of the war in Europe just a few days away, *U-853* torpedoed the SS *Black Point*, the last US-flagged merchant ship sunk in the Atlantic during the war. Twelve men were killed in the attack. In response, a group of US Navy vessels went in search of the German submarine. Once they located it, they attacked it throughout the night, before accepting in the morning signs of debris as evidence of the U-boat's destruction. The sinking of the submarine and the death of all on board was later confirmed.

Though Rhode Island played a significant role in the Cold War through, for instance, such facilities as the Naval War College at Newport, it didn't see that much actual Cold War action.

One Soviet submarine that did make it to Rhode Island was *K-77*, although it only arrived there after the end of the Cold War. After being decommissioned by the Russians, *K-77* appeared in the movie *K-19: The Widowmaker*, and then became a tourist attraction at Collier Point Park in Providence. Eventually, however, it sank and was subsequently sold for scrap.

## RHODE ISLAND
## MILITARY HISTORY SITES

### Dorr Rebellion Museum
Location: 1043 Putnam Pike, Chepachet, RI 02814
Web: www.dorrrebellionmuseum.org/index.htm

### Fort Adams State Park
Location: 84 Fort Adams Drive, Newport, RI 02840
Web: www.riparks.com/Locations/LocationFortAdams.html

### Gilbert Stuart Birthplace & Museum
Location: 815 Gilbert Stuart Road, Saunderstown, RI 02874
Web: www.gilbertstuartmuseum.org

**Hunter House**
Location: 54 Washington Street, Newport, RI 02840
Web: www.newportmansions.org/explore/hunter-house

**Naval War College Museum**
Location: Founders Hall, Building 10, Luce Avenue, Newport, RI 02841
Web: www.usnwc.edu/museum

**Roger Williams National Memorial**
Location: 282 North Main Street, Providence, RI 02903
Web: www.nps.gov/rowi/index.htm

**Seabee Museum and Memorial Park**
Location: 21 Iafrate Way, North Kingstown, RI 02852
Web: www.seabeesmuseum.com

**Spell Hall—The Major General Nathanael Greene Homestead**
Location: 50 Taft Street, Coventry, RI 02816
Web: www.nathanaelgreenehomestead.org

**Tomaquag Indian Memorial Museum**
Location: 390 A Summit Road, Exeter, RI 02822
Web: www.tomaquagmuseum.org

**Westerly Armory**
Location: 41 Railroad Avenue, Westerly, RI 02891
Web: www.westerlyarmory.com

Nickname: The Ocean State
Statehood: 1790
Capital: Providence

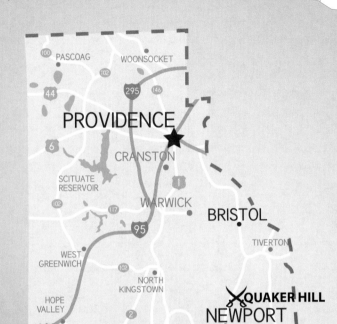

PASCOAG
WOONSOCKET
PROVIDENCE
CRANSTON
SCITUATE
RESERVOIR
WARWICK
BRISTOL
TIVERTON
WEST
GREENWICH
NORTH
KINGSTOWN
HOPE
VALLEY
**QUAKER HILL**
NEWPORT
KINGSTON
**FORT GEORGE**
GOAT ISLAND
**GREAT SWAMP FIGHT**
WAKEFIELD
BRADFORD
**POINT JUDITH**

BLOCK
ISLAND

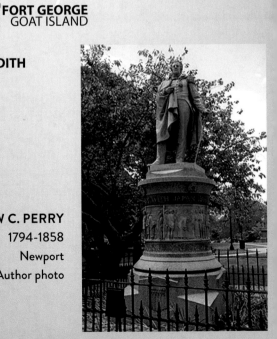

**MATTHEW C. PERRY**
1794-1858
Newport
Source: Author photo

# SOUTH CAROLINA

South Carolina, the Palmetto State, boasts a rich military history and tradition. The state was the probable birthplace of Andrew Jackson, the victor in the Battle of New Orleans. It was fought over extensively during the American Revolution. The Confederate attack on Fort Sumter marked the commencement of the American Civil War.

The area was inhabited long before the arrival of Europeans. The Catawba, Cherokee, Choctaw, Creek, and Yamasee are just some of the Native American tribes that the first Europeans encountered in South Carolina.

The Spanish took an interest in the area in the sixteenth century. Spanish explorer Hernando de Soto, for instance, cruised along the coast of South Carolina in 1540. In 1566, a Spanish settlement, Santa Elena, was established on what is today Parris Island. European diseases began to ravage the Native American population. Ten years later, the indigenous people attacked and burned Santa Elena to the ground. The Spaniards abandoned the swampy shores of Carolina.

In 1670, around 148 English colonists led by Joseph West arrived at Albemarle Point. They were the founders of Charles Town. Spanish complaints that this constituted an "invasion" of their Florida territory were disregarded.

During Queen Anne's War of 1702–1713, attacks were launched south from South Carolina into Spanish-controlled territory. The Spanish decided to take more direct action against Charles Town than just complain. In 1706, a joint French-Spanish attack was launched on Charles Town. However, the attack was repulsed, and a French ship was captured.

English settlers then had to contend with the indigenous people of the Carolinas. From 1715 to 1717, the Yamasee tribe launched attacks on South Carolina settlers. The Pocotaligo Massacre claimed the lives of over one hundred colonists. Governor Craven called the Carolina Militia to arms, but around 7 percent of the total colonial population was killed. The Creeks joined the Yamassee War in 1716, but made a separate peace with the colonists in 1717. Yamasee raids, however, would continue until 1728.

And it wasn't just the Yamassee who were attacking. In 1718, Edward Teach, aka the pirate Blackbeard, sailed into Charles Town Harbor with four ships, capturing hostages to ransom them.

Meanwhile, hostilities had begun between Creeks and Cherokees, with South Carolina supporting the Cherokees. In 1727, a peace deal was arranged with the help of South Carolina between the Creeks and Cherokees, but hostilities would resume later. In 1739, the War of Jenkins' Ear broke out between Britain and Spain, causing clashes to the south.

Also in 1739 was the Stono Rebellion, in which enslaved Africans rebelled in the name of freedom before being crushed by local Carolina militiamen.

During the Seven Years' War, British colonists in South Carolina defeated the Cherokee uprising, which lasted from 1758 until a treaty was signed in Charleston in 1762.

The start of the American Revolution in 1775 placed South Carolina in an uncomfortable position. Due to the massive superiority of the Royal Navy, its coastlines and ports were vulnerable to a British amphibious assault, and its population was divided over which side to support. The Tidewater dwellers of the coast inclined to the rebel side, as did the frontiersmen of Appalachia. The Piedmont colonists in the middle, however, tended to remain loyal to the crown. Charleston even flirted with the idea of becoming an open or neutral city at the beginning of the conflict.

Early in the war, in 1776, a British attempt to capture Charleston was repulsed at the Battle of Sullivan's Island.

The American Revolution in South Carolina soon degenerated into a brutal civil war. From 1775 on, Loyalists and rebels skirmished repeatedly at Ninety Six in Greenwood County. In 1781, General Nathaniel Greene would lay siege (unsuccessfully) to a British force in Ninety Six.

In 1779, the British government identified the southern colonies as being a softer target, holding more Loyalist or Tory supporters than the hardscrabble colonies of New England and the mid-Atlantic.

In December of 1779, Henry Clinton led a British invasion force of 8,500 men that set out to subdue Charleston. On February 11, 1780, they landed on Johns Island thirty miles south of the city. Over 5,500 Patriot troops (including many Carolina militia), commanded by Benjamin Lincoln, were besieged from March 28 until their surrender on May 12. It was the worst American reverse of the war and the third largest surrender of American forces in history, only exceeded by Bataan in World War II and Harper's Ferry in the Civil War.

In 1780, Colonel Banastre Tarleton, whose portrait by Joshua Reynolds hangs today in London's National Gallery, emerged as one of the most infamous and controversial British invaders in Carolina history. He was born in 1754 in Liverpool, the son of a wealthy slave trader. He attended Oxford University. In 1773, he inherited the sum of 5,000 pounds on his father's death, which he quickly squandered by gambling. In 1775, he purchased an officer's commission in the 1st Dragoon Guards.

Tarelton became a colonel of the British Legion and the head of Tarleton's Raiders. His most notorious action was on May 29, 1780, at the Battle of Waxhaws in South Carolina. Tarleton's request for Colonel Abraham Buford to surrender was rejected. Tarleton then led a cavalry charge that killed 113 rebels, with many more wounded or made prisoner. Tarleton's men were subsequently accused of having cut down Americans who were attempting to surrender. "Tarleton's Quarter" became a Patriot rallying cry that was used to justify swift justice for captured Loyalist and Redcoat forces in the south.

Tarleton had an affair with the actress Mary Robinson, whom he initially seduced on a wager. The villain in the 2000 film *The Patriot*, Colonel Tavington, was loosely based on Tarleton. Unlike Tavington, Tarleton survived the war, serving as an MP in Parliament and engaging in the slave trade.

On August 16, 1780, Lord Cornwallis led an outnumbered British Army to victory against Horatio Gates at the Battle of Camden. "Granny" Gates fled from the battle, covering 180 miles over the next three days. Alexander Hamilton remarked witheringly, "Was there ever an instance of a general running away … from his whole army?"

Many Cherokee Indians allied themselves with the British during the Revolutionary War, putting additional pressure on the Carolina colonists.

Despite the setback at Charleston and the humiliation at Camden, rebel resistance in the Carolinas continued and even stiffened. Mariners from Carolina fitted out as privateers to harass British shipping in the Caribbean. In the summer of 1780, a series of skirmishes were fought in South Carolina at Williamson's Plantation, McDowell's Camp, and Hanging Rock. The largest of these was the American victory gained by Brigadier General Thomas Sumter at the Battle of Hanging Rock. Years later, a fort at the mouth of Charleston Harbor would be named in his honor.

On October 7, 1780, Carolina militia won a surprising and decisive victory over British regulars at the Battle of Kings Mountain. The British commander of the 91st Foot, Major Ferguson, was killed, and most of his men were captured.

Francis Marion, a Carolinian veteran of the Cherokee Uprising in the Seven Years' War, emerged as a talented guerrilla leader in the southern campaign. Leaving Charleston due to an ankle injury, Marion was one of the few rebel soldiers in Carolina not captured with Major General Benjamin Lincoln's surrender. Tarleton, having pursued Marion without success, declared, "As for this damned old fox, the devil himself could not catch him." Marion was known thereafter as the Swamp Fox. After the Charleston surrender, he led a small band of rebels that engaged in hit-and-run Indian-style raids on the British and their Loyalist supporters. Marion led the Patriot's right wing at the Battle of Eutaw Springs on September 8, 1781, where General Nathaniel Greene fought the British to a draw. The British under Colonel Alexander Stewart withdrew, having suffered a 40 percent loss of their force. This would prove to be the last major battle of the American Revolution in the South.

On January 17, 1781, General Morgan, though outnumbered, won a decisive victory over Colonel Tarleton at the Battle of Cowpens. Most of the British and Tory forces were compelled to surrender. The tide in South Carolina had turned decisively in favor of the Patriots.

On December 14, 1782, the British evacuated Charleston, ending the war in South Carolina.

During the War of 1812, the Royal Navy blockaded the ports of South Carolina. The state contributed 5,000 soldiers to the war effort. Castle Pinckney near Charleston had been completed in 1810 to protect the Carolina coast from foreign invasion. The British did not, however, really target South Carolina.

The Citadel was established in Charleston as the South Carolina Military Academy in 1842 to educate young Southerners in military science.

In 1860 the slave population of South Carolina exceeded the white population, and fears of a slave uprising were ever present. In December of 1860, following the election of Abraham Lincoln to the White House but preceding his inauguration, South Carolina became the first state to secede from the Union. Just a week after secession was announced, on December 27, 1860, a South Carolina militia unit seized Castle Pinckney, a federal fort, near Charleston. The small Union garrison withdrew to Fort Sumter. The pot was beginning to simmer.

In the early morning hours of April 12, 1861, Confederate guns began firing on Sumter, an island fortress in the midst of Charleston Harbor. Fort Sumter was occupied by Union forces under the command of Major Robert Anderson. During the morning, 3,341 rounds were lobbed at the fort, and the garrison responded with a thousand shots of their own. In spite of all this cannonading, the only fatality on the fateful day that launched the bloodiest war in American history was an unfortunate mule! Major Anderson surrendered the fort and evacuated his men. Governor Pickens proclaimed, "The war is commenced and we will triumph or perish."

Beginning in August of 1861, the Union, with naval supremacy, struck back at South Carolina, shelling Forts Clark and Hatteras. A seventy-seven ship fleet carrying 12,000 troops and commanded by Samuel Du Pont bombarded Fort Beauregard and captured Port Royal. Possession of Port Royal made it easier for the Union to enforce a blockade of Southern ports, such as Charleston and Savannah. The Union's Anaconda strategy would gradually throttle the Confederacy, shutting down its lucrative cotton trade and starving it of supplies.

Union forces attempted an invasion of Charleston in 1862. Brigadier General Nathan Evans led Confederate forces to victory at the Battle of Secessionville on June 16, 1862, inflicting casualties at a rate of more than three to one. Union forces withdrew, and Southern newspapers crowed.

In 1863, the Union again attempted to take Charleston. More clashes followed, including two attempts to storm Fort Wagner. The second try saw heroic efforts by the 54th Massachusetts Volunteer Infantry, one of the first major African-American army units. Despite the 54th's bravery and the heavy casualties it took, the Confederate defenders managed to retain control of the fort. Colonel Robert Gould Shaw of Boston was killed in the fighting on Morris Island at age twenty-five.

Various attempts were also made by Union forces to land and then cut the

Charleston-Savannah railroad, with mixed results.

But much harder times were ahead for South Carolina. In late 1864, General Sherman, already in Atlanta, was beginning his famous—or infamous—March to the Sea. A cadet battalion from the Citadel was mustered to fight the Battle of Tulifinny on December 6, 1864, in Jasper County. The Confederates, although outnumbered five to one, managed to hold off the Union advance along a key railroad line. In January of 1865, however, General Ulysses S. Grant advanced north from Savannah into South Carolina. On February 17, Union troops captured the state capital at Columbia. Fires, set either by federal troops or rebels igniting cotton supplies, destroyed much of the city. The Arsenal in Columbia, which formed part of the Citadel, was burned to the ground. Charleston was abandoned, allowing "Billy Yank" to occupy the wellspring of the Confederacy at last.

An "invasion" of Yankee carpetbaggers swept into South Carolina after the surrender at Appomattox Courthouse. And South Carolina would see significant violence as the state adjusted to the new realities after the war. In 1882, the Citadel was reopened.

During the Spanish-American War of 1898, infantry from South Carolina fought alongside their Yankee countrymen for the first time since the Civil War and joined in occupying Cuba. Many more Carolinians would answer the call in the First World War. Meanwhile, the German Kaiser's U-boats began to hunt for merchant ships along the Carolina coast in 1917–1918.

German U-boats would again prowl the South Carolina coast during World War II. In September of 1942, Captain Hans-Heinrich Giessler of the Kriegsmarine arrived off the coast of Charleston. He noted in his diary that streetlights illuminated the bridge over the Cooper River and that the "Charleston lighthouse burns as in peacetime." Giessler, unlike most of his fellow U-boat captains, survived the war.

## SOUTH CAROLINA
## MILITARY HISTORY SITES

### The Citadel—The Military College of South Carolina
Location: 171 Moultrie Street, Charleston, SC 29409
Web: www.citadel.edu/root/visit-the-citadel

# America Invaded: SOUTH CAROLINA

Nickname: The Palmetto State
Statehood: 1788
Capital: Columbia

## BANASTRE TARLETON

1754-1833
National Gallery, London
Artist: Sir Joshua Reynolds
Source: akg-images

## FORT SUMTER

Battle of Fort Sumter
April 12-13, 1861
Source: iStock/Juanmonino

## ROBERT GOULD SHAW

1837-1863
Died on Morris Island
July 18, 1863
Memorial Boston Common, MA
Source: Author photo

**The Confederate Museum**
Location: 188 Meeting Street, Charleston, SC 29413
Web: www.confederatemuseumcharlestonsc.com

**Cowpens National Battlefield**
Location: 4001 Chesnee Highway, Gaffney, SC 29341
Web: www.nps.gov/cowp/index.htm

**Fort Sumter National Monument**
Location: 1214 Middle Street, Charleston, SC 29482
Web: www.nps.gov/fosu/index.htm

**Historic Camden Revolutionary War Site**
Location: 222 Broad Street, Camden, SC 29020
Web: www.discoversouthcarolina.com/products/1657

**Kings Mountain National Military Park**
Location: 2300 Park Road, Blacksburg, SC 29702
Web: www.nps.gov/kimo/index.htm

**Ninety Six National Historic Site**
Location: 1103 Highway 248, Ninety Six, SC 29666
Web: www.nps.gov/nisi/index.htm

**Parris Island Museum**
Location: 283 Boulevard De France, Parris Island, SC 29905
Web: www.mcrdpimuseum.com/index.cfm

**South Carolina Military Museum**
Location: 1225 Bluff Road, Columbia, SC 29201
Web: www.scmilitarymuseum.com

**War Between the States Museum**
Location: 107 South Guerry Street, Florence, SC 29501
Web: www.discoversouthcarolina.com/products/252

# SOUTH DAKOTA

South Dakota, the home of Mount Rushmore, is named after Native American tribes. Before the arrival of Europeans in what is now South Dakota, the area had already seen different Native American peoples competing for control of territory, as Sioux migrated westward and came into contact with peoples like the Arikara.

It was the French who were the first Europeans to venture into the area. Contact began in the late seventeenth and early eighteenth centuries, and in 1743, the Vérendrye brothers set off from Lake Manitoba on a journey intended to take them as far as the Pacific. En route, they buried a lead plaque near what is now Fort Pierre. Today Pierre, named after the French fur trader Pierre Chouteau, is the state capital.

Soon after that, though, the French were temporarily out of the picture. They handed over their claims to the area to Spain under a deal made in 1762, though a lot of the locals didn't find out about it until 1764. In some locations, power wasn't handed over until 1770.

The Spanish had (among others) two major problems. Firstly, exploring and exploiting the territory Spain claimed to control; and secondly, preventing Britain from exploring and exploiting the territory Spain claimed to control. In 1793, what is often known as the Missouri Company was formed in St. Louis to explore areas, including parts of what is now South Dakota. In autumn 1794, an expedition under Jean-Baptiste Truteau established Ponca House on the Missouri. And in the spring of 1795, a more ambitious expedition set off under Antoine Simon Lecuyer. However, the Poncas were not happy about it, and Lecuyer didn't entirely distinguish himself. And worse (from the Spanish point of view) was to come. News arrived that the British and Canadians were expanding their links with the Mandan people.

Somewhat confusingly, at this point the Missouri Company in Spanish St. Louis sent an expedition led by Scotsman James Mackay and Welshman John Thomas Evans to counter the growing British influence. Well, business is business.

This latest expedition built Fort Charles near present-day Sioux City; and a team under Evans made it as far as the mouth of the White River before being forced by local opposition to withdraw. In the summer of 1796, Evans finally made it as far as the territory of the Mandan and temporarily expelled the Canadian traders. But elsewhere, Mackay was withdrawing to St. Louis and the Missouri Company was going bankrupt. In the end, Evans too retreated to St. Louis.

There wasn't much future for the Spanish colonial authorities in the region. In 1800, Spain handed over Louisiana to France again, and in 1803, the young United States bought it in the Louisiana Purchase. It would be the United States, not France or Spain or Britain, that would, as an invading power, take full control of the area.

At this point, we come to, yes, Lewis and Clark again. Their expedition set off from St. Louis in 1804, and they passed through what is now South Dakota both en route to the Pacific and on their return journey as well. They had various encounters with the local peoples of the area, and they held a meeting with the Teton Sioux near what is now Fort Pierre, trying to ensure that the United States would have more influence in the area than Britain.

In the period after Lewis and Clark's historic expedition, American traders and trappers began to explore and exploit the area. Among others interested in the territory were William Henry Ashley and Andrew Henry, who established the Rocky Mountain Fur Company. And after the arrival of the traders and trappers, the US Army showed up. By 1856, they had established Fort Randall. Demands for the area to be opened up to American settlement grew and, in the end, the Yankton Sioux decided that selling millions of acres in eastern South Dakota and moving to a reservation was better than trying to stop, by force, the overwhelming military might of the expanding United States. In 1858, Struck-by-the-Ree and other leaders signed the deal. In 1859, it was implemented.

But war would come to the region. In 1862, the Sioux Uprising erupted in Minnesota, and as it was crushed there, fighting spread westward. The main focus of this phase of fighting was in North Dakota, but South Dakota also saw battles.

In 1874, an expedition led by George Armstrong Custer entered the Black Hills. It found gold, and miners raced into the area in search of riches, despite the fact that the western half of South Dakota was a Sioux reservation. Soon the US government was putting pressure on the Lakota to sell their land. When the Lakota refused, the US Army advanced. Most of the fighting, including Custer's defeat at Little Bighorn in Montana, took place elsewhere; but in September 1876, Brigadier General George Crook destroyed an Oglala village at Slim Buttes and then brushed aside an assault led by Crazy Horse. In the end, Native American resistance could not sustain itself against greater American military power. By 1877, the fighting was over as the Native American war bands surrendered, scattered, or fled.

But even this was not the end of Native American resistance to the invaders. In 1890, about 3,000 Ghost Dancers, consisting of Lakota, Oglala, and Sicangu, gathered in a place called the Stronghold. Sitting Bull was killed during an attempt to arrest him because it was feared he was about to join them. In December of that year, a group of Lakota under Chief Big Foot, the majority of whom were women and children, were stopped by the US Army and ordered to camp at Wounded Knee Creek. They complied, and forces from the 7th Cavalry surrounded them. When soldiers attempted to search for weapons and disarm the Lakota, fighting broke out, and the US forces turned their devastating Hotchkiss machine guns on the Lakota, massacring 153 of them. More violent actions occurred, including at White Clay Creek; and by the time it was all over, armed, organized Native American resistance in South Dakota was effectively at an end.

However, South Dakota was to see one more attack from abroad. During the Japanese balloon-bombing campaign of World War II, at least eight balloons reached South Dakota, including one that landed near Buffalo.

And the 1973 occupation of Wounded Knee by Oglala Lakota would show that ghosts from the past live on in the present.

## SOUTH DAKOTA
## MILITARY HISTORY SITES

### Crazy Horse Memorial
Location: 12151 Avenue of the Chiefs, Crazy Horse, SD 57730
Web: www.crazyhorsememorial.org

### Custer State Park
Location: 13329 US Highway 16A, Custer, SD 57730
Web: www.gfp.sd.gov/state-parks/directory/custer/default.aspx

### Fort Sisseton Historic State Park
Location: 11907 434th Avenue, Lake City, SD 57247
Web: www.gfp.sd.gov/state-parks/directory/fort-sisseton/

### Mount Rushmore National Memorial
Location: 13000 Highway 244, Keystone, SD 57751
Web: www.nps.gov/moru/index.htm

### Sitting Bull Monument
Location: 7 miles southwest of Mobridge, SD 57601
Web: www.mobridge.org/mobridge.php?subid=8

### Soldiers & Sailors World War Memorial
Location: 425 East Capitol Avenue, Pierre, SD 57501
Web: www.nps.gov/nr/travel/pierre_fortpierre/soldiers_sailors_world_war_memorial_pierre.html

### South Dakota Air & Space Museum
Location: 2890 Rushmore Drive, Ellsworth Air Force Base, SD 57706
Web: www.sdairandspacemuseum.com

### South Dakota National Guard Museum
Location: 301 East Dakota, Pierre, SD 57501
Web: www.military.sd.gov/natl_guard_museum.html

Nickname: The Mount Rushmore State
Statehood: 1889
Capital: Pierre

## MOUNT RUSHMORE NATIONAL MEMORIAL

Keystone

Source: akg-images

**Battleship USS *South Dakota* Memorial**
Location: 12th & Kiwanis, Sioux Falls, SD 57101
Web: www.usssouthdakota.com

**Wounded Knee Massacre Monument**
Location: Big Foot Memorial Highway, Wounded Knee, SD 57794

# TENNESSEE

Tennessee is known as the Volunteer State because of the enthusiastic role Tennesseans have played in America's battles, so it is not surprising that this state has seen its share of invasions and fighting.

The first humans in Tennessee arrived thousands of years ago. The Tennessee Path was a network of footpaths that stretched throughout the woodlands of Tennessee and beyond. The Mississippian culture built mounds in eastern Tennessee around AD 1200.

The Shawnee, Cherokee, and Chickasaw were some of the most important tribes native to Tennessee.

The Spanish explorer Hernando de Soto was the first European to "invade" Tennessee in 1540 on his circuit through the southeast. Other Spanish explorers would also enter the area. For instance, Tristán de Luna led a small expedition into the Tennessee Valley, which managed to subdue the Napochie tribe temporarily. However, in the long term it was Europeans from elsewhere who would have an impact on Tennessee.

The French were also interested in Tennessee. In 1673, Father Jacques Marquette and Louis Joliet set off on their expedition down the Mississippi. Robert de La Salle explored the area on a 1682 expedition, building a stockade at Fort Prudhomme. In 1739, the French also built Fort Assumption near present-day Memphis in order to fend off the Chickasaw.

And the British were taking an interest in the area too. For instance, they built Fort Loudoun. However, in 1760, a few years after the fort was built, the

Cherokee besieged the fort, and the garrison was forced to abandon it. While withdrawing from the camp after negotiating their surrender, the garrison was attacked by Cherokee warriors.

The end of the French and Indian War saw the end of French colonial hopes in the area. Subsequently, despite Native American claims to the land and despite British restrictions on settlement, numerous settlers began to move into the region. A tree in Washington County is inscribed "D. Boon Cilled a. Bar on tree in the year 1760." So, Daniel Boone may have "invaded" this part of Tennessee in 1760. Certainly, Daniel Boone and frontiersmen like him were a major feature of the region in this period. Boone was involved to some extent with the 1775 Transylvania Purchase, which was supposed to buy land from the Cherokee, but the deal caused trouble with colonial authorities.

The first American fort, Watauga, was built near what is currently Elizabethton from 1775–6 in order to protect the frontier settlers from attacks by Native Americans, who were being subsidized by British gold during the American Revolution. More Americans migrated to the Tennessee frontier after the American victory in the Revolutionary War.

Parts of Tennessee were under the control of North Carolina, while eastern Tennessee declared its independence as the short-lived state of Franklin. The 1794 Nickajack Expedition saw frontiersmen inflict a significant defeat on the Chickamauga Cherokee.

Tennessee became the sixteenth state to join the Union in 1796. As more settlers moved in, the process of bribing and pressuring Native Americans to cede their land began. The period from 1798 to 1806 saw a number of land cession agreements with Chickasaw and Cherokee.

Andrew Jackson, a veteran of the American Revolution, was elected one of Tennessee's first congressmen in 1796. He grew cotton on the Hermitage, a plantation near Nashville, which he purchased in 1804. He was elected as president of the United States in 1829, the first to come from Tennessee. His path to the White House was paved by his remarkable military career. During the War of 1812, Jackson led bands of Tennessee volunteers in the Creek War (see Alabama) and the Battle of New Orleans (see Louisiana). "Old Hickory" was the most distinguished American land commander of the war.

Davy Crockett, a former congressman, led a group of Tennesseans who defended and died at the Alamo in 1836 (see Texas).

Major areas of land under Native American control in Tennessee soon disappeared. The last portion of Chickasaw land between the Tennessee and Mississippi Rivers was bought in 1818. And in 1838, almost all the Cherokee in Tennessee were forced out on the Trail of Tears.

In June 1861, Tennessee voted by referendum to become the last state to join the Confederacy. Most of eastern Tennessee, however, opposed secession. Thirty-one thousand Tennesseans fought in the Union ranks, while many more served in Confederate gray. Over 20,000 freed slaves from Tennessee joined the Union Army.

Tennessee's geographic location in the Upper Confederacy and its extensive rail and river networks made it a strategic target for both sides during the Civil War. More battles were fought in Tennessee than in any state other than Virginia. Over 2,000 engagements were waged within the borders of Tennessee, and this volume can touch on only some key events.

General Albert Sidney Johnston assumed responsibility for the defense of Tennessee from Yankee invasion in September 1861.

The Cumberland and Tennessee Rivers were vital strategic routes, and in early 1862, Union forces mounted a successful campaign along them. Ulysses S. Grant, an Ohioan, was a bold, aggressive commander who said, "I will take no backward step." His meteoric career was launched in Tennessee. On February 6, 1862, with the aid of Union gunboats, he captured Fort Henry. From February 13–16, the Battle of Fort Donelson was fought. When the Confederate commander, General Buckner, asked for terms of surrender, Grant offered "no terms except an unconditional and immediate surrender." Although Tennessee's own Nathan Bedford Forest did manage to escape with about 2,500 cavalry, around 15,000 Confederate soldiers did lay down their arms. Henceforth, the Union general would be known as "Unconditional Surrender" Grant.

On February 25, 1862, Union forces captured Nashville—the first Confederate state capital to fall into Union hands.

The Battle of Shiloh was fought in April 1862 on the banks of the Tennessee River near Pittsburgh Landing. Shiloh's Baptist church was a prominent battlefield landmark that was used as a command post. Ironically, *shiloh* means *place of peace* in Hebrew. The Confederates surprised the Union forces, winning the first day of the battle on April 6. Union Major General Prentiss and the 2,200 men of his division were captured at the Hornet's Nest.

The Confederate commander, Albert Sidney Johnston, was, however, killed shortly after declaring, "We must this day conquer or perish."

On the rainy night of April 6, General Sherman observed to Grant, "We've had the devil's own day, haven't we?" Grant replied, "Yes, lick 'em tomorrow though."

On April 7, the second day of Shiloh, Grant proved as good as his word. Having been reinforced by new troops, Grant's Army of Tennessee enjoyed a substantial numerical advantage. Union General Lew Wallace, later known as the author of *Ben Hur*, had brought 7,000 fresh troops. They had previously taken a wrong turn and missed the fighting on April 6. When the Minié balls finally stopped flying, over 3,400 soldiers had been killed on both sides, with many more wounded. Though casualties were roughly even, Beauregard, Johnston's replacement, ordered a retreat. Delighted to have discovered a winning general, Lincoln exclaimed of Grant, "I cannot spare this man. He fights."

Grant's 1862 victories in Tennessee established a base for the Union to invade Mississippi and capture Vicksburg in 1863, effectively cutting the Confederacy in two.

Murfreesboro saw numerous clashes during the war, and the second battle there, though inconclusive, resulted in major losses on both sides.

In 1863, Union forces captured Chattanooga. A Confederate victory at the Battle of Chickamauga then led to the siege of Chattanooga. However, Union reinforcements led by Grant launched a campaign that eradicated the Confederate threat to Chattanooga and forced the Confederate's Army of Tennessee to retreat to Georgia.

In April 1864, Confederates captured Fort Pillow. The Confederate forces are accused of massacring surrendering African-American Union troops.

General John Bell Hood launched a desperate bid to recapture Tennessee for the Confederacy in 1864. On November 30, the Battle of Franklin was fought between Hood and Union Major General John Schofield. A plantation belonging to the Carter family and the home of a German carpenter named Lotz were at the center of the Union's entrenched positions. Confederate General Patrick Cleburne, born in County Cork, declared, "If we are to die, let us die like men." Nearly 2,000 rebel soldiers would die in the frontal assault, including Cleburne and 51 percent of his division. Confederate casualties for the battle exceeded those of the Union by nearly three to one. Nevertheless, Union troops withdrew that night back to Nashville.

My ancestor (CRK), Captain Cortlandt Van Rensselaer, who was described by the *New York Times* as "one of the most meritorious officers in our army," died near Nashville on October 7, 1864. He had been wounded previously at the Battle of Missionary Ridge and is buried at the Albany Rural Cemetery in New York. He was twenty-seven years old, and a veteran of Chickamauga and Vicksburg.

In one last desperate bid, Hood launched his Army of Tennessee toward Nashville. In the two-day Battle of Nashville, fought on December 15–16, 1864, Hood's army was crushed, and 150 Confederate guns were captured. Five months later, Lee surrendered at the Appomattox Courthouse.

In World War I, around 100,000 Tennesseans would join the American Expeditionary Force to fight "Over There" in Europe. Alvin York, from Pall Mall, became the most decorated American soldier of the Great War.

Tennessee was not, of course, invaded during World War II. More than 300,000 Tennesseans, however, served in American armed forces in the war. The Manhattan Project built plutonium for the bomb dropped on Hiroshima in Oak Ridge from 1942 to the war's end.

On Memorial Day 1994, the mortal remains of Lieutenant Simeon Cummings were brought to Tennessee for burial with full military honors under the Stars and Bars. On August 3, 1863, the unfortunate Cummings accidentally shot himself while serving aboard the CSS *Alabama* off the coast of Cape Town, South Africa (see Alabama). Though he had been born in Connecticut, Cummings became the only Confederate serviceman to have died and been buried outside of the United States. His body was transferred from the private cemetery on the Kliprug Farm in South Africa to Elm Springs.

On July 16, 2015, Muhammad Youssef Abdulazeez, a twenty-four-year-old naturalized American citizen born in Kuwait, opened fire on a naval recruiting station and a naval reserve center in Chattanooga. Four US marines and one sailor were killed in the attack, as well as the gunman. The FBI identified the attack as an act directed by "foreign terrorist propaganda."

## TENNESSEE
## MILITARY HISTORY SITES

### Carter House
Location: 1140 Columbia Avenue, Franklin, TN 37064
Web: boft.org

### David Crockett Cabin—Museum
Location: 219 North Trenton Street, Old Highway 45 West, Rutherford, TN 38369
Web: www.tnvacation.com/local/rutherford-davy-crockett-cabin-museum

### Fort Donelson National Battlefield
Location: 174 National Cemetery Drive, Dover, TN 37058
Web: www.nps.gov/fodo

### Fort Pillow State Historic Park
Location: 3122 Park Road, Henning, TN 38041
Web: tnstateparks.com/parks/about/fort-pillow

### The Hermitage—Andrew Jackson's Home
Location: 4580 Rachel's Lane, Nashville, TN 37076
Web: thehermitage.com

### Lotz House: Civil War House Museum
Location: 1111 Columbia Avenue, Franklin, TN 37064
Web: www.lotzhouse.com

### Oak Ridge Site—Manhattan Project National Historical Park
Location: 300 South Tulane, Oak Ridge, TN 37830 (tours depart from American Museum of Science & Energy)
Web: www.nps.gov/mapr/oakridge.htm

### American Museum of Science & Energy
Web: amse.org

**President James K. Polk Home & Museum**
Location: 301 West 7th Street, Columbia, TN 38401
Web: jameskpolk.com

**Shiloh National Military Park**
Location: 1055 Pittsburg Landing Road, Shiloh, TN 38376
Web: www.nps.gov/shil

**Tennessee State Museum and Military Museum**
Location: 505 Deaderick Street, Nashville, TN 37243
Web: www.tnmuseum.org
Web: www.tnmuseum.org/Exhibits/Military_Branch_Museum/

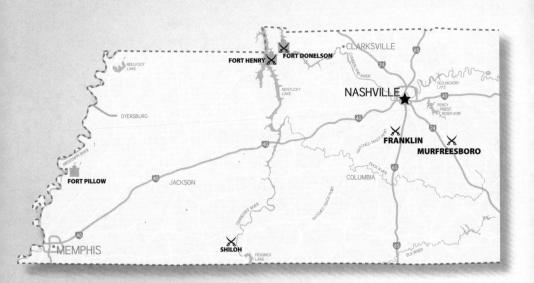

**ANDREW JACKSON**
1767-1845
Source: iStock/
GeorgiosArt

**LOTZ HOUSE**
Battle of Franklin
November 30, 1864
Source: Author photo

**CARTER HOUSE**
Battle of Franklin
November 30, 1864
Source: Author photo

Nickname: Volunteer State
Statehood: 1796
Capital: Nashville

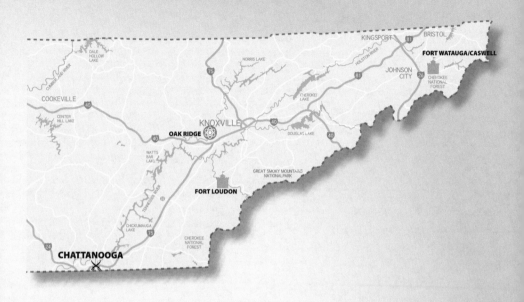

**WAR MEMORIAL PLAZA**
Dedicated 1925
Nashville
Source: Author photo

**OAK RIDGE**
Manhattan Project
National Historical Park
Source: US Department
of Energy, Ed Westcott,
Photographer

**OAK RIDGE**
Manhattan Project
National Historical Park
Source: US Department
of Energy, Ed Westcott,
Photographer

# TEXAS

Archaeologists have found evidence of human habitation along Buttermilk Creek in central Texas that is many thousands of years old. Among the findings are stone spear points and knives, suggesting the distinct possibility of warfare from man's first stirrings in Texas.

Many Native Americans made their homes in the area now known as Texas. These include the Comanche, the Apache, the Wichita, and the Caddo tribes. The word *Texas* derives, in fact, from the Caddoan word *taysha*, meaning *friend*.

The first Europeans to "invade" Texas were, of course, Spanish. The explorer Alonso Álvarez de Pineda sailed along the coast of Texas in 1519. Arriving on a Catholic feast day, he named the bay he had discovered Corpus Christi Bay. In 1528, the unfortunate Cabeza de Vaca was shipwrecked on Galveston Island. Over the next few months, most of his eighty-man crew perished on the island that they labeled *Malhado*, or Island of Doom.

Other Spanish explorers would follow. For instance, in 1541 Coronado passed through; and in 1598, Oñate held a ceremony of thanksgiving near what is now El Paso.

Diseases introduced as a result of early contact with European explorers devastated indigenous Texas tribes, setting the stage for invasion of the Texas region by stronger tribes from the Great Plains and the Mississippi and Missouri River valleys. The Apache, long dominant along what is now the Texas-New Mexico border before 1680, had, by 1700, been driven south into the Edwards Plateau area of central Texas by the better mounted and armed Comanche.

*French Texas* sounds like an oxymoron today, but the French were, in fact, the first Europeans to actually attempt to colonize Texas. The French explorer Robert de La Salle, after his 1684 expedition, claimed Texas and the Mississippi Valley on behalf of his patron, Louis XIV, the Sun King. Fort St. Louis was established by the French in 1685 in what is Victoria County today. In April 1689, a Spanish Army arrived to capture the fort, but found that the Karankawa had already attacked and destroyed it. A handful of Frenchmen were able to return to France, but French Texas was finished. The Spanish proceeded to build another fort on the location of Fort St Louis.

In fact, the Spanish would build many presidios, or fortifications, around Texas. Presidio La Bahia, site of the later Goliad massacre, is the best known Texas presidio.

They also established eighteen missions inside Spanish Texas. The most famous of these, built in 1744, was the Misión San Antonio de Valero, which is better known to us as simply the Alamo. The Spanish worked to convert the indigenous people of Texas to Christianity. The indigenous people often struck back. On March 16, 1758, for example, a group of mainly Comanche attacked the San Saba Mission, killing Father Terreros and setting fire to its buildings. Only a handful of the Spanish survived.

A Spanish commander, Diego Ortiz Parrilla, led a punitive expedition against the Indians in retaliation for the attack on San Saba. Parilla's force was, however, defeated at the battle of the Twin Villages, fought near Red River on October 7, 1759. The Wichita, Comanche, and other Plains Indians seized the Spanish supply train, and the Spanish were compelled to withdraw to the safety of their presidios.

However, in 1790, Spanish forces with local allies won a major victory over Apache forces in a battle at Soledad Creek.

New Spain exercised at best only a partial control over Texas, limited to their mission and presidio system. Spain was itself invaded by Napoleon in 1808, further weakening Spain's grip on its distant colonies.

In 1813, rebels fighting for Mexican independence were defeated by Spanish forces in the bloody Battle of Medina.

By 1821, however, New Spain was overthrown with the Mexican Revolution. Texas would be governed, for a while, by Mexico City rather than Madrid, although it remained a desolate land with few settlers. The new Mexican government launched a campaign to bring more people to Texas by offering generous land grants. The only catch was that new settlers had to convert to Catholicism and that slavery was illegal. This brought many Americans, mostly from the Southern states, to Texas. Stephen Austin of Virginia immigrated to the Texas territory and became an American impresario who actually changed his first name to Estaban.

In 1826, the short-lived Fredonian Rebellion, led by Haden Edwards, briefly declared an independent state in Texas before it was crushed by Mexican forces.

Mexican attempts to control further Anglo immigration into Texas created tensions that would lead to violence. In 1832, Texas insurgents rose once again against the Mexican authorities, and more was to come.

The wide-open spaces of Texas seemed to promise almost unlimited opportunity for those adventuresome souls who dared to make the trek to the western frontier. Texas drew an assortment of adventurers.

There was, for example, Jim Bowie, a forger and land swindler from Kentucky who was wanted in several US states. He had also invented the Bowie knife.

Texas also attracted William Travis, an Alabama schoolteacher who abandoned his pregnant wife and child to make his way to Texas. The Alamo would be the twenty-six-year-old's first command.

David Crockett, a legendary frontiersman from Tennessee, ended up in Texas. He was elected to Congress in 1826, but lost his reelection bid in 1834. Crockett responded to his defeat with: "I told the people of my district that I would serve them as faithfully as I had done; but if not, they might go to hell, and I would go to Texas."

Texas was also a magnet for Antonio de Padua María Severino López de Santa Anna y Pérez de Lebrón, who is better known to us simply as Santa Anna. In 1836, he was the president and dictator of Mexico. He also styled himself the "Napoleon of the West." With Texas beginning to stir into open rebellion, Santa Anna led what would prove to be one of the most fateful invasions of Texas and, indeed, American territory.

By 1836, the Anglo population of Texas outnumbered the Mexicans by more than three to one. On March 2, 1836, Texas declared its independence from Mexico. General Sam Houston was selected to lead the military forces of the newly created Republic of Texas.

But as Texas declared its independence, General Santa Anna and an army of over 3,000 men were laying siege to the Alamo.

On February 28, 1836, William Travis wrote this famous letter from the Alamo:

> To the People of Texas & All Americans in the World—
> Fellow citizens & compatriots—
> I am besieged, by a thousand or more of the Mexicans under Santa Anna — I have sustained a continual Bombardment & cannonade for 24 hours & have not lost a man — The enemy has demanded a surrender at discretion, otherwise, the garrison are to be put to the sword, if the fort is taken — I have answered the demand with a cannon shot, & our flag still waves proudly from the walls — I shall never surrender or retreat. Then, I call on you in the name of Liberty, of patriotism & everything dear to the American character, to come to our aid, with all dispatch — The enemy is receiving reinforcements daily & will no doubt increase to three or four thousand in four or five days. If this call is neglected, I am determined to sustain myself as long as possible & die like a soldier who never forgets what is due to his own honor & that of his country — Victory or Death.

On March 6, the presidio was stormed, and all 187 defenders, including Travis, Bowie, and Crockett, were slain. "Remember the Alamo" would become the rallying cry of the new Texas Republic.

Even worse atrocities, though, would soon follow the fall of the Alamo.

Mexican forces won the Battle of Coleto Creek on March 19–20, 1836. Colonel James Fannin was compelled to surrender his force of about three hundred Texans. The Mexican Congress had ordered captured rebels to be treated as pirates. On March 27, over 340 Texans were summarily executed in what became known as the Goliad massacre.

In 1836, Sam Houston was a hard-drinking politician with limited military experience. He had failed to come to the relief of William Travis and the defenders of the Alamo. He was powerless to prevent the Goliad Massacre. But he would succeed spectacularly at San Jacinto.

Houston was opposed by Santa Anna, and Santa Anna's forces outnumbered the Texans by about 1,300 to 900. Santa Anna, however, had violated two of the cardinal rules of military strategy: he had divided his forces, and he had camped his army with its back to a swampy river.[8] Finally, Santa Anna had neglected to post pickets around the Mexican encampment, and that allowed the Texans to launch a surprise attack. On April 21, 1836, Sam Houston decisively defeated Santa Anna at the Battle of San Jacinto, which was near the town of La Porte. The battle lasted only eighteen minutes and resulted in the deaths of 630 and the capture of 730 Mexican troops, along with Santa Anna himself. Only nine Texans were killed in the engagement. Santa Anna would be ransomed back to Mexico in exchange for the independence of Texas.

During 1836—the year of the Texas Revolution—other conflicts were also brewing in Texas. On May 19, 1836, Comanche attacked the Parker home near what is today Groesbeck. John Parker, the seventy-seven-year-old family patriarch and a veteran of the American Revolution, was scalped, castrated, and killed that day. Cynthia Ann Parker, a young girl, was abducted by the Comanche. She would subsequently marry Peta Nocona, a Comanche chief, and become the mother of Quanah Parker. Her story would inspire John Ford's 1954 classic western, *The Searchers*. Quanah Parker would become one of the legends of Texas, in a league with Travis and Crockett.

One of the veterans of San Jacinto, Mirabeau Bonaparte Lamar, was elected president of the Republic of Texas in 1838. Lamar moved the capital to Austin and called for an "exterminating war" against the Indians. Lamar was brutally frank, insisting on a war that would "admit of no compromise, and have no termination except in their total extinction, or total expulsion." Incidents such as the Parker Ranch Massacre were used to justify Lamar's genocidal policy.

The Texans attacked a Cherokee village on July 15, 1839. Chief Bowles of the Cherokee nation was killed the following day. The villages and cornfields of various Indian tribes in eastern Texas were burnt. Colonel John Moore, a hero of the Texas Revolution, led an 1839 campaign against the Comanche.

On March 19, 1840, a negotiation over hostages degenerated into the Council House Fight in San Antonio between Texans and Comanche. Spirit Talker, the Comanche chief, was killed along with over thirty Indians, including some women and children. Seven Texans were also killed.

---

8        On my 2011 visit to the San Jacinto Battlefield in La Porte, Texas, I noticed signs near the picnic tables that warned visitors to beware of alligators. (CRK)

And Mexico had not given up hope of recovering land in Texas. In 1842, Mexican troops invaded the Republic, but they were decisively defeated at the Battle of Salado Creek.

In 1845, Texas became the twenty-eighth state, joining the Union as a slave state. However, its border with Mexico was not yet agreed upon by Mexico and the United States, and more violence was coming.

In 1846, the Paredes government in Mexico City ordered attacks on American forces operating along the Texas-Mexico border. In April of that year, in the Thornton Affair, US forces were ambushed near Brownsville by Mexican forces; and in May, Mexican and US forces clashed nearby in the Battle of Palo Alto, the first major battle of the Mexican-American War.

The 1848 peace deal that ended the war would finally establish the agreed-upon international border between Texas and Mexico.

In the Cortina War, which began in 1859, local Mexican leader Juan Nepomuceno Cortina skirmished with assorted American forces.

On December 18, 1860, the Battle of Pease River was fought between Texans and the Comanche. Peta Nocona was likely killed at this engagement, and his wife, Cynthia Ann Parker, was recaptured after twenty-four years of captivity.

In February 1861, Texans voted by referendum to secede from the Union, joining the Confederacy.

Texas was the base from which the Confederates invaded New Mexico during the Civil War. Texas was also a vital source of livestock for the Confederacy. After the capture of Vicksburg, Arkansas and Texas were effectively cut off from the rest of the Confederacy.

A number of battles took place in Texas during the war.

For instance, in 1862, the Union Navy bombarded Corpus Christi. Union forces also took Galveston that year, but it was subsequently retaken by Confederate forces. In 1863, at the Second Battle of Sabine Pass, Union forces attempting to cut Confederate supply lines suffered a severe defeat.

During the Civil War, other conflicts continued to rage in Texas. The First Battle of Adobe Walls was fought in the northern Texas Panhandle on November 25, 1864. In this engagement, Kit Carson led about three hundred US troops against a much larger group of Indians. Carson withdrew.

The last significant battle of the Civil War was fought in Texas at the Palmito Ranch, on the Rio Grande near Brownsville, on May 13, 1865. This battle, or skirmish, really, featured the 62nd US Colored Troops versus the 2nd Texas Cavalry Battalion, with fewer than a handful killed. The battle of Palmito Ranch was also noteworthy for being the last time a US military prisoner was captured by Confederate Army forces.

On June 27, 1874, Quanah Parker led the Comanche against a trading post at the Second Battle of Adobe Walls. In this remarkable engagement, twenty-eight men in the post managed to hold off hundreds of mounted Comanche warriors. The defenders included William "Bat" Masterson, who would later become the sheriff of Dodge City. They were armed with Sharp's "Big Fifties" rifles, whose 50-calibre munition was designed to drop buffalo. Quanah had his horse shot from underneath him, and was wounded but survived. The Comanche withdrew in frustration after suffering heavy losses.

The Red River War broke out in the late summer of 1874. Colonel Ranald Mackenzie, a Union veteran of the Civil War, vanquished a larger Indian force at the Battle of Palo Duro Canyon. Casualties were light, but a hidden Comanche village on the canyon floor was burned. After this battle, the Comanche were compelled to abandon their nomadic ways and retire to life on a reservation. The buffalo around which they had built their society had been hunted to near extinction.

Astonishingly, Quanah Parker, the half-white half-Native American Comanche chief, led his people to the reservation. Parker settled down and converted to Christianity. In 1905, he accompanied Geronimo (see Arizona) and other Indian chiefs to the inauguration of President Teddy Roosevelt in Washington. Parker died of natural causes in Cache, Oklahoma, in 1911. The town of Quanah in Texas is named in honor of the last chief of the Quahada Comanche tribe.

The 1877 El Paso Salt War saw locals from both sides of the Texas-Mexico border seize the ranger's fort at San Elizario, before US troops and a posse violently restored government control.

The Jaybird-Woodpecker War of 1888–1889 was another post-Reconstruction feud that eventually saw white political control of Fort Bend County reimposed.

In 1912, the battleship *Texas*, the last dreadnought still afloat, was launched. In World War I, she provided convoy escort in defense against German submarines in the Atlantic. In World War II, she supplied naval gunfire for the Normandy invasion and at Iwo Jima in the Pacific. Many

Texans served on board the ship, which can be found today in a Texas state park in La Porte.

The 1911–1920 Mexican Civil War occasionally encroached on Texas, and tensions simmered along the Texas-Mexico border during World War I. In 1915, the Plan of San Diego called for raids by Mexican revolutionaries into southwestern states, including Texas. In the summer of 1915, a Texas deputy was murdered in Brownsville. The following year, four American soldiers were killed by Mexican revolutionaries in San Ygnacio along the Rio Grande. Texas Rangers were called up to defend the border.

In May 1916, the towns of Glen Springs and Boquillas were attacked. President Woodrow Wilson, under increasing pressure to improve border security, ordered Brigadier General John J. Pershing to capture Francisco (Pancho) Villa and his men. In addition to the 10,000 men under General Pershing, Wilson also activated National Guard units from Texas, Arizona, and New Mexico, around 115,000 men total. The Guard units were federalized on May 8. Texas units included the 2nd, 3rd, and 4th Texas Infantry. Known as the Mexican or Punitive Expedition, the campaign officially ended in February 1917. However, isolated clashes continued into 1919. The results of the Punitive Expedition were mixed: Villa was never captured, but war with Mexico was averted.

In 1917, the Zimmerman Telegram (intercepted by the British government and passed to the Americans) exposed German plans to ally itself with Mexico against the United States.

At least two Japanese balloon bombs are known to have landed in Texas during World War II, one near Desdemona, the other near Woodson.

In 2014, the oceanographer Robert Ballard (of *Titanic* fame) mapped the final resting place of *U-166*, a German submarine that sank off the coast of Texas on July 30, 1942. *U-166* had torpedoed the *Robert E. Lee,* a 5,000-ton passenger ship, just hours before the sub itself was sunk by depth charges fired by a US Navy patrol craft. At least twenty-two Axis submarines fought in the Gulf of Mexico in World War II.

# TEXAS
## MILITARY HISTORY SITES

**Alamo**
Location: 300 Alamo Plaza, San Antonio, TX 78205
Web: www.thealamo.org

**Battleship *Texas* State Historic Site**
Location: 3523 Independence Parkway South, La Porte, TX 77571
Web: www.tpwd.texas.gov/state-parks/battleship-texas

**George H. W. Bush Presidential Library and Museum**
Location: 1000 George Bush Drive West, College Station, TX 77845
Web: www.bush41.org

**George W. Bush Presidential Library and Museum**
Location: 2943 SMU Boulevard, Dallas, TX 75205
Web: www.georgewbushlibrary.smu.edu

**Lyndon Baines Johnson Library & Museum**
Location: 2313 Red River Street, Austin, TX 78705
Web: www.lbjlibrary.org

**National Museum of the Pacific War**
Location: 340 East Main Street, Fredericksburg, TX 78624
Web: www.pacificwarmuseum.org

**Presidio La Bahia**
Location: 217 US-183, Goliad, TX 77963
Web: www.nps.gov/nr/travel/tx/tx20.htm

**San Jacinto Battleground State Historic Site**
Location: 3523 Independence Parkway South, La Porte, TX 77571
Web: www.tpwd.texas.gov/state-parks/san-jacinto-battleground

**Texas Military Forces Museum**
Location: 2200 West 35th Street, Austin, TX 78703
Web: www.texasmilitaryforcesmuseum.org

# America Invaded: TEXAS

**ALAMO MEMORIAL**
San Antonio
Source: iStock/Alex Stork

**JIM BOWIE**
1796-1836
Source: akg-images

**BATTLESHIP TEXAS (BB-35)**
Launched 1912
Battleship Texas State Historic Site
Source: Author photo

**SAM HOUSTON**
1793-1863
Photo by
Matthew Brady,
1861
Source:
Public Domain

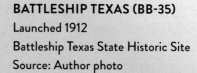

Nickname: The Lone Star State
Statehood: 1845
Capital: Austin

ADOBE WALLS (X2) ✗

✗ PALO DURO CANYON

PEASE RIVER ✗

DALLAS

FORT WORTH

SAN SABA MISSION ✗

AUSTIN

HOUSTON

LA PORTE
SAN JACINTO ✗

THE ALAMO ✗ ✗ SAN ANTONIO
MEDINA ✗ ✗ COUNCIL HOUSE FIGHT

✗ COLETO CREEK

FORT PRESIDIO LA BAHIA ✗
GOLIAD MASSACRE

SOLEDAD CREEK ✗

CORPUS
CHRISTI

PALMITO RANCH ✗

**WILLIAM TRAVIS, 1809-1836**
Source: Texas State Library and
Archives Commission

# UTAH

Utah is best known for being the headquarters of the Mormon Church, the home of the Bonneville Salt Flats, and the location of the Great Salt Lake. Utah, however, had a long and rich history of occupation by a number of different Native American peoples before the arrival of Europeans.

The first Europeans who did make it to the region were Spanish. Coronado's 1540–1542 expedition came close to the borders of modern Utah. And certainly in the eighteenth century, Spanish explorers entered the area itself. The 1776 Dominguez-Escalante expedition, led by two Franciscan fathers, was an attempt to find a route from Santa Fe to the California coast. They didn't make it that far, but they did make it into what is now Utah, and they met some of the locals.

Spanish claims in the region were succeeded by Mexican claims, when Mexico became independent from Spain. But that didn't stop American trappers and buyers from pursuing their fur trade in the region. Figures like Jim Bridger and Jedediah Smith feature in the history of the area.

Even though the region was still technically Mexican, the US government was already eying it. In 1843, John C. Frémont, known as the Pathfinder, explored northern Utah on behalf of the US government; and in 1845, he explored the Western Great Salt Lake Area. But war was about to arrive.

In the Mexican-American War of 1846–8, the United States would send military forces into what is now Utah; and in the peace deal that ended the war, it officially got to keep it. But even before that peace deal, a new people had arrived in the area who would transform its history.

Part of the US forces fighting the war was a volunteer Mormon Battalion. In 1846, they had made an epic march from Kansas to San Diego. When the battalion was disbanded in 1847 after its service, the return route some of the soldiers took toward home led through Utah. Mormons had also been moving west from Illinois since 1846. In 1847, Brigham Young with his wagonloads of Mormon pioneers entered the Valley of the Salt Lake for the first time. They rapidly set about building settlements and establishing viable agriculture. Soon after that they were petitioning the United States for recognition of a new large state (much larger than current-day Utah) to be called Deseret. Congress refused.

Soon more wars, of sorts, would come.

Tensions between the new settlers and some of the local Native Americans led to the Walker War of 1853-4, in which Native Americans led by local leader Walkara attacked settler outposts, and the settlers responded. In other violence, in 1853, a US surveying party was attacked.

Uneasy about Mormon practices like polygamy, the US government decided in 1857 to impose a non-Mormon governor and station US troops in the area to support him. Stresses surrounding this and around the increasing numbers of migrants traveling through the area were part of what led to the Mountain Meadows Massacre of September 1857, in which a group of Mormons led by John Doyle Lee teamed up with a group of Paiute to attack a group of migrants and kill all but the young children.

The massacre was part of the so-called Utah War, which wasn't much of a war. There were some attacks on army wagon trains, but in the end, by agreement with the Mormons, the new governor, Alfred Cumming, assumed office, and Fort Floyd was established.

Utah was far removed from the focus of the Civil War, but the conflict to the east did have ramifications in the region. US troops were initially withdrawn to take part in the war, as happened in some other parts of the west. At the same time, tensions with the Shoshone were rising over disputes with immigrants and a lack of food.

As volunteers swelled the ranks of the Union army and its initial manpower shortage eased, US troops returned to Utah, ordered to protect communication routes to California. In response to attacks on wagon trains, Colonel

Patrick Connor launched an expedition against Bannocks and Shoshone. The result was the Bear River Massacre. In deep snow in January 1863, Connor's men attacked the encampment of Shoshone leader Bear Hunter. When the Shoshone defenders ran out of ammunition, the attackers moved in, butchering many men, women, and children.

Widespread violence would soon break out. Again, local Native Americans were suffering from a lack of food. Black Hawk's War started in a dispute over stolen and eaten cattle, and cattle would remain a prime target of the war. Ute leader Black Hawk assembled a loose alliance of local peoples who would raid Mormon settlements, primarily aiming to steal cattle, but also occasionally causing human casualties. Settlements were deserted, and Mormon militiamen attempted to strike back, sometimes causing their own civilian casualties in the process. In April 1866, militiamen in Circleville, a town that had come under attack from Ute raiders, rounded up members of the Piede tribe from a local encampment. An attempted escape by the Piede men ended in some being killed. Most of the rest of the men, women, and children were then killed as potential witnesses.

Black Hawk himself made peace in 1867, but the attacks continued at a lesser pace until federal troops were finally sent in, in 1872, to deal with the situation.

In 1895, after the mainstream Mormons had adjusted their stance on polygamy, Utah's application for statehood was granted. It became a state in 1896.

However, Utah was to suffer one more attack from outside its borders. During the Japanese balloon-bomb campaign of World War II, at least five of the weapons reached Utah, although nobody was actually injured.

# UTAH
## MILITARY HISTORY SITES

### Bluff Fort Historic Site
Location: 550 Black Locust Avenue, Bluff, UT 84512
Web: www.bluffutah.org/bluff-fort

**Brigham Young Winter Home**
Location: 67 West 200 North, St George, UT 84770
Web: www.utah.com/mormon/brigham-young-winter-home

**CAF Utah Wing Air Museum**
Location: Airport Road, Heber Valley, UT 84032
Web: www.cafutahwing.org/heber-valley-caf-museum.html

**Camp Floyd State Park Museum**
Location: 18035 West 1540 North, Fairfield, UT 84013
Web: www.stateparks.utah.gov/parks/camp-floyd

**Cove Fort Historic Site**
Location: Highway 161se, Beaver, UT 84713
Web: www.covefort.com

**Fort Buenaventura State Park**
Location: 2450 A Avenue, Ogden, UT 84401
Web: www.utah.com/fort-buenaventura-state-park

**Fort Douglas Military Museum**
Location: 32 Potter Street, Salt Lake City, UT 84113
Web: www.fortdouglas.org

**Hill Aerospace Museum**
Location: 7961 Wardleigh Road, Building 1955, Hill Air Force Base, UT 84056
Web: www.aerospaceutah.org

**John M. Browning Firearms Museum**
Location: 2501 Wall Avenue, Suite 201, Ogden, UT 84401
Web: www.theunionstation.org/museums/john-m-browning-firearms-museum

**Mountain Meadows Massacre Site**
Location: US Highway 18, St. George, UT 84770
Web: www.mtn-meadows-assoc.com/Direc_Maps/directio.htm

# America Invaded: UTAH

Nickname: Beehive State
Statehood: 1896
Capital: Salt Lake City

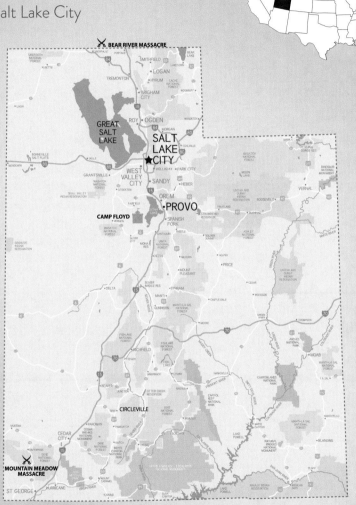

**BRIGHAM YOUNG**
1801-1877
Source: iStock/duncan1890

# VERMONT

Vermont is better known today for maple syrup and teddy bears, but it has seen a surprising number of invasions and a considerable amount of fighting over its history.

When Europeans first entered what is now Vermont, they found a number of American peoples inhabiting the region. The area was mainly occupied by Abenaki, with Lake Champlain marking the boundary between their area of control and that of the Iroquois to the west. The first Europeans to take a determined interest in the area were the French; in particular, Samuel de Champlain. Yes, the guy after whom the lake is named. And the name *Vermont* itself is of French derivation too. Champlain had mapped out the *Verd Mont*, or *Green Mountain*, on an early map of the region. Champlain also helped the Abenaki against the Iroquois, on one occasion killing two Iroquois leaders with his arquebus. This, unsurprisingly, endeared the French to the Abenaki and, equally unsurprisingly, left the Iroquois less than enthusiastic. Make that a lot less enthusiastic about the new European power trying to muscle in on territory they wanted to control.

The French would find other enemies in the region apart from the Iroquois, because while the French were pushing down into the area from the north, the English would soon be pushing into the area from the south. At the heart of the struggles for control was that strategic Lake Champlain, with its links to north-south river routes. To help establish and defend their claim to the northern part of the territory, the French built Fort St. Anne on Isle la Motte in 1666.

The position of the Vermont area between French and English colonial empires means that it saw invading troops pass through in each direction. For instance, during King William's War of 1689–97, English troops crossed through en route to attacking French positions in the St. Lawrence River area. In 1690, an Anglo-Dutch force of New York militia built Captain Jacobus de Warm's stockade to keep French activities under some kind of surveillance. Similarly, during Queen Anne's War of 1702–1713, French forces with local American allies passed through on their way to attack British settlements farther south.

And the next fifty years would see more raiding throughout the territory, as well as slow expansion into it. During Father Rale's War, Abenaki leader Gray Lock led raids that targeted English settlements in a number of areas, including Massachusetts. In 1724, Fort Dummer was built near what is now Brattleboro to try to impede such raids. Ten years later, the French constructed Fort St. Frédéric just on the other side of the present-day New York-Vermont border.

In the end, the French would lose out to Britain in the battle for control of both Vermont and North America as a whole. The French and Indian War, the name of the North American front in the Seven Years' War, saw some fierce fighting in and around Vermont. In 1755, the French built Fort Carillon. The British tried to take it in 1758 and failed, but did seize control of it the next year after and renamed it Fort Ticonderoga. Also in 1759, after a number of attempts, British forces captured Fort St. Frédéric, or what was left of it after the French destroyed and abandoned it. In the 1763 peace deal that ended the Seven Years' War, New France ceded control of Vermont.

But while the dispute between France and Britain over control of the territory was finished, the dispute over which colonies would have control was not. A number of colonies competed for authority over the region, in particular New Hampshire and New York. Under Ethan Allen, the famous Green Mountain Boys—developed as a militia recruited from settlers—was authorized by New Hampshire to defend their claims against attempts by New York authorities to impose their domination. Tensions between New Hampshire settlers and the New York authorities who had British support led to the so-called Westminster Massacre of 1775, which wasn't so much a massacre as a brawl in a courthouse in which two people died. Some, however, have been inclined to see it as the first bloodshed of the American Revolution.

Certainly the Revolution was coming to Vermont. In May 1775, the Green Mountain Boys along with Benedict Arnold captured Fort Ticonderoga, in New York, from the British. In January 1777, the area declared itself the Republic of New Connecticut, and shortly thereafter changed its name to the more familiar Republic of Vermont.

In the summer of that year, General Burgoyne's forces moved south from Canada, aiming to take control of the Hudson Valley. Fort Ticonderoga fell to the advancing British, as did the American defensive works that had been laboriously built on nearby Mount Independence in Vermont. On July 7, 1777, American troops that had retreated from their positions in the north clashed with pursuing British forces at the Battle of Hubbardton in Vermont—the only battle of the American Revolution fought in the state. In the end, after German reinforcements arrived to assist the British, it was a tactical defeat for the American forces but not a major one, as most of the American soldiers escaped. British and German losses were high, and Simon Fraser, the capable British commander at Hubbardton, would soon be killed in the Saratoga campaign. And the future was not bright for Burgoyne's invasion. On August 16, he was defeated by John Stark at the Battle of Bennington which, despite being named after Bennington, Vermont, was actually fought across the border in New York territory. And on October 17, Burgoyne was forced to surrender at Saratoga, a decisive blow to British hopes in the war. Nevertheless, the war was not entirely finished, and Vermont would see more fighting.

In October 1778, British Major Christopher Carleton led a raiding force south on Lake Champlain, intending to attack a number of targets in Vermont. After achieving some successes, the raiders withdrew north again.

More raids into the area followed, including one on October 16, 1780, when Lieutenant Houghton and hundreds of Mohawk warriors attacked Royalton, Sharon, and Tunbridge.

Even at this late stage, the possibility was raised that rather than become part of the new United States, the Vermont Republic might once again come under British control. The so-called Haldimand Affair saw the British governor of Quebec, Sir Frederick Haldimand, engage in communications on this question with representatives of the Vermont Republic, who were also interested in discussing a possible prisoner deal. It's a murky affair, so it's unclear at times what was really going on, but whatever might have been, the British surrender at Yorktown in 1781 and the end of the war helped dictate that it never was.

But even the end of the war did not leave Vermont as part of the United States. It left it as the Vermont Republic. Its slightly uncertain status and future was, however, soon resolved. In 1791, it joined the Union as the fourteenth state.

British defeat in the War of Independence, however, did not bring lasting peace to Vermont. In 1812, the United States declared war on Britain, and soon Vermont was dragged into the fighting. Lake Champlain became a focus for the conflict, and Vermont's shoreline was host to a number of clashes. For instance, in August 1813, British ships attacked Swanton and Burlington. Later the area became a staging ground for an unsuccessful invasion of Canada. In May 1814, British ships exchanged gunfire with Fort Cassin, which was protecting US Navy ships in Otter Creek, before withdrawing, having accomplished nothing. The US victory at Cumberland Bay in September of the same year gave America superiority; and on Christmas Eve, the war ended.

You might have thought that that would be the end of military action in Vermont. Vermonters did play a major role in the American Civil War on the Union side, supplying many Union generals and brave figures like Willie Johnston, a Vermonter drummer boy who, at thirteen, was the youngest person to be granted the Congressional Medal of Honor (for bravery shown when he was even younger). In all, some 34,000 Vermonters wore the Union blue during the war. If you thought that Vermont was far too far north for action during the Civil War, though, you'd be wrong.

On October 19, 1864, twenty-two Confederates soldiers infiltrated St. Albans from Canada, pretending to be civilians. On October 19, openly declaring themselves Confederate soldiers, they robbed the town's three banks of $208,000. Bennet Young, their commanding officer, had stated, "I take possession of St Albans, Vermont, in the name of the Confederate States of America." And then, having failed to set light to the town, they were chased across the border into Canada by a local posse. Some of them were eventually arrested by Canadian authorities, and some of the money ($80,000) they still had on them was returned. The men themselves were eventually set free because it was concluded Canada did not have the right to extradite serving Confederate soldiers. The St Albans raid was the northernmost fighting of the American Civil War. It was, however, the last raid of its kind, because fears of turning Canada against the Confederacy prevented any further such operations.

Vermonters would go on to serve with distinction in America's subsequent wars, but the fighting would take place well beyond Vermont's borders.

## VERMONT
## MILITARY HISTORY SITES

### Bennington Battle Monument
Location: 15 Monument Circle, Bennington, VT 05201
Web: www.benningtonbattlemonument.com/

### Ethan Allen Homestead Museum
Location: 1 Ethan Allen Homestead, Burlington, VT 05408
Web: www.ethanallenhomestead.org

### Hubbardton Battlefield State Historic Site
Location: 5696 Monument Hill Road, Castleton, VT 05735
Web: historicsites.vermont.gov/directory/hubbardton

### Lake Champlain Maritime Museum
Location: 4472 Basin Harbor Road, Vergennes, VT 05491
Web: www.lcmm.org

### President Calvin Coolidge State Historic Site
Location: 3780 Route 100A, Plymouth, VT 05056
Web: historicsites.vermont.gov/directory/coolidge

### President Chester A. Arthur's Home
Location: 455 Chester Arthur Road, East Fairfield, VT 05455
Web: historicsites.vermont.gov/directory/arthur

**Saint Albans Museum**
Location: 9 Church Street, St. Albans, VT 05478
Web: www.stamuseum.org

**Vermont History Museum**
Location: 109 State Street, Montpelier, VT 05609
Web: www.vermonthistory.org

**Vermont National Guard Library and Museum**
Location: 789 Vermont National Guard Road, Camp Johnson, Colchester, VT 05446
Web: www.vtguard.com/museum

# America Invaded: **VERMONT**

Nickname: The Green Mountain State
Statehood: 1791
Capital: Montpelier

**ETHAN ALLEN STATUE**
1738-1789
Fort Ticonderoga, NY
Source: Author photo

**BENNINGTON MONUMENT**
Battle of Bennington
August 16, 1777
Fought in NY, Commemorated in VT
Source: Author photo

# VIRGINIA

Virginia is a state with a proud military tradition and an enduring military presence. From its founding, the Commonwealth was pretty much baptized in the blood of multiple invasions.

The Algonquin, Iroquoian, and Siouan people dominated the area before the arrival of Europeans.

Many historians have remarked on the asymmetry of European and American conflicts with Native Americans over a long, bloody, and tragic history. During the early colonial period, however, the asymmetry was on the other foot, with indigenous people vastly outnumbering the European settlers clinging precariously to their forts along the Atlantic shoreline.

The first Europeans to arrive in the area we now know as Virginia were the Spanish. A number of different expeditions explored the region. For instance, in 1561, a Spanish ship landed near Tsenacommacah. Some attempts were made at converting the natives to Christianity. The small settlement was, however, attacked by the Algonquin people and wiped out in 1571.

The English would be the next to arrive. In 1584, Sir Walter Raleigh, armed with a royal charter from Elizabeth I, sent colonists to Roanoke Island. Relations with the indigenous people were problematic from the start. A silver cup was stolen by the natives, and the village of Aquascogoc was burned in retaliation. Roanoke was abandoned, becoming known as the Lost Colony. The circumstances of its disappearance remain a bit of a mystery.

In 1607, the Virginia Company of London established Jamestown, the first successful British colony in the New World. It was located in the heart of the Powhatan Confederacy, near the York River. Powhatan was also the leader of about fourteen thousand Indians from as many as thirty different tribes around Jamestown. It was Powhatan's twelve-year-old daughter, Mataoka or Pocahontas, who allegedly rescued Captain John Smith. The colony was named *Virginia* in honor of Elizabeth I, the Virgin Queen.

In 1609, Smith quotes Powhatan as saying: "Some doubt I have of your coming hither … for many do informe me, your comming is not for trade, but to invade my people, and possesse my Country."[9]

The English came to Jamestown hoping to find gold and gems. Instead they found cold, starvation, and thousands of hostile Indians. Some even resorted to cannibalism. They built James Fort, and the Indians besieged the colonists inside the fort. On the verge of abandoning Jamestown, the English colonists were refortified by the arrival of Lord De La Warr with supplies and soldiers in the spring of 1610.

Still, violence had broken out between the colonists and the Algonquin people. In December 1609, Captain John Ratcliffe was gruesomely skinned with mussel shells and eventually burned.

The first Anglo-Powhatan war raged from 1610 until 1614. Disease also decimated the indigenous population.

Pocahontas, by then a Christian convert, married one of the new arrivals—an Englishman by the name of John Rolfe—in 1614, bringing the Peace of Pocahontas. Just two years earlier, Rolfe had begun growing tobacco in Jamestown. Agriculture, and especially tobacco, would eventually save the colony from extinction, transforming Virginia in the process.

Powhatan died in 1618 and was succeeded by Chief Opchanacanough, who despised the English settlers. He bided his time, and then on March 22, 1622, he struck. On that one day, 347 colonists, nearly a third of Jamestown's population, were massacred. The Second Anglo-Powhatan War would last from 1622 until 1632.

The third and final Anglo-Powhatan War was launched in 1644. It raged until 1646, killing around five hundred colonists and many more Indians. Trust between the English and the Powhatan never recovered.

---

9    Scott Weidensaul, *The First Frontier: The Forgotten History of Struggle, Savagery, and Endurance in Early America* (Boston: Houghton Mifflin Harcourt, 2012), 92.

Virginia was largely pro-Royalist during the English Civil War; but in 1652, Cromwell sent a force to Virginia to impose the rule of the Commonwealth.

Additional internal conflict was to come. After the restoration of the monarch in Britain, a Royalist governor was also restored in Virginia. In 1676, rebels, discontented with the governor's attitude to Native American raids, seized Jamestown in Bacon's Rebellion. The rebellion was crushed but Jamestown was burned during the process.

On February 22, 1732, George Washington was born in Westmoreland County. He was an excellent horseman who surveyed land throughout the colony and on the western frontier. During the Seven Year's War, he would rise to become a colonel of the Virginia Regiment, fighting in numerous engagements, although he was disappointed not to receive a commission in the British Army. In 1754, he inherited Mount Vernon from his older half-brother Lawrence, who had served under Admiral Edward Vernon at the 1741 assault on Cartagena during the War of Jenkins' Ear. The Second Continental Congress selected Washington to be commander in chief of the Continental Army in 1775.

Washington was an imperfect military commander—he lost more battles than he won. He was, however, a tremendous motivator of men, who endured their hardships while on campaign at Valley Forge and elsewhere. He was a paragon of integrity. Moreover, he won the really important battles of the war. Washington became the "indispensable man" of the American Revolution.

The colony of Virginia was by far the richest and most populous of any of the thirteen colonies at the start of the American Revolution. In 1775, Governor Dunmore was forced out of Virginia after British defeat at the Battle of Great Bridge. However, conflict would return to Virginia later in the war.

In 1779, Lord Cornwallis dispatched Major General Edward Matthews to Virginia with a force of 1,800 Redcoats. Starting from Portsmouth, Matthews captured Norfolk and Suffolk, burning barns and crops along the way. In December 1780, Brigadier General Benedict Arnold, now fighting for the British, arrived at Hampton Roads. Arnold captured Richmond and set the city ablaze.

Washington responded by sending Marquis de Lafayette with 1,200 American troops to defend Virginia. Lafayette was outnumbered by over 7,000 British troops. Colonel Banastre Tarleton (see South Carolina) very nearly captured the colonial governor of Virginia, Thomas Jefferson, in a raid on Charlottesville. Washington soon reinforced American forces in Virginia with "Mad" Anthony Wayne's Pennsylvanians and other troops, bringing the American total to around 5,000. Baron von Steuben, the Prussian drillmaster of the Continental Army, also joined Lafayette.

The Battle of Virginia Capes, fought on September 5, 1781, was the most decisive naval engagement of the American Revolution, and it was fought in Virginia waters near the mouth the Chesapeake Bay. Twenty-four French ships under Comte de Grasse and nineteen British ships under Admiral Graves pounded each other for about two hours. Only one British ship sank—the seventy-four gun *Thunderer*—but Admiral Graves retreated to New York, leaving Lord Cornwallis stranded and besieged at Yorktown.

George Washington marched south to assume command of the forces under Lafayette in Virginia. On September 17, 1781, Washington met with de Grasse aboard his flagship, the *Ville de Paris,* to plot strategy against Lord Cornwallis. The landing of about 4,000 French troops and many cannon under the command of Rochambeau finally gave the numerical edge to the Patriots. The combined Franco-American force began besieging the British at Yorktown. On the night of October 14, Lafayette and Alexander Hamilton, Washington's aide de camp and future Treasury Secretary, led a daring night assault on Redoubt No. 10, capturing it. The French Grand Battery fired over 15,000 cannonballs at the British over eight days. On October 19, 1781, Lord Cornwallis signed the surrender documents, and over 7,000 British soldiers laid down their arms, according to legend, to the tune of "The World Turned Upside Down." Though the Treaty of Paris, which ended the war, would not be signed until 1783, Yorktown marked the last major battle of the American Revolution. The Declaration of Independence, signed on July 4, 1776, may have declared American independence, but it was victory at Yorktown that made it a reality.

After serving two terms as the first American president, George Washington retired to his farm at Mount Vernon on the Potomac. Many Virginians would follow in his footsteps, with eight American presidents hailing from the Old Dominion.

The War of 1812 was initiated by Virginian James Madison. During this war, the British imposed a naval blockade on Virginia ports and attacked many American vessels. The Chesapeake Bay was a vital strategic area. British landing parties also launched a large number of raids on Virginia territory. Some of these resulted in serious fighting. In June 1813, thousands of British troops attacked Craney Island with the intention of seizing Norfolk, but they were repulsed. A few days later, they seized Hampton and sacked it, but eventually withdrew, having suffered significant casualties. In April 1814, they seized and occupied Tangier Island. And then in August, a British fleet captured and plundered Alexandria.

Virginia saw a number of slave rebellions or plans for them, but perhaps the most famous is the one led by Nat Turner in Southampton County in August 1831. The rebellion was crushed by local militiamen and some artillerymen.

In 1839, the Virginia Military Institute was founded in Lexington.

Virginia was the largest state in the Confederacy, and Richmond was, from June of 1861, its capital. This made it an obvious strategic target for the Union. Virginia's proximity to the capital of the United States also made the state a continual source of anxiety for Northern planners. Virginia would become the most fought over state during the Civil War. It is therefore impossible to note here every action. It is only possible to concentrate on some of the main events.

Many Virginians, such as Robert E. Lee, Thomas "Stonewall" Jackson, and Jeb Stuart, rallied to their state after its announced secession. On the other hand, many distinguished Virginians fought on the Union side, including Winfield Scott, David Farragut, and Sergeant William Carney—the first African-American recipient of the Medal of Honor. The western portion of the state was not supportive of secession and voted to secede from the secession, forming West Virginia in 1861 (see West Virginia).

On July 21, 1861, at First Bull Run (called Manassas by the South), the first major battle of the war was fought. "A throng of sightseers"—politicians and some women—rode carriages equipped with picnic baskets twenty-five miles from Washington to observe the spectacle of the Union Army teaching a lesson to "Johnny Reb." Instead, they witnessed the bloodiest day in US history up to that point, as the Confederates whupped the Yankees, who skedaddled from the field. The Congressional picnickers fled back to Washington. Major General Irvin McDowell proved to be first in a long line of Union commanders destined to disappoint Lincoln and try the patience of the North.

In 1862, General McClellan sought to exploit the Union's naval advantage by launching a bold amphibious invasion by 105,000 soldiers of the Army of the Potomac. The Peninsula campaign began with a landing at Fort Monroe by the Hampton roads. Confederate troops led by General Magruder occupied some of the same defensive works that had been used by the British at Yorktown in 1781. Hot air balloons and Pinkerton detectives were employed to gather intelligence. McClellan dithered rather than assaulting the vastly outnumbered Confederates. Union forces advanced slowly up the Peninsula, winning on May 5 a small battle at Williamsburg, which had been Virginia's original capital. Robert E. Lee assumed command of the Army of Northern Virginia on June 2, 1862. The Seven Days' Battles were fought near Richmond from June 25 to July 1. Confederate losses over the battles exceeded Union by 20,204 to 15,855. Nevertheless, McClellan, mistakenly believing himself outnumbered, embarked his army and withdrew from the Peninsula.

In March 1862, the Battle of Hampton Roads, the most important naval engagement of the Civil War, was fought off the Virginia coast. The CSS *Virginia* (formerly *Merrimack*), armored by the Tredegar Ironworks of Richmond, was the first ironclad ship to ever steam into battle. On March 8, she managed to sink two Union ships while Union shot bounced off her ironclad deck. The next day, she encountered the Union's ironclad *Monitor*, which mounted an 11-inch gun on a revolving turret. After two hours of ineffectual bombardment, both ships withdrew from history's first battle between ironclad warships. The *Virginia* was captured and scuttled later that year by McClellan's forces in Norfolk. The *Monitor* also sank in a storm off the coast of North Carolina that same year.

On August 29–30, 1862, Lee sent Stonewall Jackson on a flanking maneuver that defeated Major John Pope at the Second Battle of Bull Run. Union casualties were almost double Confederate losses (about 16,000 versus 9,000), and casualties for Second Bull Run on both sides far exceeded those of First Bull Run. Pope withdrew and was soon sacked by Lincoln. Lee advanced north into Maryland, bound for Antietam.

The year 1862 ended with another Confederate victory in Virginia at the Battle of Fredericksburg on December 13. An outnumbered Lee managed to inflict a crushing defeat on Major General Ambrose Burnside, who is mainly remembered today for his sideburns. Burnside has delayed his attack, allowing Lee to build up a superior defensive position. By the shores of the Rappahannock, over 1,700 Union troops were captured, along with 11,000 rifles. Lincoln would sack Burnside, replacing him with Joseph Hooker.

From May 1–3, 1863, Lee, although again outnumbered by more than two to one, would defeat Hooker at the Battle of Chancellorsville in Virginia.

Lee sent Jeb Stuart to attack Hooker's right flank while Stonewall Jackson drove onto his left, surrounding the Union position. The battle that many regard as Lee's masterpiece cost the Confederacy General Jackson, who died from wounds inflicted by friendly fire shot by troops from North Carolina. Lincoln swiftly replaced Hooker with George Meade (see Pennsylvania), but Lee would never successfully replace Jackson.

In 1864, Lincoln put Ulysses S. Grant, victor of many western battles, in command of the Army of the Potomac and charged him with the capture of Richmond and destruction of the Rebel Army. In the Overland Campaign, the Army of the Potomac crossed the Rapidan River and fought the Army of Northern Virginia in a series of attritional battles in Virginia. Finally, these battles pitted Grant, the greatest Union general of the war, against Lee, the greatest Confederate commander. Grant's forces outnumbered Lee's by about 115,000 to 60,000. Bloody engagements were fought that May at the Battle of the Wilderness, Spotsylvania Court House, and at Cold Harbor. Union losses were higher than those of the Confederates, but the South found it increasingly difficult to replace its troops. Some losses, such as the death of Jeb Stuart at Yellow Tavern, were irreplaceable.

On May 15, 1864, ten cadets from VMI were killed at the Battle of New Market in Virginia. The Institute would be burned by Union forces later that year.

Though Confederate cavalry led by Jubal Early threatened Washington in July, that did not deter Grant from initiating the long siege of Petersburg. And on April 2, 1865, Union troops finally entered Richmond. The Tredegar Ironworks that had produced 1,100 pieces of artillery in the war was finally captured by the Union. Ten days later, Grant and Lee met to sign the articles of surrender at the Appomattox Court House, bringing to an end the great tragedy of the American Civil War.

In 1898, Fort Hunt on the Potomac was made operational. It was built to defend against invasions that never materialized. Today, like many former defense installations on American coasts, it is a recreational facility run by the National Park Service.

Battles would be fought in Virginia waters in both world wars. On May 25, 1918, *U-151*, a German submarine, surfaced off the coast of Virginia and stopped three schooners. All three were sunk by naval gunfire after their crews were allowed to evacuate. On June 15, 1942, tourists along Virginia Beach were horrified to witness the sinking of two merchant ships by torpedoes launched by *U-701* of the German Navy.

The US Pentagon was built in Arlington County and dedicated in 1943. Arlington National Cemetery, established in 1864, is a constant reminder of the American sacrifice in wars in America and around the world.

## VIRGINIA
## MILITARY HISTORY SITES

### American Civil War Museum—Historic Tredegar
Location: 500 Tredegar Street, Richmond, VA 23219
Web: www.acwm.org

### Arlington National Cemetery
Location: Entrance at Arlington Memorial Bridge, Arlington, VA 22211
Web: www.arlingtoncemetery.mil

### Cold Harbor Battlefield
Location: 5515 Anderson Wright Drive, Mechanicsville, VA 23111
Web: www.nps.gov/rich/learn/historyculture/cold-harbor-tour.htm

### Colonial Williamsburg
Location: 101 Visitor Center Drive, Wilmington, VA 23185
Web: www.colonialwilliamsburg.com

### Manassas National Battlefield Park
Location: 6511 Sudley Road, Manassas, VA 20109
Web: www.nps.gov/mana/index.htm

### Monticello
Location: 931 Thomas Jefferson Parkway, Charlottesville, VA 22902
Web: home.monticello.org

**Mount Vernon**
Location: 3200 Mount Vernon Memorial Highway, Mount Vernon, VA 22121
Web: www.mountvernon.org

**National Museum of the Marine Corps**
Location: 18900 Jefferson Davis Highway, Triangle, VA 22172
Web: www.usmcmuseum.com

**Richmond National Battlefied Park**
Location: 470 Tredegar Street, Richmond, VA 23219
Web: www.nps.gov/rich/index.htm

**Yorktown Battlefield**
Location: 1000 Colonial Parkway, Yorktown, VA 23690
Web: www.nps.gov/york/planyourvisit/visitorcenters.htm

### POCAHONTAS
c. 1596-1617
Source: iStock/traveler1116

### YORKTOWN MONUMENT
Colonial National Historical Park
Source: Author photo

### TREDEGAR IRONWORKS
Richmond
Source: Author photo

### GEORGE WASHINGTON'S MOUNT VERNON
Source: Author photo

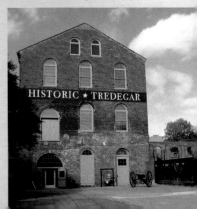

Nickname: Old Dominion
Statehood: 1788
Capital: Richmond

WINCHESTER
LEEBURG
ARLINGTON CEMETERY
ARLINGTON
FORT HUNT
STRASBURG
THE PLAINS
ALEXANDRIA
WASHINGTON
BULL RUN X2
MT JACKSON
NEW MARKET
REMINGTON
SHENANDOAH NATIONAL PARK
QUANTICO
HARRISONBURG
CHANCELLORSVILLE
WILDERNESS
FREDERICKSBURG
MONTEREY
STANARDSVILLE
ORANGE
SPOTSYLVANIA
SPOTSYLVANIA COURT HOUSE
GEORGE WASHINGTON NATIONAL FOREST
STAUNTON
WAYNESBORO
CHARLOTTESVILLE
BOWLING GREEN
WARSAW
TANGIER ISLAND
WARM SPRINGS
SHERANDO
ASHLAND
TAPPAHANNOCK
REEDVILLE
GOSHEN
COVESVILLE
COLD HARBOR
KILMARNOCK
ONANCOCK
VA MILITARY INSTITUTE
CLOVERDALE
TUCKOHOE
RICHMOND
WEST POINT
EXMORE
LEXINGTON
AMHERST
MT RUSH
JAMES RIVER
BON AIR
CHESAPEAKE
HOG ISLAND
DANOKE
LYNCHBURG
CUMBERLAND
CHESTER
WILLIAMSBURG
SUSAN
VIRGINIA CAPES
APPOMATOX COURTHOUSE
JETERSVILLE
WILLIAMSBURG
YORKTOWN
YORKTOWN
SMITH MOUNTAIN LAKE
BROOKNEAL
BLACKSTONE
SIEGE OF PETERSBURG
FORT MONROE
PENHOOK
GRETNA
KEYSVILLE
MCKENNEY
WAVERLY
FORT JAMES
NORFOLK
HAMPTON ROADS
CRANEY ISLAND
VIRGINIA BEACH
HALIFAX
JARRATT
SUSSEX
CHESAPEAKE
VILLE
DANVILLE
KERR LAKE
SOUTH HILL
CLARKSVILLE
LAKE GASTON
EMPORIA
COURTLAND
SUFFOLK
GREAT BRIDGE
ATLANTIC OCEAN

## ROBERT E. LEE
1807-1870
Source: iStock/traveler1116

## APPOMATTOX COURTHOUSE
Appomattox Court House
National Historical Park
Source: iStock/visionsofmaine

# WASHINGTON

Humans have been living in the area that we know today as Washington State for many millennia. Tribes such as the Salish, Klickitat, Chinook, and Yakama subsisted on a diet of salmon, oysters, clams, and halibut. They built longhouses and totem poles using the abundant cedar that grew around them. They reshaped the landscape of their environment with middens made of discarded shells.

Europeans may have reached the seas off Washington as early as 1579, when Sir Francis Drake was exploring the Pacific coast.

Bruno de Heceta, a Spanish explorer from Bilbao, actually set foot on the Washington coast and encountered the mouth of the Columbia River in 1775, when he led a squadron of two Spanish ships north. Relations between the Europeans and the Native Americans did not get off to a great start. After an attack by the local Quinault Indians on the Spanish ships, the Basque captain named the area *Punta de los Martires*, or Point of the Martyrs. It is today known as Point Grenville.

The Spaniards claimed the Pacific as a vast Spanish lake with their rights blessed by God himself. The Borgia Pope, Alexander VI, in the 1494 Treaty of Tordesillas divided the New World into Spanish and Portuguese spheres of his most Catholic majesties. The Spanish influence on the state of Washington persists in the names of many geographic locations, such as the Straits of Juan de Fuca, San Juan Island, and Rosario.

But other colonial powers were taking an interest in the area as well, and soon they would challenge those who were attempting to claim the area for Spain. In 1778, Captain James Cook reached Cape Flattery on the Olympic Peninsula and claimed it for Britain.

In 1787, Captain Robert Gray of the US Navy set out from Boston in the *Lady Washington,* bound for the Pacific Northwest. He reached the Columbia River the next year, approaching but not entering the mighty river flowing into the Pacific. Grays Harbor, the bay near Aberdeen, and the town of Grayland were named in honor of the captain from Rhode Island. Gray's voyages formed the basis for subsequent American claims to the Oregon Territory, which later included Washington.

In 1790, the Nootka Sound Treaty between Britain and Spain decided claims in the area in favor of Britain. And in 1792, Captain George Vancouver anchored off what is now Seattle and named Puget Sound. That same year, the Spanish fort at Neah Bay, which was supposed to protect the Strait of Juan de Fuca against the British, was abandoned.

The following decades would see both American and British Canadian explorers entering the area over land, and a competition for influence in the area between the Unites States and Britain.

In October 1805, the Lewis and Clark expedition reached what is now Washington State. By 1811, Canadian David Thompson had reached the Pacific after navigating the whole length of the Columbia River. The Hudson's Bay Company set up a string of fur trading posts along the river, controlled from Fort Vancouver, what is now Vancouver, Washington. American fur traders set up their own forts.

Russia was also interested in the area and laid claim to it, but its efforts to establish a presence there failed to make much progress. In 1808, for instance, the ship *Saint Nicholas*, carrying a party of twenty Russians to set up a fort at the mouth of the Columbia River, was wrecked on the Olympic Peninsula.

The War of 1812 didn't exactly have a huge impact on the area, although, afraid of attack by British ships, the American owners of Fort Astoria sold it to the British North West Company. It was renamed Fort George.

After the War of 1812, in an agreement of 1818, Britain and the United States decided to administer the area jointly, but ultimately this arrangement would not last. After James K. Polk made US control of the area one of the main policies in his successful 1844 presidential campaign, tensions in the area escalated in 1845 and 1846, and there was even talk of war.

In the end, though, the 1846 Treaty of Oregon established the 49th parallel as the northern border of Washington State, separating it from Canada. Vancouver Island, though south of the 49th parallel, was carved out as British territory. The terms of the treaty were ambiguous in regard to the disposition of the San Juan Archipelago in the strait of San Juan de Fuca. The Hudson's Bay Company established a sheep farm on San Juan Island while some Americans also moved to the disputed island.

Many skirmishes were fought between settlers and indigenous people in Washington from 1846 to 1858. In the 1840s, a measles epidemic killed about half of the Cayuse population near Walla Walla. The Cayuse responded with the Whitman Massacre on November 29, 1847, which killed thirteen civilians, including Dr. Marcus Whitman and his wife at a mission. A punitive expedition set out from Oregon City, and several small battles were fought in 1848. The 1850s would see much heavier fighting as more settlers entered the area.

Americans in the Oregon Territory responded to the Indian threat by constructing defensive works, such as Fort Steilacoom in 1849 and Fort Bellingham in 1856.

In November 1851, a small group of Americans arrived on Alki Point in what is today West Seattle. Chief Seattle of the Suquamish tribe welcomed the settlers, forming a friendship with "Doc" Maynard, a founder of Seattle and the city's first doctor.

Starting in 1855, the next few years were busy times in what is now Washington State, as clashes erupted between US forces and a number of different Native American groups.

In 1855, war with the Yakima began after the killing of Indian Agent Andrew J. Bolon. A retaliatory expedition led by Major Haller was ambushed in the Yakima Valley and forced to retreat.

Chief Leschi began rallying tribes in the Puget Sound area and launching raids. On January 26, 1856, Native Americans attacked in what became known as the Battle of Seattle. The US Navy 's 16-gun sloop *Decatur* (named after Stephen Decatur, who famously said, "Our country, right or wrong,") shelled the attackers while its marines clashed with them on land. Two American settlers and twenty-eight Native Americans were killed.[10] Eventually, the attackers withdrew.

---

10    Lorraine McConaghy, *Warship under Sail: The USS* Decatur *in the Pacific West* (Seattle: University of Washington Press, 2009), 141.

In November, US forces commanded by Major Gabriel Rains used artillery in a significant victory over Yakima forces led by Kamiakin.

In March of the next year, settlers at the Upper Cascades were attacked, and soldiers in the small fort in the Middle Cascades had to battle to hold out until a relief party arrived. In August, General Wool closed off eastern Washington to settlers, hoping to end the fighting. Governor Stevens also declared martial law in the Puget Sound area in an attempt to deal with Native American raids.

In February 1858, Chief Leschi of the Nisqually was hanged after being controversially convicted of murder.

On May 17, 1858, Brevet Colonel Edward Steptoe and his forces were ambushed by a group of Cayuse, Spokane, Yakama, and other Native Americans warriors. The Battle of Pine Creek in Rosalia was a rare defeat for American regular Army forces, which lost their artillery. Fewer than a hundred were killed on both sides in what amounted to a skirmish.

However, in September 1858, US troops equipped with new long-range rifles inflicted a crushing defeat on the Spokane in the Battle of Four lakes. And at the Battle of Spokane Plains shortly thereafter, US forces captured over eight hundred Spokane horses and slaughtered them all. In the end, resistance from Native Americans crumbled, a peace deal was imposed on them, and reservations were created.

And war with another power in the area was about to become a possibility.

On June 15, 1859, Lyman Cutlar, an American squatter on San Juan Island, shot a Berkshire boar that belonged to the Hudson's Bay Company. Cutlar felt that the pig was trespassing onto the 160-acre homestead that he was tending with his Indian wife. This rash act triggered an escalation by both the Americans and the English authorities on the island. Captain George Pickett, the subsequent leader of a disastrous charge at the Battle of Gettysburg in 1863, was dispatched from Fort Bellingham to San Juan Island. A company of Royal Marines landed on the island and garrisoned at English Camp. It seemed, for a time, that Britain and America might be again at war. Both sides consulted respective elder military figures—Rear Admiral R. Lambert Baynes, Pacific Station Commander of the Royal Navy, and Lieutenant General Winfield Scott, head of the US Army. Both men advised extreme caution, and both nations backed away from war. Fortunately, the only casualty of the Pig War was porcine.

For twelve years, from 1860 until 1872, San Juan Island was subject to joint occupation by American and British forces. In 1872, the boundary dispute was mediated by the German emperor William I, whose three-member commission awarded the island permanently to America.

In the late nineteenth century, there was an explosion in the popularity of invasion fiction. Erskine Childer's 1903 *Riddle of the Sands* is, perhaps, the most well-known example. Over in Europe, a naval race to build dreadnoughts was being waged between Britain and Imperial Germany before World War I. The United States was also swept up in the period of imperial expansion following the Spanish-American War. Alfred Thayer Mahan's *The Influence of Sea Power upon History* dominated thinking in naval circles around the world. Americans discovered that their coastline was vulnerable to naval gunfire from enemy battleships. Those on the West Coast felt particularly vulnerable, since even Chile's fleet was, for a time, stronger than the US Navy's West Coast squadron.

In 1889, Washington became the forty-second state to join the Union.

The solution to the predicament of the vulnerable coast was to build fortifications. In 1897, construction on Fort Casey on the western side of Whidbey Island began. Its 10-inch guns on disappearing carriages commanded sweeping views of Admiralty Inlet. Other installations were built at Fort Ebey, Fort Flagler, and Fort Worden. Today Fort Casey is a state park and a wildlife sanctuary that is often visited by seals.

On July 5, 1917, less than three months after the United States declared war on the Central Powers in WWI, construction began on Fort Lewis. At an astonishing cost of just over $7 million, 1,757 buildings and 422 other structures were erected in ninety days. Many generations of recruits would learn to become soldiers under the shadow of Mount Rainier.

The 91st Division, known as the Wild West Division, trained at Fort Lewis prior to being sent "Over There" to fight in Europe. The 91st was drawn mainly from soldiers from Western states. In spite of the segregation of the US Army at that time, many ethnic groups trained at Fort Lewis. Squa De Lah, for example, was a Native American who trained at Fort Lewis and was killed on Christmas Day, 1917, on the Western Front.

After WWI, Fort Lewis was allowed to languish, effectively becoming a ghost town. During the 1930s, however, the pace of military activity picked up significantly there.

From November 1940 to June 1941, Lieutenant Colonel Dwight Eisenhower served as chief of staff of the IX Army Corps based at Fort Lewis. He was regarded as "amiable and efficient." Likable Ike would, of course, become the leader of Operation Overlord—the Allied invasion of Nazi-occupied Europe and, later, president.

Shortly after the Pearl Harbor attack, two Japanese submarines began hunting for Allied shipping targets off Washington waters. The Imperial Japanese Navy's *I-26* lurked off the Strait of Juan de Fuca, while the *I-25* patrolled near the mouth of the Columbia. Commander Yokota of the *I-26* was still prowling near the Strait of Juan de Fuca on June 7, 1942, when it fired a Long Lance torpedo into the *Coast Trader*. The ship, laden with a cargo of newsprint, soon sank. The crew of the American vessel was eventually rescued and taken to a US Navy post on Neah Bay.

At least twenty Japanese Fu-Go balloon bombs landed in Washington State from 1944 to 1945. In March of 1945, one bomb even landed at the Hanford Engineer Works in Cold Creek, near the site where plutonium was produced that would later be used in the atomic bomb dropped on Nagasaki. The plant was briefly shut down due to enemy action—the only time this ever occurred to an American atomic facility. Due to censorship, the Japanese never learned of their brief success during the war.

Warren Magnuson, a US Navy vet from World War II, served as a US Senator from 1944 until his death in 1981. He gained seniority and sat for many years on the Senate Committee on Appropriations, steering many projects toward his home state.

In 1973, Bangor became the home of a Trident Nuclear Submarine base for the navy. World War II bases at Whidbey Island and Spokane (Fairchild AFB) were strengthened.

During the Cold War, the Soviets set up joint commercial ventures with American companies to harvest white fish off the northwest coasts. Some of their "fishing ships" were undoubtedly engaged in espionage activities.

In the late twentieth century, relations between Native Americans and other Americans made enormous progress in Washington State and throughout the country. In 1970, Sonny Sixkiller, a member of the Cherokee Nation, became the quarterback of the University of Washington's Huskies football team. Today Washington State has been "invaded" by many successful Indian gambling casinos.

The *Windjammer*, a commercial fishing vessel trawling about twelve miles off Washington's coast, caught a Soviet hydrophone during the Cold War. It can be found today outside a fishing supply store in Ballard, where a sign identifies it as "Putin's hearing aid." In fact, it is more likely a souvenir of the Brezhnev era.

In 1999, another Battle of Seattle was fought when many protested globalization at the World Trade Organization (WTO) convention. Chief Seattle was long dead by that time, but Seattle's chief of police was ousted as a result of the riots.

## WASHINGTON
## MILITARY HISTORY SITES

### B Reactor National Historic Landmark
Location: Hanford, WA (tours start from 2000 Logston Boulevard, Richland, WA 99354)
Web: manhattanprojectbreactor.hanford.gov

### Fort Casey Historical State Park
Location: 1280 Engle Road, Coupeville, WA 98239
Web: parks.state.wa.us/505/Fort-Casey

### Fort Ebey State Park
Location: 400 Hill Valley Drive, Coupeville, WA 98239
Web: parks.state.wa.us/507/Fort-Ebey

### Fort Nisqually
Location: Point Defiance Park, 5400 North Pearl Street, Tacoma, WA 98407
Web: www.metroparkstacoma.org/history-fort-nisqually

### Flying Heritage & Combat Armor Museum
Location: 3407 109th Street SW, Everett, WA 98204
Web: www.flyingheritage.com

BLAINE

FORT BELLINGHAM

BELLINGHAM

MT BAKER NATIONAL FOREST

NORTH CASCADES NP

ROSS LAKE

SAN JUAN ISLANDS

SKAGIT RIVER

CONCRETE

LA CONNER

OZETTE LAKE

PORT ANGELES

FORT EBEY

FORT CASEY

WENATCHEE NATIONAL FOREST

FORKS

FORT WORDEN
FORT FLAGLER

PORT LUDLOW

**EVERETT**

OLYMPIC NATIONAL FOREST

EDMONDS

**SEATTLE**

QUINAULT RIVER

**SEATTLE**

BELLEVUE

U.S. 2

QUINAULT INDIAN RESERVATION

QUINAULT

HOODSPORT

RENTON

SNOQUALMIE NATIONAL FOREST

POINT GRENVILLE

**FORT LEWIS**
(NOW JOINT BASE LEWIS–MCCHORD)

**TACOMA**

CLE ELUM

PACIFIC OCEAN

HOQUIAM

**OLYMPIA**

**FORT STEILACOOM**

LA GRANDE

NACHES RIVER

RAYMOND

CHEHALIS

ASHFORD

12

PACKWOOD

LONG BEACH

TOLEDO

RIFFE LAKE

12

GIFFORD PINCHOT NATIONAL FOREST

YAKIMA INDIAN RESERVATION

LONGVIEW

MOUNT ST HELENS

COUGAR

GLENWOOD

VANCOUVER

COLUMBIA RIVER

WHITE SALMON

## CAPTAIN ROBERT GRAY
1756-1806
Statue, Garibaldi, OR
Source: Author photo

## CHIEF SEATTLE
c. 1786-1866, Statue,
Downtown Seattle
Source: Vincent Driano

## TOTEM POLE
San Juan Island
Source: Author photo

Nickname: The Evergreen State
Statehood: 1889
Capital: Olympia

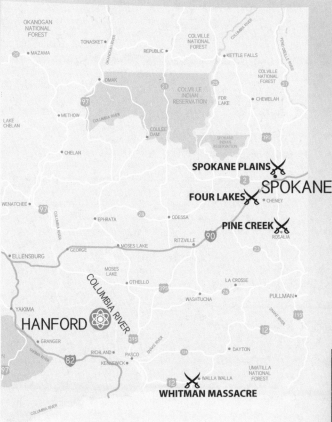

SPOKANE PLAINS ⚔
SPOKANE
FOUR LAKES ⚔
PINE CREEK ⚔

COLUMBIA RIVER

HANFORD ⚛

WHITMAN MASSACRE ⚔

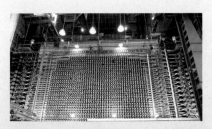

## HANFORD REACTOR CORE

Manhattan Project
National Historical
Park, Hanford
Source: Author photo

## SOVIET HYDROPHONE

Ballard
Source: Author photo

### ENGLISH CAMP

In 1859 the killing of a pig on
San Juan Island brought England and the
United States to the brink of war over
the issue of territorial rights here.

By agreement, both nations' troops
were permitted to occupy this area
while the problem was studied.

British soldiers established camp
at Garrison Bay, just west of here, while
American troops camped at the southern
end of the island.

Peaceful arbitration of the dispute
in 1872 placed the San Juan Islands
within the territorial United States.

In October of that year the British
garrison was abandoned.

## THE PIG WAR ENGLISH CAMP

San Juan Island
Source: Author photo

**Historic Flight**
Location: 10719 Bernie Webber Drive, Mukilteo, WA 98275
Web: historicflight.org

**Lewis Army Museum**
Location: 4320 Main Street and Constitution Drive, Joint Base Lewis-Mc-Chord, WA 98433
Web: https://lewisarmymuseum.com

**Museum of History & Industry (MOHAI)**
Location: 860 Terry Avenue North, Seattle, WA 98109
Web: mohai.org

**Museum of Flight**
Location: 9404 East Marginal Way South, Seattle, WA 98108
Web: museumofflight.org

**United States Naval Undersea Museum**
Location: 1 Garnett Way, Keyport, WA 98345
Web: www.navalunderseamuseum.org

**San Juan Island National Historic Park—American Camp and English Camp (Pig War)**
Location: San Juan Island, 4668 Cattle Point Road, Friday Harbor, WA 98250
Web: www.nps.gov/sajh/learn/historyculture/american-camp.htm
Web: www.nps.gov/sajh/learn/historyculture/english-camp.htm

**Puget Sound Navy Museum**
Location: 251 First Street, Bremerton, WA 98337
Web: www.pugetsoundnavymuseum.org

**Veterans Memorial Museum**
Location: 100 SW Veterans Way, Chehalis, WA 98532
Web: veteransmuseum.org

# WASHINGTON DC

What is now Washington DC was once a piece of marshy land inhabited by Native Americans of the Conoy, or people linked to them. Then it became part of the colony of Maryland. Assorted settlements appeared, most notably Georgetown, which was founded in 1751.

Although it remained a part of Maryland until after the American Revolution and after events like the Pennsylvania Mutiny of 1783 (see Pennsylvania), it became increasingly clear that Congress needed its own territory outside the control of any individual state.

The result was the creation, from some land in Virginia and some land in Maryland, of the original ten-mile by ten-mile rectangular District of Columbia, named after Christopher Columbus. The land taken from Virginia would later be returned, leaving the irregular borders that the current District of Columbia has.

In 1800, the government moved to the new city of Washington; and just a few years later, the British invaded.

The District of Columbia's most famous invasion occurred during the War of 1812. It was a somewhat difficult time in the war from the American point of view. In Europe, Napoleon had surrendered, and thousands of experienced British troops crossed the Atlantic to join the fight. Rear Admiral George Cockburn saw an opportunity to strike a devastating blow against the United States.

In August 1814, British forces that had landed at Benedict clashed with American militia at the Battle of Bladensburg (see Maryland). President Madison rode out to witness the battle. He probably shouldn't have bothered. The British regular troops brushed aside the inexperienced militia, even though the Americans outnumbered them, and marched into Washington. Madison and the rest of the US government fled.

The commander of the city's defenses, Brigadier General William Winder—a lawyer with good political connections but minor military experience—decided he had no option but to abandon the city to the attackers. British troops were seeking revenge for the sacking of York (Toronto), and while largely leaving private buildings intact, they burned the Capitol, the White House, and other key buildings, including the US Treasury. Just over twenty-four hours after arriving, they departed and the invasion was finished.

As the center of political life in the United States, over the years Washington DC has inevitably been the focus of a significant number of acts of political violence. For instance, in June 1857, rioting broke out as gangs from the anti-immigrant American Party (popularly known as the Know-Nothing Party) clashed with opponents. Eventually, US marines opened fire, killing ten.

On May 22, 1856, fighting erupted in the Senate chamber of the US Capitol. Representative Preston Brooks of South Carolina attacked Senator Charles Sumner of Massachusetts with a cane. Sumner had earlier delivered a fiery abolitionist speech. Some have labeled this the incident, nearly five years before Fort Sumter, as the opening blows of the American Civil War.

During the Civil War, though, the District of Columbia would once more face military invasion. In July 1864, the forces of Confederate Lieutenant Jubal A. Early reached as far as Fort Stevens, inside the District of Columbia. For two days, his forces skirmished around the fort; and at one stage, the entourage of President Lincoln, who had come to observe, came under Confederate fire. In the end, though, Early decided that the fort's defenses were too strong and he withdrew.

But Lincoln himself had only a little time left to live. On April 14, 1865, five days after General Lee surrendered to General Grant, John Wilkes Booth shot Lincoln at Ford's Theatre as part of a plot to decapitate the Union government at a time when the complete collapse of the Confederacy seemed inevitable. However, while Booth managed to kill the president, his fellow conspirators were not so successful. Lewis Powell only wounded Secretary of

State William H. Seward in his home. George Atzerodt abandoned his attempt to kill Vice President Andrew Johnson almost before he even started. And ultimately, Lincoln's death could not prevent the collapse of the Confederacy.

More acts of political violence in Washington would follow, but in terms of actual major attacks on the district, that was pretty much it. Until, of course, 9/11. American Airlines Flight 77 hit the Pentagon at 9:37 a.m. One hundred and eighty-nine were killed, including the plane's passengers and hijackers. At 10:03 a.m., near Shanksville, Pennsylvania, United Airlines Flight 93 hit the ground after heroic passengers tried to regain control of the aircraft from the attackers. The intended target of the Flight 93 hijackers is thought to have been either the Capitol or the White House.

## WASHINGTON DC
## MILITARY HISTORY SITES

### African American Civil War Museum
Location: 1925 Vermont Ave NW, Washington, DC 20001
Web: www.afroamcivilwar.org/

### Ford's Theatre
Location: 511 10th Street NW, Washington, DC 20004
Web: www.fords.org

### Lincoln Memorial
Location: 2 Lincoln Memorial Circle NW, Washington, DC 20037
Web: www.nps.gov/linc/index.htm

### National Air and Space Museum
Location: 600 Independence Avenue SW, Washington, DC 20560
Web: www.airandspace.si.edu

### National Guard Memorial Museum
Location:  1 Massachusetts Ave NW, Washington, DC 20001
Web: www.ngef.org/national-guard-memorial-museum/

### FORD'S THEATRE
Site of Lincoln Assassination
April 14, 1865
Source: iStock/SeanPavonePhoto

### LINCOLN MEMORIAL
Washington DC
Source: iStock/TylerFairbank

Motto: Justitia Omnibus
Approved: 1790
District of Columbia

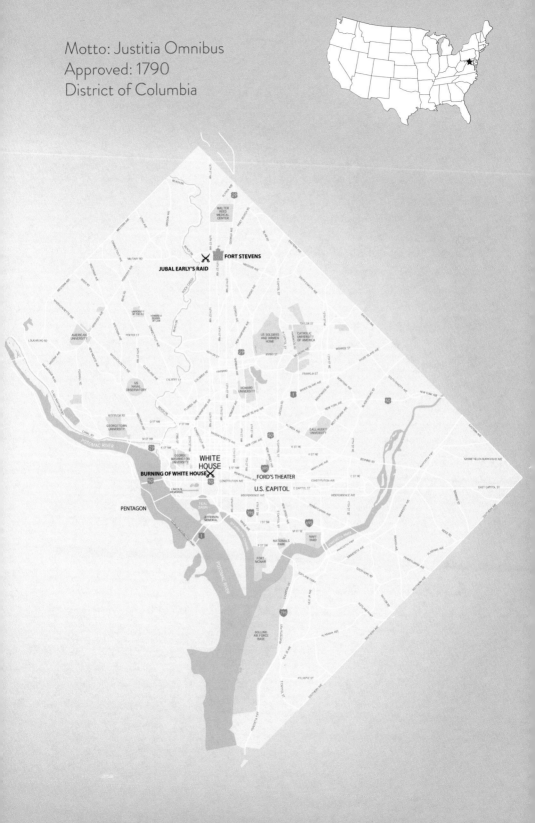

**National Museum of American History**
Location: 14th Street & Constitution Avenue NW, Washington, DC 20001
Web: americanhistory.si.edu/

**National Museum of the American Indian**
Location: 4th Street SW & Independence Avenue SW, Washington, DC 20560
Web: www.nmai.si.edu/

**National Museum of the United States Navy**
Location: 736 Sicard Street SE, Washington, DC 20374
Web: www.history.navy.mil/content/history/museums/nmusn.html

**United States Naval Observatory**
Location: 3450 Massachusetts Avenue NW, Washington, DC 20392
Web: www.usno.navy.mil/USNO

**Washington Monument**
Location: 2 15th Street NW, Washington, DC 20024
Web: www.nps.gov/wamo/index.htm

# WEST VIRGINIA

The Mountaineer State of West Virginia, created as a direct result of the Civil War, is a constant reminder of the fluidity of US state borders. Formerly, West Virginia formed part of the colony and then state of Virginia. Robert Dinwiddie, the lieutenant governor of colonial Virginia, had an expansive vision, claiming that, "Virginia resumes its ancient Breadth, and has no other limits to the West ... to the South Sea, including the Isl'd of California."

The Shawnee, Delaware, Susquehanna, and Cherokee were some of the tribes living in West Virginia before the arrival of Europeans

English explorers pushed westward in the region in the period after the English civil war, until problems in Virginia caused a halt.

There was renewed interest in the area, however, in the eighteenth century, and settlers began to arrive, including a Welshman, Colonel Morgan Morgan.

The expansion of the settlement region eventually led to tension between Virginia and Pennsylvania, and, more significantly, between Britain and France.

Dinwiddie is best known for dispatching George Washington for an expedition to the Ohio River Valley, which ignited the French and Indian War. Young George Washington surveyed the Appalachians and the Kanawha Valley from horseback.

In 1774, Lord Dunmore's War broke out between the colony of Virginia and Native Americans (principally Shawnee). The most significant battle of this war, the Battle of Point Pleasant, was fought on October 10, 1774, in present-day West Virginia. A thousand Indian warriors led by Chief Cornstalk surprised a group of colonial militia. As a result of this war, the Indians were pushed west of the Ohio River.

Fort Henry was constructed in 1774 during Lord Dunmore's War, near what is Wheeling today. During the American Revolution, Fort Henry would be subjected to two sieges. The first took place in 1777 and was led by Shawnee and Mingo Indians sympathetic to the British cause. This siege was notable for McCulloch's extraordinary and, perhaps, mythological leap. Major Samuel McCulloch found himself on the wrong side of the closed gates of Fort Henry, surrounded by hostile Indians. The militia leader galloped away to a three-hundred-foot precipice. After he plunged over the cliff, the pursuing Indians were astonished to note that he and his horse somehow managed to survive. McCulloch's Leap is marked by a plaque today.

In 1782, a force of Indians and Redcoats again besieged Fort Henry. When the fort's ammunition was running low, Betty Zane, a seventeen-year-old farm girl, came to the rescue by fetching gunpowder in a tablecloth from her nearby home. The fort never surrendered.

John Brown, a fervent abolitionist, led an unsuccessful raid on the federal armory at Harper's Ferry in western Virginia in 1859. He had planned to supply arms to slaves in hopes of inciting a rebellion. The armory was, however, defended by Colonel Robert E. Lee, who commanded US Marines and local militia. Brown was later apprehended and executed in Charles Town. His death made him a martyr for the Union cause, and "John Brown's body lies a-mouldering in the grave" became an anthem for the North in the coming Civil War.

West Virginia was, in fact, part of Virginia up until the Civil War. But the western part of the state was very different from the Tidewater shore of Chesapeake Bay. There were, for example, no plantations and very few slaves in western Virginia. On May 23, 1861, Virginia voted to secede from the Union. West Virginia, on the other hand, chose to secede from the secession.

Two Wheeling conventions were held in May and June of 1861. Supporters of the Union won a referendum, and a state constitution was adopted. On June 20, 1863, West Virginia became the thirty-fifth state to join the Union.

In the summer of 1861, George McClellan won three small battles in western Virginia—at Philippi, Rich Mountain, and Carrick's Ford. These battles helped to preserve western Virginia for the Union. They also helped launched McLellan's career, which proved to be a mixed blessing for the Union.

Jefferson Davis sent Robert E. Lee to western Virginia in late summer to restore Confederate control of the area. The Battle of Cheat Mountain, fought in a forested mountainous region from September 11–13, 1861, was Lee's inauspicious debut as a Confederate field commander. Though he outnumbered Union forces, Lee was defeated by Brigadier General Reynolds and withdrew his forces from western Virginia. Confederate casualties were fewer than a hundred.

A year later, in September of 1862, General Thomas "Stonewall" Jackson, a native of western Virginia, managed to exact a measure of revenge for Lee's humiliation at Cheat Mountain. Jackson led the rebels to victory at the Battle of Harper's Ferry on September 12–15, 1862, capturing 12,419 Union soldiers and around 13,000 firearms at the arsenal. It was the second greatest surrender of American forces, exceeded only by the surrender at Corregidor in 1942. Belle Boyd, an eighteen-year-old Confederate spy from western Virginia, had supplied valuable information to Jackson earlier that year.

Confederates occupied Charleston for six weeks after the Battle of Charleston on September 13, 1862. Confederate-sympathizing guerrillas and cavalry raiders kept up a low level of sustained violence in West Virginia for the remainder of the war. The railways were frequently targeted. After the Union victory at the Battle of Droop Mountain on November 6, 1863, Union control of West Virginia went largely undisputed.

Over 30,000 West Virginians would serve in the Union Army in the Civil War. Many more would go on to serve in a variety of American wars.

For many years, coal from West Virginia was shipped via railway to Hampton, Virginia, to power ships of the US Navy.

On December 7, 1941, the USS *West Virginia* was struck by six Japanese torpedoes and two bombs and sank at Pearl Harbor. The Colorado-class battleship was later salvaged and repaired.

## WEST VIRGINIA
## MILITARY HISTORY SITES

### Arsenal Square
Location: Shenandoah & High Street, Harpers Ferry, WV 25425
Web: www.nps.gov/hafe/learn/historyculture/harpers-ferry-armory-and-arsenal.htm

### Belle Boyd House
Location: 126 East Race Street, Martinsburg, WV 25402
Web: www.bchs.org/belle-boyd-house.html

### Carnifex Ferry Battlefield State Park
Location: RR 2, Summersville, WV 26651
Web: www.carnifexferrybattlefieldstatepark.com

### Droop Mountain Battlefield State Park
Location: 683 Droop Park Road, Hillsboro, WV 24946
Web: www.droopmountainbattlefield.com

### Harpers Ferry National Historical Park
Location: 171 Shoreline Drive, Harpers Ferry, WV 25425
Web: www.nps.gov/hafe/planyourvisit/index.htm

### Mountaineer Military Museum
Location: 345 Center Avenue, Weston, WV 26452
Web: www.mountaineermilitarymuseum.com

### Philippi Covered Bridge
Location: 26416 US-250, Philippi, WV 26416
Web: www.civilwar.org/visit/heritage-site/philippi-covered-bridge

### Rich Mountain Battlefield
Location: Rich Mountain Road, Beverly, WV 26253
Web: www.richmountain.org

Nickname: Mountain State
Statehood: 1863
Capital: Charleston

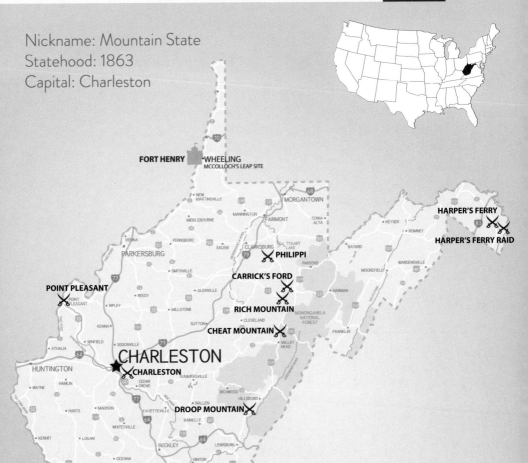

FORT HENRY — WHEELING
MCCOLLOCH'S LEAP SITE

HARPER'S FERRY

HARPER'S FERRY RAID

PHILIPPI

CARRICK'S FORD

POINT PLEASANT

RICH MOUNTAIN

CHEAT MOUNTAIN

CHARLESTON

DROOP MOUNTAIN

**HARPERS FERRY**
Harpers Ferry National Historic Park
Source: iStockphoto/drnadig

**Top Kick's Military Museum**
Location: 149 Army Lane, Petersburg, WV 26847
Web: www.topkicksmilitarymuseum.com

**West Virginia State Museum at the Culture Center**
Location: 1900 Kanawha Boulevard East, Capitol Complex, Charleston, WV 25305
Web: www.wvculture.org/museum/education/EDUindex.html

# WISCONSIN

Today Wisconsin is known for its cheese, its Badgers, and its Packers, but it has seen its share of invaders too.

Long before the arrival of Europeans to what is now Wisconsin, the territory was occupied by a complex mix of cultures that included outstanding sites like Aztalan. Over a thousand years ago, the Mississippian culture constructed mounds at Aztalan.

The first European in the area may have been Frenchman Jean Nicolet in 1634, though claims have been made for earlier visits. Nicolet met Ho-Chunk/Winnebago and Menominee people and found a land that would have great attraction for French fur traders—but they were going to have to wait for a lull in fighting. The Iroquois Wars, fought largely over control of the fur trade, threw Native American society in much of the Great Lakes area into turmoil, and led to some peoples moving substantial distances from their homes.

When French explorers, fur traders, and missionaries started expanding in the area later in the seventeenth century, they found a number of different native American peoples living there, including Ho-Chunk/Winnebago, Menominee, Potawatomi, Sauk, Meskwaki, and Ojibwa.

In 1686, Nicholas Perrot set up Fort St. Nicholas. Two more forts in and around Lake Pepin followed soon after.

And this was not a land at peace. Different Native American peoples competed for preeminence in a tribal landscape transformed by the influx of peoples, refugees of the Iroquois Wars. In the middle of it all were the French trying to promote their own interests.

The French found themselves particularly in conflict with the Meskwaki/Fox, leading to prolonged periods of clashes.

The early eighteenth century saw battles around the Detroit area; and farther north, in the Green Bay area, the Meskwaki/Fox prevented French fur trading. In response, Louis de la Porte led a detachment of eight hundred men to Green Bay and then up the Fox River to a Meskwaki/Fox village near Lake Butte des Morts, where the locals came to terms with him temporarily. But the calm was not to last. Further fighting on the Fox River would follow, and by the 1730s, a significant proportion of the Fox were either dead or enslaved. Meskwaki/Fox leader Kiala was enslaved and taken to the West Indies. The weakened Fox teamed up with the Sauk, and in 1733, Commandant de Villiers was killed at a Sauk village in Green Bay.

But French rule in the area was about to come to an end. In 1761, during the French and Indian War, Captain Henry Balfour and a party of British troops seized Green Bay and renamed the French stockade there Fort Edward Augustus. And the 1763 peace deal that ended the war officially made Britain the colonial power in the land. Having said that, a lot of the locals weren't too keen on the idea, and during Pontiac's Rebellion in 1763 (see Michigan), Fort Edward Augustus was abandoned because it was regarded as too remote and insecure.

The situation did settle down a bit, but official British rule in the region would not last for long. By the end of the War of Independence, the new Unites States was, at least according to the peace deal that ended the war, the new power in what would become Wisconsin. In reality, not that much had changed, with the British still controlling much of the fur trade, and Native Americans in control of most of the land.

The new country did, however, have to decide how to administer the new territory it had acquired. In 1788, what is now Wisconsin became part of the US's Northwest Territory. After that, it would become part of assorted other territories.

In 1800, fearing a British-inspired attack by Native Americans, the Spanish in St. Louis were running gunboat patrols up the Mississippi River as far as Prairie du Chien.

And another war was coming to what is now Wisconsin. Yes, the War of 1812.

The area wasn't exactly the main focus of the action, but it did mean another invasion, even if it wasn't exactly the most dramatic of invasions.

America was fairly unprepared to defend the region against Britain. So in 1814, William Clark—the Clark of the Lewis and Clark Expedition—decided he would do something to protect American interests in the local fur trade. So, on St. Feriole Island at Prairie du Chien, he built Fort Shelby. That summer, a British force headed from Mackinac to Green Bay, and then on to the fort to attack it. After some fairly low-key attempts at combat, the British eventually incapacitated the Americans' gunboat; and after a siege of a few weeks, the fort surrendered. The British renamed it Fort McKay and then, at the end of the war, before withdrawing from the land they had captured, they burned the fort.

In the period after the war, the American military decided on a more serious presence in the area. In 1816, troops were stationed at Fort Crawford at Prairie du Chien and Fort Howard at Green Bay. And in 1828, they would build Fort Winnebago at Portage, but only after there had been more fighting.

As settlers moved into the area, tensions grew, and so did opportunities for misunderstandings. American riverboat crews were accused of raping Ho-Chunk women, and Ho-Chunk prisoners who had been accused of attacking settlers were mistakenly believed by some Ho-Chunks to have been executed. In this atmosphere of suspicion, Ho-Chunk warriors attacked a settler's house at Prairie du Chien in June 1827. Later the same month, Ho-Chunks attacked American keelboats too.

In response, US military reinforcements were sent into the area, and local militiamen assembled. By late August, the American forces were targeting Ho-Chunks assembled at Portage. In early September, Ho-Chunk leaders surrendered Red Bird and five others to the US authorities, and the so-called Winnebago War was over.

It hadn't been much of a war, though a few people did die in it. But more widespread violence was coming. The Black Hawk War of 1832 was a much more major matter.

The war started in Illinois and is dealt with in more depth there, but fundamentally it was caused by aggressive attempts by US authorities to exercise disputed land rights and to open up land for new settlers. Black

Hawk was an experienced war leader who had already fought against the Americans, in alliance with the British during the War of 1812 (see Missouri).

After an initial clash at Stillman's Run (in Illinois), which involved hundreds of mostly Sauk led by Black Hawk on one side, and Illinois militiamen and US troops on the other, Black Hawk eventually led his group north into what is now the state of Wisconsin. They were pursued by American forces, and a number of battles followed as Black Hawk's group tried to elude their pursuers and cross the Mississippi. The clashes coincided with and sometimes overlapped with continuing violence that involved other groups of Native American resisting American settlers.

Eventually, Black Hawk's group reached the Mississippi where it meets the Bad Axe River, and were caught there between pursuers and an American gunboat, the *Warrior*. What followed was a massacre. Black Hawk tried to negotiate under a flag of truce, but the Americans opened fire. When the US troops caught the main body of Black Hawk's people, the Native Americans attempted to surrender. Instead, hundreds of men, women, and children were massacred. The *Warrior* shot at people trying to cross the river, and Lakota Sioux attacked those who did make it across. Black Hawk was taken prisoner, and the war was over. And after 1832, serious military resistance by Native Americans in Wisconsin was over too.

Under pressure from the US government and in return for often minimal compensation, Native Americans ceded their rights to almost all land in Wisconsin in the first half of the nineteenth century.

Although fighting with Native Americans was pretty much at an end in Wisconsin, there was one more "war" to come. In 1845, the Milwaukee Bridge War erupted. Or, at least, *happened*.

The city of Milwaukee grew mainly out of two settlements on either side of the Milwaukee River—Juneau Town on one side and Kilbourn Town on the other. As the settlements grew, continuing to rely on ferries to connect them became a problem, so bridges were built. But without cooperation between the two settlements, disputes soon arose over the location and operation of the bridges, which led to the destruction of a number of them. Peace was finally restored, bridge building was properly planned, and in January 1846, Milwaukee was established.

In 1848, Wisconsin became the thirtieth state in the Union.

People from Wisconsin fought bravely in the Civil War and many subsequent conflicts outside the United States, but the fighting took place elsewhere.

The USS *Wisconsin* (BB-64), which served in World War II, the Korean War, and the Gulf War, is berthed today in Norfolk, Virginia.


## WISCONSIN
## MILITARY HISTORY SITES

**Civil War Museum**
Location: 5400 First Avenue, Kenosha, WI 53140
Web: museums.kenosha.org/civilwar

**EAA Aviation Museum**
Location: 3000 Poberezny Road, Oshkosh, WI 54902
Web: www.eaa.org/en/eaa-museum

**Fort Crawford Museum**
Location: 717 South Beaumont Road, Prairie du Chien, WI 53821
Web: www.fortcrawfordmuseum.com

**Fort Winnebago Surgeon's Quarters** Historic Site
Location: 1824 East State Road 33, Portage, WI 53901
Web: www.fortwinnebagosurgeonsquarters.org

**Pabst Mansion**
Location: 2000 West Wisconsin Avenue, Milwaukee, WI 53233
Web: www.pabstmansion.com

**Portage WWII History Museum**
Location: 119 West Cook Street (Highway 33), Portage, WI 53901
Web: www.travelwisconsin.com/history-heritage/portage-wwii-history-museum-192742

**Swiss Historical Village**
Location: 612 7th Avenue, New Glarus, WI 53574
Web: www.swisshistoricalvillage.org

**Villa Louis**
Location: 521 North Villa Louis Road, Prairie du Chien, WI 53821
Web: villalouis.wisconsinhistory.org

**Wisconsin Maritime Museum**
Location: 75 Maritime Drive, Manitowoc, WI 54220
Web: www.wisconsinmaritime.org

**Wisconsin Veterans Museum**
Location: 30 West Mifflin Street, Madison, WI 53703
Web: www.wisvetsmuseum.com

# America Invaded: WISCONSIN

Nickname: Badger State
Statehood: 1848
Capital: Madison

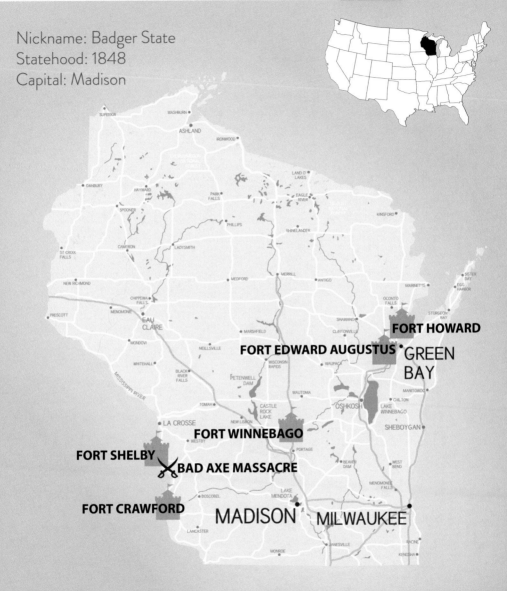

FORT HOWARD

FORT EDWARD AUGUSTUS

GREEN BAY

FORT WINNEBAGO

FORT SHELBY

BAD AXE MASSACRE

FORT CRAWFORD

MADISON

MILWAUKEE

**AMERICAN BADGER**
Source: iStockphoto/Lynn Bystrom

# WYOMING

Native Americans had a long history in what is now Wyoming, over many thousands of years, before the arrival of Europeans in North America.

When people of European heritage did finally make it to the region, they found a number of Native American peoples living there, including Arapaho, Blackfeet, Cheyenne, Crow, Kiowa, Shoshone, Sioux, and Ute.

It wasn't until the eighteenth century that the first Europeans arrived, though. On their 1743 expedition, for instance, the Vérendrye brothers probably visited bits of Wyoming, although if so, it's hard to be entirely sure which.

The Lewis and Clark Expedition didn't go through Wyoming, but John Colter separated from the main expedition and explored parts of Wyoming, including an area of geysers that would later become part of Yellowstone National Park.

Meanwhile, despite comparatively few people of European heritage actually having been there, the area acquired quite a tangled list of outside powers eager to claim parts of it. The Spanish claimed the territory to the east of the Rockies. Then the French made its claim—but with their defeat in the French and Indian War, France ceded that to Spain. Then in 1792, Lieutenant Broughton claimed the Columbia River basin for Britain. The Spanish ceded most of their claims in Wyoming to the French, who promptly sold them to the United States under the Louisiana Purchase. But the confusion wasn't entirely finished. Britain and the United States jointly administered a small section of what is now Wyoming as part of their Oregon Country compromise, until 1846. Mexico had a claim on another small piece of Wyoming, and then the Republic of Texas had a claim, until finally after 1848, the entire territory was internationally recognized as part of the United States. This process almost completely ignored the rights and interests of the Native Americans who actually lived on the land.

But gradually, as the nineteenth century progressed, more and more outsiders entered Wyoming. At first, these were mainly trappers and traders. For instance, Jedediah Smith explored parts of the area. But once the South Pass through the Rockies became known among the outsiders, Wyoming became a through route as emigrants traversed it on their journeys to elsewhere.

And with the trappers and traders and emigrants came the US Army.

In 1849, the army purchased a fort originally built privately for fur trading and renamed it Fort Laramie.

The 1851 Treaty of Fort Laramie signed between the US and local Native Americans aimed to define the indigenous people's land rights, protect settlers on the trails, and provide for the United States to build forts and roads.

However, early on there were signs that the process was not going to be entirely peaceful. In 1854, in what is now Goshen County, a dispute over a dead cow and an ensuing clumsy attempt by twenty-nine soldiers under Lieutenant John Grattan to arrest the man responsible led to the killing of all thirty Americans and their interpreter.

As increasing numbers of settlers and migrants flowed through Wyoming, much more violence was to come.

In July 1865, after the Sand Creek Massacre in November the year before, Lakota Sioux and Cheyenne attacked US forces in the Battles of Platte Bridge Station and Red Buttes, hitting both troops at the bridge and a wagon train, and killing twenty-eight American soldiers. In retaliation, the Powder River Expedition was sent out by the US military. A number of clashes ensued, including a major incident on August 29. Brigadier General Connor's forces attacked an Arapaho village at what is now Ranchester, killing sixty-three before the Arapaho, under Black Bear, counterattacked and forced Connor to withdraw. In the end, the expedition failed to destroy Native American resistance.

In 1866, the army established three forts—Reno, Phil Kearny, and C. F. Smith—on the Bozeman Trail, which connected with gold-rush territory in

Montana and the Oregon Trail. Sioux leader Red Cloud commenced a guerrilla campaign against the forts, and he got support from other Native American leaders, including Black Bear, Sitting Bull, Crazy Horse, and Hump.

On December 21, 1866, warriors under Crazy Horse and Hump attacked wagons carrying timber. An eighty-one-man military force under Captain William Fetterman raced to rescue it, but the US detachment was ambushed and wiped out. In August 1867, a Cheyenne force attacked hay cutters and their guards near Fort C. F. Smith, but due to their new breech-loading Springfield rifles, the hay-cutting party managed to hold off the attackers in the Hayfield Fight.

The day after this attack, Red Cloud, Crazy Horse, and American Horse attacked a wood-cutting party near Fort Phil Kearny.

Although the Native American forces could not defeat the might of the US military, the US military was besieged in its forts and unable to protect the Bozeman Trail.

In the end, the federal government was forced to accept that negotiating with the Native Americans was the only realistic option. Various agreements were signed with various peoples, and in November 1868, Red Cloud signed the Fort Laramie Treaty. Under its terms, the Great Sioux Nation Reservation was established, and the three forts along the Bozeman Trail were abandoned. After their abandonment, the Sioux burned them.

It was not, however, the end of fighting in Wyoming.

The Black Hills War erupted in 1876 after Custer and gold miners invaded the Black Hills, which were Sioux territory. The war was mainly fought beyond the borders of Wyoming, but forts in Wyoming did play a role, acting as US bases. In June, Custer's force was defeated at the Battle of Little Bighorn in Montana. In November 1876, Colonel Ranald Mackenzie attacked a Cheyenne village on the Red Fork of the Powder River. Escaping Cheyenne waded through deep snow to Crazy Horse's camp 150 miles away from the battle site.

By July 1877, the Black Hills War was officially declared finished.

Gradually, some of the key elements of the future of Wyoming were emerging. In 1869, women in Wyoming Territory got the right to vote. In 1890, Wyoming became the forty-fourth state in the Union.

But there was at least one more war to be fought in Wyoming. Well, sort of. Yes, it's the 1892 Johnson County War, known also as the Wyoming Range War, or the War on Powder River. Powerful ranchers and some of their employees and hired gunmen set out to attack and kill a number of small-scale settlers and farmers, who then teamed up with local lawmen to resist the ranchers' hired gunmen. In the end, President Benjamin Harrison had to send in the US Cavalry to sort out the situation.

And in 1922, US marines invaded Wyoming. Well, sort of. Assistant Secretary of the Navy, Theodore Roosevelt Jr., sent in the marines to expel an oil prospector's crew from Teapot Dome, also known as US Naval Petroleum Reserve No. 3. That is, he sent in four marines under Captain George Shuler. The invasion was quickly (and peacefully) successful.

The last foreign invasion of Wyoming was yet to come. During World War II, Japanese balloon bombs did make it as far as Wyoming. One of the first Fu-Gos to arrive in the continental United States was spotted near Thermopolis in December 1944.

Fort D. A. Russell in Wyoming was first built in 1867, and troops from there fought in the Black Hills War. "Black Jack" Pershing was once stationed here, and eventually the fort was renamed Fort F. E. Warren after his father-in-law, a Wyoming senator. Then it became F. E. Warren Air Force Base, and after World War II, it became one of the biggest missile-command bases in the United States.

## WYOMING
## MILITARY HISTORY SITES

### Buffalo Bill Center of the West & Cody Firearms Museum
Location: 720 Sheridan Avenue, Cody, WY 82414
Web: www.centerofthewest.org

### Fort Caspar Museum and Historic Site
Location: 4001 Fort Caspar Road, Casper, WY 82604
Web: http://www.fortcasparwyoming.com/

### Fort Fetterman Historic Site
Location: 752 Wyoming-93, Douglas, WY 82633
Web: wyoparks.state.wy.us/Site/SiteInfo.aspx?siteID=19

# America Invaded: WYOMING

Nickname: Equality State
Statehood: 1890
Capital: Cheyenne

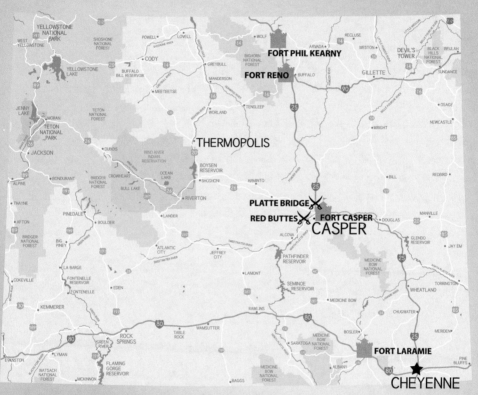

FORT PHIL KEARNY
FORT RENO
THERMOPOLIS
PLATTE BRIDGE
RED BUTTES
FORT CASPER
CASPER
FORT LARAMIE
CHEYENNE

**FORT LARAMIE**
Fort Laramie
National Historic
Site
Source: iStock/
milehightraveler

**Fort Laramie National Historic Site**
Location: 965 Gray Rocks Road, Fort Laramie, WY 82212
Web: www.nps.gov/fola/planyourvisit/visitorcenters.htm

**Fort Phil Kearny State Historic Site**
Location: 528 Wagon Box Road, Banner, WY 82832
Web: www.fortphilkearny.com

**Fort Yellowstone Historic District**
Location: Yellowstone State Park, Yellowstone National Park, WY 82190
Web: www.nps.gov/yell/learn/historyculture/fortyellowstone.htm

**Heart Mountain Intepretive Center**
Location: 1539 Road 19, Powell, WY 82435
Web: www.heartmountain.org

**War Birds Museum**
Location: 8220 Fuller Street, Casper, WY 82601
Web: visitcasper.com/places/war-birds-museum

**Wyoming State Museum**
Location: Barrett Building, 2301 Central Avenue, Cheyenne, WY 82002
Web: wyomuseum.state.wy.us

**Wyoming Veterans Memorial Museum**
Location: 3740 Jourgensen Avenue, Casper, WY 82604
Web: wyomilitary.wyo.gov/veterans/museums/vets-museum

# CONCLUSION

*by Christopher Kelly*

Winners, we are told, write history. This is, at best, a half truth. Ultimately, it is survivors who write the history, whether they were conquerors or conquered, aggressors or victims, or even those who simply tried to stay on the sidelines of history. All survivors have their war stories to tell, their pain to share. Historians are grateful that some of these survivors make the effort to remember their experiences and have their recollections recorded on paper or in other ways.

We Americans tend to think of ourselves not merely as survivors but as winners. We root for our athletes at the Olympics, paying attention to the country medal count. We remove our caps for "The Star-Spangled Banner"—which was written on the occasion of a British invasion in the War of 1812. We do not really like to think of ourselves as ever having been conquered or invaded.

But it is clear that America has been subjected to many waves of invasion. Nearly every square yard of the country seems to have been contested over the course of history. These invasions, these struggles for dominance, have shaped our country in many ways. The legacy of these conflicts can be found in battlefields, monuments, cemeteries, and memorials in all fifty states. We hope that *America Invaded* will be a kind of passport that invites the reader to explore further this rich history. Please visit our website, www.americainvaded. com, for fuller tourist information.

Of course, invasions are, in many ways, in the eye of the beholder.

The difference between an exploration and invasion is often merely a matter of perspective. Captain Cook saw himself as an explorer. Native Hawaiians saw him as an invader.

From the Texan perspective, Santa Anna "invaded" Texas. From the Mexican perspective, the sovereignty of Mexican territory was violated by the rebel Texans. Both of these propositions are coherent and valid from their respective perspectives.

Many generations of Southern pupils were taught about the "War of Northern Aggression" that devastated their region. The South was, in fact, ravaged near the end of the Civil War in a way that prefigured the horror of the world wars of the twentieth century. Sherman's brutal invasions directly targeted the infrastructure and civilian population of the South.

Readers of this volume will, however, also recognize the extent to which there was a "War of Southern Aggression" as well. The Confederates were the first to attack at Fort Sumter. Lee's Gettysburg Campaign was a massive invasion of Pennsylvania. Over the course of the war, Confederates launched many forays into Union territory, from robbing banks in Vermont to raising the Stars and Bars over Tucson.

Both Southern and Northern perspectives on the Civil War are worthy of our respect and study.

American territory was invaded in the twentieth century when the Japanese waded ashore on Attu and Kiska in the frigid Aleutian Islands in 1942. Guam was invaded and occupied as well. Thousands of American merchant mariners were killed off the East Coast in the so-called "Happy Days" that followed the attack on Pearl Harbor. Even the United States' West Coast was attacked by a few intrepid Japanese submarines and seaplanes. Late in the war, Japanese balloon bombs—Fu-Go—descended on many American states.

In the twenty-first century, the War on Terror has involved not conventional invasions, but rather multiple attacks on the American homeland. We continue to face grave threats from home-grown terror inspired by radical, militant philosophies found on the Internet, and from cyberinvasions by foreign powers.

We must conclude that Americans have invaded and that America has been invaded as well. We have paid a price for our liberty. We have paid the cost of all those invasions in terms of blood and treasure.

Our unique American story has involved great endeavor, great bravery, great ambition, great greed, and great suffering. It has produced an extraordinary country, a country that has also had a profound effect for both good and bad in the rest of the world. We have already explored the military aspect of that in the partner book to this, *America Invades*.

And while we know that *America Invades* will soon need updating, as America's military conducts further operations, it is easy to assume that the story of major combat within the United States is a finished one, a past one. But this would be unwise. If history shows anything, it shows that making too many assumptions about future threats is rarely a good option. Even as we go to press, North Korea seems on the verge of testing ICBMs that could reach the states of Alaska, Hawaii, and even Washington.

It is not inconceivable that some future dispute will so divide the nation that civil war will once again tear our country apart. It is not inconceivable that some group will feel so strongly about its beliefs, taking up arms in a major rebellion will seem the only option. And it is not inconceivable, as the power politics of the world change and shift through this twenty-first century, that some new foreign military force will arrive on the shores of the United States, and America will be invaded yet again.

# SUGGESTED READING

Many, many sources informed this work. The following is but a very partial listing of works to which we are grateful.

Ambrose, Stephen. *Undaunted Courage: Meriwether Lewis, Thomas Jefferson, and the Opening of the American West*. New York: Simon and Schuster, 1996.

Ambrose, Stephen. *Crazy Horse and Custer: The Parallel Lives of Two American Warriors*. New York: Anchor Books, 1996.

Boyd, Carl, and Akihiko Yoshida. *The Japanese Submarine Force and World War II*. Annapolis, MD: Naval Institute Press, 1995.

Bradlow, Edna, and Frank Bradlow. *Here Comes the Alabama*. Cape Town, South Africa: Westby Nunn Publishers, 1958.

Brown, Dee. *Bury My Heart at Wounded Knee: An Indian History of the American West*. New York: Vintage Books, 1991.

Cook, Captain James. *The Journals of Captain Cook*. New York: Penguin Classics, 2000.

Coen, Ross. *Fu-go: The Curious History of Japan's Balloon Bomb Attack on America*. Lincoln, NE: University of Nebraska Press, 2014.

Cusick, James G. *The Other War of 1812: The Patriotic War and the American Invasion of Spanish East Florida*. Athens, GA: University of Georgia Press, 2007.

Daughan, George C. *1812: The Navy's War*. New York: Basic Books, 2011.

Dugard, Martin. *Farther Than Any Man: The Rise and Fall of Captain James Cook*. New York: Washington Square Press, 2001.

Dukas, Neil Bernard. *A Military History of Sovereign Hawaii*. Honolulu: Mutual Publishing, 2004.

Felton, Mark. *The Fujita Plan: Japanese Attacks on the United States and Australia During the Second World War*. Barnsley, UK: Pen and Sword Books, 2006.

Gannon, Michael. *Operation Drumbeat: The Dramatic True Story of Germany's First U-Boat Attacks Along the American Coast in World War II*. Annapolis, MD: Naval Institute Press, 1990.

Grant, John, and Ray Jones. *The War of 1812: A Guide to Battlefields and Historic Sites*. Buffalo, NY: Western New York Public Broadcasting Association, 2011.

Grant, Ulysses S. *The Complete Personal Memoirs of Ulysses S. Grant*. New York: Charles L. Webster & Company, 1885.

Groom, Winston. *Patriotic Fire: Andrew Jackson and Jean Lafitte at the Battle of New Orleans*. New York: Vintage Books, 2006.

Gwynne S. C. *Empire of the Summer Moon: Quanah Parker and the Rise and Fall of the Comanches, the Most Powerful Indian Tribe in American History*. London: Constable, 2010.

Harlow, Neal. *California Conquered: The Annexation of a Mexican Province 1846–1850*. Berkeley, CA: University of California Press, 1982.

Keegan, John. *The American Civil War: A Military History*. New York: Vintage Books, 2010.

Ketchum, Richard M. *Saratoga: Turning Point of America's Revolutionary War*. New York: Henry Holt and Company, 1997.

Knight, James R. *The Battle of Franklin: When the Devil Had Full Possession of the Earth*. Stroud, UK: The History Press, 2009.

Knight, James R. *Hood's Tennessee Campaign: The Desperate Venture of a Desperate Man*. Stroud, UK: The History Press, 2014.

Lewis, Meriwether, and William Clark. *The Journals of Lewis and Clark (Lewis & Clark Expedition)*. Edited by Bernard DeVoto. Boston: Mariner Books, 1997.

McConaghy, Lorraine. *Warship under Sail: The USS Decatur in the Pacific West*. Seattle: University of Washington Press, 2009.

McDonough, James Lee. *Shiloh—In Hell before Night*. Knoxville, TN: University of Tennessee Press, 1977.

Polhemus, Richard V. and John F. Polhemus. *Stark: The Life and Wars of John Stark, French and Indian War Ranger, Revolutionary War General*. Delmar, NH: Black Dome Press, 2014.

Rimini, Robert. *The Battle of New Orleans: Andrew Jackson and America's First Military Victory*. New York: Penguin Books, 2001.

Richards, Leonard L. *The California Gold Rush and the Coming of the Civil War*. New York: Vintage Books, 2007.

Ross, John F. *War on the Run: The Epic Story of Robert Rogers and the Conquest of America's First Frontier*. New York: Bantam Books, 2011.

Steinbeck, John. *Tortilla Flat*. New York: Penguin Books, 1997.

Stephenson, Michael. *Patriot Battles: How the Revolutionary War Was Fought*. New York: HarperCollins Publishers, 2007.

Tucker, Spencer C. *Almanac of American Military History*. 4 vols. Santa Barbara, CA: ABC-CLIO, 2013.

Vinkovetsky, Ilya. *Russian America: An Overseas Colony of a Continental Empire, 1804–1868*. Oxford UK: Oxford University Press, 2011.

Vouri, Mike. *The Pig War: Standoff at Griffin Bay*. Seattle: University of Washington Press, 1999.

Weidensaul, Scott. *The First Frontier: The Forgotten History of Struggle, Savagery, and Endurance in Early America*. Boston: Houghton Mifflin Harcourt, 2012.